DIALOGUE ACROSS DIFFERENCE

DIALOGUE ACROSS DIFFERENCE

Practice, Theory, and Research on Intergroup Dialogue

Patricia Gurin, Biren (Ratnesh) A. Nagda,
and Ximena Zúñiga

Russell Sage Foundation • New York

The Russell Sage Foundation

The Russell Sage Foundation, one of the oldest of America's general purpose foundations, was established in 1907 by Mrs. Margaret Olivia Sage for "the improvement of social and living conditions in the United States." The Foundation seeks to fulfill this mandate by fostering the development and dissemination of knowledge about the country's political, social, and economic problems. While the Foundation endeavors to assure the accuracy and objectivity of each book it publishes, the conclusions and interpretations in Russell Sage Foundation publications are those of the authors and not of the Foundation, its Trustees, or its staff. Publication by Russell Sage, therefore, does not imply Foundation endorsement.

Library of Congress Cataloging-in-Publication Data

Gurin, Patricia.
    Dialogue across difference : practice, theory and research on intergroup dialogue / Patricia Gurin, Biren (Ratnesh) A. Nagda, Ximena Zúñiga.
    p. cm.
    Includes bibliographical references and index.
    ISBN 978-0-87154-476-6 (pb : alk. paper) — ISBN 978-1-61044-805-5 (epub)
1. Communication in education.   2. Interpersonal communication   3. Intercultural communication.   I. Nagda, Biren A., 1965-   II. Zúñiga, Ximena.   III. Title.
    LB1033.5.G876 2013
    371.102'2—dc23   2012046114

Text design by Suzanne Nichols.

RUSSELL SAGE FOUNDATION
112 East 64th Street, New York, New York 10065

10 9 8 7 6 5 4 3 2 1

to all who came before us, walk with us, and will come after us this book honors the legacies of those who paved the roads of dialogue, affirms those doing the everyday work of promoting diversity and justice, and celebrates the courage of all the students who, by stepping out of their comfort zones, will be leaders in our diverse democracies

CONTENTS

TABLES AND FIGURES

ABOUT THE AUTHORS

PATRICIA GURIN is the Nancy Cantor Distinguished University Professor of Psychology and Women's Studies Emerita at the University of Michigan.

BIREN (RATNESH) A. NAGDA is associate professor of social work and director of the Intergroup Dialogue, Education and Action (IDEA) Center at the University of Washington, Seattle.

XIMENA ZÚÑIGA is associate professor in the Social Justice Education Concentration in the Student Development Department at the School of Education of the University of Massachusetts Amherst.

GARY ANDERSON is a lecturer and director of the Intergroup Relations Program (2003–2012) at the University of California, San Diego.

GLORIA BOUIS is executive director of the Office of Human Relations Programs in the Office of the President at the University of Maryland.

KERI DEJONG is a doctoral candidate in the Social Justice Education Concentration in the Student Development Department at the School of Education of the University of Massachusetts Amherst.

AMY CARPENTER FORD is assistant professor in the School of Education at Central Michigan University.

RICHARD GONZALEZ is professor of psychology at the University of Michigan.

CHLOÉ GURIN-SANDS is a graduate of the University of Michigan and program coordinator of the Spectrum Center at the University of Michigan.

MOLLY KEEHN is a doctoral candidate in the Social Justice Education Concentration in the Student Development Department at the School of Education of the University of Massachusetts Amherst.

GRETCHEN LOPEZ is assistant professor in the School of Education and director of the Program on Intergroup Relations at Syracuse University.

KELLY MAXWELL is codirector of the Program on Intergroup Relations and lecturer in the Department of Psychology at the University of Michigan.

CARMEN MCCALLUM is academic research specialist in the Office of the Provost for Undergraduate Education at Michigan State University.

ELIZABETH MEIER is a National Institute of Drug Abuse Postdoctoral Fellow at the University of Michigan.

JANE MILDRED is professor in the School of Social Work at Westfield State University.

ROSIE PEREZ is a graduate student in the School of Education at the University of Michigan.

JACLYN RODRIGUEZ is professor of psychology at Occidental College.

DELIA SAENZ is vice provost for international and institutional inclusion and associate professor of psychology at Arizona State University.

NICHOLAS SORENSEN is a researcher in the Education Division of American Institutes for Research.

MARTHA STASSEN is assistant provost for assessment and educational effectiveness at the University of Massachusetts Amherst.

COOKIE WHITE STEPHAN is professor of sociology emerita at New Mexico State University.

WALTER G. STEPHAN is professor of psychology emeritus at New Mexico State University.

KATHLEEN WONG (Lau) is lecturer at Western Michigan University.

RANI VARGHESE is a doctoral candidate in the Social Justice Education Concentration in the Student Development Department at the School of Education of the University of Massachusetts Amherst.

ACKNOWLEDGMENTS

At its heart, intergroup dialogue is a sustained, intentional effort to bring diverse people together to collectively build something greater than any of us as individuals may accomplish. It requires respect for divergent voices, value for the unique and shared responsibilities individuals bring to the collective good, and a concerted effort to listen and understand multiple experiences and perspectives that derive from people's different connections to power and privilege. These very characteristics defined the relationships among colleagues that created the Multi-University Intergroup Dialogue Research (MIGR) Project. The project began in a gathering of colleagues from different universities and colleges in the United States who were running intergroup dialogue programs on their campuses. Some colleagues had their intergroup dialogue roots at the University of Michigan and then initiated similar efforts when they took new positions at other institutions of higher education. Others had developed intergroup dialogue courses and programs after consulting with Michigan's Program on Intergroup Relations. Some of the participating universities were focused primarily on intergroup dialogue practice, while a few were also involved in evaluating their practice. None, however, had conducted experimental studies that would allow effects to be attributed to intergroup dialogue itself, rather than to the kinds of students who select intergroup dialogue courses. None of us had conducted intergroup dialogue research studies beyond our own institutions. It quickly became obvious that we could leverage our different faculty, staff, and student positions and experiences to create a research project that spanned the ten universities that were initially involved (University of Illinois later dropped out), utilized our range of qualitative and quantitative skills, and used an experimental design capable of producing a rigorous test of the possible impact of intergroup dialogue.

Such an undertaking would have been impossible without the committed partnership of our campus collaborators: Delia Saenz, Thomas Walker and Kathleen Wong (Lau) from Arizona State University; Jaclyn Rodriguez from Occidental College; Gretchen Lopez from Syracuse University; Gary Anderson from the University of California, San Diego; Joycelyn Landrum-Brown from the University of Illinois at Urbana-Champaign; Gloria Bouis from the University of Maryland, College Park; Teresa Brett and Margarita M. Arellano from the University of Texas; Martha Stassen and Ximena Zuñiga from the University of Massachusetts Amherst; Patricia Gurin, Kelly Maxwell, Nicholas Sorensen, and Elizabeth Meier from the University of Michigan, Ann Arbor; and, Biren (Ratnesh) Nagda from the University of Washington, Seattle. Walter Stephan and Cookie White Stephan provided invaluable consultation from the very first meeting to the culmination of the project and this volume. Nearly all of these collaborators, and some other colleagues, co-authored different book chapters and are noted as appropriate in footnotes to chapter titles.

Other partners who were involved at the local campus level and sometimes at national meetings were: Andrea Rodriguez-Scheel and Kenjus Watson from Occidental College; Judy Hamilton and Sigrid Davison from Syracuse University; Anna Yeakley and Brett Robertson from the University of California, San Diego; Dominic Cobb and Joseph Mienko from the University of Illinois at Urbana-Champaign; Craig Alimo from the University of Maryland, College Park; Shuli Archer, Stephanie Burrell, Keri DeJong, Larissa Hopkins, Molly Keehn, Romina Pacheco, and Taj Smith from the University of Massachusetts Amherst; Charles Behling, Roger Fisher, Taryn Petryk, Chloé Gurin-Sands, and Monita Thompson from the University of Michigan, Ann Arbor; and, Akua Campanella and Rebecca Hedrix Cate from the University of Washington, Seattle.

The entire project team, at times comprising thirty colleagues, met at least twice a year from 2003–2008. We met at each of the participating campuses, and we thank each of the hosting institutions and offices for the hospitality they extended to us. Given the complexity of the project, we had three main working groups and we wish to thank all the members for their hard work. The curriculum team, comprised of Craig Alimo, Gary Anderson, Margarita

M. Arellano, Gloria J. Bouis, Teresa Brett, Dominic Cobb, Eva Fatigoni, Patricia Gurin, Joycelyn Landrum-Brown, Gretchen Lopez, Kelly Maxwell, Biren (Ratnesh) A. Nagda, Jaclyn Rodriguez, Thomas Walker, Kathleen Wong (Lau), Anna Yeakley, and Ximena Zúñiga, created the standardized curriculum (readings, assignments, and in-class active learning activities) that was used across all participating institutions. The qualitative research team, comprised of Craig Alimo, Kelly Maxwell, Elizabeth Meier, Jaclyn Rodriguez, Kathleen Wong (Lau), Anna Yeakley, Martha Stassen, and Ximena Zúñiga, with consultation from Mark Chesler, designed the qualitative protocols for the study. The quantitative team, comprised of Patricia Gurin, Gretchen Lopez, Biren (Ratnesh) A. Nagda, Nicholas Sorensen, Cookie White Stephan, and Walter Stephan, with the consultation of Richard Gonzalez, designed the survey instrumentation and analysis approach for the study. We thank all the working groups for their dedicated work.

Graduate students and undergraduate students served as research assistants at the three universities (Michigan, Massachusetts, and Washington) that carried out various project-related tasks, including the coding and analysis of the surveys, interviews, final papers, and videotapes. At Michigan, the team included Carmen McCallum, Rosie Perez, Amy Ford, Chloé Gurin-Sands, Shardae Osuna, Aesha Mustafa, and Andrea Coombes plus over thirty undergraduates who coded paper and interview protocols for a semester or longer. At Washington, it included Diane Arnold, Rebecca Hedrix Cate, Akua Campanella, Amelia Derr, Taura Greenfield, Shawn Mincer, Ebasa Sarka, and Norma Timbang. At Massachusetts, it included Shuli Archer, Elaine Brigham, Keri DeJong, Dre Domingue, Laura Henderson, Chris Hughbanks, Larissa Hopkins, Molly Keehn, Joy Miller, Lubna Mostafa, Kyle Oldham, Romina Pacheco, Morgan Ray, Davey Shlasko, Taj Smith, and Alina Torres-Zickler.

We especially thank Susan Lorand, librarian at the University of Michigan, who checked citations and quotations, and created the final references for the book. We are grateful to Walter and Cookie Stephan who served as consultants throughout the project, and provided editorial assistance for the entire book, including chapters on which they are not authors. They are notable scholars in the social psychology of intergroup relations who brought wisdom and rigor to this project. The analysis of the survey data could not have been carried out without the continual consultation by Richard Gonzalez, who gave many hours to this project while he simultaneously served as chair of Michigan's Department of Psychology. Special thanks goes to Gerald Gurin, who was involved in all aspects of the study, especially construction of the surveys. Although not an author on any chapter, he collaborated in framing the book and edited nearly all of the chapters. He is a virtual author and real colleague.

Select former intergroup dialogue facilitators responded immediately and fully to our request to reflect on the impact of intergroup dialogue in how they are addressing the three challenges that frame the book. Their responses form the bases of the Epilogue and some of them have also volunteered to have their statements used in presentations the authors have made. Our special gratitude to Colleen Campbell, Denny Chan, Annabel Cholico, Adam Falkner, Chloé Gurin-Sands, Tara Hackel, Aaron James, Joshua Johnson, Jaimée Marsh, Kartik Sidhar, Nathaniel Swartz and Clare Wrobel.

We three authors of the book also wish to express appreciation for support we received from our home institutions during the implementation of the research project and the crafting of this book. The University of Michigan, the home institution of Patricia Gurin, hosted all the research workshops during the first two years of the project, and also the National Institute held at the end of the project that was attended by representatives of thirty-five colleges and universities. The Division of Student Affairs, the Department of Psychology, and the College of Liberal Arts provided institutional funds that supplemented external funds throughout the project. Dr. Gurin is especially grateful to her colleagues in the Program on Intergroup Relations and in the Department of Psychology, LS&A Assistant Dean Evans Young, LS&A Dean Terrence McDonald, Vice-Provost Lester Monts, and Philip Bowman, director of the National Center for Institutional Diversity at the University of Michigan, who provided funds for completing this book project.

Biren (Ratnesh) Nagda expresses gratitude to colleagues at the University of Washington and associates of the Intergroup Dialogue, Education and Action (IDEA) Center. Dean Edwina Uehara of the School of Social Work has been an erstwhile supporter of intergroup dialogues as have Professors Eugene Aisenberg, Sue Sohng and Stan de Mello. He also thanks colleagues and advisors at the Office of Minority Affairs & Diversity (OMAD) and Undergraduate Academic Affairs for promoting interest in intergroup dialogues among undergraduates. Dr. Nagda appreciates Glenda Wildschut and honors the memory of the late Clem Van Wyk, both dear friends at the Desmond Tutu Peace Centre in Cape Town, where he was working while also finalizing the research proposals for this project. Dr. Nagda thanks the University of Michigan School of Social Work for welcoming him as a visiting scholar while completing this book.

Ximena Zúñiga expresses her deep appreciation to colleagues and graduate students at the University of Massachusetts Amherst, and to Dean Effrat and Dean McCormick of the School of Education for providing the funds to support our participation in the study. She is especially grateful to Martha Stassen, assistant provost for Assessment and Educational Effectiveness, for her clear guidance, unequivocal support, and collaborative spirit through the various phases of this research endeavor. Dr. Zúñiga is also grateful to all the graduate students in the Social Justice Education concentration who participated in various roles in the study, and to her dear faculty colleagues—Maurianne Adams, Bailey Jackson, and Barbara Love—for all the support and encouragement provided over the years to incorporate the practice of intergroup dialogue in the undergraduate and graduate curriculum on the University of Massachusetts campus.

Finally, we are especially grateful to the William T. Grant Foundation and to the Ford Foundation for funding this project. Both foundations took some risk in that it was not obvious that fifty-two experiments involving pairs of intergroup dialogue courses and control groups, along with social science comparison groups, could actually be implemented across the nine institutions (excepting University of Illinois) that collaborated on this project. We are proud to have met that goal, to have conducted interviews and videotaping in twenty of the intergroup dialogue courses, and to have content analyzed 720 final papers of the intergroup dialogue students. The Russell Sage Foundation, and its director of publications, Suzanne Nichols, has provided extraordinary guidance throughout the reviewing and publication process of this book.

The picture on the cover of the book was taken by Laura Sanchez Parkinson, an undergraduate staff member in Michigan's Program on Intergroup Relations. The students who appear on the cover include: Silvena Chan, Evalyn Carter, Adrienne Clabin, Dan Green, Nader Hakim, and Nora Stephens. All of them are facilitators of dialogue courses and CommonGround Workshops at the University of Michigan.

INTRODUCTION

Intergroup Dialogue and the Multi-University Intergroup Dialogue Research Project

I came to this class hoping to better understand racial relationships and to be able to talk honestly about race. I came to this class having gone through many stages in the past about race, thinking that if I could just explain the true history of my people, other people would understand. Failing that, I often became enraged, then not caring what other people think. The stage I was at when I came to this class was being slightly bitter, slightly sarcastic, and completely disillusioned. What I hoped for was a small community where I could speak about racial issues without feeling like people would point to me as the "angry, black woman." In fact, I did get a place to speak comfortably about issues of race. I know for a fact that we have talked honestly and truthfully.

I wanted to find a place in this university to openly communicate while learning and discussing issues that are universally relevant. I saw this as an opportunity to converse honestly while gaining knowledge about the broader dynamics of gender relationships and the social system in which I exist. I have been stimulated intellectually and emotionally by the content and the relationships in my dialogue. I have learned more in this class than I ever dreamed possible because it was both academic and personal.

Before this class, I was nervous about talking about gender or race. I was apprehensive about speaking about these topics because I didn't want to offend anyone. I didn't want to appear ignorant. Talking about a subject as sensitive as gender is hard enough with friends and family, but to open up in a class—to trust people enough to do that—that was hard. But I was surrounded by people who were just as nervous as I. Everyone was eager to listen to and learn from each other. And we did. My fears were put to rest because of the constructive facilitation of the course, the course readings, the participation of the rest of the members of the class, and my willingness to be open-minded.

I can have very strong opinions and I wasn't sure how I would react with people who might have opposite thoughts from mine. It is always hard to share thoughts in depth with anyone. In my experience on this campus that does not happen very often. Some of it comes from being uneasy about expressing conflicting views. But, after a few sessions of my dialogue class, the walls of apprehension were gone. We were very open and we actually began to see that you don't learn anything unless there is conflict.

These statements are extracted from narratives students wrote about their experiences learning about race-ethnicity and gender in intergroup dialogue (IGD). Intergroup dialogue is a facilitated educational effort that brings an equal number of students from two social identity groups—white students and students of color, men and women—together in quarter- or semester-long, credit-earning courses. Since their inception in the late 1980s, intergroup dialogues have sought to educate students proactively to understand and work with intergroup conflicts that are not only historical and structural but persistent and present in their daily college lives. IGD aims for students to gain knowledge of intergroup issues, especially group-based social identities and inequalities; to improve and deepen intergroup communication and relationships; and to develop skills in and commitment to intergroup collaboration (Nagda and Gurin 2007; Schoem et al. 2001; Zúñiga et al. 2007; Zúñiga, Nagda, and Sevig 2002). Today intergroup dialogue is in place at many colleges and universities in the United States, usually offered as credit-earning courses led by trained facilitators (Dessel, Rogge, and Garlington 2006). Since 2003, collaborators in the research project discussed in this book, as well as staff at the University of Michigan's Program on Intergroup Relations (IGR), have consulted with 110 higher education institutions via summer institutes, usually lasting three to four days, and campus trainings, usually lasting two to three days, for faculty and staff interested in developing intergroup dialogue courses or programs.

Intergroup dialogue involves diverse groups of students in learning about social justice. By social justice, we mean learning that involves understanding social identities and group-based inequalities, encourages building of cross-group relationships, and cultivates social responsibility. Thus, intergroup dialogue fosters engagement that is intellectual and affective, self-reflective and in dialogic relation with others, personal and structural, and that connects dialogue to action (Zúñiga et al. 2007). The IGD courses conducted across the nine participating institutions followed a standardized curriculum developed by collaborators from these institutions. Within the context of small and diverse groups led by trained facilitators, the IGD curriculum included in-class structured activities and opportunities for critical reflection, and out-of-class reading, writing, and group assignments. Because intergroup dialogue fosters learning through interaction, it builds specific skills of dialogic communication among students that encourage listening and learning from others, reflecting and sharing experiences and perspectives, and asking questions to discern similarities and differences in experiences. Additionally, because the groups in dialogue are usually defined by strained and conflictual relationships, current or historical, IGD draws on specific content about social identities and inequalities. The dialogic communication processes are coupled with critical communication processes whereby students critically analyze how larger social structures create or perpetuate power inequalities, affect intergroup relations and personal lives, and how they can be involved in individual and collective efforts aimed at greater social justice (Nagda 2006). Throughout the dialogue, facilitators pay special attention to equalizing participation by fully involving students from both identity groups.

Students conveyed that learning in intergroup dialogue was not easy. It often involved disagreements and discomfort. It required them to risk going beyond their comfort zones. It challenged them to form relationships, not just coexist, across differences. The students said that the typical cross-racial and gender-based interactions on their college campuses rarely involved exploring what difference means—differences in life experiences, differences in what students call their realities, that is, differences in cultural expectations and visions, and especially differences embedded in social, economic, and political inequalities. In the IGD courses students learned to talk, think, feel,

and work across racial-ethnic and gender differences as they also simultaneously discovered commonalities as well.

This volume presents the educational practices and the theoretical rationale
for intergroup dialogue. It further discusses how those practices share elements
of other intergroup relations programs and also differ from other programs.
Primarily, it presents the results from a multi-university field experiment on
intergroup dialogue that was carried out by nine universities over three years—
the Multi-University Intergroup Dialogue Research (MIGR) Project.

The project had two goals: to determine whether intergroup dialogues have
the predicted effects of increasing students' intergroup understanding, intergroup relationships, and intergroup action, and to examine how the dialogues
produce effects—the processes that take place within dialogue courses that
account for their effects on these three sets of outcomes. The nine participating institutions were Arizona State University, Occidental College, Syracuse
University, University of California (San Diego), University of Maryland,
University of Massachusetts Amherst, University of Michigan, University of
Texas, and University of Washington. These institutions were selected to be
part of the research project because they already offered intergroup dialogue
courses. Race-ethnicity and gender intergroup dialogues were selected as the
focus of the research for two reasons. First, all of the nine participating institutions were already conducting courses on race-ethnicity and gender. Although some institutions also offered dialogue courses focused on other social
identities (class, religion, sexuality), there was too little consistency across the
nine institutions to include these other identities. Second, although race-
ethnicity and gender are important identities among college students, talk
about them is often avoided except at the most superficial levels.

Fifty-two parallel pairings of dialogue courses and control groups were
conducted across the nine participating institutions. Twenty-six pairings
tested the effects of race-ethnicity dialogues; another twenty-six tested the
effects of gender dialogues. In each, approximately an equal number of white
women, white men, women of color, and men of color, not exceeding a total
of sixteen, were randomly assigned to the dialogue courses or to control
groups from the pool of students who applied to take these courses. Altogether, 1,437 students participated in the experiment. The importance of the
study's experimental design cannot be overstated. To the best of our knowledge, ours is the first random assignment experiment on the effects of intergroup dialogue.

The research also tested whether effects could be attributed to the dialogue method or simply to learning about race-ethnicity or gender by also studying a comparison group of students enrolled in fourteen traditional social science classes on race-ethnicity and thirteen social science classes on gender. If students in the dialogue courses changed significantly on more measures of the outcomes than the students in the social science classes did, the results would suggest that IGD had effects that extended beyond the content on race-ethnicity and gender that both types of courses had in common. Students in each of the social science classes were randomly chosen from volunteers to be part of the study. A total of 438 of these students made up a comparison group that matched the demographic composition of the dialogue and control groups. All three groups completed a survey at the beginning and the end of the semester in which the dialogue and comparison courses were held. Dialogue participants and students in the control groups also completed a longitudinal survey a year later so that we could test the longer-term as well as the immediate effects of intergroup dialogue.

We show in this book that intergroup dialogue increased the students' intergroup understanding, positive intergroup relationships, and intergroup action. Of the twenty-four multi-item measures on which we assessed positive change from the beginning to the end of the semester, students randomly assigned to the dialogue courses showed significantly greater change than those randomly assigned to the control groups on all but four measures. We also show that the IGD courses had significantly greater impact than social science courses on two-thirds of these measures. Most impressive, we show that the differences between the intergroup dialogue and control group students were still present a year later on all but three of the twenty-four measures. We also relate how students, through their final papers and interviews, appraised their experiences in intergroup dialogue.

OVERVIEW OF THE BOOK

Chapter 1 positions intergroup dialogue within the long tradition of research on intergroup relations. It places the research project within continuing controversies about the educational value of diversity that were brought to national attention by the Supreme Court ruling on affirmative action in Grutter v. Bollinger in 2003 and by Fisher v. University of Texas in 2012. It discusses why talking across race and gender in more than superficial ways has proven difficult, and how intergroup dialogue addresses those difficulties.

It situates IGD within three important challenges facing the United States and particularly higher education. These challenges also provide the framework for discussing the implications for higher education of the research project in the book's concluding chapter.

Chapter 2 presents the practice model of intergroup dialogue and discusses how intergroup dialogue differs from other approaches to intergroup relations. It specifically describes the pedagogy that characterizes IGD and how that pedagogy is implemented over four stages over the course of a semester. Excerpts from the students' final papers in the dialogue courses are used to illustrate the pedagogy in these four stages of dialogue.

Chapter 3 lays out the theoretical framework that guided the project. It highlights the crucial role of communication processes in intergroup dialogue that foster psychological processes within participants (both cognitive and affective) that lead to the primary outcomes of interest in the study: intergroup understanding, intergroup relationships, and intergroup action. Excerpts from the students' final papers are used again to illustrate how the students understood the communication processes, their connection to psychological processes, and the connection of both sets of processes to the three sets of outcomes. This theoretical approach frames the rest of the book.

Chapter 4 describes the design and methods, and shows how they address limitations in prior research on intergroup relations and intergroup dialogue. It details both the quantitative and qualitative approaches that combine to make this project a mixed-methods investigation. It also presents the methodological issues that this project was not able to resolve.

Chapter 5 presents the effects of dialogue through the experiments conducted across the nine participating institutions. These effects show differential changes from the beginning to end of a term, and a year later, by students who had been randomly assigned to the dialogues relative to those randomly assigned to the control groups. This chapter also provides evidence supporting the generalizability of the effects of dialogue across both race-ethnicity and gender dialogues and across students from groups with more or less societal privilege. Evidence is also presented showing that the effects of dialogue are generally larger than the effects of more traditional race-ethnicity and gender social science courses, and thus that the impact of the dialogue courses involves their method and not merely the race-ethnicity and gender content that the dialogue courses shared with the social science courses. Results presented in chapter 5 further indicate that the effects present immediately after the dialogue courses ended were still evident a year later, although they were somewhat smaller. Chapter 5 also presents a test of the theoretical framework delineated in chapter 3, using structural equation modeling to focus on how pedagogy, communication processes, and psychological processes together increased intergroup empathy, structural understanding of inequality, and action.

Chapters 6, 7, and 8 present mixed-method analyses, emphasizing the qualitative data collected as part of an intensive substudy of ten gender and ten race-ethnicity dialogues (described in chapter 4). These analyses illustrate how students experienced dialogue. Using both student interviews and final papers, chapter 6 examines how intergroup empathy was expressed in intergroup dialogues and reveals a distinction not evident in the survey measures and analysis. As the students talked and wrote about their experiences, we discerned two kinds of intergroup empathy. One, *relational empathy*, was toward a specific individual, usually another student. The second, *critical empathy*, included an understanding of that individual's position in a system of power and privilege. Using the interviews, chapter 7 focuses on engagement in the dialogues and distinguishes listening, speaking, and active thinking engagement, and details features of intergroup pedagogy that seem to foster each of these types of engagement. Chapter 8 then uses material coded from videotapes of the dialogues that were part of the intensive substudy to show how students participated in the dialogues, how facilitators participated, and how facilitator behaviors were related to student behaviors. At the end of chapter 8, we summarize what these three mixed-method chapters demonstrate about the practice model of intergroup dialogue.

Chapter 9 draws together the conclusions from the analyses of the surveys and qualitative materials, showing how they generally support the critical-dialogic model of intergroup dialogue. It also presents practice implications of the findings, and discusses criticisms of intergroup dialogue and why the results generally do not support those criticisms.

Chapter 10 returns to the three challenges—demographic, democratic, and dispersion—that frame the book, and emphasizes the implications of those challenges specifically for higher education and how intergroup dialogue is an effective educational approach for addressing them.

Authored by Patricia Gurin, Biren (Ratnesh) A. Nagda, and Ximena Zúñiga.

PART I

What Is Intergroup Dialogue?

CHAPTER 1

Intergroup Dialogue: Its Role in Contemporary Society

In this chapter, we position intergroup dialogue (IGD) within the programs and studies on intergroup relations and discuss what motivated the research on which this book is based. We discuss both why talking across differences of race-ethnicity and gender in more than superficial ways has proven difficult, and how intergroup dialogue addresses those difficulties. We also look at broader challenges facing the United States and particularly higher education that underscore the importance of intergroup dialogue in contemporary society.

HISTORICAL CONTEXT

Intergroup dialogues have evolved from a long tradition of programs designed to improve intergroup relations. These programs first appeared after World War II, but became much more common after the Supreme Court's decision in Brown v. Board of Education in 1954, which outlawed segregation in America's schools.[1] The implementation of that decision, however, was slow and eventually ground to a halt in the face of opposition to school desegregation and to a number of later decisions by the Court that eroded the original mandate (Stephan and Feagin 1980). As a result, the problem that the Brown decision was designed to overcome, segregation in the schools, persisted. In response, a large number of new intergroup relations programs was created by educators and social scientists to improve race and ethnic relations among school-age children. At the same time, intergroup relations programs were developed for other settings, particularly the military and the workplace, to train people going to work or study in foreign cultures.

A major thrust of early intergroup relations efforts was in the realm of anti-bias education and prejudice reduction. Scholars and educators located the problem of intergroup tensions in stereotypes and misinformation about groups, particularly minority groups, but differed in the goals and methods of their programs. Three major approaches were evident. One, enlightenment programs were based on the premise that a lack of knowledge about other groups was the basic origin of problems in intergroup relations. The goals were to increase intergroup understanding, as well as reduce prejudice, stereotyping, discrimination, and other negative behaviors toward out-groups (Dovidio et al. 2004). In various ways, although mostly direct and didactic, these programs provided knowledge about the history, culture, social norms, and values of other groups. Two, contact programs provided opportunities for members of different social groups to interact with one another in controlled settings. Most of these programs can trace their origins to Gordon Allport's (1954) contact theory with a focus on face-to-face contact that was sanctioned by authorities. Many focused on knowing others through interaction but did not directly provide information on the other group. Three, skill-based programs involved teaching skills that promoted positive intergroup relations, and skills to manage differences and to lessen or resolve interpersonal conflicts in a peaceful manner. In some programs, the participants were taught mediation skills they could use to deal with their conflicts or in mediating conflicts between others (Johnson and Johnson 1996). The approach to teaching was usually highly interactive, involving practicing and role-playing conflict resolution.

Intergroup dialogue is thus positioned in a history of social science efforts to apply research-based knowledge about group interactions to real-world intergroup situations (Stephan and Stephan 2001, 2004). The anti-bias education efforts—goals, methods, and approaches—provide a backdrop for the origins of intergroup dialogue. In chapter 2, we discuss in greater detail the roots of intergroup dialogue in the social psychology of intergroup relations and in diversity and social justice education efforts. We also discuss how IGD is a distinct approach even though it has elements common to the different approaches to anti-bias education.

WHAT MOTIVATED THE MULTI-UNIVERSITY INTERGROUP DIALOGUE RESEARCH PROJECT

The motivation for conducting this research project lay in the arguments and social science evidence on the educational benefits of diversity that was marshaled by the University of Michigan in defending its use of race as one of many factors in admissions. In 2003, the Supreme Court upheld in Grutter v. Bollinger the University of Michigan's use of affirmative action in admission to its law school.[2] The university argued that diversity in curricular initiatives and in peer interactions is critical for learning, for ensuring multiracial leadership for our society, and for fostering an engaged citizenry in a diverse and participatory democracy (Gurin 1999). Seventy-four amicus briefs submitted to the Supreme Court on behalf of the University of Michigan supported that argument. They all stressed, in language unique to their particular societal missions, the importance of students acquiring an understanding of different life experiences and group perspectives, and developing the cultural competencies that are needed to be effective leaders in the world of work, governmental as well as nongovernmental agencies, corporations, the military, and international organizations.

Justice Sandra Day O'Connor, writing for the majority, delineated why the Court found that achieving diversity is a compelling national interest. Referring to the University of Michigan Law School's claims of educational benefits that diversity is designed to produce, she wrote:

> The Law School's claim is further bolstered by numerous expert studies and reports showing that such diversity promotes learning outcomes and better · prepares students for an increasingly diverse workforce, for society, and for the legal profession. Major American businesses have made clear that the skills needed in today's increasingly global marketplace can only be developed through exposure to widely diverse people, cultures, ideas, and viewpoints. High-ranking retired officers and civilian military leaders assert that a highly qualified, racially diverse officer corps is essential to national security.[3]

One of the authors of this book, Patricia Gurin, was the University of Michigan's expert witness on the educational benefits of diversity and well aware of deficiencies in the evidentiary base that was available in social science at the point of submitting her expert report. Two deficiencies were particularly relevant to launching this intergroup dialogue research project. First, experimental evidence on the effects of diversity experience was mostly lacking at the time. Yet, if diversity has educational benefits, it is important to show greater educational gains among students randomly assigned to a diversity course or program compared to equally motivated students randomly assigned to control groups. Second, although Gurin (1999) and others argued that institutions needed to make full use of diversity as an institutional resource if it is to have educational benefits,[4] empirical evidence on the impact of diversity in curricular initiatives was scant. Like other resources, such as an excellent library or an outstanding faculty, racial and ethnic diversity is an institutional resource that needs to be leveraged, for example, by creating innovative courses and other academic initiatives that foster cross-racial-ethnic interaction and learning from diverse peers.

Gurin, together with Biren (Ratnesh) Nagda and Ximena Zúñiga, the developers of the original intergroup dialogue curricular model at the University of Michigan, proposed to the Ford Foundation and the W. T. Grant Foundation a research project that would address both of these inadequacies. It was a project with an experimental design that would assess the possible effects of a diversity initiative that explicitly uses student diversity. Leaders of intergroup dialogue programs or courses at nine universities agreed to work together to craft the proposed project.

As it turned out, the 2003 Supreme Court decision did not settle either the constitutionality of affirmative action or the value of diversity as a rationale for utilizing affirmative action in higher education. As this book goes to press, once again the Supreme Court will decide the constitutionality of using race as one factor in university admissions in Fisher v. University of Texas at Austin et al. The claim that diversity has educational benefits will once again figure prominently in the Court's decision. Thus, what originally motivated the study—to evaluate experimentally what educational outcomes are produced when student diversity is explicitly used in an educational program—continues to be highly relevant and important for higher education.

Two widely read and highly regarded social science works published since the 2003 Supreme Court affirmative action decision are worth noting here because they relate to our argument that diversity is an institutional resource that must be explicitly used if it is to produce positive outcomes for students.

One is cited in amicus briefs supporting the University of Texas's use of race in law school admissions (Page 2007, 2011), and one is cited in amicus briefs supporting the plaintiff in Fisher v. University of Texas at Austin et al. (Putnam 2007).

Scott Page, a political scientist at the University of Michigan, has explored in two books, *The Difference: How the Power of Diversity Creates Better Groups, Firms, Schools, and Societies* (2007) and *Diversity and Complexity* (2011), whether and how diversity contributes to effectiveness and productivity. His work, which is primarily theoretical and mathematical, concerns cognitive-intellectual diversity, and his demonstration of problem solving and organizational benefits from diversity is limited to its impact in complex or difficult tasks. On routine tasks, homogeneity wins because, as Page puts it, the profit bottom line is increased when every bagger at Wal-Mart packs groceries in the same, efficient way (private communication). On complex tasks, Page theorizes and demonstrates mathematically that more cognitive diversity produces more robust outcomes. One might ask whether cognitive diversity has anything to do with social diversity. To some extent, the connection between social and cognitive diversity seems obvious, and Page argues that his work does relate to social diversity. He reflects on the expansion of ideas he encountered on meeting people in college from backgrounds so different from his small town in western Michigan.[5] Perhaps a trivial but powerful example, Page recalls that everyone he knew in his hometown had seen or read *Paddle to the Sea*, a story of a canoe that makes it to the ocean from Lake Superior. Students he met from California didn't know the acronym HOMES standing for the Great Lakes. What they knew was grist for the mill in those many conversations, "You don't really do that in California (or Michigan or New York or Pakistan) do you?" When conditions support such interactions and conversations, the connection between social and cognitive diversity seems transparent. That connection is well established by scholars in higher education (Bowman 2010; Chang 2003; Daye et al. forthcoming; Denson and Chang 2009; Deo 2011; Jayakumar 2008; Milem, Chang, and Antonio 2005).

Page's work (2007, 2011) focuses on the mechanisms that explain the value of diversity. Among them are three that he concludes have been well established: insurance against bad outcomes that results from the presence of more possibilities when diversity is present; responsiveness that results from the presence of more ideas about how to adapt to environmental challenges, demands, and emergencies; and collective knowledge that results from broader forecasts or predictions that occur more readily when multiple, diverse individual predictions are on the table. Empirical support for such mechanisms has been demonstrated with racially diverse and homogeneous decision-making groups in that members of the more diverse groups perceived the information available to them as more unique, and they also spent more time on the tasks given to them than members of the homogeneous groups (Phillips, Northcraft, and Neale 2006). Dissenters in the diverse groups also spoke up more frequently than dissenters in the homogeneous groups, resulting it would seem in having more varied perspectives on the table in the diverse groups (Phillips and Loyd 2006).

Page discusses possible downsides to diversity as well. For one, people in diverse groups or organizations are usually not as satisfied with their performances or experiences as are those in homogeneous ones. Thus, although people perform better in diverse problem-solving groups, their members are less confident in their performance and perceive their interactions as less effective than members of homogeneous groups (Phillips, Liljenquist, and Neale 2009). The most important negative Page (2011) noted, one especially relevant to this book, is that people in a diverse setting may not actually interact with each other, yet the greatest possibility of positive outcomes from diversity occurs when they do.

In accord with the premise of intergroup dialogue, Page stresses the importance of actual interaction and sharing of perspectives when people from diverse backgrounds end up in the same physical space. Just as scholars contended in materials submitted to the Court a decade ago, and still stress in materials submitted in the 2012 affirmative action case, diversity needs to be tapped so that diverse people interact with each other (Chang et al. 2006; Denson and Chang 2009; Milem, Chang, and Antonio 2005; Sorensen et al. 2009). Intergroup dialogue can be implemented in higher education and more broadly in other societal institutions to ensure that people from diverse backgrounds do interact with each other, and that they do so over a sustained period in a setting in which the interaction is facilitated for maximal benefit to occur. When those conditions are met, the impact of diversity is robust, as we show in this book.

The second post-2003 example is the well-known research by Robert Putnam, professor of public policy at Harvard's Kennedy School, showing a negative relationship between living in neighborhoods characterized by greater ethnic-racial diversity and what he calls social capital. Based on a survey carried out with roughly 30,000 individuals that included both a nationwide representative sample and smaller samples representative of forty-one communities (census tracts) that varied greatly in their ethnic diversity, Putnam (2007) found that residents of the most diverse communities hunker down, distrust their neighbors, withdraw from social interaction, volunteer less, contribute less to charity, less often register to vote and in all these ways have less social capital than residents of the most homogeneous communities. These findings demonstrate that compositional diversity—living in the same physical space—by itself does not produce social capital. Moreover, Putnam's results proved to be robust rather than reduced or erased when he controlled for many other characteristics that might affect social capital, such as neighborhood poverty, crime levels, and resources such as libraries, schools, and religious institutions.

Putnam's findings should not surprise scholars who have studied the impact of diversity in higher education. They have generally stressed that diversity needs to be utilized in explicit ways in the institution's curriculum, residence halls, and campus organizations. For students to learn from each other, they need to interact and explore each other's experiences and perspectives. Support for the argument that actual interaction needs to take place if diversity is likely to promote positive outcomes comes from a study in Great Britain, which is related to the Putnam study. The study in Great Britain examines what happens to trust when people in neighborhoods varying in diversity do or do not have social contact with each other (Sturgis et al. 2011). In a survey of 25,000 individuals in neighborhoods in Great Britain, social contact, measured as being acquainted with people in the neighborhood, was positively related to trust in neighbors at all levels of ethnic diversity of the neighborhood. Social contact was more important than diversity itself, or, as the authors explain, "In substantive terms, the social contact variable dominates" (77). To the limited extent that societal well-being is threatened by the ethnic diversity of local communities, Patrick Sturgis and colleagues conclude that "the solution would not appear to lie in reducing, or restricting, the ethnic diversity of neighbourhoods but in fostering increased contact and communication" (2011, 80). The main point is that compositional diversity by itself may or may not produce positive outcomes. Instead, attention must be given to conditions that promote interaction and especially promote the sharing of diverse points of view. Intergroup dialogue is one educational program in which diversity has been used to promote nonsuperficial, substantive communication across differences, with significant and consistent positive effects we detail in this book.

TALKING ACROSS DIFFERENCES

Intergroup dialogue arose in a particular context within higher education in which students in the mid- to late 1980s pressed for courses and programs that would address diversity. At the University of Michigan, where the first formal intergroup dialogue courses were created in 1989, campus tensions had led the university administration to craft a vision for diversity in the university, one that centered the role of the university in addressing issues of diversity and democracy constructively. James Duderstadt, then the president of the university, launched the Michigan Mandate, an initiative that provided funds for faculty, staff, and students to develop academic programs to foster diversity and inclusiveness in all aspects of campus life. Intergroup dialogues emerged as one initiative under the Michigan Mandate with the explicit goal of creating opportunities for members of the Michigan community to talk across differences to foster intergroup understanding, relationships, and action. The first dialogues focused on race-ethnicity because that was the focus of both campus tensions and student activism to make the university more inclusive and effective as an increasingly multicultural institution. Even now the majority of the intergroup dialogue initiatives now under way on higher education campuses focus on race-ethnicity.

Race continues to be the major social divide in the United States (Bobo 2011), and a topic often avoided or at best dealt with superficially. The political scientist Katherine Cramer Walsh describes the behavior of ordinary citizens taking part in face-to-face interracial conversations about race as striking for a number of reasons: "First, these folks were about to voluntarily take part in an interracial discussion, not a typical behavior for most Americans. Second, they were not just engaging in interracial discussion; they were doing so *about race*. Bringing up the topic of race in interracial settings is generally treated as a potential for disaster by politicians and ordinary citizens alike" (2007, 2).

Writing about the difficulties in talking about race, Paula Moya and Hazel Markus stress that ·

even though race and ethnicity pervade every aspect of our daily lives, many of us become deeply uncomfortable whenever the conversation turns to those topics. The discomfort takes a variety of forms and affects people differently. Some people believe that the United States has successfully moved beyond what were painful racially conflicted chapters in its national history; others think that race and ethnicity are unrelated to their own lives. . . . Some . . . avoid talking about [race and ethnicity] for fear of being thought racist. Yet others think that even noticing race and ethnicity is wrong. . . . Still others believe that U.S. Americans have not begun to talk seriously about these topics and that no one can understand society without analyzing how race and ethnicity are linked and deeply intertwined with wealth, status, life chances, and well-being in general. (2010, 3–4)

Moya and Markus (2010) delineate eight conversation stoppers that make talking about race difficult. Among these conversation stoppers are comments such as "We're beyond race," or "Everyone's a little bit racist," or "That's just identity politics." Moya and Markus believe that to proceed from such comments requires offering accurate information, such as understanding the distinctions between the bio-geographical concept of ancestry groups and the sociohistorical bases of race, and understanding the group and power bases of inequalities versus individual explanations of inequalities. However, we believe that many people are not able to bring forward such information even if they know it because they may be so aroused emotionally by such comments that they remain silent. Others may feel hopeless about countering these kinds of cultural axioms that frame the national discourse about race because these axioms seem so resistant to information and knowledge (Tatum 1997). Sheryl Watt (2007), Derald Wing Sue and colleagues (2007), and Uma Narayan (1988) elaborate on the difficulties in dialogue and interacting across differences, including emotional challenges. The more privileged are seen to be highly anxious and defensive in such interactions, and in turn many interactions are experienced as microaggressions by the less privileged who may feel their identities invalidated and denigrated. Perhaps for all these reasons, the conversation stoppers noted by Moya and Markus (2010) appear to prevent reasonable and informed discourse about race. Not only is accurate information necessary, so is the need to expect some uneasy emotional experiences as we talk about what we know and do not know, and what is easy to talk about and what is difficult to talk about.

Why are differences, especially race differences, so difficult to talk about? It is not because there are no differences to discuss. So what accounts for avoidance of talk about and across differences? With respect to race-ethnicity, it comes at least partially from segregation. Although residential integration exists in some places in the United States, large proportions of all racial-ethnic groups still live fairly separately. John Iceland (2004) shows that residential segregation in metropolitan areas declined 26 percent overall between 1980 and 2000, and that African Americans were moderately more evenly distributed across neighborhoods in 2000 than in 1980. However, even in 2000 the dissimilarity index for those two groups was still sixty-four, that is, the percentage of a group's population that would have to change residences for the group to be evenly distributed across neighborhoods. Iceland further shows that although Hispanics and Asians and Pacific Islanders are significantly less segregated than African Americans, their level of segregation changed very little and, for Asian Americans, actually increased somewhat. According to data released by the Census Bureau in 2011 that reality has been reinforced, showing that black and white Americans still tend to live in separate neighborhoods (Denvir 2011). Segregation is decreasing slowly, although the dividing lines have shifted from urban centers to once all-white suburbs where middle-income blacks, Latinos, and Asians have moved as whites have moved to outlying suburbs. Talking about race or ethnicity across differences is made difficult by the large proportions of racial-ethnic groups who live separately in homogeneous urban situations.

Racial segregation, however, is only part of the explanation. In writing about community-wide conversations about race, Walsh emphasizes that people of different racial backgrounds have not only lived separately but interpret life in the *same* city differently. They don't see the same city the same way. "When they confront race head-on . . . the participants compel each other to face the reality of different realities. As they listen to and scrutinize each other, they hear that everyday life in their city can vary starkly by race" (2007, 8).

Separation, be it residential or relational, creates difficulties for conversations that are more than superficial across race and other social, demographic, and cultural differences. The goal is not necessarily to see the same city in the same way but to understand why people of different backgrounds may see it differently.

Differences in perspectives involving gender are often avoided as well, but not because men and women live separately. On the contrary, gender relationships—between men and women, fathers and daughters, mothers and sons, sisters and brothers—are wholly integrated and involve intimacy. That intimacy can inhibit examination of gender-based issues that involve power and inequality. The frequent, familial, and intimate relationships among men and women have helped explain why income and occupational disparities across gender are less easily interpreted as unjust, compared to such disparities across race (Crosby 1984; Gurin, Miller, and Gurin 1980; Rudman and Glick 2008). With race, it is often segregation that leads to lack of contact and avoidance of talking across difference; with gender, it is intimacy rather than lack of contact that leads to avoidance of talking across differences.

Avoidance of talking about group-based differences may also result from a fear of what acknowledgment of differences might mean for civil society. If, as some people believe, the stability and viability of democracy depend on harmony and unity, democracy could be threatened when differences are acknowledged. This view is supported by critics of multiculturalism. Arthur Schlesinger, a thoughtful and prolific critic of multiculturalism, especially in educational settings, wrote that if "the assumption that ethnicity is the defining experience for every American . . . [if] we must discard the idea of a common culture and celebrate, reinforce and perpetuate separate ethnic and racial communities, then multiculturalism not only betrays history but undermines the theory of America as one people" (1991, 13–14). Race in particular arouses discomfort because of our long history of racial inequality, because of reverberations from slavery, because of continuing discrimination, and because of a belief held by some that the United States is now a postracial society in which race no longer matters.

The question of whether racial differences can be addressed effectively is itself contentious. Two major perspectives—color-blindness and multiculturalism—suggest different answers to that question. They differ in their view of the significance that race-ethnicity and other social identities play in the life chances of people in the United States. They differ in whether or not it is productive or destructive to talk about these social differences.

According to the sociologist Eduardo Bonilla-Silva (2003), color-blindness involves the belief that: only minimal, if any, racial disparities still exist; the few that exist are caused by cultural deficiencies in certain racial groups and not by structural constraints that unfairly impinge on different groups; obvious patterns of racial segregation simply reflect the natural tendency of people to prefer to associate with similar others; and meritocracy assures equality if individuals, assumed to play on a level field, take advantage of opportunities and work hard. Because proponents of color-blindness believe that intergroup relations are hampered by attention to group membership, they argue against race-conscious educational initiatives, including specifically intergroup dialogue courses (Wood 2008).

The multicultural perspective does not reject the ideal of color-blindness but asserts that the United States is not a color-blind society. Rather than ignoring race and acting as though the United States is already a postracial society, the multicultural position is that race and other kinds of inequalities, including gender, should be analyzed and understood as critical features of the current social structure and social life that should be changed to produce a more equitable society. Multiculturalism, as a policy position, envisions a "pluralized public sphere—where cultural, linguistic, and religious diversity could be actively and positively accommodated" (May 2009, 33).

A parallel controversy regarding gender also exists, the idea that the United States is now a postgender society. For some, gender discrimination is thought to be a thing of the past or that gender disparities are simply the normal features of social life, perhaps even biologically ordained that women do the majority of childcare and domestic work, and that men express violence against women because of their biologically based aggressiveness. The naturalness of gender disparities may also reflect gender-based socialization that produces gender differences in the interests and choices of men and women. Many fewer women than men, for example, are interested in becoming candidates for political office (Lawless and Fox 2010). Many fewer are interested in science, technology, and math (Hill, Corbett, and St. Rose 2010).

For others, gender discrimination is thought to still affect the outcomes of women and men. Pay differences continue to exist, for example, even when comparing women and men with equivalent preparation and experience and in equivalent job categories (Eagly and Carli 2007). In 2010, women still earned only 77 percent as much as men (American Association of University Women 2012). Cultural expectations of men and women who hold identical jobs or other positions in society are also different (Risman 2004). Male and female politicians are held to different expectations about expressing emotion. Crying by male politicians is tolerated, sometimes even applauded, because it is perceived as demonstrating sensitivity and humanity. Crying by female politicians, in contrast, is disapproved of, if not ridiculed, because it is seen as demonstrating weakness and instability, something Hilary Clinton learned during the 2008 presidential election.

Why, then is the idea of a postgender society believable? In part, it is believed because gender-based equality is far greater than it has been. It is also fostered by benevolent sexism—the idea that women are not derogated or constrained as much as they are idealized and protected. Yet benevolent sexism does constrain women's choices and behaviors (Glick and Fiske 2001). Men effectively maintain power through what Barbara Risman calls "politeness norms," behaviors that "construct women as 'others' in need of special favors, such as protection" (2004, 438). A white man in a gender dialogue described how he had never thought of his "gentlemanly" behaviors as anything that might constrain a woman's development. "I was rather shocked when we read about benevolent sexism and that I had been such a part of this phenomenon. I was always taught to protect and take care of women. In this I thought I was just respecting them. I never realized that I may have prevented a woman from fully realizing what she is capable of or may dream of wanting to be." So both benevolent sexism and today's genuinely greater equality justify a belief in a postgender society for many people. They make talking about gender inequalities as uncomfortable for some as talking about racial inequalities, although of course for different reasons.

Intergroup dialogue wrestles in both theory and practice with the problems of talking across differences and integrating two goals that are often viewed as conflicting: how to address the degree of unity and common purpose required for democracy, and how to give sufficient attention to racial and gender identities and inequalities.

CHALLENGES THAT INCREASE THE IMPORTANCE OF TALKING ACROSS DIFFERENCES

Three challenges facing the United States, and other countries as well, increase the importance of knowing how to talk in productive, collaborative ways with people from different walks of life. These broad challenges speak to the need for intergroup dialogue, especially in higher education institutions, which we argue are best suited to the task of improving intergroup relations. Due to residential segregation here and in other countries, diversity in everyday life is minimal. Where it does exist, levels of intergroup contact tend to be low. As we detail in chapter 10, many K-12 institutions are largely segregated. Business organizations have mounted initiatives to improve intergroup relations, the effects of which depend on the extent to which organizational responsibility exists for increasing managerial diversity (Kalev, Dobbin, and Kelly 2006), and on whether diverse work teams that exist include shared objectives, feelings of safety, and effective conflict management (Jackson, Joshi, and Erhardt 2003). The business case for increasing diversity and instituting such initiatives has received mixed research support, although an especially impressive study of 506 representative for-profit business organizations provides overall positive results showing that diversity is associated with increased sales revenue, more customers, greater market share, and greater relative profits (Herring 2009). Still, it is arguable whether improving intergroup relations can or should be a primary mission of for-profit business organizations. The one institution in our society, and probably in other societies, that is best suited to educating people to function effectively in diverse societies is higher education. But these institutions, too, cannot simply assume that creating a diverse student body will be enough to educate students to understand the perspectives held by students in other groups, to work effectively across groups, and to work together for the benefit of their communities, states, countries, and the world. Creating a diverse student body provides the raw materials for reaping the benefits that can be derived from diversity, but institutions of higher education have to find ways of making diversity work, and that is where intergroup dialogue becomes relevant to addressing these three challenges. The three are

the demographic challenge brought about by the changing demographics in the United States;

the democracy challenge of assuring the engagement of people from all backgrounds in civic life despite persistent and growing economic inequality; and

the dispersion challenge represented by what Fareed Zakaria (2008) calls the "rise of the rest" in a post-American world. The United States, though still a mighty force in the world, will not be the exclusive world superpower in the twenty-first century.

The Demographic Challenge

Even before the middle of the twenty-first century the United States will no longer have a majority of white people. It is estimated that by 2042 the demographic composition of the United States will make it a minority-majority country. Slightly less than half will be white and slightly more than half will be from other racial-ethnic groups. A *Wall Street Journal* article estimates that racial-ethnic minorities will become the majority of the population aged zero to seventeen years of age even sooner, in 2023 (Conor Dougherty, "Whites to Lose Majority Status in U.S. by 2042," August 14, 2008, A3). In 2010, the majority of the population in four states—Texas, Hawaii, California, and New Mexico—had minority racial-ethnic backgrounds. In eight more—Arizona, Florida, Georgia, Maryland, Mississippi, Nevada, New York, and New Jersey—the percentage of non-Hispanic whites had fallen below 60 percent.

The Hispanic population is driving minority growth. By 2050, about one in three U.S. residents will be Hispanic (Dougherty 2008). These demographic shifts have implications for politics, education, economic growth, residential diversity, and intergroup relationships. The old terms, minority and majority groups, will likely have different meanings or be meaningless by the end of the first half of the twenty-first century. People will need to be able to talk, listen to, and understand the perspectives, interests, and needs of a vastly more multiracial, multi-ethnic, and multicultural society.

The Democracy Challenge

The United States has become not only more demographically complex but also a more unequal society in terms of income since the Great Depression. Larry Bartels (2008), writing about inequalities over the past three decades, summarizes that as the rich became vastly richer—80 percent of net income gains since 1980 going to the top 1 percent of the income distribution—working-class wages stagnated. In 2011, the *New York Times* reported Congressional Budget Office numbers that "the top 1 percent of earners more than doubled their share of the nation's income over the last three decades" (Robert Pear, "Top Earners Doubled Share of Nation's Income, Study Finds," October 15, 2011; Congressional Budget Office 2011). Average inflation-adjusted after-tax income grew by 275 percent for the top 1 percent, whereas for the top 20 percent it grew by 65 percent, and for the bot-

tom 20 percent only 18 percent. Moreover, although income inequality usually shrinks during a recession, Don Peck (2011) points out that excluding
capital gains, top earners saw their share of national income rise even in
2008. At the same time that the income of people at the top has soared,
Sabrina Tavernise points out in the *New York Times*, poverty also has soared
to its highest level since 1993 ("Soaring Poverty Casts Spotlight on 'Lost
Decade,'" September 13, 2011).

Democracy does best when most people believe that they have a stake—
economically and politically—in its future, and thus democracy is particularly threatened when poverty and affluence are disproportionately located in
certain groups in society. The National Urban League's 2009 report, *The State
of Black America*, shows that blacks are twice as likely to be unemployed,
three times as likely to live in poverty, and more than six times as likely to be
incarcerated as whites. The report concludes that economics remains the
most significant domain of inequality African Americans face. The Center for
American Progress reports that though the unemployment rate has risen for
all groups since the beginning of the 2008 recession, it increased much faster
for minorities than for whites (Logan and Weller 2009). This was true for
both African Americans and Latinos. Family incomes in 2007 for whites
were about 30 percent greater than for Latinos and 36 percent greater than
for African Americans. The poverty rate among Latinos in 2007 was also
nearly three times that of whites. Minority groups were hit the hardest from
the 2008 recession and by 2010 African Americans had a poverty rate of 27
percent, Latinos 25 percent, Asians 12.1 percent, and whites 9.9 percent (Tavernise 2011). The wealth gap between whites, African Americans, and Latinos
has also increased. The Pew Research Center reports that "the median wealth
of white households is 20 times that of black households and 18 times that of
Hispanic households" (Kochhar, Fry, and Taylor 2011, 1), and these wealth
ratios are the largest since the government began publishing such data twenty-
five years ago.

Although women in the United States have made major gains in education (more undergraduate degrees now go to women than to men), and the
labor force participation of women has nearly doubled since 1950, the rate
for women (61 percent) is still lower than the rate for men (75 percent) (U.S.
Department of Commerce and OMB 2011). Historically, more women than
men have been poor and the poverty among female heads of households is
especially high—two to three times as high as the overall male and female

rate of poverty ever since 1966 (U.S. Department of Commerce and OMB 2011). The most dramatic gender inequalities in the United States relate to violence and victimization. A report on the prevalence, incidence, and consequences of violence against women, published by the National Institute of Justice (Tjaden and Thoennes 2000), gives statistics for both childhood and years after eighteen for men and women. During childhood, boys (66 percent) were physically assaulted more than girls (52 percent) but girls (9 percent) were raped more than boys (2 percent). Reporting experiences over their lifetimes after age eighteen, 9.6 percent of women but only 0.8 percent of men say they have been raped. Adding physical assault to rape, 25 percent of women and 8 percent of men report victimization by an intimate partner during their lifetimes. Violence against women, in fact, is primarily initiated by an intimate partner. Nearly two-thirds of the women who have experienced rape, physical assault, or stalking, but only 16 percent of men who have experienced the same assaults say that they have come from a current or former spouse, cohabiting partner, or dating partner (Tjaden and Thoennes 2000).

All of these inequalities present important challenges for the United States that people need to be able to discuss. The causes of increasing inequality are many, and conservatives and liberals have different views about what should be done about inequality, if anything. Whatever one's perspective on the causes and the importance of doing something to reduce inequality, talking about its implications for the personal lives of Americans and for the vitality of our democracy could not be more important for society generally. It is certainly important for institutions of higher education to educate students about this democratic challenge. Intergroup dialogue's method of promoting critical analysis of inequality is one way for that to happen.

The Dispersion Challenge: The Rise of the Rest

A third challenge that increases the importance of learning to dialogue comes from the expectation that the dominance of the United States will decrease as other countries—notably China, India, Brazil, and South Africa, but others as well—become more powerful globally. The rise of these countries is an outcome of the creation of a global economy. It is also a symbol of globalization more broadly, not only in business but also in our concerns for global problems such as pollution, the extinction of species, global warming, the transmission of diseases, interconnections through social media, and the internationalization of regional and local conflicts. Moreover, the United States faces greater challenges with globalization than many other countries do because of our greater geographic isolation. On the other hand, the United States has advantages as well. English is the de facto world language. The United States has the largest economy and the largest army in the world. And because the United States has been, and continues to be, a magnet for immigrants, it is among the most culturally diverse countries in the world. This is a real asset in meeting the dispersion challenge, and this book presents a way to make the most of this advantage.

Fareed Zakaria argues that the United States will not lose all influence because "at the politico-military level, we remain in a single-superworld world. But in every other dimension—industrial, financial, educational, social, cultural—the distribution of power is shifting, moving away from American dominance" (2008, 4–5). We are moving into a post-American world in which leaders will need to understand events and interact with leaders from many places in the world. The "rise of the rest" will require leaders who can relate with leaders from other countries at both governmental and nongovernmental levels on a more equal footing than at any time in our history. Going forward, we cannot dictate the terms of those relationships by using economic and military strength to enforce our will. We have to learn to work and communicate more effectively across cultures, not just in business but in diplomacy, to collaborate in solving global problems and in dealing with regional conflicts, and to promote human rights and social justice. Never before has the need to deal with the diversity of the world been so urgent. Intergroup dialogue offers a method for educating future leaders in how to communicate, negotiate, and collaborate with people in these other increasingly influential countries.

INCLUSION OF MULTIPLE VOICES: DIALOGUE AND DEMOCRATIC PRACTICE

However difficult talking about differences and inequalities may be, the voices of people from many groups in society and from many countries must be included for democratic practice and multinational relationships to be effective. But what kind of communication can simultaneously acknowledge differences, inequalities, and conflicts as well as foster a capacity for collaboration and broad democratic engagement? We argue in this book that intergroup dialogue accomplishes these dual, sometimes seemingly contradictory, objectives.

Dialogue is collaborative and honors the intellectual and experiential diversity among participants. It strives for understanding, not agreement. Unlike debate, which is usually oppositional and in which people try to convince each other so that one side wins, dialogue strives to build mutual understanding. In dialogue, differences are not taken as points of division; rather, they serve as a means to identify assumptions, encourage inquiry and develop mutual understanding.

Discussion, as it occurs in many settings, be it in family living rooms, corporate board rooms, or university classrooms, also differs from dialogue. Although discussion does attempt to raise and work through multiple opinions and perspectives, it is a format in which each person typically waits before speaking for another to stop talking. Those who have led discussion classes in higher education rarely see students probing the ideas of others in an attempt to understand the bases of the ideas and the reasoning that undergirds them. Instead, discussion is often characterized by debate or involves serial monologues in which participants wait their turns to present their ideas and arguments as cogently and logically as possible.

Dialogue has as much to do with listening to others and asking them questions as with sharing one's ideas. This is not to say that debate and discussion do not involve listening, but the purpose of listening is different. In debate, one may listen to identify weaknesses in others' arguments in order to counter them. In discussion, one may listen just to know when it is time to enter and express a point of view. In dialogue, one is able to listen and share in a connected way. Listening in dialogue is joined with sharing, partly because listening allows people to hear, see, or feel something similar to what others are experiencing even if it is a familiar sentiment or a parallel experience or not a shared perspective, and partly because it helps people see how differences are interconnected and related. Individuals listen with the interest in understanding another's perspective. Listening also leads to reflection, sometimes privately and sometimes publicly, on how another person's perspective relates to and affects one's own perspective. In dialogue, listening also helps participants learn how their individual narratives are connected to larger societal narratives, and how inquiry and openness lead to a deeper understanding of differences and similarities.

Intergroup dialogue provides a hopeful blueprint for engaging in difficult and often avoided conversations. Yet, there is an additional question. How do we deal with differences within dialogue groups that mirror the differences and inequalities in the wider society? Intergroup dialogue has a social justice framework that interrogates why inequalities exist across social groups. Students are challenged to understand that race-ethnicity and gender differences that they read about and encounter usually reflect differences in the lived experiences and the social realities of various groups from which participants come to dialogue courses. Disagreements in dialogue often emerge from differential access to social power and from social inequalities in society. Participants inevitably bring their social experiences with privilege and disadvantage into the dialogue. Those experiences can affect who speaks, who interrupts, who remains silent, and who dominates the discourse, especially at the outset of dialogue.

The late social, political, and feminist philosopher Iris Marion Young (1997) was well known for her critique of how democratic projects such as community problem-solving groups, school parent-teacher associations, and others are conducted. She charged that they too often fail to attend explicitly to inequality and imbalances of power in discourse. In her conception of democratic endeavors, called communicative democracy, Young focused on how power often enters speech. She is openly critical of the idea that people from diverse backgrounds can simply be brought together without first defining the ground rules of engagement so as to promote genuine equality of communication.

In many formal situations, the better-educated white middle-class people, moreover, often act as though they have a right to speak and that their words carry authority. Those of other groups, on the other hand, often feel intimidated by the argument requirements and the formality and rules of parliamentary procedure, so they do not speak, or speak only in a way that those in charge find disruptive. Norms of assertiveness, combativeness, and speaking by the contest rules are powerful silencers or evaluators of speech in many situations where culturally differentiated and socially unequal groups live together. The dominant groups, moreover, often fail entirely to notice this devaluation and silencing, and the less privileged often feel put down or frustrated, either losing confidence in themselves or becoming angry (Young 1997, 64).

Marion Young prescribes three preconditions, which characterize intergroup dialogue, that foster effective communication across wide cultural and social differences: significant interdependence, equal respect, and agreed-upon rules for fair discussion and decision making. "A richer understanding of processes of democratic discussion results," she informs us, "if we assume that differences of social position and identity perspective function as a resource for public reason rather than as divisions that public reason transcends" (1997, 67). The importance of ground rules is made evident by a woman of color who described how difficult it had previously been for her to express her ideas in interracial communication situations given the norms that define how talk is supposed to be conducted. "It hasn't been easy because in general people are not able to understand other people who do not express themselves easily and quickly." In accord with the conditions Young delineated, this student emphasized that in her race-ethnicity dialogue, the students "respected different styles of talking. You didn't have to speak quickly or confidently to be heard." A white man in a gender dialogue described that learning how to respect different styles had been difficult for him. "I have always been a talker, someone who thinks quickly on his feet, and someone who is known as articulate. So it came as a big challenge for me to slow down, ask questions, and be patient if others were not so quick in what they were saying. I'd say that I have become much more tolerant and that I will be much more effective in campus organizations now that I have learned to respect people's different personal styles." All of these preconditions, which are important for discourse across both race-ethnicity and gender, are made explicit in the design of intergroup dialogue in chapter 2.

CONCLUSION

In this chapter, we have traced the history of intergroup dialogue to its roots in the early intergroup relations and anti-bias education programs geared toward prejudice reduction. We have situated intergroup dialogue within controversies surrounding the educational value of diversity and in the growing importance of learning to talk across differences. Finally, we framed this book by three challenges—demographic, democratic, and dispersion— that both higher education and the society at large must address. We turn in chapter 2 to the practice model of intergroup dialogue.

Authored by Patricia Gurin, Biren (Ratnesh) A. Nagda, Cookie White Stephan, and Walter G. Stephan.

CHAPTER 2

The Practice of Intergroup Dialogue

In this chapter, we describe more fully the intergroup dialogue (IGD) practice model that addresses the divides and challenges of talking across and about race and gender highlighted in chapter 1. We have four goals: to place the foundations of intergroup dialogue in the context of social psychological research on intergroup relations and of multicultural education concerned with diversity and social justice; to draw on approaches to reflective, relational, and integrative learning that inform and undergird dialogue pedagogy; to show how intentional intergroup interactions can be supported by content and facilitation to achieve the major goals of IGD; and to provide in-depth information on the educational design of intergroup dialogues.

FOUNDATIONS OF INTERGROUP DIALOGUE PRACTICE

Social Psychology of Intergroup Relations

The major theories of intergroup relations in social psychology derive from the classic work on intergroup contact (Allport 1954), which hypothesizes that intergroup harmony can be fostered by having members of different groups interact with each other under specified conditions. These conditions include equal status between the groups in the contact situation, intergroup cooperation toward common goals, opportunities to get to know members of the out-group personally, and knowledge that the contact is positively sanctioned and supported by relevant authorities. More than a thousand research studies have supported these ideas (for reviews, see Pettigrew and Tropp 2011; Tropp and Pettigrew 2005). Following Gordon Allport's statement of conditions for beneficial intergroup contact, much of social psychology's theoretical and empirical work on intergroup relations was directed at understanding ways to achieve intergroup harmony and reduce bias and prejudice by creating ideal contact conditions. One enduring question in creating the ideal conditions has been how salient separate group identities are and should be in the contact situation.

Patricia Gurin and Biren (Ratnesh) Nagda (2006) summarize three approaches to this question. These approaches indicate how in recent years theory and research on social identity have been incorporated into the contact hypothesis. The initial view is that intergroup harmony depends on de-emphasizing separate group identities so that members of different identity groups will treat each other as individuals, rather than as group members. The ultimate goal is to create a comprehensive group identity that overrides their separate group identities.

One theoretical approach, called decategorization or personalization, suggests that members of groups need to personalize and get to know out-group members as individuals rather than as group members (Brewer and Miller 1984; Wilder 1981). The goal is to promote differentiated conceptions of out-group members so that they "slide even further toward the individual side of the self as individual–group member continuum" (Gaertner and Dovidio 2000, 43). According to the decategorization model, anything that makes groups salient and encourages thinking about groups rather than individuals—group competitiveness, seating arrangements, resource allocation, discussion of cultures and histories, and attention to group identities—fosters intergroup prejudice, bias, and discrimination.

A second approach, called recategorization or the common in-group identity model (Gaertner and Dovidio 2000), draws on well-documented evidence that members of groups show bias in favor of others in their in-groups in evaluating and allocating resources. Because of this in-group positivity bias, recategorization theorists argue that "once outgroup members are perceived as ingroup members, it is proposed that they would be accorded the benefits of ingroup status" (Gaertner and Dovidio 2000, 48). The way to achieve a superordinate, overall group identity is through common activities and tasks, rewards based on cooperative behavior, integrated seating and living patterns, and symbols such as a T-shirt with a group logo for the new inclusive group. Research shows that when the common in-group identity model guides intergroup interactions, prejudice and intergroup bias are reduced, and both helping and self-disclosure to former out-group members are enhanced.

These two approaches, advanced by many social psychologists as the most effective for achieving intergroup harmony, do not distinguish among the identities or statuses of the groups involved (for overviews of these models, see Gaertner et al. 1999; Stephan and Stephan 2001). In both models, all group identities, whether privileged in the social structure or not, are deemphasized so that group members think about each other as individuals or as part of a newly formed deracialized or nongendered in-group. Original in-group identities are deemphasized as a trade-off to improve intergroup harmony. However, it is not always possible or even desirable, outside of the laboratory, to rely completely on these two models for positive intergroup relations because many people continue to find their racial, gender, ethnic, and nationality identities important in their lives every day.

A third approach uses Henri Tajfel's (1974) social identity theory to argue that group identities can foster positive social outcomes because in-group solidarity can become a basis for promoting social change. Thus, rather than aiming for intergroup harmony, an in-group solidarity model aims to create more equal relationships through group mobilization for social change, and through those altered relationships to create harmony based on justice. In-group solidarity derives from Tajfel's emphasis on positive psychological distinctiveness. Members of groups compare their groups with other groups, and when that comparison is positive, individuals are motivated to stay in the group. They usually are unaware of the importance of groups and group identity, which they take for granted. When the group a person identifies with is devalued or wields less power than other groups, individuals face two choices. They may try to leave the group or bring about social change so that their group has more status. Historically, some people have passed out of devalued groups. Others have tried to raise group consciousness and solidarity to strengthen group ties based on an understanding of how groups are affected by systems of power and inequality (Gurin, Hatchett, and Jackson 1989; Gurin, Miller, and Gurin 1980; Gutiérrez and Lewis 1999). In orienting to social change, individuals often alter their evaluations of their in-group and its relationship to other groups, such as by reinterpreting negative stereotypes as positive and creating new cultural images for the group (for example, Black is Beautiful, Woman Power). In this model, group consciousness and solidarity provide social psychological resources for collective action by groups that lack certain political, economic, and social resources. The goal of such collective action is greater equality and social justice in society. This goal contrasts markedly with the outcome of intergroup harmony in the standard models of intergroup relations, wherein group members are expected to de-emphasize their original group identity in the name of increased intergroup harmony (Wright 2009). Recent research summarized in a special issue of the *Journal of Social Issues* (Van Zomeren and Iyer 2009) supports the importance of social identity for motivating collective action among low power groups.

Continuing with the considerations of identity saliency, we note two additional recent trends in social psychology (Nagda and Gurin 2012; Rodriguez, Gurin, and Sorensen, under review). First, recognition is increasing that, along with identity salience, societal power statuses affect intergroup contact. Thomas Pettigrew's and Linda Tropp's (2011) meta-analysis of intergroup contact efforts confirmed the long-standing belief that intergroup contact, especially cross-group friendships, helps reduce prejudice. However, they also found that more than 85 percent of the studies looked at the benefits of prejudice reduction only for majority group members. The benefits of intergroup contact have been framed primarily from the perspective of advantaged group members. More research needs to consider the perspectives of disadvantaged groups. Recent research has begun to identify misunderstandings or asymmetries in intergroup contact and how people in diametric power positions may perceive, experience, and evaluate intergroup contact differently (Demoulin, Leyens, and Dovidio 2009). For example, privileged group members prefer the contact or interactions to focus on commonalties, whereas disadvantaged group members prefer a focus on both differences and commonalties (see Saguy, Dovidio, and Pratto 2008). Advantaged group members more often want to be liked in intergroup contact, and disadvantaged group members to be respected (Bergsieker, Shelton, and Richeson 2010). In thinking about inequalities, disadvantaged group members are more likely to make structural attributions for inequality and advantaged members to make system-justification and individualistic explanations for inequality (Bobo 2011; Cohen 2011; Gurin, Miller, and Gurin 1980). Although disadvantaged group members are more likely to feel anger and resentment at the inequalities, their advantaged counterparts either are fearful of being labeled prejudiced or feel ashamed and guilty (Richeson and Trawalter 2005). In terms of the goal of contact and action, privileged group members seem more to prefer contact for attitude change and prejudice reduction, whereas disadvantaged group members are more likely to prefer efforts for social change (Dixon et al. 2010; Maoz 2011; Wright and Lubensky 2009).

Second, social psychologists have now begun to move beyond prejudice reduction as the gold standard for successful intergroup contact. Linda Tropp and Robyn Mallett (2011), for example, note that research and practice of intergroup contact emphasize preventing prejudice, but that little attention, if any, has been paid to how intergroup contact can promote positive majority-minority group relationships. In other words, prejudice reduction efforts have not provided alternatives that promote more positive intergroup relationships. Combining this with the increased attention to identity and power promotes intergroup contact efforts geared toward forgiveness (Hewstone et al. 2006), reconciliation (Nadler 2012), and alliance building (Nagda 2006). All three are concerned centrally with the relationship among groups with different access to power and privilege; all three acknowledge the salience of identities and power differentials among the groups in contact; and all three specify particular social or interactional processes that can help move beyond fractured relationships toward greater social justice by bridging differences and enhancing relationships (Nagda and Gurin 2012). Reciprocal self-disclosure and empathy in forgiveness, removal of identity threats in reconciliation, and critical-dialogic communication processes in intergroup dialogue are deemed necessary to restoring relationships.

The intergroup dialogue practice model uses elements of decategorization, recategorization, and social identity theories and extends the recent work on power in contact and on promoting positive relationships across differences in contact. Most important, it builds on theorizing reflected in the dual identity approach offered by Samuel Gaertner and John Dovidio (2000) and the mutual differentiation approach delineated by Miles Hewstone and Rupert Brown (1986). In these two studies, it is argued that members of groups can be thought of simultaneously as separate groups and still be capable of engaging in common tasks with members of other groups. In fact, when members of groups for whom history, culture, and group identity are central to a sense of self are asked to forsake their group identities, strong negative reactions and worsened intergroup relations—not intergroup harmony—may actually be aroused (Gaertner and Dovidio 2000; Schofield 1986). Some experiments demonstrate that the dual identity and mutual differentiation models are often just as effective as the common in-group model in reducing intergroup bias. Sometimes they are more effective in helping group members generalize the positive feelings developed in the original intergroup situation toward other out-group members who were not present at the time (Gaertner and Dovidio 2000; Hewstone, Rubin, and Willis 2002). Recognizing that it is not always possible to mute or eliminate social categories, even if that were desirable, David Deffenbacher and his colleagues have shown that it is possible to "increase the salience of boundaries that separate two groups without simultaneously increasing the magnitude of intergroup bias expressed by group members" (2009, 189).

Multicultural Education

Over the last half century, higher education has supported many forms of education that have to do with learning about the "other." Both James Banks's (2009) and Christine Sleeter's and Carl Grant's (2009) typologies of multicultural education have helped delineate both the particular evolution of these approaches in education and the contributions of different practices over time. Earlier forms of multicultural education were remedial or focused on learning about single groups and the development of single group programs (such as Black Studies, Asian Studies, Women's Studies), what Kevin Kumashiro (2000) has termed "education for the other" or "education about the other." Later forms of multicultural education brought in more social structural analyses and moved toward "education that is critical of privileging and othering" and "education that changes students and society" (Kumashiro 2000, 25). Most relevant for our consideration are the two approaches that have developed within this later multicultural tradition: social diversity and social justice education.

Diversity education aims to promote feelings of unity, tolerance, and acceptance; it focuses on enhancing positive relations among students, reducing stereotyping and promoting positive self-concepts for all students. Typical curricula include readings with multiple perspectives representing the diverse students in the classroom. What is frequently lacking is a structural analysis of group-based inequalities and attention to how inequalities may be altered (Hardiman, Jackson, and Griffin 2007; Sleeter and Grant 2009). Like many of the interventions suggested by social psychologists who have built on Allport's contact theory, the diversity educational approach generally de-emphasizes separate group identities in favor of mechanisms to create cooperation and the development of superordinate group identities (Gaertner and Dovidio 2000).

Social justice education, on the other hand, teaches students "to develop the critical analytical tools necessary to understand oppression and their own socialization within oppressive systems, and to develop a sense of agency and capacity to interrupt and change oppressive patterns and behaviors" (Bell 2007, 2). It teaches about group-based inequalities through exploration of social identities (such as race, ethnicity, gender, and others) and positionalities (place in the stratification system) in systems of power and privilege. Typically, the curriculum is organized around various *isms* (such as racism, sexism, heterosexism, ethnocentrism, and others) as a way to examine systemic privilege and oppression. Pedagogically, students' life experiences are brought into the classroom as a starting point for raising consciousness (Adams 2007). Perspective taking, critical thinking, and social action skills are important outcomes of social justice education (Sleeter and Grant 2009). Students generally learn how they can be allies to work in collaboration with or on behalf of individuals and groups that have been disadvantaged, and thus learn how to practice anti-oppression actions and build "allyships" (Adams, Bell, and Griffin 2007).

Diversity and social justice education, as forms of multicultural education, share a foundation in the early anti-bias education efforts discussed in chapter 1. They attempt to teach students from diverse backgrounds about each other but do so in distinctive ways. Diversity education stresses relationship building, sometimes with an emphasis on similarities while downplaying group identities and differences, and other times with an emphasis on cultural differences not contextualized in power relations. The aim is to build friendships across differences. Social justice education focuses instead on developing critical consciousness and translating that into action and building alliances (Bell 2007). Yet the concern in social justice education with understanding power and inequalities, applying that understanding to social and political issues, and then connecting that to action may rely more on individual learning and less on collective learning through building relationships across differences.

Approaches to Learning

Social psychology of intergroup relations and the diversity and social justice approaches to education help define the dialogic and critical focus of intergroup dialogue. They, however, do not provide specific pedagogical approaches that will achieve the goals of these various approaches. The pedagogy of intergroup dialogue is characterized as learner-centered rather than teacher-centered. Paulo Freire (1993) terms teacher-centered education as banking education, relying exclusively on the expertise of teachers to deposit knowledge and to transmit it to students. By contrast, a learner-centered approach, which Freire calls dialogic education, considers who the students are and what learning practices will best promote motivation, learning, and achievement among them (McCombs and Whisler 1997). In learner-centered classrooms, students are active rather than passive; they engage in deep learning and understanding rather than simply master information; they individualize their learning but also participate collectively in group learning; they interact in a learning climate characterized by mutual respect and reflexivity (Lea, Stephenson, and Troy 2003; O'Neill and McMahon 2005). Learner-centered approaches aim to bridge learning in the classroom with students' lives outside of the classroom. Intergroup dialogue uses learner-centered processes. To illustrate how such processes operate in intergroup dialogue, we draw on three major approaches to learning that deal with the what and how of learning: relational, reflective, and integrative learning.

The psychologists Elizabeth and Robert Bjork of the University of California at Los Angeles have written widely about how learning occurs. Learning "is something we [have to] infer," they explain; it is "the more or less permanent change in knowledge or understanding that is the target of instruction" (2011, 57). The Bjorks stress that certain conditions under which people learn will increase the probability that what is being learned will get into storage, what some might refer to as long-term memory, with enough strength to decrease forgetting and enhance long-term retention of learning. In general, those learning conditions present what they call *desirable difficulties*—situations that may make it seem harder to learn at the moment but promote storage strength. They have delineated numerous such conditions—varying conditions of practice, including where one practices; interweaving instruction on separate topics rather than grouping by topic; spacing rather than massing (cramming) study sessions; using practice tests rather than presentations as study events; and what might be called an active orientation to learning, such as looking up answers, generating ideas, and making connections across readings. These are all strategies to increase storage strength—to get what we learn into long-term memory. One of the authors of this book, Patricia Gurin (2011), has argued that social diversity in the learning environment may productively be thought of as one of these desirable difficulties that increases the probability of learning having enough strength to be retained. Because diversity, for most students arriving at college from fairly segregated environments, is novel or at the very least somewhat unfamiliar and discontinuous from previous life experiences (Gurin 1999), diversity fosters attention and the kind of thinking that correlates with what produces high storage strength, namely active, systematic, minded, conscious thinking.

The strategies suggested by the Bjorks, demonstrated through a program of empirical research to enhance retention and transfer of learning to new situations, say nothing about what is to be learned. The strategies are especially useful when study sheets, practice tests, or PowerPoint lecture slides are given to students, defining what they are to learn. But that is not what happens in intergroup dialogue. Its goals—to increase intergroup understanding, relationship building, and action—are defined in a general way but we do not give students specific fact or informational sheets to be learned. Instructors design the dialogue curriculum, which includes informational as well as theory-based readings. Much of the what that is to be learned is co-constructed by the students and facilitators, however, through active learning exercises, facilitative inquiry, and dialogic and critical communication processes that the dialogue curriculum sets up. In this sense, learning in the critical-dialogic model of intergroup dialogue involves relational, reflective, and integrative approaches to learning.

Relational learning occurs when students, mentors, and instructors co-construct knowledge (Konrad 2010). Relational learning derives from the intellectual contributions of Lev Vygotsky, a Russian psychologist who began his work following the Russian Revolution of 1917. Vygotsky emphasized the interdependence between individual and social processes and the importance of learning in a social situation in which more knowledgeable people and the learner both bring something to the interaction (Scott and Palincsar 2009). In our model of intergroup dialogue, these co-learners include the participants and the facilitators who, guided by readings and prestructured learning activities, construct together what is to be learned. Learning about identity is an excellent example of what we mean by co-constructing knowledge. Dialogue participants learn that their multiple and complex identities are socially defined. Through both their interactions with each other and collective critical analyses, they can and usually do construct new identities as collaborators in social justice. They gain knowledge of exemplars who have identified with social justice; they construct what it may mean for them to think of themselves in that way.

Intergroup dialogue also involves reflective learning: stepping back to ponder what has just transpired and what sense can be made of what has occurred. In most dialogue sessions, three kinds of reflection take place, what Jack Mezirow (1991, cited in Reilly 2010) defines as content reflection (a review of what is understood), process reflection (a review of how that is understood), and premise reflection (questioning the assumptions that are revealed). All three may occur privately, as in reflection papers that are part of the learning in IGD, and especially may occur publicly, as in the dialogue about the learning in dialogue that takes place at the end of each session. In the dialogue about the dialogue, participants "step back, ponder, and make explicit the meaning to self and others, what has recently transpired, been planned, observed, and achieved in practice" (Reilly 2010, 2, paraphrasing Raelin 2000). The power of public reflection, or what we refer to in intergroup dialogue as collective reflection, is through interaction with others, not simply because one reflects in the presence of others. Thus, public or collective reflection in intergroup dialogue is itself a relational form of learning. The skills needed for public reflection, according to Joseph Raelin (2001), are exactly what the dialogic and communication processes demand of dialogue participants: listening, speaking, disclosing, testing ideas, probing, and inquiry.

Integrative learning usually is thought to include making connections across concepts, disciplines, or contexts and applying what is learned in one situation to another. Mary Huber and Pat Hutchings, in the most widely cited article on integrative learning, state that it involves "learning across contexts and time," "the capacity to connect," "integrating and interpreting knowledge from disciplines," and "applying knowledge through real-world engagements" (2004, 1; see also Peet et al. 2011). Too often students see their courses as separate bodies of knowledge and their co-curricular, research, and community involvements as discrete experiences. IGD courses constantly ask students to use integrative learning. Because the pedagogy of intergroup dialogue uses active learning exercises, participants can articulate what they have learned and see how they can use their learning outside the dialogue class. IGD also promotes integrative learning by using analytical, emotional, and behavioral learning. Because the communication processes continually engage students in reflecting on their learning, listening and probing the ideas of others, critically analyzing what they read and what their collective discourse reveals, and testing how to build alliances, students become able to tell what they know, see connections between their dialogue experiences and other learning experiences at college, and adapt and apply what they are learning to other situations. They are encouraged to bring experiences from their lives on campus into the dialogue and to apply learning in dialogue to their lives outside the course.

Intergroup dialogue integrates these three learning approaches with the social psychology research on intergroup contact and social identity, the diversity education emphasis on relationships across differences, and the social justice education emphasis on consciousness-raising. Intergroup dialogue involves all three approaches—reflective, relational, and integrative—and it leverages diversity into a learning environment with qualities of desirable difficulty. In line with the contact approach to intergroup relations, IGD's explicit pairing of two groups of students from different backgrounds elicits the students' attention and active involvement because this environment strikes students as different from the environments in which they have usually lived and studied. The novelty of the dialogue environment and especially the facilitated interactions across groups pull the students out of their comfort zones and motivate them to think hard about what they know and don't know. Students also build knowledge through enlightenment approaches, especially readings. Novelty and interactions across difference stimulate them to think and take an active role in their learning, both consequences that should enhance retention and application of learning. Being expected to be active learners, students also build skills not only for interacting across difference, but personal reflection and social action skills as well.

In the multifaceted integration of social psychology, diversity and social justice education, and learning processes traditions, intergroup dialogue distinguishes itself from the anti-bias education efforts discussed in chapter 1. The most distinctive aspect of intergroup dialogue is that it moves beyond the focus on reducing prejudice, implicit or explicit, to foster understanding of identity and inequality, to build relationships with and across differences, and to strengthen collaborative capacity for change. To reiterate what Linda Tropp and Robyn Mallett (2011) noted, most intergroup contact approaches have focused on preventing prejudice but not on promoting positive intergroup relationships in the context of unequal power relations. Intergroup dialogue promotes positive intergroup relationships as it consistently takes account of power and privilege. The critical-dialogic practice model of intergroup dialogue is an approach to intergroup relations and intergroup education that conceives of relationship building, critical consciousness, and action in a more coordinated way. It draws on and extends the work of David Schoem and Marshall Stevenson 1990; Ximena Zúñiga and Biren (Ratnesh) Nagda 1993; Ximena Zúñiga, Biren (Ratnesh) Nagda, and Todd Sevig 2002; see also Schoem et al. 2001.

A CRITICAL-DIALOGIC PRACTICE MODEL OF INTERGROUP DIALOGUE

Intergroup dialogue integrates the various social psychological and multicultural educational approaches. Social identity is kept salient and an intentional pedagogy is used that encourages students with different identities to get to know each other personally and as members of groups. IGD also promotes understanding one's racial-ethnic, gender and other social identities as well as understanding those of others. A collective learning environment helps students explore these identities in relation to their peers, and thus allows them to appreciate diversity among them. Although diversity education does emphasize building relationships, intergroup dialogue acknowledges identities and differences in these relationships. Furthermore, these identities are located in systems of power and privilege, which are not viewed as static but rather as dynamic and allowing for change (see also Zúñiga et al. 2007). Thus, as in social justice education, a critical analysis of inequality and commitment to social responsibility and action are tied to identities as central issues in intergroup dialogue. Through alliance building, what may be considered a common group identity as social justice allies is developed that allows for both in-group identity affirmation and cross-group collaborations. Alliance building does not require members of the two identity groups to deemphasize or forgo their group-based identities. It is based on both common commitments and recognition of differential access to power and privilege (Nagda 2006).

Defining our approach to intergroup dialogue as a critical-dialogic model captures its strong emphasis on both relationship building across differences and critical analyses of inequalities, as well as their integration in the service of action and change (Nagda 2006; Zúñiga et al. 2007). By *critical*, we mean a conscientious effort to examine how individual and group life are embedded within a structural system of inequality and privilege, and to connect that analytical understanding to action. We aim to raise critical consciousness by facilitating individual and collective reflections on readings, the experiences students share about how power and privilege influence their lives, and the power dynamics that emerge during the dialogue. This joint focus on person and structure means that students reflect on their social identities and on the larger systems of inequalities. As in critical consciousness (Freire 1970) and critical race theory (Delgado and Stefancic 2001), students learn about racial and gender inequalities not only through informational sources (documentaries, readings), but also through personalization, that is, an examination of how their and other students' lives are affected by race and gender. They reflect on key socialization experiences in their lives—from family to peers, teachers, and media—that influence how they think about themselves as individuals who simultaneously are also members of racial, ethnic, and gender groups. They tell their stories of individual and collective resiliency and resistance in dealing with privilege, inequalities, and structural constraints. Thus, in our work, *critical* means illuminating the connection of the individual and the group to systems of inequality and prejudice and further connects that understanding to action.

By *dialogic*, we mean a focus on building substantive relationships between and within groups through communication. Because estranged intergroup relationships are marked by lack of contact and lack of constructive engagement across differences, a primary task of intergroup dialogue is to create engaged interaction. This embraces the importance of personalization from social psychology but does so by keeping a group focus—individuals as members of social groups. Students build dialogic skills through active listening, personal sharing, perspective taking, and asking questions of each other. These basic communication skills serve as a foundation for deepened learning about one's own and other people's experiences and perspectives. Dialogue offers students a way to understand the complexities of their identities and self-other relationships. The goal of dialogue is neither agreement nor consensus decision making. Instead, it aims to create understanding through exploring meaning, identifying assumptions that inform perspectives, and fostering a willingness to reappraise one's thinking in light of these exchanges. In the traditions of dialogue, students do not take the relationships between themselves and others for granted but instead actively participate in jointly constructing both the meaning and process of building relationships across and within differences (Baxter 2004; Buber 1970). Martin Buber (1970), one of the most influential writers about dialogue, stresses the importance of mutual respect, listening, and building relationships in dialogue. The focus on dialogic, interactional learning does not undermine the focus on structural analysis of group inequalities and action in social justice education, nor does it blindly embrace the goal of harmonious intergroup relationships emphasized by diversity education and many social psychological approaches to intergroup contact.

Our critical-dialogic pedagogical model aims to facilitate critical analyses and dialogic relationships not simply as ends unto themselves or as separate goals, but to integrate them with a commitment to collaborative action and change. Readings, classroom activities, and written reflections during the dialogue link relationships to the larger social structure and help students recognize, understand, and connect across identity differences and inequalities. In intergroup dialogue, relationships are conceptualized in both broader and more complex ways than merely being aimed at creating intergroup harmony or at reducing unconscious prejudice that are the primary outcomes of several social psychological models of intergroup contact. Instead in intergroup dialogue, relationships are mechanisms for grasping how social structures operate to create and maintain inequality. At the same time, focusing on critical analyses in the context of sharing stories about the impact of power on the students' lives actually fosters motivation to bridge differences and individual and collective agency.

PEDAGOGICAL FEATURES OF INTERGROUP DIALOGUE

Intergroup dialogue directly responds to the conclusion drawn by many scholars of higher education that diversity must involve active engagement if it is to have educational benefits for students (Gurin et al. 2002; Milem, Chang, and Antonio 2005). Actual interaction, not mere coexistence, is important for diversity to promote learning. Students from diverse backgrounds need to be actively guided to learn from each other in courses, research projects, community work, and co-curricular activities. In courses, they need to grapple with materials that contextualize diversity in sociopolitical systems and they also need to get to know each other in depth rather than in superficial ways. In this study, the IGD courses were designed to accomplish both of these goals through content learning, structured interaction, and facilitation.

Content

Content learning refers to ways in which students are involved in learning key concepts and information, largely through readings. Referred to as enlightenment (Dovidio et al. 2004) and informational learning (Parker 2003), readings and written assignments in intergroup dialogue engage students in content learning. The assigned readings are diverse both in the social backgrounds and disciplines of the authors as well as in the content—theoretical, conceptual, narrative, case studies, and poems. Students read assigned readings in preparation for each class session. For example, because of its focus on critical, sociopolitical analysis, students read Bobbie Harro's (2000a) *Cycle of Socialization* in the second stage to examine their socialization into identities that accord more or less privilege (such as being white, affluent, and heterosexual or being an Asian immigrant, low-income, and a nonnative English speaker). Accompanying readings may also include socialization narratives of authors from diverse backgrounds.

Students were asked to use the readings as a reference point for writing their reflection papers. To carry the example of the cycle of socialization forward, students are asked to use that reading as a basis to write a testimonial of their socialization on the focal identity of their intergroup dialogue (race or gender) as well as other social identities that were salient for them. They then use their reflection papers as a basis of sharing their testimonials in class. In this example, but also in other in-class activities and exercises, written assignments and readings are fully integrated into classroom dialogue and into the students' reflective learning. Readings are not treated as a separate locus of learning or discussed as a separate part of the dialogue session but instead are brought into every aspect of what happens in the dialogue session.

In their final papers, students are asked to mention specific readings that especially helped them understand how privilege operates in society. One student commented on a quote from Harro's *Cycle of Socialization*: "if we are members of the groups that benefit from the rules, we may not notice that they aren't fair" (2000a, 18).

I believed that we all existed only as individuals—individual experiences, individual accomplishments, individual responsibility, and individual failure. Of course, we are all individuals but we are also more or less privileged by the circumstances in which we grew up. I could see from my socialization that I was very privileged and that many of those privileges had little to do with what I had personally done. (White woman, race-ethnicity dialogue)

Don Sabo's (1995) *Pigskin, Patriarchy, and Pain* was particularly meaningful for another student. Quoting Sabo, "one more man among many men who got swallowed up by a social system predicated on male domination" (229), the student reflected on his socialization as a boy and as a man:

Before the dialogue, I felt dominant and I was happy that I was. I was unaware about the extent of negative effects this had on the females I was in contact with. . . . In middle school I felt the need, very much like Sabo, to join the football team to prove myself to be a man. I was often teased about being a "mama's boy," being fat and goofy. . . . Being on the team, my coach would say comments like "you're big for nothing." Through embarrassment, punishment and pain, he was able to mold me into an aggressive competitive player contradictory to myself as a child. (White man, gender dialogue)

Not only did the students find the readings helpful in raising awareness about socialization and inequality, they were also inspired by them. One student wrote,

I see myself further practicing not being a "silent witness" and not only pointing out but also educating about oppressive behavior as mentioned in McClintock's *How to Interrupt Oppressive Behavior* (2000). McClintock said that it wouldn't be easy but I am up for the challenge. I have already begun but am also inspired both by this reading and what other students are already beginning to do. It will help me be a more knowledgeable mentor against violence as a peer trainer. (Woman of color, gender dialogue)

Structured Interaction

In intergroup dialogue, *structured interaction*, also referred to as encounter by Jack Dovidio and colleagues (2004) and as interactional learning by Walter Parker (2003), is the intentional creation of group structures and activities to involve students from different backgrounds in active learning. In structured interaction, explicit attention is given to constructing intergroup dialogues so as to equalize the group structure of the dialogue classroom. The interactions are designed to fulfill Allport's conditions for intergroup contact without losing sight of the larger context of inequality. Intergroup contact theory and practice have stressed conditions that promote positive interactions: equal status, authority sanction, acquaintance potential and interdependence (Allport 1954; Stephan and Stephan 1996). To accomplish equal status in the dialogue, we strive to have equal numbers of students from the two identity groups, such as an equal number of men and women, or of people of color and white people. Enrollment is kept low, usually fourteen to sixteen students, to allow the most opportunities for getting acquainted. In addition, each group is guided by two facilitators, one from each of the two focal identity groups. Building relationships and interdependence among participants are further fostered by ground rules—such as mutuality, sharing, listening, respectful inquiry, confidentiality, and open acknowledgment of disagreements and conflicts—that the participants create for themselves. Further, in-class activities and exercises are used to actively engage students and allow them to get to know one another on a personal basis.

The learning activities, many of which are described in more detail in the next section on the four-stage model of intergroup dialogue, provide common reference points to reflect and dialogue about similar and dissimilar experiences, and help build trust in the group. One student commented,

> I was in no way comfortable giving away a piece of myself when I thought about giving my testimonial. But I overcame this fear. I was able to grow in that ten minutes more than I have the whole time here at college. What really helped me was the sincerity of other students when they gave their testimonials and also how the group received them. It made the ideas of safety and trust real. I felt safe, secure, and confident in this group after that. (Man of color, race-ethnicity dialogue)

To connect individual testimonials to collective experiences in systems of privilege and disadvantage, facilitators guide the students in two related dialogues—an intragroup and an intergroup dialogue. Intragroup dialogues, known as caucuses or affinity groups, are made up of students sharing identities, either race or gender as relevant for the dialogue focus. Students meet first in separate caucuses to explore similarities and differences in experiences and to situate these experiences in systems of stratification that advantage some groups and disadvantage others (Zúñiga and Nagda 1993). Then both caucuses return to the whole group where each of them shares the themes that their caucuses considered important for everyone to understand. The intergroup part of dialogue is stimulated by an activity called fishbowl.

In the intragroup caucus group, the facilitator who shares the identity of that group guides the interaction. First, she or he will usually check to see how the students react to meeting in separate groups. Men and white people are sometimes uncomfortable about having to meet separately, whereas women and people of color are usually more comfortable. Facilitators ask the students to be aware of those feelings and to bring them up later in the intergroup dialogue. In these caucus groups, students explore issues of privilege, discrimination, stereotypes, vertical and horizontal inequalities, often making lists of how they feel advantaged and disadvantaged (McIntosh 1989; Pincus 2000). Members of disadvantaged groups usually find this an easy task, and often reveal a litany of experiences of feeling of being on the outside, marginalized, and discriminated against. Some of the students find that they can finish each other's sentences because of their many shared experiences. Others may find themselves understanding for the first time that their experiences are not merely attributable to their individual circumstances, but are part of a wider fabric that affects many others like them. Students in advantaged caucus groups often struggle to recognize the privileges that their group status has brought them or that their successes and achievements reflect special opportunities as well as hard work. The facilitator asks questions that encourage students to understand that the stratification system produces privilege and affects everyone, not just the disadvantaged group. Instead, students need to recognize that privilege exists and that they have likely internalized messages and practices that reflect the stratification system. Both groups find that they are able to voice their trepidations and experiences more freely in the caucus groups. A student stressed this benefit of the caucus groups both for understanding the complexity of her identity group and making a connection with the other group.

It was such a relief to talk honestly among ourselves about being viewed simplistically as just white people. We *are* white people. Of course, people see us as white. But we have very different families and backgrounds and ways of thinking. The caucus group helped us see how different we are, how upset we get when we are stereotyped, and yet how our anger, even fury, helped us understand how angry and furious students of color must feel when they are constantly treated as a glob. (White woman, race-ethnicity dialogue)

Another student wrote explicitly about the benefit of talking with other students of color like herself about expectations of prejudice from white students and how angry she often feels.

I knew coming into this class that race was a very sensitive subject to most people. My previous experiences in talking about this topic had been very tense and controversial. I admitted in my caucus group that I become angry and frustrated when people say ignorant things. It helped to talk about these barriers and go back to the group ready to have a deeper dialogue that acknowledges everyone's fears. (Woman of color, race-ethnicity dialogue)

Students also find that advantages and disadvantages are complex and that even those whose identity groups have been more advantaged in society may have some identities that have brought them disadvantages, whereas students whose identity groups have been more disadvantaged may have certain advantages.

The intragroup caucus group dialogue is later shifted to an intergroup context through the fishbowl activity (Schoem, Zúñiga, and Nagda 1993). In this structured dialogue, sharing starts with members of one identity group seated in an inner circle to dialogue within the fishbowl about their insights from the caucus group dialogue. They converse about how it felt to be engaged in the intragroup dialogue and the insights they gained. Members of the other group are seated in an outer circle and asked to listen to the dialogue in the inner circle. They may jot down questions or comments. At the end of the first group's sharing, each member in the outer group acknowledges one thing they heard in listening to the inner group. The two groups then switch roles and follow the same procedure. Following the structured fishbowl activity, facilitators invite the students to share what they learned, and how it felt to be speaking and listened to in the inner circle. During the ensuing intergroup dialogue, students ask each other additional questions and connect the readings to their observations. Their earlier experiences in dyadic active listening are now expanded to group-level listening, offering a unique opportunity to understand the complexity of identity within and across groups. As one student put it,

> I learned through the caucus groups and fishbowl that women, men, and other genders are completely different. Within each one gender there are diverse goals, emotions, and identities. In the caucus group, I heard women having very different ways of thinking about family and career. In the fishbowls, I saw how men view themselves and others, and that men differed a lot from each other too. (White woman, gender dialogue)

In the large group, facilitators also encourage students to consider within-caucus differences. Students in the disadvantaged caucus are asked to dialogue about ways in which they also experience privilege, such as socioeconomic privilege by the fact that they are college students. Students in the advantaged caucus group are asked to dialogue about ways in which they may also experience disadvantages and challenges based on their other identities, such as gender, class, religion, or sexual orientation. Such inquiry helps broaden students' understanding of themselves and the dynamics of power and privilege. It also allows for perspective taking across differences and empathy for the different cognitive and emotional challenges experienced in acknowledging how privilege and inequality affect students' daily lives.

Facilitation

Because interactions between students of different backgrounds and life experiences can replicate the dynamics of inequality on the campus and in the larger society, skilled *facilitation* is imperative to ensure that dialogue promotes open, equal exchanges and deepened learning (Nagda, Zúñiga, and Sevig 1995; Schoem et al. 2001). Co-facilitators, one from each of the identity groups present in the dialogue, help create an inclusive space for dialogue (Nagda and Zúñiga 2003). Biren (Ratnesh) Nagda and Kelly Maxwell (2011) lay out three principles for intergroup dialogue facilitation. First, facilitation refers to the guidance, not didactic teaching, provided in IGD to maximize the potential of content-based learning and structured interactions in diverse settings. Facilitators model dialogic communication and an equal relationship between themselves as a co-facilitation team. This design allows for support for diverse group members in the leadership of the dialogues. Even though co-facilitators represent the different groups, they are required to be neither impartial nor partial, but to practice multipartiality that lends support and challenge within and across group identities (Wing and Rifkin 2001). Facilitators strive to integrate content and process into the dialogues. Informational content is accessed through readings, short video clips, and conceptual organizers. Students also generate content by sharing their learning and perspectives. Process refers to the individual and group processes that unfold in diverse learning groups. Facilitators bring content and process together by attending to how different people respond to the content and the group dynamics unfolding in the dialogue process, by focusing on how the content is closely tied to people's identities, and by providing supportive frames of reference to understand individual experiences.

Second, IGD facilitators work not only from a place of being empowered, but also in ways that empower students in their dialogues (Nagda and Maxwell 2011). Facilitators can share their experiences and perspectives, which other forms of facilitation do not permit. Special care must be taken, however, that the dialogues do not become facilitator-centered and that facilitators do not become advocates for particular positions. A productive use of self as a facilitator can be purposive in guiding and deepening the dialogue. Facilitators also use their knowledge in framing and naming individual and group dynamics. For example, they can support participants by normalizing thoughts (such as dissonance and ambivalence) and emotions (such as anger, guilt, shame, and hopelessness) that arise in dialogues about inequalities intimately connected to students' lives. Additionally, by framing the emergent group dynamics in ways that shed light on how patterns of power and privilege are reflected among participants, facilitators can allow students to connect content and process to deepen the dialogue. Naming and framing are especially productive when facilitators ask questions to guide students in sharing their observations about group processes and dynamics, rather than facilitators making pronouncements. Facilitators, in bringing an empowering intentionality to their work with students, model and foster students' facilitative engagement so that the students can also guide the dialogue process and engage with one another directly.

Third, facilitators pay keen attention not only to the procedures of dialogue and learning agendas, but also to the communication processes that can encourage deeper analysis, feeling, and sharing in the dialogues at the collective level (Nagda and Maxwell 2011). Facilitators have to manage time, get through the learning agendas and activities for particular sessions, and ensure the logistics are clear for all participants. These procedures, however, need not override the importance of the critical-dialogic communication in interactions among the students. These processes, expanded on in chapter 3, are crucial for the focus of the learning on process, especially the important phase of collective reflection. Dialogic processes refer to fostering self-other relationships. Dialogic communication can be cultivated by encouraging relational speaking and responsive listening that enable students to validate and build on each other's contributions. For example, facilitators may ask, "How are your different perspectives related to each other? How do you relate to what has been shared thus far?" Critical communication processes refer to connecting consciousness of power and privilege to the dialogue learning. Facilitators may ask, "What do you think accounts for the different perspectives shared in our dialogue? How do power and privilege play into our experiences of the activity?" Critical-dialogic communication bridges the dialogue to action. Facilitators may ask, "What are our responsibilities as members of privileged and less privileged groups to extend our learning in the dialogue to our spheres of influence outside the dialogue? What would it take for us to build alliances and sustain our social justice work?" The dialogic, critical, and critical-dialogic inquiry each have a quality of deepening the dialogue and encouraging students to think of themselves not as isolated individuals but as people in relation to their peers, their societal context, and a responsibility for fostering social change. When facilitators model critical-dialogic engagement and especially inquiry, the learning process is deepened in the very ways we hope that the participating students interact with each other and in the world outside the classroom.

These three principles—guidance, empowering students, and attention to communication processes—provide an overview of the facilitation approach particular to IGD. Students often wrote about the importance of facilitators for their learning, for example, in reminding students to speak from personal experience and not generalize:

At the suggestion of the facilitators, we focused on the usage of "I" statements. "I" statements ensure that the person speaking remains the essential figure in the comment. There was no "black male view" or "white female perspective" in this dialogue, as I had experienced in most prior classes. (Woman of color, race-ethnicity dialogue)

Students also wrote about facilitators encouraging them to take ownership of their learning. At the beginning of most dialogues, students tend to direct their comments to the facilitators and wait for the facilitators to ask questions. Over time, students learn that dialogue requires a more democratic process, one that teaches them to inquire of each other rather than to depend on facilitators.

We got really great at asking each other to "please explain that further" or "is this what you mean by that." Becoming comfortable asking each other for these clarifications greatly enhanced our understanding of each other and what it meant to have a dialogue. (White man, gender dialogue)

Many students credit facilitators with helping them take risks in stating their opinions, especially when they worried that those opinions might reveal ignorance or prejudice. A white woman described how one day her facilitators helped her talk openly about a behavior that she worried would be seen as prejudiced:

The facilitators decided to make things more interesting by asking us to write down something that we "don't want to talk about". . . that we were afraid of bringing up. After we had all written something down, we put the [unsigned] cards up on the wall for everyone to see. Then we chose a few common themes for dialoguing. I decided to write something that had been on my mind for a long time but I never found a good time to bring it up. . . . I had been pretty cautious about saying anything. It was about how I am overly friendly or overly nice to people of color. Too often I just wasn't natural. I thought I would be seen as prejudiced. (White woman, race-ethnicity dialogue)

Students stressed the importance of both facilitator inquiry and facilitative interventions that encouraged deeper reflection.

Our facilitator was really good in providing priming questions, which led to monumental dialogues. It also helped the rest of us see that asking questions can go a long way in encouraging people to talk and listen; it isn't just saying what is on our minds but delving into other people's ideas. (White man, gender dialogue)

When most of the students of color spoke, their comments tended to be heavily grounded in personal experience and represented their individual interpretation of a given phenomenon. When the white students spoke, their comments were more generic . . . [or] hypothetical, which then depersonalizes them from the discussion. The facilitators asked questions about what patterns we saw. Everyone agreed that we should speak personally and everyone tried. (Man of color, race-ethnicity dialogue)

After everyone had given their testimonials, our facilitators asked us if we saw any general patterns in what students had shared. It wasn't very hard to see them once we were asked to think about patterns. One was that nearly all of the white students talked about not having a racial identity. Another was the opposite, how easily the students of color talked about identity. That doesn't mean that every white person and every student of color disclosed exactly the same stories. The stories were rich and individual. But still the pattern was clear. Maybe we would have seen it even without the facilitators but just being asked to reflect on the general patterns really helped. (White woman, race-ethnicity dialogue)

The students' reflections about facilitators show a balance between facilitator guidance and group member responsibility for assuring positive dynamics in the dialogue. On one hand, facilitators ask questions that lead to naming and framing the group dynamics; they redirect the dialogue to foster trust and risk taking, recognizing intergroup patterns and deepening the dialogue. On the other hand, group members also ask questions and redirect the dialogue as they learn to become facilitators themselves.

Content, structured interactions, and facilitation provide the steady pedagogical foundation for each intergroup dialogue session. Each dialogue group is unique in its composition and dynamics as well as substantive issues, but two practice road maps are particularly important. The first, a learning guide template for each session explicates the flow of an individual session. The second, a four-stage IGD model, spans the the entire dialogue over the academic term, usually between ten and fourteen individual sessions. We describe both in detail in the following section.

INDIVIDUAL SESSION LEARNING GUIDE FOR INTERGROUP DIALOGUE

As described in the pedagogy of intergroup dialogue, learning in IGD occurs at both individual and group levels, each informing the other. IGD strives to involve students actively in their learning rather than to let them be passive recipients, to provide opportunities to both listen and speak, to connect individual experiences to more collective experiences by exploring similarities and differences among participants, and to connect in-group processes to larger societal dynamics. These learning principles guided the design of IGD sessions and the four-stage curriculum of the courses implemented as part of the study.

A typical session is organized thus:

- introduction and check-in

- common language and conceptual organizers

- structured learning activity

- collective reflection and dialogue on learning from activity

- dialogue about the dialogue: collective reflection on learning from the entire dialogue session

- check-out and transitions to next session

We describe each section in greater detail in the following sections.

Introduction and Check-in

Facilitators usually start each session by welcoming the students to the session. In the beginning, as a way of inviting people into the dialogic space and allowing for a transition from other classes or activities that the students are involved in, facilitators use one of several different quick check-ins. Some examples include icebreakers that allow students to share parts of themselves that may not be related to the dialogue content but that do allow for a more interpersonal connecting with classmates before the heart of the session. Other times, facilitators conduct more intentional check-ins that are connected to the dialogue, such as asking students to share what they have been reflecting on from the past session, an insight they gained from the readings for the week and so on. Facilitators do check-ins using either rounds in which each student gets to share and listen to others in the large group, or dyads or small groups. Large group check-ins may involve kinesthetic activities that require students to move around. Such check-ins can allow for reconnecting as a group, provide a common stimulus for individual responses, and maximize participation from the beginning of the dialogue.

After the check-in, facilitators introduce the learning goals for the particular session. They usually find some connections either to what the participants share during the check-in or to themes present in the previous dialogue session.

Common Language and Conceptual Organizers

For sessions that require definitions and conceptual organizers, facilitators introduce these in the beginning to ensure participants start with a common base (Adams 2007). Participants receive a handout with definitions or a visual aid, such as Harro's cycle of socialization. They may ask participants to read over the list of definitions or alternatively post the definitions on the walls of the room. They may ask participants to give some examples of the definitions, connect definitions to the readings, or offer some examples themselves. Although common language is important, facilitators remain careful not to get bogged down in this aspect of the session.

Structured Learning Activity

Intergroup dialogue uses learning activities to engage students in integrating different modes of learning. Included as part of structured interactions, the intention of learning activities is to provide a common reference point for all participants, an in vivo experience that everyone can reflect on based on their own experience (Zúñiga et al. 2007). Examples of learning activities include testimonials, caucus groups and fishbowls we described earlier. We describe a few more learning activities in the four-stage model. Particular facilitation skills are important in engaging all students in learning activities. Facilitators need to think beforehand about accessibility and inclusion of all participants. Visual aids or demonstrations or modeling participation in activities are usually helpful. Most important, facilitators need to keep in mind that the learning activity is a stimulus for dialogue, and not an end in itself. Learning activities are intended to lead to the next part of the dialogue session—reflection on learning from the activity.

Collective Reflection and Dialogue on Learning from the Activity

A strong theme in how students learn is the role of reflection in learning (Reilly 2010). Specifically, two types of reflection, which Raelin (2001) refers to as private and public reflection and we call individual and collective reflection, are deemed important. Substantive reflection on learning from the activity is crucial for two reasons: to foster active, affective, analytical, and applied thinking, and to connect students' individual experiences to the collective experience of the activity for all group members. Individual reflection is done through free-writing, journal writing, or in-class reflection papers. Collective reflection happens in two ways: one, sharing and listening to individual reflections in the large group but without interactive engagement; and, two, sharing, listening and inquiring in a highly interactive dialogue among all participants. Collective reflection enables students to examine their experiences and perspectives in relation to each other, explore similarities and differences, examine what influences their perspectives including social identities and social power relations, and what the learning means for their lives on campus and beyond. It also gives students an opportunity to share ways in which they are integrating their learning across multiple learning sources (such as readings, activities, dialogues) and across multiple arenas of their life (such as other courses, campus life, family and community life). The goal of collective reflection is neither to simply advance individual perspectives nor to come to a preconceived end of the dialogue session. Rather, it is to foster a generative dialogue that allows for both divergent and convergent insights, and an excitement to continue learning individually and collectively inside and outside the dialogue groups.

Given that students may process their learning in different ways and with different comfort levels, facilitators use free-writing (one-minute reflection papers), dyad check-ins, or rounds for students in their individual reflections on learning from the activity. If students start by giving feedback about the activity, facilitators redirect them to share more about their experiences. In other words, the engagement is to be a reflection and dialogue about the experience in the activity and not feedback about the activity.

Dialogue about the Dialogue: Collective Reflection on Learning from the Entire Session

Dialogue on learning from the entire session involves an interactive, collective reflection. In this collective reflection, the facilitators guide students to think and dialogue about the dialogue process itself, including the dynamics in the dialogue (see Zúñiga et al. 2007). It includes listening, sharing, inquiry, identifying assumptions, probing, critical reflection, and bridge building across perspectives and identities. Facilitators are encouraged to keep an eye on who is participating and how they are participating, the emotional climate of the group, and the ways in which students participate from their comfort zones and how much they meet their learning edge (Nagda and Maxwell 2011). Inquiry at this level may involve asking students about observations at the personal or group level: "In what ways did we engage our learning edges today? In what ways did we support each other working at our learning edges? How can we all work together to take the dialogue deeper in the upcoming sessions? Are there any particular dynamics or tensions that affected our ability to dialogue fully?" The discussion that emerges from these questions encourages participants not only to identify any underlying dynamics but also to link them to dynamics in society.

Throughout the session, and especially in the individual and collective reflection and dialogue on learning, facilitation skills of active listening, encouraging, inquiry, reflection, redirection, clarifying, summarizing, and observing and naming group dynamics are crucial. For the dialogue to go beyond just the simple sharing of experience in the activity, facilitators use inquiry and foster student inquiry to deepen the learning.

Check-outs and Transitions

The final part of each dialogue session involves a check-out and transition. Check-outs are a way of closing the dialogue. Because participants may not have processed all their thoughts and emotions, we normalize this process by saying that learning will continue after the session. We may not always put an end to a conversation in one session and start a completely new one the next. A final check-in can allow participants to share one insight they had in the dialogue, one new thing they learned, one former assumption or idea they challenged, or even one thing they would like to share with their roommate or friend. If the facilitators decide something light would be helpful, they may just ask questions: "What are your plans for the upcoming weekend? What is one fun and rejuvenating thing you would like to do before next session?"

To end the session and transition to the next one, facilitators may highlight work the students need to do in preparation for the next dialogue session, any announcements of speakers and events, and share some general affirmative (if appropriate) comments with the students.

THE FOUR-STAGE DESIGN OF INTERGROUP DIALOGUE

Because intergroup dialogues are learner- and learning-centered, and rely on sustained contact to make meaningful relationships possible, we use a developmental stage-model of dialogue (Saunders 1999; Stephan and Stephan 1996; Zúñiga and Nagda 2001). The four stages unfold over the time of contact, starting with group beginnings and getting acquainted to exploring socialization, to dialoguing about hot topics or difficult questions, and ending with alliance building and taking action.[1] We discuss in the following sections the goals and key content and process issues for each stage of the intergroup dialogue curriculum used in this study.

Stage 1. Group Beginnings: Forming and Building Relationships

The goals of the first stage are to set the context for dialogue engagement. At the first meeting, students are introduced to the course and to the facilitators. But because IGD is based on building substantive relationships across differences and grappling with issues of identities and inequalities, special attention is paid to both framing the course and creating an inclusive learning community.

In the first session, co-facilitators introduce students to the goals of the course and frame the course as an opportunity to actively and collaboratively learn about racial-ethnic or gender inequalities. They emphasize the importance of active learning through structured activities and dialogic exchange. The class is usually seated in a circle so that everyone can see each other, the facilitators sitting across from one another. This arrangement conveys a different learning environment for most undergraduates, who may be more used to large lectures and discussion classes that may have chairs arranged in rows with the instructor or instructors at the front of the room. As a way of getting acquainted, students and facilitators share briefly their formal and informal experiences of diversity on campus, and discuss their motivations for taking the course. This helps set the context for what they may expect from the course, and how it may be different from or build on their previous learning. The co-facilitators also talk about their roles and how facilitating IGD fits into their learning and commitments to social justice.

To engage students immediately in active learning, the facilitators ask them individually to think about their understanding of debate and dialogue. They then divide the class into two groups, instructing one to focus on debate and the other on dialogue. They are asked to meet in their groups, discuss their ideas about debate or dialogue, and construct a role-play of debate and dialogue around a simple question (such as "Should one year of national community service be required of all graduates?"). They then perform the role-play in front of the whole class, and the facilitators help the entire group debrief both performances, asking for observations from both the participants and the observers, and comparing and contrasting the two. This activity conveys that the students are active participants and agents in the learning process, helps draw the distinctions between debate and dialogue (as elaborated in chapter 1), and sets the foundation for a quick, experiential understanding of dialogic engagement. The students and facilitators then reflect on and share their hopes and fears for the dialogue experience about to ensue.

These two experiences—a role-play and sharing hopes and fears—set the stage for the students to collectively develop guidelines for meaningful engagement to build a learning community. Facilitators ask the students, in small groups and then in the full group, to reflect on the kinds of interactions that would help them actualize their hopes and diminish their fears. Students think about what would allow them to participate honestly and to learn productively in the dialogues, as well as what they would like to contribute to make it productive for everybody. The facilitators encourage the students to frame their guidelines as much as possible as behaviors. For example, students often bring up respect and openness as two guidelines. Obviously, the meaning and understanding of these two important qualities vary among the students. Facilitator inquiry helps students be more specific about the guidelines, for example, what behaviors would convey respect and openness. Some guidelines that commonly emerge are using *I* statements, asking clarification questions and not assuming meaning or intent, responding to or building on others' comments, acknowledging emotions, engaging conflicts as opportunities for learning, taking ownership of one's impact on others, and respecting the personal confidentiality of what is shared in the dialogue group.

In the session following the role-play and setting of guidelines, facilitators involve the students in an active listening activity to build the students' capacities for both listening and purposeful speaking. The students are usually struck by a simple realization that they often are not fully listening to people because they want to share their perspectives. Jeanne Weiler's (1995) *Finding a Shared Meaning: Reflections on Dialogue* provides helpful content for students to deepen their understanding of dialogue. Thus, at the end of the first stage, the students have begun to get to know their peers through personal sharing, and to conceptually and experientially distinguish between debate and dialogue; they have established guidelines for engagement, and developed some skills for listening and speaking in the group.

In their final papers, students wrote about how the sessions in stage 1 fostered their learning about what dialogue means and demands. Students referred directly to the activities in their group that helped set an inclusive environment for dialogue instead of debate:

> The behaviors we practiced in role-playing a debate and a dialogue helped me get what dialogue means right at the beginning of the course. I could see in the role-playing what [Weiler] meant when she wrote, "Dialogue creates an openminded attitude; an openness to being wrong and an openness to change," as well as the other side of it, that "Debate creates a closed-minded attitude, a determination to be right." From then on, we knew when we were slipping into debate because we understood what it looks and feels like. (White woman, race-ethnicity dialogue)

> For the most part, the guidelines we established were accepted by all and helped us dialogue instead of debate. The most important one was our agreement to use *I* statements. Every time someone started speaking on behalf of a group of people, someone referred to that guideline—say it for yourself. (White man, gender dialogue)

Students also wrote about their recognition of the importance of active listening for understanding and insights into their own listening styles before intergroup dialogue:

Two-way listening—learning about someone from actually listening to them and having them learn about you from actually listening—creates connections that automatically make the situation more comfortable. Having a group of people take time to listen to each other proves that they will be willing to listen to opinions they disagree with. It isn't that dialogue is always better than debate, just when people really want to understand each other. (Man of color, gender dialogue)

Being in the dialogue made me a better listener. Active listening is more than just seeming to be interested in what the speaker is saying; rather it is being attentive to the speaker in every way—verbally and nonverbally. Before this class I would find my mind wandering off after listening to someone for a couple of minutes. Now I can really focus and listen in depth. (Woman of color, race-ethnicity dialogue)

The students' reflections speak to the newness of engaging in IGD and the foundational knowledge and skills that made them part of a learning community and not simply a group of individual learners.

Stage 2. Exploring Differences and Commonalities of Experience

The foundation for dialogic communication having been set in the first stage, the second stage centers the conversation on identities and inequalities. The goals are threefold: one, to recognize and analyze through relationships and stories told in the dialogue how race, ethnicity, gender, and other identities develop; two, to explore how these identities and stories reflect social group memberships and are located in the larger structural systems of power and privilege; and three, to discover how group-based identities are implicated in relationships that emerge within the dialogue itself.

Given that many students may not think about themselves in social identity terms or may not talk about these social identities with others who are different from themselves, students are asked to describe themselves through both a personal and social identity lens. The personal identity wheel activity asks students to share information about their hobbies, birth order, favorite book, family life, and aspirations, among other things. The social identity wheel activity asks students to reflect upon their multiple social group memberships (race, ethnicity, gender, sex, class, age, sexual orientation, national origin, religion, ability, and others) and to share with each other which identities are most and least influential in their lives, ones that they think about the most and least, and ones that they would like to learn about more. Not only does this activity enable students to build relationships with each other by sharing their identities and their meaning in their lives, it also helps them differentiate between personal identity and social identity. These two exercises—coupled with reading Tatum's (1997) *The Complexity of Identity: 'Who Am I?'*—help them reflect on questions such as "How do I usually see myself? How do others usually see me? How are the two lenses connected or separated? How do my experiences of privilege and inequality influence the lens that I feel more comfortable with? How do others in the group identify themselves and why?"

Sharing their identity wheels then leads them to examine socialization into particular social identities. Using Harro's (2000a) cycle of socialization as conceptual organizer, students write personal testimonials about both an identity that is the focus of the dialogue and another. If the students are from a racial-ethnic or gender identity group with less societal power, they are asked to write about a second identity in which they are privileged, and vice versa. For each of these identities, students write about initially coming to understand themselves as members of that particular identity group, including the early influences from parents and siblings. Students bring these testimonials to the classroom and take turns sharing them, as much or as little as is comfortable for them. Facilitators reinforce the importance of listening attentively to and acknowledging one's own connection with each person's sharing. Facilitators stress that connection does not have to be similarity but could be difference; the important point is to acknowledge the emotional and cognitive connection between self and other. As students listen to others, they are encouraged to try as much as possible to suspend their judgments and listen for both the content and meaning of the testimonials. As part of the debriefing and learning from the shared testimonials, facilitators ask questions such as "How did it feel to present your testimonial? How did it feel to listen to others' testimonials? What struck you about the commonalties and differences in the testimonials? In what ways did you see or feel connections between you and others in the dialogue? How has socialization shaped us, and why? How can the impact of socialization be challenged?"

A student, reflecting a widespread sentiment among others, wrote in his final paper about the profoundness of the testimonial activity for learning about his identities and those of other students:

> Now that the course has come to a close, I can say that all of us have deeper understandings of our identities. That has come partly from readings but it began very early in the testimonials when we saw how personal identity and social identity were different. The testimonials when everyone shared about their own lives and how their identities were formed and affected them, that was a turning point for me. I could see how identity is part of everyone's make-up. (Man of color, race-ethnicity dialogue)

In expanding learning about inequality to the structural level, facilitators use the web of oppression activity to guide students to think deeply about the readings and concretize how privilege and inequality are created and maintained (see Bell, Love, and Roberts 2007). Students brainstorm a list of institutions, such as education, media, legal system, health care, and so on. They then think of examples of a particular kind of inequality (racial, ethnic, gender, or class) that may be created or reinforced by these institutions. Standing in a circle, students hold on to one part of a preconstructed web on which there are labels of the different institutions. On each label are statements—current or historical—that show aspects of institutional inequality. Students take turns reading examples from the different institutions. Sequentially, they can see the interconnections among the institutions and the historical and structural maintenance of inequalities. In this activity, many students ask, "How do some institutions create and maintain inequality? Can the web be altered? What can we as students do to change how the web operates?" They can also see what happens when one link of the web is dropped through social change. The point is to help them visualize the creation, maintenance, and change of structural and institutional policies and practices involving inequalities.

The power of this active learning activity is its visual depiction of the complexity and interconnection of institutional sources of inequality and how every individual is implicated in the web, something that is usually hard for people to understand at an abstract level. It also engages students in actively considering their own roles in maintaining or challenging the web. As an avenue to reflect on and analyze the activity to deepen learning, facilitators ask questions, such as "What do you think accounts for the different experiences and perspectives with the web? How do our identities affect our perspectives? What different feelings come up as we examine the systematic nature of inequality? What is the personal impact of socially structured privilege and inequality?"

Students reported learning a great deal from the web of oppression activity. A white woman in a gender dialogue wrote about how she came to understand sexism:

> For the first time I grasped the disadvantages I face as a woman. Sexism is so institutionalized that I did not realize that a lot of my everyday activities and relationships with men are constructed in a manner in which they dominate. (White woman, gender dialogue)

Supported by readings, the dialogues help students make sense of the multilevel nature of privilege and inequality. It is neither simply institutional nor solely individual; the reverberations of advantage and disadvantage are reinforced and felt at each level. It is as important for students to understand the impact of their interpersonal relationships and dynamics on the sociopolitical context as it is to understand the impact of sociopolitically structured inequalities on individuals.

> Racism is not hate for no reason. It is a system made to give advantages based on race alone. This totally separates racism and prejudice. Prejudice is a personal ideology and racism is a system with institutional policies, beliefs, and practices. (Man of color, race-ethnicity dialogue)

One male student wrote about a new understanding and awareness about male privilege, and how that operates institutionally and in the dialogue itself:

> The biggest impact of dialogue was increasing my understanding of privileges and discriminatory practices that affect social, gender, ethnic, and religious groups. I am much more aware of the glass ceiling in business and the overall effect of the web of oppression on women's self esteem and social stature. (White man, gender dialogue)

Another male student wrote,

Now I question nearly everything. Why did I speak out more in class than the woman beside me? Why didn't I get interrupted as much as the women in my dialogue? (Man of color, gender dialogue)

Stage 3. Exploring and Dialoguing about Hot Topics

The third stage in IGD design engages students in controversial issues related to the dialogue topic. The goals of the third stage are for students to apply both their dialogic skills and their analytic understanding of social identities, inequalities, and collective dynamics in the dialogue to these controversial issues in the hot topics activity. Examples of these hot topics in the race dialogues are interracial relationships, separation and self-segregation on campus, racial profiling, and immigration. In gender dialogues, such topics might include friendships and intimate relations, sexual harassment, and gender in the media. Even when issues may be personally or politically charged, and students feel pressured to agree or disagree on an issue, facilitators guide them to try to understand the different positions and why students hold them. They help students examine their perspectives on issues and listen to those of others with curiosity and openness to broaden their thinking. Facilitators encourage students to look at assumptions—their own and those of other students—that result in particular perspectives. Dialoguing about controversial issues allows students to practice what dialogue means in a situation where argument usually prevails; analyze how power and privilege affect real issues; conduct a multilevel analysis of social issues, connecting historical and structural factors to current issues and lived realities; and grasp how relationships that were built during stages 1 and 2 provide a foundation for dialogue. In some cases, students may also examine possible solutions to policy issues, and also what their views of these issues mean for their relations with each other.

Students themselves suggest hot topics they would like to address. The only parameters the facilitators provide are to choose one topic that may be seen from an interpersonal perspective (such as interracial relationships), and another from an institutional or policy-related perspective (such as gender and media). For the topic that is more interpersonally oriented and aimed at more dialogic connecting, facilitators use the uncommon ground activity to stimulate the dialogue (see Botkin, Jones, and Kachwaha 2007). Facilitators call out statements that relate to the topic. If it applies to any student or facilitator and if they feel comfortable, they step inside a circle. Everyone is instructed to be aware of the emotions evoked by the statements and whether they feel these emotions when they are inside or outside the circle. Everyone also observes who is in the circle and who is outside. After the facilitators read some statements, they invite the participants to call out something that applies to them in relation to the topic and about which they would like to know who else shares that experience or perspective. Again, the students step into the circle if the statement applies to them. Facilitators debrief this exercise by asking students to individually write down how they felt, what statement or statements were most striking to them, and what they were struck by about the unfolding dynamic of who was in the circle and who was outside. Facilitators ask students to share reflections, observations, and the meaning they derived from the activity. This part of the dialogue is geared toward understanding how the statements and students' responses to them help students see a connection between identities and perspectives on social issues. Facilitators encourage students to ask each other questions and to relate to each other's experiences within the context of racial-ethnic and gender identities, societal inequalities, and the readings assigned for the week.

The next hot topic activity aims to highlight an institutional issue, such as the impact of media in socializing gender-based expectations or the impact of urban schooling on racial and ethnic disparities in high school graduation and college enrollment. Students are asked to bring in images, articles, and other visual materials that depict the topic for this dialogue in preparation for an activity called the gallery walk (see Zúñiga et al. 2007, 99). They post their items around the room in what looks like a gallery. Facilitators may also add video clips or other audiovisual materials related to the topic. Participants circle the gallery in silence. After all participants have looked at the entire gallery, participants share reactions, either verbally or by creating another gallery for participants to write reactions and questions on Post-it notes, which are placed next to the appropriate images. For example, they may write responses to questions such as "What are you struck by?" and "How does it feel to see all these images?" Participants recircle the gallery and read everyone's responses. Facilitators then debrief the activity by asking students to share and listen to each of the students' reactions in the gallery walk. They challenge students to make connections between institutions and their impact on individuals.

Students' writings about the hot topics activity convey their deepened learning and engagement with these issues. In particular, they reported becoming more comfortable in conversing about contentious issues. One student wrote,

> The hot topics activity was a big learning for me because it helped me see that one can get different impressions if you look at something from different angles. I pretty much avoided confrontations before, but now I know that it is important to name what the conflict is and look at it from other people's perspectives as well as my own. (Woman of color, race-ethnicity dialogue)

Students also wrote about how the hot topics sessions made visible the differences that exist and provided an avenue for them to engage with them more productively as individuals and in dialogue with others.

> One thing I learned in our hot topics activity is that white people will avoid and ignore race and pretend like it doesn't exist. That doesn't help the problem. Everyone has to be willing to lay it out there and then see how others react to it. That takes courage, which we got to in our dialogue, including the white people. (Man of color, race-ethnicity dialogue)

> Putting up those examples from magazines that showed so much sexism has stayed with me. I used to read those magazines at the gym without paying attention but now I go through them and point out how women are portrayed, men too, in sexist ways. I now understand the role of media in enforcing gender stereotypes. (White woman, gender dialogue)

Stage 4. Action Planning and Collaboration

The fourth stage in IGD allows students to apply learning about dialogue, identity, and inequalities to their responsibilities to advance social justice, sometimes by themselves individually and sometimes in concert with others. The goal of the fourth stage is to make explicit the connections between dialogue and action. This stage is crucial because it allows students to talk about ways in which they can have an impact on the inequalities that they have been learning about, to realize that recognizing and understanding their own positions of advantage and disadvantage are not goals but necessary conditions for them to make the world more just, and to embrace lifelong learning rather than imagining that they have arrived. Many students feel either extremely motivated to change the world or too overwhelmed by the enormity of injustices. Facilitators guide students to think about action and alliance building that can be both individual and collective, and to make use of the readings that discuss action, participation in democratic processes, and alliance building. Harro's (2000b) *Cycle of Liberation* enables students to see how individual actions can be joined with those of others to work toward institutional and cultural change.

The spheres of influence activity helps students see the multiple areas of influence they have in the present and the future (Goodman and Schapiro 1997; Tatum 1997). Other readings on alliance building, Judit's (1987) *Alliances* and Andrea Ayvazian's (2007) *Interrupting the Cycle of Oppression* show how positions of relative privilege and relative disadvantage carry similar as well as different responsibilities for redressing inequalities and promoting change. Further, students also dialogue about their ongoing commitments toward justice.

In this stage, a learning activity called the Intergroup Collaborative Project (ICP) is used to foster alliance building (see Zúñiga et al. 2007, 102). Early in the intergroup dialogue process, students are assigned to small groups of four students, two each from the two identities participating in the dialogue. The primary task for the group is to plan, implement, and reflect on a small action project to be accomplished in the last three weeks of the term. These groups also serve as spaces for small-group dialogic communication throughout the term. They also meet outside class to continue the in-class dialogues and to plan their projects. Group members collectively develop ideas for action projects that will push them out of their comfort zones. Examples include conducting dialogues among their friends on controversial issues or on a provocative movie, surveying public opinion, creating a multimedia presentation on contentious issues such as sexual harassment or affirmative action, and holding a public event to educate others about safety and violence on campus. In the final sessions of the dialogues, students present their ICP projects and dialogue about the rewards and risks of taking action to promote justice, and the impact of taking action on themselves. They also share what they had learned about the dynamics of working across difference. They dialogue about how that action would be different if they had done it individually or collectively. The primary point the facilitators try to make during this session is that students have learned about cross-group alliances, not how successful their action project proved to be.

In dialoguing about the ICPs, facilitators probe how students reflect on their action projects: "What identity-based dynamics arose in your ICP group? How did the group deal with those dynamics? What have you learned about alliance building? How can internalized inferiority and superiority impede our abilities to build alliances across power differences? How can different groups work together in ways that build stronger alliances and empower everyone?"

Referring specifically in their papers to the intergroup collaboration projects, students wrote that the ICP allowed them to become more involved in the entire intergroup dialogue experience and to extend it beyond the dialogue group:

> Earlier in the semester I was more conscious about what I said, trying not to offend other people, but as the semester went on and we got more involved in our ICP groups, I realized that the best way to work in a group of diverse people is to embrace the differences among us rather than pretending that they do not exist. By acknowledging that we were all different, some of us more privileged and others less privileged, we created an open and honest atmosphere where we were all free to give our ideas for our project. (White woman, gender dialogue)

> Beyond learning how to engage in the formalities of dialogue, I also felt that the opportunity to collaborate on the ICP helped me grow. . . . What I found remarkable about the project was that it provided us an outlet to promote awareness on campus of different cultures and cultural issues. . . . It is usually difficult to get others to listen, but the ICP gave us a way to affect some type of change. (White man, race-ethnicity dialogue)

Other students wrote about how working together throughout the dialogue allowed them to understand more realistically about what it takes to be allies.

> The reason that trust is important is that it helps us expose our vulnerabilities. We built up trust so that we could admit that we needed allies. Everyone can be an ally. (Woman of color, race-ethnicity dialogue)

[It] requires much more than just laying down demands on a few issues. It takes full commitment and determination from all parties. Such alliances are formed out of desire and passion for bettering our world, not because of sympathy. Instead, these relationships should revolve around empathy. (Man of color, gender dialogue)

In this last stage, it is also important that participants recognize that the learning community that they have built will come to an end in its current form. They are invited to show appreciation for their learning in two ways—through self-reflection on their learning and an appreciation of others' contributions to their learning. An assignment that helps students do this is to write a letter to themselves in two parts. In preparation for the last session, they write the first part about their most important learning in the dialogues; they describe one or two key lessons from the dialogue and what made them important for them. Then, during the last session in class, they write the second part about what they would like to apply to their life on campus and the larger community, and how they see themselves sustaining their learning. Students bring a self-addressed stamped envelope to class, seal the two-part letter in it, and hand the envelope to the facilitator. The facilitators mail the letters to the students three to six months later. Then, as a way of affirming other students' contributions to their learning, students write or verbally share specific appreciations of different members in the group. These activities terminate and round out the dialogue experience.

CONCLUSION

We have discussed the core elements of the IGD pedagogy with examples of key activities and the collective reflection that is crucial for students' learning. We have also highlighted examples of such learning in the four stages defined in the curriculum. The developmental nature of the four-stage IGD model allows for both individual and collective learning to unfold over time, and for students to develop relationships through personal sharing, social inquiry, collective reflection, and collaborative projects. Because the IGD pedagogy places a heavy emphasis on learning and co-learning rather than performing, the sustained process allows for thinking and rethinking one's perspectives and experiences as well as influencing and being influenced by others. Although we have defined and noted separately the special significance of content learning, structured interactions, and facilitation, they operate in concert to maximize learning for students. Facilitators are key participants in helping integrate the dialogic and critical elements that distinguish intergroup dialogue from other intergroup contact approaches and other diversity and social justice education approaches. In the next chapter, we present the critical-dialogic theoretical framework that guided the multi-university research project, highlighting communication processes that are fostered by the pedagogical features of content learning, structured interaction, and facilitation presented in this chapter.

Authored by Biren (Ratnesh) A. Nagda and Patricia Gurin.

CHAPTER 3

A Critical-Dialogic Theoretical Framework for Intergroup Dialogue

[We] often hate each other because we fear each other;
we fear each other because we don't know each other;
we don't know each other because we cannot communicate;
we cannot communicate because we are separated.

—Martin Luther King Jr.

In the previous chapter, we described the critical-dialogic practice model of intergroup dialogue (IGD). The pedagogical features of IGD—content learning, structured interaction, and facilitation—are intentionally integrated to foster communication processes that play the central theoretical role in how IGD increases intergroup understanding, intergroup relationships, and intergroup collaboration.

As noted in chapter 1, talking about race and gender across race and gender is challenging. Such conversations are often avoided or approached superficially, yet the rewards are great when these conversations are intentional and supported by facilitators. On college campuses, for example, students often interact across differences and power simply as acquaintances or classmates, superficially greeting each other with a variety of casual expressions: "What's up?" "What'd you do Saturday night?" "Saw you tagged on Facebook!" Even when they interact with greater depth, they sometimes create misunderstandings or reinforce tensions because of their limited skills for conversing across differences. Intergroup dialogue, in contrast, aims to encourage deep conversations about and across social divides of race and gender. In small group learning environments, students interact across social boundaries to develop more substantive relationships that may not be available in other spaces on campus. The communication processes that are the heart of what happens in IGD produce an interaction that students sometimes describe as "relating under the skin." Instead of staying at a superficial level, they learn to communicate in new ways. In intergroup dialogue, they learn to ask about each other's life experiences, and what it means for them to build community with each other. They ask, "How do you feel about that?" "What does hearing about that experience mean to you?" "How do our different life experiences affect our perspectives, beliefs, and how we interpret what we read?" "How can we work together across our differences?" Engaging these questions are starting points to develop more meaningful and connective relationships that require knowing and practicing relational skills we believe are the substrate for other learning in intergroup dialogues. Such learning may be thought of as "an ecology of relationships with people who value diversity and transformative discourse" (Parks Daloz 2000, 116).

In this chapter, we present a theoretical framework for intergroup dialogue that guided both the implementation and the research investigation of gender and race-ethnicity dialogues at the nine participating universities. We emphasize communication processes in our theoretical framework as the central mechanisms of change. They are the processes that take place in interactions among participants that then foster changes that individuals undergo in the IGD experience.

Figure 3.1 shows this theoretical framework. It differentiates the communication processes that occur among individuals and the psychological processes that occur within individuals (Nagda 2006; Sorensen et al. 2009; Stephan 2008). Our theoretical framework posits that the IGD pedagogy fosters the communication processes, which in turn lead to psychological processes. Together, the communication and psychological processes lead to the outcomes of intergroup relationships, understanding, and collaboration.

We begin our description of the framework with the conceptualization and definition of the communication processes.

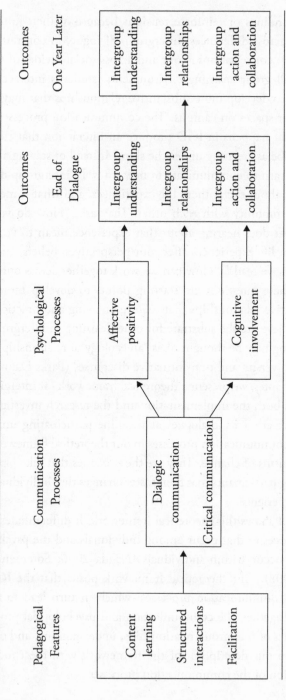

Figure 3.1 A Critical-Dialogic Theoretical Framework of Intergroup Dialogue

Pedagogical Features	Communication Processes	Psychological Processes	Outcomes End of Dialogue	Outcomes One Year Later
Content learning	Dialogic communication	Affective positivity	Intergroup understanding	Intergroup understanding
Structured interactions	Critical communication	Cognitive involvement	Intergroup relationships	Intergroup relationships
Facilitation			Intergroup action and collaboration	Intergroup action and collaboration

Source: Authors' compilation.

COMMUNICATION PROCESSES IN INTERGROUP DIALOGUE

Recent work in intergroup contact and intergroup relations interventions has moved from solely understanding outcomes to understanding the mechanisms that help explain how interventions work to produce desired outcomes (Dovidio et al. 2004; Stephan 2008; Pettigrew and Tropp 2011). Given the long-standing tradition of research on intergroup contact in social psychology, most of these intervening processes are considered to be psychological, that is, they refer to what happens within individuals. For example, intergroup anxiety as experienced by individuals is often considered as an explanation for when intergroup contact has positive versus negative effects (Stephan 2008). Research on diversity in higher education also emphasizes mechanisms that explain the impact of college on students. Influenced by Alexander Astin's (1993) I-E-O (input-environment-output) model, research on the impact of student body diversity treats diversity activities in the educational environment—classes, workshops, programs—as the intervening processes that explain how student body diversity produces learning outcomes.

Biren (Ratnesh) Nagda (2006), in his study of intergroup dialogues, focused on communication processes that occur in the interactional situation between and among participants. These communication processes can be conceptualized as social processes that foster psychological processes. Four communication processes—appreciating difference, engaging self, critical reflection, and alliance building—have been identified and found to mediate the effects of participation in intergroup dialogues on motivation to bridge differences (Nagda 2006).

Why does the critical-dialogic model of IGD focus on communication? In his formulation of the intergroup contact hypothesis in *The Nature of Prejudice*, Gordon Allport noted the centrality of communication in relationships: "It is not the mere fact of living together that is decisive. It is the forms of resulting communication that matter" (1954, 272). More recently, in the introduction to *Doing Race*, Paula Moya and Hazel Markus (2010) stress the importance of the social self. They understand that the social self is central in shifting the conception of racial identity (and gender and other identities) from a static element to one in which identities exist in relation to each other and are considered dynamic elements of social interaction.

All people form bonds with other people; they love, help, depend on, learn from, teach, and compare themselves to those around them. They experience the world through other people's images, ideas, and words. Becoming a person is a social project; in a very real way, people make each other up. (Moya and Markus 2010, 47).

Communication scholars and symbolic interactionists within sociology also emphasize the self as social (Bakhtin 1981; Baxter 2004; Littlejohn 2004; McNamee and Gergen 1999; Stryker 1980). Stephen Littlejohn addresses the importance of communication processes in becoming social:

We make our social realities through social interaction and live in a world co-constructed in our relations with other people.

The strong commitment to communication process is bolstered by the importance of the *how* of communication. What happens "between" people is a significant force in the establishment of the social worlds in which they live, love, and work. Communication does more than manage "content" or achieve "objectives." It literally creates the larger worlds or frames within which we understand and act on our content and objectives. (2004, 340)

Communication allows a larger, social truth to emerge between and among individuals in which everyone recognizes themselves as social selves rather than autonomous beings, or what Leslie Baxter (2011) terms relational rather than sovereign selves. Communication allows participants to engage in relational practice (Barge and Little 2002) aimed at understanding rather than assuming, connection rather than separation, and active co-construction rather than passive engagement in relationships. In the critical-dialogic communications we elaborate in this chapter, participants expand ways of seeing others, themselves, and their relationships as embedded in larger social structures. In IGD, participants also go beyond recognizing ways in which their relationships are defined by societal power relations to ways in which they can redefine these relationships to produce more equality. Critical-dialogic communication helps participants engage questions such as "What would be different if we framed our talk, our descriptions, our explanations about self and social life in relational rather than individual terms? What new conversational opportunities might a relational orientation offer? How might we talk differently about ourselves, our relationships, and our everyday interactions, politics, policies, education if we foregrounded these assumptions and their implications?" (McNamee and Gergen 1999, 29).

Defining Dialogic and Critical Communication Processes

In developing how communication processes operate within IGD, Nagda (2006) proposed that the four communication processes can be distinguished as primarily involving dialogic self-other processes or involving critical analysis-action processes. Thus, as noted in chapter 2, intergroup dialogue in this study is referred to as a critical-dialogic model, with the four communication processes defining how this model is both dialogic and critical.

The term *dialogic* denotes a relationship "between self and other, a simultaneity of sameness and difference out of which knowing becomes possible" (Baxter 2004, 109). The dialogic part of our framework stresses how students learn with each other to co-create or constitute themselves and their relationships through communication (Bakhtin 1981; Buber 1970; Ziegahn 2007). Drawing from current theorizing about feminist conceptions of citizenship and ethics, Mary Dietz (2003) defines one line of feminist theories, associational feminism, that has much in common with dialogic approaches within communication studies. Associational feminists take a dialogic approach in analyzing the negotiation and coordination of multiple intersecting identities when people from different backgrounds communicate with each other. They argue that this type of communication, negotiation, and coordination are crucial for enabling full participation in a democracy (see also Benhabib 2002).

The dialogic processes focus on how people speak with and listen to each other. Sometimes in sensitive conversations among people with diverse experiences, particular stories and perspectives may not be acknowledged due to a lack of understanding. Even when they are acknowledged, such stories or perspectives may not be met with interest or curiosity. The stories may not be received in the ways the speaker intended them to be received. Such breakdowns in communication constitute breakdowns in human relationships (McNamee and Gergen 1999), have emotional costs (Narayan 1988), and are potentially experienced as microaggressions (Sue et al. 2009).

David Bohm (1996) offered dialogue as a response to social breakdowns that often occur when people talk across difference. He proposed four elements for effective dialogue practice: suspending judgments, deep listening, identifying assumptions, and reflecting with inquiry. Suspending judgments speaks to openness to others and their perspectives regardless of whether they are similar or radically different from one's own. It is an attempt to undo the ways in which expectations and prejudices about others create problems in communicating and relating. By having an awareness of one's judgments, such as racial and gender stereotypes, one may be more mindful of the biases that hamper understanding. Deep listening calls for focusing on and paying attention to others to fully understand what they are saying; it involves stopping the inner chatter that gets in the way of fully listening to others. Inner chatter may be as simple as worrying about an upcoming deadline, thinking about what one would like to say, or as difficult as becoming anxious when talking about race or gender. Deep listening involves suspending judgments so as to create openness and receptivity to others in communicative interactions. Deep listening builds relationship because it fosters recognition and validation of the other person's experience.

Identifying assumptions refers to understanding how inferences are based on available information. At times, assumptions involve attaching meaning or value to an observation. Often, these assumptions are based on cultural beliefs that may not apply to a particular interaction. For example, racial and gender biases may lead to a conclusion that a person is not intelligent enough or is too emotional. It may include individual or cultural assumptions. Identifying assumptions means understanding how one's judgment led to the inferences that it did, and thus identifying the ways in which communication may have been impaired.

Reflection and inquiry involve trying to make sense of ongoing communication and asking questions of others to make sense together. Reflecting is not mirroring the content of what has been said, but involves considering how that content and interaction have affected the listener. Together, identifying assumptions and reflection and inquiry deepen and expand the dialogue through insights and new questions; they encourage deeper relationships as people learn to "talk *about* the paradoxes, misunderstandings, and conflicts" and "talk *with* culturally different others" (Ziegahn 2007, 3, emphasis in original). They are crucial to the dialogic processes in our model of intergroup dialogue.

The *critical processes* refer to exchanges that illuminate how power and privilege influence the lives of people in different social groups. This aspect of our framework draws on Paulo Freire's (1970) concept of critical consciousness, which uses analysis of unequal power and action to bring about greater social and economic justice. Critical consciousness involves questioning and "meaning-making in particular situations, instead of passively accepting taken-for-granted social realities" (Ziegahn 2007, 3). We are also influenced here by theoretical analyses and writing by critical race scholars, critical feminist scholars, and black feminist scholars who particularly emphasize how structures in the law and other institutions influence the operation and impact in society of race, gender, and social class (Anzaldúa and Keating 2002; Benhabib 2002; Collins 2000; Delgado and Stefancic 2001; Dietz 2003; Taylor, Gillborn, and Ladson-Billings 2009). These critical theorists stress the importance of power and privilege in shaping life experiences and outcomes of different groups of people. Rather than being exceptional or idiosyncratic, racism and sexism and, by extension, other forms of inequalities are seen as embedded and endemic features of social life. Critical communication processes thus have to make visible—bring to consciousness—the ways in which racism, sexism, and other inequalities operate and affect different people and relationships. When communicating critically, "a person [may also] become more empowered in acting within and upon her or his social world" (Fook and Askeland 2007, 522).

Storytelling is one communicative device that shows how structural inequality affects members of different groups. Because storytelling involves freedom of expression, open-endedness, and imagining oneself in another person's situation, it helps students from both privileged and less privileged backgrounds personalize and understand each other. Storytelling is especially powerful as a way to learn from marginalized groups whose voices are too often unheard and unheeded in discourse that takes place in many social institutions. Freire stresses that dialogue cannot occur "between those who deny other [people] the right to speak their word and those whose right to speak has been denied them" (1970, 76–77). By giving voice to people from marginalized groups, storytelling can illuminate their structural and internalized oppression. By giving voice to members of privileged groups, storytelling can make clear their often unexamined statuses and privileges. Through these stories, members of both less and more privileged groups can learn how and why privilege is so rarely perceived or understood by the more privileged in society. Thus, in our model storytelling and other narrative communication techniques are used to foster critical reflection on the role of power and privilege among members of both the more and less privileged groups in the dialogue.

In joint critical-dialogic communication, participants build relationships that are interpersonally affective and critically aware of the impact of power imbalances on communication and relationship building. This type of communication allows students to critique what is and offers possible alternatives for other ways of being. Relationships built within this context provide alternative experiences and possibilities to what are often estranged and separate group existences, and open possibilities for building alliance across differences.

> Dialogue . . . aims to achieve . . . transformation of the relationship or system of communication in which the parties are engaged. . . . In dialogue, we may not change our opinions, but we do undergo a radical shift in how we view ourselves, others, and the relationship. In dialogue, we find new ways to manage both our differences and our interdependencies. (Littlejohn 2004, 339)

We turn now to the two dialogic and two critical communication processes, and illustrate each with student narratives.

DIALOGIC COMMUNICATION PROCESSES: APPRECIATING DIFFERENCE AND ENGAGING SELF   Our theoretical framework includes two specific dialogic processes: *appreciating difference* and *engaging self* that relate to David Bohm's (1996) conceptualization of building blocks for dialogue. Appreciating difference involves intentional listening and learning from others, especially those whose experiences and perspectives differ from one's own. It also involves being open, curious, and inquiring about others' ideas and experiences. Students, in their final papers, highlighted listening to others and suspending judgment as important ingredients for learning from each other.

> Coming into the course, I had a hard time listening to white people's complaints and concerns about whether or not they actually hold privilege in society. This class taught me to be patient and be there for people along their journeys to reconciling identities, just as I was helped as well. I have become more receptive to the comments of my peers as I have begun to understand that learning is a two-way street and we both benefit from listening to each other. (Man of color, race-ethnicity dialogue)

Listening actively allows for a deepened conversation through asking questions to build understanding. Sometimes the questions simply attempt to clarify what someone else has said. At other times, the questions are intended to understand *why* another student thinks as she or he does.

——— was quick to announce his discomfort with cross-dressing. When I asked him why, he responded, "Just cuz." I pressed, "But *why*? Think about it." He began to explain that it greatly defied the gender norms he was accustomed to. Then I asked why stepping out of gender norms made him so uneasy. He said he turned to religion for an answer, that God made man one way and woman another, and that these distinctions should not be blurred by what people look like. His conceptualization of these norms is grounded in his fundamental understanding of the world as created and dictated by God, and for him to instantly be ready and willing to put that into question is a lot to ask. I don't agree with him but I learned why he thinks the way he does. (White woman, gender dialogue)

As the student conveyed, being open to others does not mean agreeing with their perspectives, but attempting to understand them as much as possible.

A sole emphasis on simply appreciating difference or learning from or about difference can result in voyeurism. An individual can focus on others but not share perspectives, feelings, and opinions. At the same time, a sole focus on self can become narcissistic. Thus, as stressed in the field of communication, mutuality in dialogue is necessary to build reciprocal relationships that counter unequal relationships. Mutuality is the basis of forming I-Thou relations, not I-It relations (Buber 1970). Reciprocity means that learning from others must be complemented with engaging self, our second dialogic process, so that as one listens and learns from others, she or he also shares and discloses personal experiences, feelings, and beliefs (Simpson, Large, and O'Brien 2004). The process of engaging self by personal sharing, taking risks, voicing disagreements, and addressing difficult issues is an important complementary process to listening to others. Rather than only learning from and about others, engaging self entails reflecting on one's own learning and opening oneself to others. Students share that the relational trust that developed over time made it safe for sharing more personal experiences, often because students learned that others were truly interested in them.

Every week when I walked into that room, I automatically felt safe. I knew that I could ask the questions that were on my mind and no one would judge me for it. We were there to learn from each other and help teach ourselves as a collective group. I felt that I could be myself in that space, more than in any other academic setting that I been in thus far. (White woman, race-ethnicity dialogue)

In dialogue I learned to open up more and realize that although there can be consequences for sharing your thoughts with others, it can also be very rewarding. Often in classes I feel that no one is interested in what I say. I learned to trust people in my dialogue that they would actually listen and care what I said. (Woman of color, race-ethnicity dialogue)

Being able to share without being judged and knowing that others will listen intently to one's contributions opens more possibilities for participants to take risks with each other and oftentimes to admit mistakes and show vulnerability. A male student wrote,

I had been so trained to take a rather authoritative perspective, especially in classrooms, that it felt strange to disarm myself and make myself fallible. It wasn't instantaneous; it took me most of the semester. But the more I could see how others were treated when they put themselves out there, the less guarded I got. It got less important to me to be right. No one stomped on me when I made mistakes. I learned that I could learn by being open and fallible. (White man, race-ethnicity dialogue)

A man of color in a gender dialogue, who demonstrated becoming less defensive as others pressed for more openness, connected engaging self with learning from others.

When —— kept asking me questions about why I think the way I do, I was pretty defensive at first. I didn't want to go very deeply, and I certainly didn't want to examine how I was coming across in the dialogue. But as I got more introspective, I tried to look at it from another standpoint and now I am glad that I see that I have a lot more work to do in order to understand other people. When I actually dug into my feelings on the matter, I realized it helped me to have to listen to how other students thought I was behaving in the class. (Man of color, gender dialogue)

These reciprocal exchanges allow for risk-taking and trust building, which are often mutually reinforcing. These students touch on vulnerability but, as the next student conveyed, seeing others take risks in the social space of dialogue inspired her courage to do so as well.

From listening and seeing what went on in our dialogue, I learned to take risks. I saw others take risks and what they said was appreciated by others. That gave me more courage. I realize now that it is not possible to grow as a person without taking some risks. I took risks by sharing personal experiences, sharing my emotions, and standing up for my beliefs. By taking those risks and having other students ask me questions, and sometimes really pressing me, I learned and changed. (Woman of color, gender dialogue)

In the open engagement of differences, participants find commonalities, points of connection, and build trust over time. "We are not afraid to say honestly what is on our mind, but we listen genuinely to the concerns, ideas, and perspectives of others. We neither accommodate nor compete" (Littlejohn 2004, 341). Many students found the trusting, collective learning environment in intergroup dialogue markedly different from other courses.

I discovered much of myself . . . some of which was very painful for me, and I am very pleased with myself for being open and trusting enough to share so much previously uncharted territory. I felt consistently supported and validated by everyone; because we struggled with a difficult topic, we bonded in a very rare and special way. I am usually present and engaged in my classes, but during dialogue I found I brought my entire self with me each time. I felt like a whole person as opposed to fragmented and disconnected, juggling my duties as a student. I did not spend one minute of dialogue thinking of anything else. (White woman, race-ethnicity dialogue)

The practice of listening and asking clarifying and probing questions provides opportunities to revise one's perspectives in dialogues. A sense of being recognized through listening enables others to engage and share more meaningfully. Not only does this allow for trusting others, but it creates a trust in oneself to bring as much as possible of oneself to the dialogic engagement, sometimes allowing others to see parts not easily shared with others.

> By sharing our testimonials as a group, we were able to create meaning between us. Each of us had something different to tell. We built a level of trust and established understanding. I learned the personal struggles each of us carry within us. Our personal struggles are a result of our backgrounds and how we are raised. With that distinction, we connected and were able to build trust among us. (Woman of color, gender dialogue)

> For the most part, everyone kept an open mind. There was a willingness to learn from everyone and I think that is what made the class so amazing. Everyone had different viewpoints and there were several disagreements but because there was a bond made between everyone that continues to become closer each class period, we all were able to feel comfortable and have trust in knowing that we can share ourselves with one another without being judged. (Woman of color, race-ethnicity dialogue)

As explained in chapter 2, our practice of intergroup dialogue especially stresses these dialogic processes in the early stages, when students become engaged with each other through testimonials and exploration of group identities, both theirs and those of others. The students share their experiences not merely as unique individuals but also in the traditional social psychology models of intergroup relations. In dialogue, stories are situated in students' positions in the stratification system as members of groups, some advantaged by wealth, power, and privileges, and others disadvantaged by economic struggles, lesser institutional power, and fewer privileges. Thus, in the early stages of the dialogue, the critical processes, to which we turn next, emerge as students get to know each other individually and as members of groups.

CRITICAL COMMUNICATION PROCESSES: CRITICAL REFLECTION AND ALLIANCE BUILDING

Our theoretical framework includes two critical processes—*critical reflection* and *alliance building*. Critical reflection involves students actively reflecting together about how power and privilege operate in society and in their social lives. Students grapple with how their socialization and backgrounds situate them in particular structural hierarchies, how group-based power dynamics may operate in the dialogue, and how they might challenge inequalities. In intergroup dialogue, critical reflection is neither a solitary analytic endeavor nor just about understanding social systems as they affect others. The relational space in which critical reflection occurs involves students in understanding their experiences and connecting them with those of others. Critical reflection distinguishes intergroup dialogue from much of the previous work in social psychology where the focus has often been on interpersonal relationships and friendships as conditions leading to reduction of intergroup prejudice and bias. The traditional aim of intergroup contact has been the creation of intergroup harmony and reduction of bias through interpersonal relationships and friendships (Pettigrew 1998; Pettigrew and Tropp 2011). IGD assumes that an exclusively interpersonal approach that puts aside separate group identities will produce intergroup harmony, but that approach cannot support sociopolitical analyses and can promote false assumptions of equality (Saguy et al. 2009).

Recent work in social psychology has begun to affirm our view that power differences must be dealt with in intergroup interactions (Saguy, Dovidio, and Pratto 2008; Tam, Hewstone et al. 2008). These researchers have pointed out that participants from identity groups that differ in societal power and privilege usually have differing expectations of programs promoting cross-group interactions (Abu-Nimer 1999; Shelton, Richeson, and Salvatore 2005; Wright and Lubensky 2009). Communication breaks down not just when members of different groups are not equally skilled in communicating, but when those groups hold widely divergent analytic frames, especially about race (Nagda et al. 2012). Some individuals, especially members of more advantaged groups, favor the idea of a color-blind society and a postgender society, whereas others, believing that our society is not yet postracial or postgender, stress that groups matter in people's life experiences and outcomes (Bonilla-Silva 2003; Chesler, Lewis, and Crowfoot 2005; Richeson and Nussbaum 2004). Moreover, members of more privileged groups may conceive of differences as rooted in individual preferences; they may attribute differences to cultural styles only rather than to structural factors as well. Members of disadvantaged groups, on the other hand, more readily acknowledge that race and gender still matter in social life and conceive of their social realities as highly influenced by social conflicts, structures, and institutions (Bobo 2011; Tatum 1997). They want intergroup interactions to deal with inequality and social change (Jones et al. 2009). The more advantaged groups, in contrast, may prefer to talk about commonalities and similarities than group differences (Abu-Nimer 1999; Dovidio, Saguy, and Schnabel 2009; Walsh 2007).

In critical-dialogic environments, critical reflection often involves examining past experiences in light of new understanding and of questioning everyday, taken-for-granted ways of thinking and being. A woman wrote of her new conception of being a woman.

> Before entering dialogue I considered myself to be a very feminine woman and I thought that most other females thought the way I did. Now that we have talked about gender relationships in the dialogue and sort of pulled them apart, I notice that I have relied on men, such as my boyfriend, to open doors for me and to help me with other tasks, such as lifting heavy things. . . . Once we began to critically analyze how gender works in my dialogue, I began to see that I was contributing to benevolent sexism in women. Now I understand that being a female does not mean expecting people to do things for me when I can do them myself. I understand that to be a woman is to be proud of who I am and what my abilities are. (Woman of color, gender dialogue)

This observation is mirrored by another woman who wrote about how the dialogues helped her and other students reflect on their experiences and understand the structural forces that frame gender inequalities.

> In one of our class sessions, we watched a film that was one of my favorites, *The Little Mermaid*. When I was little I wanted to be just like Ariel. She was beautiful and passionate and willful, but I knew back then that Prince Eric would not have fallen in love with her if she hadn't been pretty. She couldn't even talk during the majority of the time they spent together! And, Eric was the one thing that made Ariel happy. I internalized the messages I got from this movie, and began my conceptualization of my gender identity as a girl. . . . I developed an eating disorder in high school to ensure my appearance as a fundamental way for feeling good about myself and feel in control. What was important in the dialogue is that all of us could see that individual experiences, like mine, aren't just individual. It is how society structures gender roles and how socialization through movies, books, parents, school clubs—everything— make sure that both boys and girls accept their roles. (White woman, gender dialogue)

Critical reflection deepens both analysis and sharing among students in the dialogue. The emphasis on talking with each other about power and privilege also helps create newer understandings of experiences.

Sitting in class and hearing how we as a group represented so many different relationships to privilege, I looked at my life and how no one ever sat me down and told me about my privilege. When I thought of my high school years where I actively sought conversations with the rappers in our school's sound studio, I was always curious about their anger and why their daily lives seemed to be more difficult than mine. My attraction to hip-hop snowballed into a growing exposure to the racial line between white and black. . . . But I didn't understand the line or how I benefited from that line. I am proud and confident of the fact that I am identifying my privileges. I could not have done it alone; it was the impact of everyone talking about privileges and disadvantages in their lives that I began to understand. (White woman, race-ethnicity dialogue)

My interest in the class really escalated after having great conversations with [other students] who challenged my thinking and made me look at some of the oppressions and prejudices I held within. (Man of color, gender dialogue)

In addition to examining these socialization experiences and understanding how each of them is located in a system of inequality, students also begin to understand how their privileges are enacted in society and in relations with others. They see themselves better and what they represent relationally, as individuals in society and as participants in dialogue:

I learned a lot about myself, not just myself but my presence. I've learned not only about my appearance but also the symbolism behind it and its connotations and consequences for those around me. I've learned that I am a white heterosexual, able-bodied male. I am everything championed by American society; I am a physical representation of normalcy and the standard set by which to judge deviation. I live in a world that was constructed by men like me in the sense of our western European heritage; I live in a world that is designed to give me unearned advantages over other people who don't fit into the cookie cutter mold that fits me so snugly. I didn't learn it just from reading or just thinking about it myself. I learned from all of us looking privilege in the eye. (White man, race-ethnicity dialogue)

Critical reflection means that students not only examine their socialization and past experiences, but also their everyday experiences on campus and the here-and-now dynamics of the intergroup dialogue itself. They reflect individually, often in response to something that happens in the dialogue, as the next student did. They also reflect together when the facilitators ask them to make sense of what happened in that dialogue session. In both individual and collective reflection, students attend to the experiences of others, exploring both heterogeneity and commonalities within and across identity groups.

[She] said that the conversation was focused on the dynamics of racism solely in terms of black and white people. This comment immediately sent me into self-reflection. I tried to process the comment, my first reaction was defense, but then I realized in trying to disprove [her] comments, she was completely correct. [Her] comments made me realize that I was not realizing and even contributing to the silencing and oppression of other minority groups by not including them in the conversation. (Woman of color, race-ethnicity dialogue)

When critical reflection considers how individual lives and relationships are located within social systems of privilege and inequality, it may convey a sense of futility—hopelessness concerning the enormity of the task of change. Students talk about a kind of hopelessness that sometimes occurs in taking courses that present historical and contemporary patterns of inequality, making them seem inevitable and intractable:

I have a very good grasp of racial disparities—in health, criminal justice (or injustice), underemployment, education, wealth—you name it, I know the statistics. I have had excellent sociology courses on all these facets of inequality, both here in the U.S. and around the world. Sometimes the knowledge I have acquired is just overwhelming. For me the critical question is, What can be done about this? How do we educate ourselves and others to get the political will to care, to craft social policies that increase opportunities, and to pay taxes for better schools for children in our cities, children who are not "our" children but in fact really are? (Woman of color, race-ethnicity dialogue)

In intergroup dialogue, the second critical communication process of alliance building counters the sense of hopelessness. Alliance building provides an avenue for students to channel their individual and collective energies to address inequalities with a view toward social change. It involves recognizing commonalities and differences, and working through disagreements and conflicts that often arise when identity groups interact. It also involves imagining alternate possibilities and having a sense of efficacy and a commitment to action in a context of collaboration and relational responsibility.

You build a community of people who support and educate each other. You build a coalition of people different from you. (Man of color, gender dialogue)

Participating in intergroup dialogue has convinced me that, in the effort to rid society of oppression, everyone has to be involved and maybe most importantly that everyone can make a difference. I don't just stay silent when race or gender jokes or homophobic comments are made by my friends. I have learned how to confront without putting people down. I have learned that I can be effective in these small ways, intervening with people I know. I also know that I can bring about broader changes, and I am beginning to do that right here on campus. Social change will be a big part of my life somehow and I don't doubt that I can be the change I want to see. (Woman of color, race-ethnicity dialogue)

Critical race theorists and critical feminist theorists call for solutions to inequality in which the interests of privileged groups are not given primacy over marginalized groups (Bell 1980; Collins 2000; Hurtado 1996). Solutions and actions follow from engaged and informed dialogue between members of less and more privileged groups, leading to alliances. They must find ways to bridge conflicts and differences of group interests to collaborate in joint action to achieve greater social justice. A woman wrote about the importance of embracing differences.

Earlier in the semester I was more conscious about what I said, trying not to offend other people, but as the semester went on and we got more involved in our ICP groups, I realized that the best way to work in a group of diverse people is to embrace the differences among us rather than pretending that they do not exist. By acknowledging that we were all different, some of us more privileged and others less privileged, we created an open and honest atmosphere where we were all free to give our ideas for our project. (White woman, gender dialogue)

Alliance building occurs throughout the dialogue and is especially pronounced in the Intergroup Collaboration Project (ICP), in which students join together across identity groups to extend their learning out of class.

Our ICP groups were strategically chosen for us to interact with people of a different race and ethnicity, and also possibly different gender, than ourselves. This strategy served as a catalyst to take us out of our comfort zones. It showed us how working across difference could lead to common ground. When I read the poem on alliance, the last stanza stuck out for me because it is a perfect explanation for what went on in my ICP group. "Alliances are really very simple, they arise out of the fact that we are different." (White man, race-ethnicity dialogue)

Students find that alliance building is a process, one that often moves from trepidation around differences to using those differences productively.

From these moments of conflict, I also felt a sense of hope when I realized that it was possible for diverse people to use their differences in pursuit of a common goal, which in the case of dialogue is shared meaning. (Man of color, race-ethnicity dialogue)

Drawing on the shared and collective learning in their dialogue group, students feel empowered because they are not alone in their commitments to change.

By being a role model and an ally, I partook in consciousness raising. Because other members of the class also began to struggle against sexual and domestic violence between genders, we, as a whole, served as a small force for change bound by strength in numbers. (White woman, gender dialogue)

Students commented in their papers that the ICP produced a sense of efficacy about making a difference because it required them to practice collaboration and carry out some kind of action. A white man in a race dialogue saw the possibility for an alliance between him and an African American male peer.

Good relationships between African American and white fraternities are almost nonexistent on this campus. The work that [African American classmate]
and I did in the ICP makes me sure that he and I could formulate a plan to get
those groups together on something they could productively do together. Becoming allies is something we can take beyond the dialogue. (White man,
race-ethnicity dialogue)

It is possible that a singular focus on critical reflection could lead students
to feeling overwhelmed, whereas one on alliance building could lead to re-
producing power dynamics in collaborations for social change. That could
happen because analyses of inequality and the politics of social change can
produce a sense of hopelessness, and alliance building that emphasizes commonalities over differences can result in status-quo arrangements in which
group members from more advantaged backgrounds take over the leadership
in the group. The critical reflection that continues to operate during alliance
building enables students to create a collective sense of efficacy and hope yet
remain vigilant to the power dynamics in coalitions for change.

Jointly, the critical and dialogic processes of intergroup dialogue mobilize
cross-group relationships as sites for learning. These processes also help dialogue participants relate in ways that advance personal and collective agency
for social change (Habermas 1984; Nagda 2006; Saunders 1999).

As time went on, we were able to open up to each other and reveal our wounds
to each other by sharing personal stories, experiences and examples from our
lives. I felt that the feelings and perspectives that we shared with each other
were genuine and that we developed a sense of trust that allowed us to share
our personal accounts with the group. We were also able to challenge the
thinking of others and our own method of thinking which enabled us to ask
other group members difficult questions and work through disagreements and
conflicts. (Man of color, race-ethnicity dialogue)

Pedagogy Fosters Communication Processes

The IGD pedagogy—content, structured interaction, and facilitation—that
we delineated in chapter 2—is designed to foster the dialogic and critical
communication processes. The hypothesized relationships in our theoretical
framework begin with this connection between pedagogy and communication processes. The rationale for the relationship derives from practice, spe-

cifically the facilitation and teaching experiences of the multi-university col-laborators (Zúñiga et al. 2007), and from the research that members of the multi-university team has conducted over the years (Gurin et al. 2002; Lopez, Gurin, and Nagda 1998; Nagda 2006; Nagda, Kim, and Truelove 2004; Nagda and Zúñiga 2003).

Structured interaction in various activities is used to stimulate dialogue. Readings provide key concepts and key information. Facilitation helps students debrief the activities and discuss the readings. Together, these components of pedagogy help students connect with each other (dialogic processes) and situate their learning in broader social contexts (critical processes). For example, in the first stage of dialogue, activities such as the role-play of debate and dialogue and the active listening exercise build dialogic processes because these activities help students practice listening and asking questions of each other. Appreciating difference is reinforced and deepened in the second stage as students share their identity wheels and testimonials in class, two activities that also encourage engaging self. Facilitators are not simply conducting these activities but are using them to create dialogic communication. Facilitators ask students to talk about how they responded to the activities and then to notice and comment on the commonalities and differences that are expressed in these responses. The facilitators continually connect appreciating difference and engaging self, making sure that all students are listening, speaking, and asking each other questions during these activities and in the dialogue about the activities. They try to ensure that what a participant says is acknowledged by others and that through questions the listeners help the speaker expand what she means. The students begin to see that speaking, listening, and inquiry—engaging self and appreciating difference—are inextricably connected in their communications.

As students' frames of reference expand from purely personal and individual to the larger societal context, dialogic communication begins to include critical processes. For example, the within-identity group caucuses and subsequent cross-group fishbowls require their dialogic skills to be exercised within the larger context of situating individual and group experiences in the societal dynamics of power and inequality. Students ask each other about the privilege and oppression that may be implicit in what someone says. Facilitators help students generalize understanding from personal to group experiences. They support and challenge participants to go beyond appreciating differences to examining how social inequalities affect groups differently. Students begin to hone their critical reflection communication, which is then greatly reinforced through the web of oppression activity (described in chapter 2). The web of oppression usually ends with the question, "So what do we do to dismantle the web?" This serves as a transition to the final stage in the dialogue, in which students actively think through and dialogue about alliance building, that is, practice collaboration to advance social justice. Facilitators play a crucial role in connecting pedagogy to all of these communication processes (for an elaborate discussion of intergroup dialogue facilitation, see Nagda and Maxwell 2011).

A white woman in a gender dialogue credited her facilitators with promoting dialogic processes, though of course she did not use that term. She noted that they encouraged "reflection before sharing, assuring that everyone was taking the activity seriously and thoughtfully," and that helped her "create trust" with her classmates. Other quotations from students about the role of facilitators in chapter 2 also reveal the connection between pedagogy and communication processes.

We turn next to our rationale for the particular psychological processes that are included in our theoretical framework and our rationale for why communication processes should promote these psychological processes.

PSYCHOLOGICAL PROCESSES

In the theoretical framework depicted in figure 3.1, the communication processes are expected to foster both cognitive and affective psychological processes, and through those processes occurring within individuals the three sets of outcomes of IGD. Two sets of psychological processes form the latent constructs in our theoretical framework, which is tested in chapter 5:

Cognitive involvement: complex thinking, analytical thinking about society, consideration of multiple perspectives, and identity engagement.

Affective positivity: positive intergroup interactions, positive emotions during intergroup interaction, and comfort in intergroup interaction.

We do not mean to suggest that cognitive involvement and affective positivity are separate psychological processes. Just as communication processes are intertwined, so too are psychological processes. That is to be expected because they are generally connected, something now supported by increasing evidence coming from neuroscience (Damasio 2000).

Cognitive Involvement

The latent construct of cognitive involvement includes the four listed concepts. The first two, *complex thinking* and *analytical thinking about society*, are suggested by research based on two widely used scales measuring the need for cognition and attributional complexity. Need for cognition is defined as the tendency to engage in and enjoy effortful thought (Cacioppo and Petty 1982). Attributional complexity is defined as a preference for complex explanations for behavior, including a tendency to use contemporary, external attributions such as the impact of society on individual behaviors (Fletcher et al. 1986). Research shows that these two measures are moderately to highly related, and that need for cognition is also associated with other measures of complexity and thinking: a tendency to seek out, engage in, and enjoy effortful cognitive activity; to acquire information relevant to dilemmas or problems; to engage in problem solving; to generate more thoughts in response to a stimulus; and to translate thoughts into judgments and judgments into behavior (Cacioppo et al. 1996; Petty et al. 2008). These cognitive consequences of need for cognition should produce a desire to acquire knowledge about group and societal phenomena, knowledge that Jack Dovidio and his colleagues (2004) theorize is an important cognitive mediator of the impact of intergroup contact on reducing intergroup bias. Research further shows that high levels of attributional complexity, for example, are associated with lower levels of racism and stereotyping (Schaller et al. 1995).

The third concept within our latent construct of cognitive involvement is consideration of *multiple perspectives*, which in most studies is considered cognitive empathy. It is defined as the ability to step outside the constraints of one's immediate frame of reference. The standard measure of consideration of multiple perspectives (Davis 1983), which is also used in this research, has been found to correlate with the tendency to mimic other people's nonverbal behaviors, with reduction in egocentric perceptions of fairness in competitive contests, and with adoption of strategic approaches in negotiations (Galinsky et al. 2008).

The fourth cognitive involvement concept is *identity engagement*, which is often measured by questions about cognitive centrality of identity and behaviors geared to learn more about one's identity (Gurin and Markus 1989; Crocker and Luhtanen 1990). It is conceived in this research as an indicator of the latent construct of cognitive involvement because in intergroup dialogue students are stimulated to think about their group identities and how their personal beliefs are influenced at least somewhat by the experiences and perspectives they have encountered within their identity groups. Through this cognitive work, they also begin to understand that something similar happens among students in the other identity group. Thinking about social identity provides participants with insights into the sources of their beliefs and those of others. We do not mean to imply that emotions are unimportant in the identity explorations, merely that the cognitive work explains why identity involvement is treated as an indicator of cognitive involvement in our framework.

Affective Positivity

The latent construct of affective positivity includes three concepts: *positive intergroup interactions, positive emotions during intergroup interaction,* and *comfort in intergroup interaction.* The expected relationship of affective positivity to communication processes is suggested both by dialogue practice and by studies on the role of emotions in relationships in many aspects of social life. For example, emotions such as sympathy, compassion, warmth, and tenderness comprise the core of emotional empathy (Batson et al. 1997). The dialogic communication processes of appreciating difference and engaging self inevitably include positive emotions and positive interactions. These processes ought to reduce intergroup anxiety, another emotion that has been widely studied and has played a pivotal role in the outcomes of intergroup relations (Stephan and Stephan 1985). Evidence is mounting that when intergroup anxiety is reduced, positive feelings are generated and people feel more comfortable during intergroup interaction. Unconscious prejudice and intergroup bias are also reduced (Stephan 2008; Pettigrew and Tropp 2011). Dialogic and critical communication processes by definition deal with stereotypes and prejudice, and thus ought to foster affective positivity. Additionally, both practice and previous research suggest that the communication process of alliance building ought to be related to affective positivity. For example, emotions figure prominently in accounting for why people act on behalf of their group and through alliances on behalf of other groups as well (Stürmer and Simon 2009).

Why These Psychological Processes?

The critical-dialogic framework for intergroup dialogue focuses on these two sets of psychological processes because, as indicated, research has shown them to be influential. Dialogue practice also reveals the importance of both cognitive involvement and affective positivity. Furthermore, other research has demonstrated that these particular processes are connected to intergroup interaction. Three types of research provide such evidence: field studies of the impact of interacting with diverse peers on college campuses, laboratory studies of intergroup interaction, and studies of roommates who are randomly assigned to match or not match a student's racial background. All three have focused on race, and are thus directly relevant to our emphases on the specific cognitive and emotional processes that refer mostly to race. We believe them to be generalizable to gender as well because they deal with underlying psychological processes in intergroup contact and interactions across differences.

The literature on cognitive processes reveals evidence that intergroup interaction and participation in courses with multicultural curricula are related to active thinking, as measured nearly identically to the measures used in this research (Gurin et al. 2002). Intergroup interaction and participation in multicultural courses are also associated with problem solving, consideration of multiple perspectives, attributional complexity (Antonio et al. 2004; Bowman 2010; Gurin, Nagda, and Lopez 2004; Hurtado 2005; Laird 2005), and cognitive openness as indicated by having serious conversations with students from diverse backgrounds and attending intellectual activities outside class (Gottfredson et al. 2008). Uma Jayakumar (2008), in an impressive national study that followed students six years after leaving college, found that cross-racial interaction during college—reflected by dining, dating, studying, and interacting generally across race—was associated with higher scores after college on a measure of consideration of multiple perspectives, which Jayakumar terms pluralistic orientation.

Research on the emotional implications of intergroup contact reveals evidence that intergroup interaction can have both positive and negative emotional effects. On the positive side, research indicates that intergroup interaction reduces ethnic prejudice and intergroup bias (Denson 2009; Pettigrew and Tropp 2011; Shook and Fazio 2008a; Sidanius et al. 2008; Stephan 2008), and increases positive feelings toward members of other groups (Pettigrew 1998). Studies of white students randomly assigned roommates of the same or different racial background also show a positive impact for having a roommate of color in reducing unconscious prejudice and intergroup anxiety (Shook and Fazio 2008b), on increasing positive feelings toward members of other groups (van Laar et al. 2005), and on having more heterogeneous friendships beyond the roommate (Camargo, Stinebrickner, and Stinebrickner 2010). Another of the studies involving the random assignment of room-mates shows a long-term positive emotional effect in which white students who had a nonwhite roommate during college displayed greater comfort with minorities several years later (Boisjoly et al. 2006).

On the negative side, another study of white students shows that those with a roommate of color spent less time with the roommate, had less involvement in shared activities (Towles-Schwen and Fazio 2006), and felt themselves less compatible than those with a white roommate (Phelps et al. 1998). A study specifically on emotions asked students, both white and students of color, with cross- and same-race roommates to keep a daily accounting of emotions experienced with the roommate (Trail, Shelton, and West 2009). It showed fewer positive emotions, less felt intimacy, and fewer intimacy-enhancing behaviors (smiling, talking, appearing engaged and interested, warmth, ease in conversation and pleasantness) both for whites with minority rather than white roommates, and for minorities with white rather than minority roommates.

Numerous studies also indicate that intergroup interaction increases intergroup anxiety among both majority and minority group members (Blasovich et al. 2001; Stephan and Stephan 1985). It is important, however, that intergroup contact over time mutes some of these negative effects. In particular, sustained intergroup contact reduces the intergroup anxiety initially aroused (Pettigrew and Tropp 2011; Stephan 2008; Toosi et al. 2012) or those with previous interracial contact show less physiological arousal of anxiety (Page-Gould, Mendes, and Major 2010; Page-Gould, Mendoza-Denton, and Tropp 2008). This reduction in anxiety explains, at least partially, why intergroup contact reduces unconscious prejudice (Blair, Park, and Bachelor 2003; Blascovich et al. 2001; Hewstone et al. 2006; Stephan 2008).

The effects of intergroup interaction on prejudice reduction are a source of controversy in social psychological theory and research. Specifically, research over the past two decades has drawn a distinction between prejudice as an automatic versus controlled process, also termed unconscious-implicit versus conscious-explicit prejudice respectively. A large body of research documents a steady decline in negative evaluations of racial-ethnic minority groups in North America after World War II, coupled with only a modest decrease in racial tension and conflict, leading some theorists to highlight the role of more subtle forms of prejudice and discrimination (for example, Gaertner and Dovidio 1986; McConahay 1986; Sears 1988).

Research has documented the powerful effect of automatic, implicit, and unconscious attitudes on behavior and theorists interpret these findings differently, some assuming that authentic beliefs rest in implicit attitudes and others arguing that implicit attitudes reflect only learned associations, not authentic attitudes toward members of other groups. For example, Russell Fazio's (1990) motivation and opportunity as determinants (MODE) model assumes that automatically activated attitudes influence an individual's spontaneous interpretation of a situation, which guides behavior without any awareness of the influence of the attitude. The MODE model also assumes that when an individual has the motivation and opportunity (for example, enough time) to engage in effortful processing, the relationship between the implicit attitude and behavior will be mitigated by the influence of explicit attitudes and controlled interpretations of a situation. In contrast, Patricia Devine's (1989) dissociation model makes a distinction between knowledge and belief in a stereotype, arguing that everyone, regardless of prejudice, is familiar with the content of dominant cultural stereotypes but diverges in the extent to which he or she believes in the accuracy of any of them. Because stereotypical knowledge is acquired during early childhood, the rejection of stereotypical knowledge is assumed to result from egalitarian beliefs acquired later in life (see Banse et al. 2010) and replacing automatically activated stereotypes requires controlled processing. These models imply a somewhat different perspective on the role of authentic attitudes. Although the MODE model assumes that personal attitudes are activated automatically and overt expression of these attitudes is suppressed when they conflict with social norms, the dissociation model assumes that culturally prevalent stereotypes are automatically activated and their expression is suppressed when they conflict with personal beliefs. Intergroup dialogue draws on the assumptions of both models by providing motivated students the opportunity to explore the biases that affect their behavior and attitudes toward other groups. For instance, through exploring the *Cycle of Socialization* (Harro 2000a) discussed in chapter 2, students examine the sources of their biases, and when and how their identities affect prejudicial judgments outside of their awareness. Yet IGD also helps students forge meaningful relationships with members of other groups and engage in collaborative actions to address prejudice and discrimination. In doing so, it helps students recognize that they will forever carry with them the content of cultural stereotypes, their learned (and potentially authentic) biases as well as their explicit commitments to social justice.

The cognitive processes are used to encourage students to always be mindful of when their learned biases and knowledge of cultural stereotypes might shape their behavior despite their commitment to redressing inequality and social justice.

Paying too much attention to one's implicit or explicit bias can be counterproductive in intergroup communication. Recent research has stressed the likelihood of concerns about evaluation and expression of prejudice when people interact across differences, at least across race (Vorauer 2006). Among white students, intergroup interaction sometimes fosters a fear of being evaluated and appearing prejudiced, and those concerns then result in poorer performance on cognitive tasks because these students have to use so many cognitive resources to regulate their feelings and behaviors during the interaction. Among students of color, intergroup interaction sometimes produces a corollary fear that they will have to deal once again with prejudiced white people (for a review of studies showing evidence of these types of fears, see Richeson and Shelton 2007; for evidence of depletion of cognitive resources for whites in intergroup interactions, see Richeson and Trawalter 2005).

These fears of evaluation and concern with either appearing prejudiced or being the target of prejudice often appear during the first session of the dialogue courses when students are asked about their hopes and fears as they begin the courses (see Khuri 2004). They say and also wrote in reflection papers a variety of explanations: "I was scared about what people, especially in the other group, would think about me." "I was afraid that one more time my stomach would tighten up when some ignorant, prejudiced statement would come out of the mouth of a student in the dialogue." "I hoped that I could speak about racial issues without being judged the angry black woman, but I feared that wouldn't happen anymore than in any other class." "I was apprehensive about offending people, of saying something stupid or hurtful."

In summary, these studies of intergroup interaction and accounts of students' fears when they begin to dialogue across differences support the importance of cognitive involvement and affective positivity in our theoretical framework. Cognitive involvement and affective positivity may be thought of as the foundational cognitive (mind) and affective (heart) of the psychological changes that students undergo when dialogue pedagogy is successful in fostering the four communication processes in our model, and when the communication processes are successful in addressing the psychological challenges that arise when students interact across differences and power.

Connecting Communication Processes and Psychological Processes

Having now defined both the communication and psychological processes, we turn to how communication processes are expected to foster psychological processes. The IGD sessions contain two critical elements—being sustained over time and being guided by trained facilitators—that lead to the prediction that communication processes will foster cognitive involvement and affective positivity. IGD courses are sustained over an entire academic term during which participants meet two to three hours weekly. Trained facilitators guide all sessions of the courses. They are trained to help students share, express their feelings, take risks, reappraise their views (engaging self); to encourage students to listen actively to what others say and express nonverbally, to ask questions of others, and to probe the ideas of others (appreciating difference); to examine collectively in the dialogue process and individually in self-reflection papers how privilege is involved in both identity-based stories told in the dialogue and interactions in the dialogue itself (reflecting critically); and to explore commonalities and differences (building alliances).

It is true that some studies, namely, the roommate studies, have involved sustained interaction. However, roommate interaction is not facilitated. Sustained but unguided intergroup interactions occurring naturally between roommates, or in student organizations, or at campus events, or in community settings may and indeed often do have positive intergroup effects. These effects are more likely to occur, however, when intergroup interaction is guided by trained facilitators to create the communication processes we argue are so central to IGD (Sorensen et al. 2009). Moreover, facilitation is crucial to help students understand and learn from negative interactions that the roommate studies have documented and that dialogue practice expects to occur as well.

We predicted that all four communication processes would relate positively to both cognitive involvement and affective positivity. Both the dialogic and critical processes should foster cognitive involvement. Sharing and listening to personal stories involving life experiences with inequalities, as well as critically reflecting on those stories in the dialogue, should lead students to think about race and gender in more complex ways. They should increasingly think about society's role in creating and reinforcing inequalities, and recognize the presence of multiple perspectives. In particular, they should come to understand that their identities and those of other students are connected to these different perspectives. In stressing the importance of these communication processes in producing these cognitive outcomes, we do not minimize the role of readings and written assignments (the content aspect of pedagogy). However, the communications within the dialogues make the cognitive learning especially enriching.

The dialogic and critical processes should also foster affective positivity by addressing the emotional challenges that sometimes emerge during intergroup interaction. All four communication processes combine to produce an intergroup climate comfortable for students to confront issues they usually avoid or talk about only superficially. Comfort does not mean nonchallenging, nor are students always comfortable when they and others share, take risks, admit vulnerabilities, listen actively to others, and engage in collective critical reflection. Over time, however, the four processes should increase comfort, positive emotions, and positive interactions. They should decrease intergroup anxiety, especially fears about appearing prejudiced and having to deal privately with the prejudice of other people. Through engaging self, students see others take risks, share beliefs and prejudices, and expose their ignorance without being judged. They learn to listen and ask questions themselves. They see others being listened to and responded to positively. They try to understand why peers think and feel as they do, and appreciate that others try to do that as well. They practice alliance building by exploring commonalities and differences, some of them individual, some cultural, and some power-based. Through these communication processes, students develop positive feelings for each other, feel fewer fears of judgment and other kinds of anxieties, and increase capacities for collaboration across differences.

We test the interconnection of the communication processes and psychological processes in chapter 5 as part of an overall test of the entire critical-dialogic framework. Here we draw on the students' writing in their final papers to illustrate these interconnections. The final paper assignment did not name the communication processes. It did not refer to cognitive involvement or affective positivity, or ask students to explain how dialogue might have produced such psychological effects. Nonetheless, the students seemed to tie communication processes to psychological processes.

In an example of dialogic processes fostering affective positivity, two students connected engaging self with emotions, and appreciating difference by asking questions with affective interactions among participants.

Group members asked difficult questions of each other. Questions led to people's sharing of personal experiences and deeply held ideas. Facilitators encouraged us to question each other but with the goal of hearing and feeling what others said. People sometimes cried. It was clear that emotion was ok. We learned that when people discuss their feelings and beliefs in a place where it is ok to express emotions, everyone became able to trust one another and it helped build a sense of community, bonding, and collaboration. (White man, race-ethnicity dialogue)

When students shared their testimonials, I was blown away with how everyone really listened and how each person who shared was treated with such respect and without judgment. Often someone showed real emotion as they listened to another student. That was incredible. I'm not one who feels very comfortable sharing in public but when I saw how the facilitators and students asked thoughtful and respectful questions, I was a whole lot more comfortable sharing my own story and beginning to be a fully participating member of this dialogue. It's like legitimating that everyone can take risks through seeing how others are treated. (White woman, gender dialogue)

These statements demonstrate these students' recognition of the relational climate developed in the group by participants and facilitators. Other students also reported experiencing a new kind of dialogic listening that opened them cognitively to more complex thinking and led to more personalized knowledge.

There was a new kind of listening in this class. It wasn't just hearing what the person said but *why* they said it. It was listening for more understanding. It made me realize that there is more than one aspect to listening. I used to just dismiss whatever I knew was factually incorrect or what I disagreed with after listening to a speaker. I thought that was enough. Now I want to know *why* a person feels a certain way or believes a certain thing. Appreciating differences and especially why they exist has made me more open to other people's points of views. That is huge. (Woman of color, race-ethnicity dialogue)

Hearing everyone's testimonials did something really deep in our dialogue. Everyone started listening to each other, I mean really listening and asking questions because we wanted to know more. In other classes, people depend only on a textbook or handouts or even a cheat sheet for grasping key concepts of the course. In this class, just being there did wonders in helping all of us gain a strong understanding of race and ethnicity, and not a narrow understanding of just our own race or ethnicity. We learned how race and ethnicity work in everyone's lives in this society. Race and ethnicity weren't remote concepts anymore. I always found myself thinking about what we had discussed in class for days afterwards. (Man of color, race-ethnicity dialogue)

Other students connected critical communication processes to cognitive openness. Through collective critical reflection, students were encouraged to ask why they think the way they do. Sometimes that became a question about why students in the dialogue thought differently or disagreed with each other. Other times it was about why inequality might emerge in the dynamics of the dialogue.

Since we were all different from each other, we could present ideas that others may never have thought about before. If we all agreed, it would just reaffirm our beliefs. What happens in dialogue every day is disagreement, new ideas, viewing things in new ways. But for it to mean that, we had to listen to each other and genuinely want to know why other people thought the way they did. It's about the kind of dialogue that goes on, one of trust to talk about anything without worrying about being attacked. (Woman of color, gender dialogue)

That discussion where our facilitator pressed us to see who was talking and who was silent sent us all into reflection and thinking together. We realized that our dynamics were silencing people from minority groups that weren't black, and that there were many different points of view in our dialogue. We talked about the importance of various forms and histories of oppression as being equally valid and that no one kind of inequality takes precedence over another. What we eventually got to is that all of these social identities and categories are connected somehow, intertwined to create the illusion that only one is oppressed, and that whites are always the only oppressors. Our dialogue went way beyond that simplistic thinking. (Woman of color, race-ethnicity dialogue)

Both critical reflection and alliance building also promoted expression of emotions and development of trust in the group:

Our dialogue's discussion and analysis of what gender means will stick with me a long time. I came to the conclusion that I didn't know as much as I thought I did and that gender could possibly be a state of mind and not purely biological. On the issue of gender roles, we had to face conflicting ideas about how men and women should be shown in the media. But for me it was a great relief to hear all these points of view and know that everyone was looking at the issues with critical eyes. That was important for accepting that emotions are involved also. It isn't one or the other, both ideas and emotions surface whenever people talk deeply about gender. (White man, gender dialogue)

We talked a lot about alliance building on differences. That was a point from a powerful poem we all read by Judit. It was also a point in our dialogue. . . . We already knew how everyone's lives had affected them. We knew all about those differences. And because of the differences, not despite them, we had built a lot of trust. So you can have alliances when you have built up trust. (White woman, race-ethnicity dialogue)

Finally, we predicted that all four communication processes would promote the integration of affective and cognitive processes. Intuitively, it might seem that the dialogic processes would encourage affective psychological processes, and that the critical processes would promote cognitive ones. Instead, we hypothesized that the four communication processes would occur together and connect with both psychological processes. As a student mentioned earlier, "both ideas and emotions surface whenever people talk deeply about identities."

We turn now to the three sets of IGD outcomes and how the psychological processes foster these outcomes.

OUTCOMES OF INTERGROUP DIALOGUE

The critical-dialogic model of intergroup dialogue includes three sets of outcomes that mirror the three primary aims of the practice of IGD, namely to increase intergroup relationships, intergroup understanding, and intergroup action.

Intergroup Relationships

Our framework focuses on two major relational outcomes, intergroup empathy and motivation to bridge differences. Both could be considered psychological processes rather than outcomes, but we include them as outcomes because intergroup dialogue has always had the goal of helping students feel what others feel and reciprocally learn about each other's groups.

INTERGROUP EMPATHY Intergroup empathy, which in our theoretical framework is conceptualized as emotional empathy, occurs when individuals respond to the experiences of members of other social groups by feeling what they feel or reacting emotionally to their experiences. The emphasis on empathy in intergroup relations and specifically in IGD fits within a growing view that human beings (and other mammals) are empathic by nature. Jeremy Rifkin argues in *The Empathic Civilization* that "empathy is the very means by which we create social life and advance civilization. . . . it is the extraordinary evolution of empathic consciousness that is the quintessential underlying story of human history" (2009, 10). He details the research of neuroscientists (Iacoboni 2008; Ramachandran 2006; Rizzolatti and Sinigaglia 2008) into the neural mechanisms, the mirror neuron system, by which humans are "wired for empathy" (Iacoboni 2008, 268).[1]

A biological capacity for empathy is not limited to humans. In *The Age of Reason*, Frans de Waal (2009) provides evidence from experiments and observations of many species that there is nothing unique about the human brain with respect to capacity for empathy. He concludes that "empathy is part of a heritage as ancient as the mammalian line. Empathy engages brain areas that are more than a hundred million years old. The capacity arose long ago with motor mimicry and emotional contagion, after which evolution added layer after layer, until our ancestors not only felt what others felt, but understood what others might want or need" (208). Speaking of humans, de Waal says that he derives "great optimism from empathy's evolutionary antiquity. It makes it a robust trait that will develop in virtually every human being so that society can count on it and try to foster and grow it" (209). That is exactly what intergroup dialogue is designed to do.

That neuroscience research increasingly shows empathy to be pre-wired, and that the cross-species experiments and observations show it to be evident across many mammals, does not mean that these capacities will flourish without environmental nurturing. Rifkin (2009) provides a compelling case that the biologically influenced capacity for empathy must be supported and rewarded in all social institutions, in education, the law, business, communities, government, and families. That view contrasts dramatically with the criticism of President Obama by Republicans when he suggested that a Supreme Court justice needs empathy—"the capacity to stand in somebody else's shoes and see through their eyes"—as well as intellect and commitment to the law (Society of American Law Teachers 2009). Although President Obama was referring to cognitive empathy (the capacity to understand the perspectives of other people), the outcry at his use of the term *empathy* focused on emotional empathy. During the hearings on the nomination of Sonia Sotomayor for the Supreme Court, and again during similar hearings on the nomination of Elana Kagan, President Obama was charged with urging that emotions rather than the law should prevail in decision-making in the Court.

Many studies have demonstrated the importance of intergroup empathy as a mediator of the impact that intergroup contact has on reducing prejudice and intergroup bias (Batson et al. 1997, 2003; Finlay and Stephan 2000; Galinsky and Moskowitz 2000; Vescio, Sechrist, and Paolucci 2003). Prejudice and bias are usually reduced when people of different racial-ethnic groups interact, and this happens at least partly because interacting across race-ethnicity increases intergroup empathy. Thomas Pettigrew and Linda Tropp (2008) conducted a meta-analysis of intergroup contact, covering more than 500 studies, which supports both the overall impact of contact in reducing prejudice and the role of empathy as a mediator of that effect.

Several explanations for this mediating role of intergroup empathy have been suggested. One is that increased empathy reduces perceptions of dissimilarity and feelings of threat during intergroup contact by helping members of different groups see that they share a humanity and destiny (Gaertner and Dovidio 2000). Increased intergroup empathy also helps blur distinctions between in- and out-group members and decreases stereotype activation (Galinsky and Moskowitz 2000). Intergroup empathy generates feelings (compassion, despair, anger, outrage) in response to evidence of injustice that members of some groups experience (Finlay and Stephan 2000), and thus undermines people's acceptance of hierarchies in which groups are unequal, what is called a social dominance orientation (Bäckström and Björklund 2007).

Intergroup empathy has consequences in addition to its role in reducing prejudice when intergroup interaction takes place (Sorensen, Nagda et al. 2010; Sorensen, Gonzalez et al. 2010). One of its strongest effects is fostering prosocial behavior (Batson et al. 2003), indicated by greater likelihood of helping others (Shih et al. 2009). Intergroup empathy is also associated with improved attitudes toward members of groups other than one's own (Batson et al. 1997; Finlay and Stephan 2000; Stephan and Finlay 1999; Vescio, Sechrist, and Paolucci 2003), and cross-group forgiveness (Brown, Wohl, and Exline 2008; Cehajic, Brown, and Castano 2008; Tam et al. 2008).

BRIDGING DIFFERENCES Bridging differences, the second relational outcome, refers specifically to identity-based knowledge sharing and exchanges in intergroup contact situations. In intergroup dialogue, bridging differences involves reciprocal exchanges for mutual benefit. It requires motivation to participate in such exchanges and openness to sharing one's own group-based experiences and to learning about the group-based experiences of others (Nagda, Kim, and Truelove 2004).

Bridging differences extends Pettigrew's (1998) identification of friendship potential as influential in intergroup relations. Pettigrew conceptualizes friendship potential as involving four processes: learning about the outgroup, changing behavior, generating affective ties, and in-group reappraisal. Although cross-group friendship has been identified as an important contributor to reducing prejudice (also see Pettigrew and Tropp 2011), it is not clear in that research whether identities are salient in the friendship relationship or the relationship is defined as an intergroup or an interpersonal one. As discussed earlier, the identity differences between members of societally disadvantaged and advantaged groups are usually evident in individuals' differing cognitions, emotions, and behavioral goals (Demoulin, Leyens, and Dovidio 2009). Thus, members of different groups may have different expectations in these friendships and in cross-group contact in general. There are also questions about mutuality and who benefits from the friendship. In many intergroup contact situations, members of low-power groups are in an educating role (Chesler, Lewis, and Crowfoot 2005). Sometimes when members of low-power groups share personal stories, often laden with emotion, members of high-power groups may listen but not respond emotionally (Narayan 1988). That divergence ends up favoring high-power groups, who value relationships in which they learn about the vulnerabilities of low-power groups, whereas members of low-power groups often end up resenting such one-sided relationships. Other research shows that members of high-power groups want to be liked and accepted, whereas members of low-power groups seek to be respected and empowered (Bergsieker, Shelton, and Richeson 2010; Shnabel et al. 2008, 2009). What is needed is building relationships that keep identity differences salient as actual resources in forging common ground.

Bridging differences is entirely intergroup, that is, individuals in cross-group contact interact with each other but keep their group identities salient. It is marked by mutuality and introspective reappraisal by members of each group at the same time that they form affective ties with members of another group (Nagda et al. 2004). Bridging differences may also be a vehicle for re-spect and trust-building, both of which are important processes in reconcili-ation and forgiveness in intergroup relations (Hewstone et al. 2006; Lalljee et al. 2009; Nadler and Liviatan 2006). In his work on the Truth and Reconcili-ation Commission (TRC) in South Africa, Archbishop Desmond Tutu often evoked the value of *ubuntu,* reminding South Africans and the world at large of the interconnected nature of our lives, that we are humans through each other.

We are bound up in a delicate network of interdependence because, as we say in our African idiom, a person is a person through other persons. We believe that a person is a person through another person, that my humanity is caught up, bound up, inextricably, with yours. When I dehumanize you, I inexorably dehumanize myself. (1999, 35)

Reciprocal self-disclosure, in which members of both low-power and high-power groups share, builds trust in cross-group friendships and is crucial for forgiveness. "Reciprocal self-disclosure allows for the acquisition of knowl-edge about the outgroup and the sharing of knowledge about the ingroup. It also facilitates a more in-depth understanding of the outgroup through in-creased perspective taking and subsequent feelings of empathy for the out-group" (Swart et al. 2011, 185).

Becoming motivated to bridge differences captures the idea of humanizing each other through connection and understanding the larger contexts of their lives. Rather than seeing others as stereotypical representations or merely group representatives, the personalized, reciprocal sharing of group-identity experiences provides understanding of each other's life situations and experi-ences. The idea of humanizing is related to self-other overlap (Aron and McLaughlin-Volpe 2001). However, self-other overlap also supposes that out-group friends become more similar to self. Bridging differences attends to similarities but not at the expense of differences. Tamar Saguy, Linda Tropp, and Diala Hawi (2013), in their review of power and intergroup contact, emphasize that though both low-power groups and high-power groups like to talk about similarities in their intergroup interactions, low-power groups also have a stronger preference than high-power groups for talking about differences.

Bridging differences is also consistent with Bernard Rimé's (2007) idea of a social climate of emotions, whereby a participant's emotional sharing evokes an empathic response from a listener and then stimulates even more sharing from the original participant. In IGD, the listener is also stimulated to share her or his experiences. It is through this mutuality of sharing and connecting about identity-related experiences that participants are able to discern commonalities as well as differences in their lives. Moreover, because bridging differences is built on reciprocal exchange, it is possible that participants recognize that all their lives are characterized by a common humanity and vulnerability (Watkins, Larson, and Sullivan 2007).

Research on bridging differences has generated three conclusions. One, IGD increases motivation to bridge differences (Nagda et al. 2004). Two, bridging differences increases participants' confidence in taking self- and other-directed actions to promote diversity and social equity (Nagda et al. 2004) or to act with awareness to counteract acts of prejudice (Watkins, Larson, and Sullivan 2007). Three, in intergroup dialogue, bridging differences is fostered through the four communication processes—appreciating difference, engaging self, critical self-reflection, and alliance building (Nagda 2006). IGD thus offers a social space in which students can share and learn from each other, and in so doing, think more about their groups and identities. They share both personal and politicized experiences of privilege and inequality. Sharing, listening, exploring commonalities and differences, and reappraising social identities then help build alliances and foster commitments to social justice and social action.

Intergroup Understanding

Intergroup dialogue stresses two sets of intergroup understanding outcomes: the sources of intergroup inequalities and one's and other's attitudes toward diversity.

UNDERSTANDING INEQUALITIES   Concern with social justice in intergroup dialogue requires both knowledge about racial and gender inequalities, and understanding why inequalities continue to exist and economic inequalities have increased since the 1970s (Allen and Kohut 2008; Bartels 2008; Lowenstein 2007).[2] The reasons for increased inequalities are complicated and numerous: educational gaps between groups, demands for technological skills that some groups have in greater abundance than others, the impact of globalization on raising demands domestically for skilled labor more now than in the past, the fall in the real value of the minimum wage, increased disparities between management and workers' salaries, the decline in unionization, and policies (tax and others) favoring the wealthier (Bartels 2008; Yellin 2006). In intergroup dialogue, students learn about these complex sources of intergroup inequalities. Through collective critical reflection on the readings, in-class exercises such as the web of oppression, and sharing life experiences, students obtain both an academic and an experiential understanding of these complex sources of inequalities. These features of pedagogy and communication processes especially promote cognitive processes that facilitate understanding the causes of inequalities. The goal is for students to understand that while personal qualities—such as motivation, behavior, abilities, values—of individuals play a role in inequality, structural factors—such as segregation, discrimination, unequal access to employment networks, quality of schooling, tax and other public policies, and others—are both underestimated and highly influential in accounting for inequality.

Attributions for inequalities are defined in this research as explanations for the existence of inequalities. Research on how people explain inequalities has demonstrated that people tend to favor individualistic over structural interpretations of group-based inequalities (Bobo and Fox 2003; Feagin 1975, 2006). Particular groups think more individualistically than others (Bullock 2006). White Protestants, Catholics, middle-income people, and those with moderate education are the most likely to offer individualistic explanations. They tend to focus on group differences in motivation, values, and behaviors. In contrast, African Americans, low-income people, those on welfare, and those with less education are the most likely to offer structural explanations, such as group differences in the quality of schools, location of jobs away from urban population concentrations, lack of availability of transportation to job sites, public policies, and discrimination (Bullock 1999, 2006). In polls taken over the years, African Americans have always emphasized structural factors more than whites; they still do. Matthew Hunt (2004, 2007) and Lawrence Bobo (2011) support these conclusions and demonstrate that political ideology plays a significant role in who emphasizes individualistic and structural causes of inequalities. Conservatives advance individualistic explanations more than liberals, who more often than conservatives stress structural explanations for various kinds of inequalities.

Race differences in explanations for inequality have been narrowing over time. Maria Krysan and Nakesha Faison (2008), updating analyses originally published in 1997, examined surveys conducted by the National Opinion Research Corporation from 1986 through 2005. They show changes over time among both whites and African Americans in explaining why "blacks, on average, have worse jobs, income and housing than whites." In those surveys, respondents in a national sample were given four possible explanations: discrimination, access to education, low motivation, and low ability. The percentage of both whites and African Americans who endorse the two structural explanations, discrimination and access to education, has declined since 1986. Still, in 2005, more than twice as many blacks as whites endorsed discrimination as a cause for job, income, or housing disparities, and 10 percent more attributed causality to differential access to quality education. The one explanation where the two groups now converge is that approximately 40 percent of each racial group attribute causality for racial disparities to low motivation among African Americans. However, the relative stress on motivation and discrimination still differs greatly across the two groups. Among African Americans, 20 percent more endorse discrimination than low motivation. Whites show the opposite: 20 percent more endorse low motivation than discrimination. Maria Krysan and Nakesha Faison (2008) also summarized a series of questions asked in the Gallup Poll from 1997 to 2004 about how fairly African Americans are treated in a range of venues, including on the job, in neighborhood shops, downtown, in restaurants, and by the police. The percentage of whites who acknowledge that discrimination exists ranges from 10 to 15, and that of blacks from 37 to 70 percent across these venues. Wide discrepancies also emerged in the extent to which African Americans and whites believed that racism was a cause of people's treatment in various parts of New Orleans following Hurricane Katrina (Adams, O'Brien, and Nelson 2006).

ATTITUDES TOWARD DIVERSITY Attitudes toward diversity involve feelings, positive or negative, about an institutional focus on promoting diversity. These attitudes are important because they play a role in campus climate (Chang et al. 2003; Hurtado 2005). On campuses where students support institutional efforts to increase the diversity of the student body as an avenue for enhancing students' learning and competencies needed for future diverse work settings, students also more frequently express feeling comfortable and feeling that they belong in the institution (Milem, Chang, and Antonio 2005). Intergroup dialogue provides a venue in which students can discuss their views about the value or lack of value of increasing campus diversity. It is also a place where experiences and interactions should help students perceive that various kinds of diversity—racial, gender, geographic—actually do matter in their learning and cultural competencies. The controversy about the value of diversity in higher education centers on exactly this issue. Does diversity foster learning and other valued college outcomes?

Many scholars have demonstrated positive effects of attending diverse institutions (Chang 2003; Jayakumar 2008) and especially positive effects of interacting with diverse peers (Antonio 2001, 2004; Chang et al. 2006; Denson and Chang 2009; Engberg and Hurtado 2011; Fischer 2008; Gurin et al. 2002, 2004; Milem et al. 2005). Other scholars have argued that such claims are overblown and that diversity has only minor, if any, positive effects and may result in negative effects (Rothman, Lipset, and Nevitte 2003; Wood and Sherman 2001, 2003; Wood 2008). In intergroup dialogue, students are encouraged to understand these controversies about diversity and, most important, they learn experientially that diverse backgrounds and experiences often produce different perspectives. They may come to the dialogue classes believing, or not, that social diversity is likely to bring intellectual diversity. They may come to the dialogue holding positive or negative attitudes toward practices in higher education or in corporations (where diversity initiatives are widely under way) that aim to increase social diversity (Ensari and Miller 2006). Through dialogue they see how diversity operates. They see that diverse life experiences often produce different perspectives. For them, the value of diversity is no longer abstract and merely politically contentious. By interacting across racial-gender lines in an educational environment where diversity is brought into learning in an explicit way, they understand why diversity enriches their educations.

Intergroup Action

Encouraging students to commit themselves to social responsibility and action specifically geared to reducing inequalities is a primary goal of intergroup dialogues. Acting to bring about greater social justice often entails collaboration across differences of people working toward a common cause. Of course, solidarity-based action of people within a group is also important in social change. At the very least, however, many kinds of action require members of different identities to work together. It is that kind of action that IGD courses specifically address through their emphasis on alliance building, providing practice in the Intergroup Collaboration Project, and continually asking students to reflect on their individual and collective commitments to social change. Dialogue does not mean mere talking. Dialogue, especially the critical communication processes it entails, means acting as well as talking.

Studies conducted by scholars of higher education have examined the impact of diversity curricular initiatives on increasing students' commitments to social action. A study by Thomas Nelson Laird, Mark Engberg, and Sylvia Hurtado (2005), part of a larger national study looking at how colleges prepare students for a diverse democracy, compared the ratings of the importance of social action engagement by students enrolled in a diversity course and in a business management course. They found that enrollment in a diversity course was positively related to ratings of the importance of social action engagement. In another publication, Biren (Ratnesh) Nagda and his colleagues (2009) show, based on data from the Multi-University Intergroup Dialogue Research Project, that dialogue students increased more in postcollege action commitments than both control group students and comparison group students in social science classes on race-ethnicity and gender. Such action included "influencing the political structure (such as voting, education campaigns, and get-out-the-vote)," "influencing social policy," "working to correct social and economic inequalities," "helping promote inter-racial and inter-ethnic understanding," and "working to achieve greater gender equality." Furthermore, this difference was at least partially explained by the greater presence of the four communication processes in the dialogue courses than in the social science courses.

Other higher education studies have looked at action orientations in more specific ways or situations. Although they did not assess students' action ori-

entations, Gretchen Lopez and her colleagues (1998) did ask students to endorse action options in response to intergroup conflict situations. Using a
pretest-posttest design, and comparing students in an introductory course on
intergroup relations and conflict and a matched comparison group of students not in the course, they found that students in the course endorsed
more structural level actions (such as changing the climate of the university
and societal change) as responses to the conflict situation than did their
counterparts who were not in the course. Biren (Ratnesh) Nagda, Chan-woo
Kim, and Yaffa Truelove (2004), also using a pretest-posttest design, found
that social work students in a cultural diversity and social justice course increased in both their motivation for and confidence in engaging in two kinds
of action: personal (self-directed prejudice reduction) and social (other-
directed efforts promoting diversity). Furthermore, the impact of the course
components (lecture and intergroup dialogue) was mediated through the students' motivation to bridge identity differences.

In summary, these studies by higher education researchers generally show
that diversity courses influence the importance students attach to action,
their postcollege commitments to action, and their motivation for and confidence in carrying out action. They also show that the course pedagogy and
the communication processes that take place within the courses influence
action outcomes.

In our latent construct of action, we focus on three types of action aimed
at furthering social justice that were distinguished by Nagda and his colleagues (2004): self-directed, other-directed, and collaborative action. *Self-
directed actions* are behaviors by individuals to educate themselves and to examine their biases, perspectives, and orientations toward members of other
groups. Self-directed acts make one mindful of internalized or taken-for-
granted thoughts, feelings, and behaviors that may be hurtful to others and
that reinforce stereotypes and injustice. *Other-directed actions* are behaviors
by individuals that challenge biases that others express, that support the efforts of others to act in socially just ways, or that educate others about inequality, diversity, and justice. *Collaborative actions* are behaviors by individuals that involve working with others as in joining an action group, organizing
events, and participating in community-based collective actions. In addition,
our latent construct of action in the model that we test in chapter 5 includes
postcollege commitments, the same measure referred to in the Nagda and colleagues (2009) study earlier. Research on intergroup dialogue shows a posi-

tive impact on action, particularly on the importance and confidence in self-directed and other-directed actions (Gurin-Sands et al. 2012; Nagda et al. 2009; Nagda et al. 2004). Related research on students' analyses of conflict situations reveals that intergroup dialogue increases students' advocacy of both individual and institutional actions to resolve the conflicts (Lopez et al. 1998; Nagda, Gurin, and Lopez 2003).

Connecting Psychological Processes to Outcomes

Figure 3.1 shows our expectation that both cognitive and affective processes would relate to all three of these outcomes. We turn first to our reasoning for why the cognitive involvement should foster intergroup relationships, understanding, and action.

COGNITIVE INVOLVEMENT TO OUTCOMES The latent construct of cognitive involvement should foster all three of these outcomes because each requires thinking and reflection. The rationale for this prediction is based both in intergroup dialogue practice and in research literatures related to one or more of the components of cognitive involvement. For example, consideration of multiple perspectives (that is, cognitive empathy) has been shown to lead to emotional empathy, one of the intergroup relationship outcomes of intergroup dialogue (Batson et al. 1997). As students learn to take the perspectives of members in the other identity group, they should also develop emotional empathy. This learning also involves two other components of our latent construct of cognitive involvement—complex thinking and analytical thinking about society—which should increase emotional empathy as conveyed by a student in a gender dialogue:

> I feel now whenever I look at someone and start to make an assumption about them based on social identification, I stop myself and ask why am I thinking that? I have become so much more aware of my assumptions and how simply I used to think things were. And seeing the complexity has helped me be more empathetic with other people. Because I am so much less judgmental, I let myself identify with their feelings. (White woman, gender dialogue)

Cognitive involvement should also foster intergroup understanding, especially attributions for group-based inequalities. The multiple perspectives they encounter in the dialogue, sometimes through stories and sometimes through discussion of readings and in-class activities, create greater understanding of inequality. They become aware that because of their different identities, members of various groups often differ in how they explain those disparities and as well what should be done about them. Increasingly, the students learn to think in complex ways about the shape of inequalities in society and how their social positions have given them and their classmates relative advantages and disadvantages. Considering multiple perspectives, connecting those perspectives to identities, recognizing complex causes of behavior, and thinking analytically about the role of society in people's lives are all aspects of cognitive involvement that should help students become more cognizant of structural causes of inequalities. A student speaks precisely to this in examining her life through the lens of inequality:

> There were many instances during dialogue where I felt very confused about the way our society works and I have had to think hard about things I used to take for granted. It's as though somebody had placed my whole world in a jar for me to look at and then they shook it up. Piece by piece, I had to take inventory and analyze my beliefs and opinions about gender norms and gender inequalities. This has been my "waking up," and "getting ready." (Woman of color, gender dialogue)

Cognitive involvement should lead to action commitments, the third outcome of intergroup dialogue. The rationale for this prediction concerns the fourth component of our latent construct of cognitive involvement, namely identity engagement. Research has demonstrated that identity engagement increases collective action (Kelly and Breinlinger 1996; Simon et al. 1998; Stürmer and Simon 2004; Stürmer et al. 2003; Tajfel and Turner 1986), as well as action by allies on behalf of low-power groups. Identity is especially influential when it is politicized, that is, when the identity reflects consciousness of relative deprivation and injustice or is attached specifically to a social movement (Duncan and Stewart 2007; Gurin, Hatchett, and Jackson 1989; Gurin, Miller, and Gurin 1980; Gutierrez and Lewis 1999; Stürmer and Simon 2009; van Zomeren et al. 2004; Wright 2009). Research also shows that consideration of one's identity in systems of racial power and privilege (O'Brien 2001; Reason, Millar, and Scales 2005) or in systems of gender power and privilege (Kahn and Ferguson 2009) promotes ally development.

In addition, analytical thinking about society, another component of our latent construct of cognitive involvement, should foster collective action that members of low-power groups pursue on behalf of their groups, as well as action by members of high-power groups on behalf of low-power groups (Bailey 1998; Reason, Millar, and Scales 2005). For instance, Eileen O'Brien (2001) found that thinking about the prevalence of racial inequality as contrasted to color-blindness was common among students who became racial allies. O'Brien found that students who were just beginning to analyze whiteness more often acted individually, and that those who had thought more about the privileges of whiteness were more involved in campus leadership positions to advance equity (Reason, Millar, and Scales 2005). Students appear to build a commitment to make a difference in their environments:

> I've learned how racism operates and why it is so hard to see sometimes. I've thought about how it works on this campus and that is the first step, I think, in forming alliances with other students so we can make this campus better for everyone. (White man, race-ethnicity dialogue)

AFFECTIVE POSITIVITY TO OUTCOMES   The latent construct of affective positivity should also foster all three outcomes because all of them involve emotion as well as thinking and reflection. For example, positive emotions, being comfortable in intergroup situations, and having emotionally satisfying intergroup interactions clearly promote emotional empathy. These emotions include experiences such as sharing personal feelings and problems and having had meaningful discussions outside class about ethnic or gender relations as well as feeling engaged, open, excited, and trusting (for some of the items that measure emotions, see chapter 5; Shelton et al. 2010). Previous literature shows that these kinds of self-disclosing experiences promote emotional empathy (Turner, Hewstone, and Voci 2007; Rimé 2007). The predicted connection between affective positivity and emotional empathy also comes from IGD practice. In intergroup dialogue, the expression of emotion is normalized when students relate personal stories and experiences involving their identities. Students see that emotionality is accepted, even welcomed. They and others become more comfortable with emotional expression, leading everyone to feel more empathic toward one another.

Hearing others' stories helped put me at ease. It was comforting to know that other people had similar experiences and struggle. I really felt connected to [her] story. When she mentioned feeling being called names and being publicly discriminated against, I felt so sad. How could people be so hurtful to her? (Woman of color, race-ethnicity dialogue)

Emotions, positive interactions, and comfort should also foster an understanding of inequalities. Although cognitive work may predominate in understanding inequality and its structural sources, in dialogue learning how inequality operates involves emotions as well. Personal stories, which nearly always generate emotions in both the storyteller and the listeners, help students in particular understand the importance of social structure. When peers express sadness or anger about discriminatory or isolating experiences they have had, other students learn from them because emotions compellingly convey the impact of inequality. Students become more comfortable with each other and face inequality head on, without fears or embarrassment or avoidance. This comfort and confidence in talking emotionally about inequalities extends to their relationships outside the dialogue group:

I've learned how to deal with my feelings when my buttons are triggered by what someone says. That's important to me because now I can talk with my family and my boyfriend, people I love, when they make stereotypic comments. I know that they have feelings too and we have to connect our feelings with each other. I believe I can now talk with my boyfriend about benevolent sexism and how him wanting to put me on a pedestal is a form of oppression, even though it is much harder to notice than downright discrimination. I know I will have to deal with him feeling hurt but I've seen how people bring up potentially hurtful issues in ways that others can hear it and not be hurt. I'm actually looking forward to that conversation. (Woman of color, gender dialogue)

Emotions and positivity of interactions should also be related to action. Research demonstrates that anger, guilt, and sympathy motivate actions on behalf of low-power groups by members of high-power groups (Doosje et al. 1998; Iyer, Schmader, and Lickel 2007; Leach, Iyer, and Pedersen 2006; Van Zomeren and Iyer 2009). Anger also motivates collective action by low-power groups (Ellemers and Barreto 2009; Van Zomeren et al. 2004; Iyer and Ryan 2009). A second affective process—experiencing positive inter-group interactions—is also related to a number of actions. Positive interactions that embody unconditional respect are especially important (Lalljee et al. 2009), as are interactions marked by meaningful and honest conversations about social issues (Broido 2000; O'Brien 2001; Reason et al. 2005; Tatum 2007). Such interactions embolden students to take positive steps toward addressing inequalities in their immediate environments, sometimes even against peer pressure:

> I've learned so much, especially about how women feel in various situations. One of the really good things about my dialogue is that the women never took out against us men but just shared their feelings in ways that I felt included and accepted. And I'm a different person now. Just yesterday my fraternity brothers wanted to go to Hooters. I said they would be welcome to go but I would not step a foot in there. I told them that Hooters is sexism at its finest. They understood where I am coming from because they could see my emotions, that I really care. (Man of color, gender dialogue)

CONCLUSION

In this chapter, we have presented the theoretical framework that has guided both the dialogue practice intervention and the research project. In describing this framework, we have drawn from communication studies, social psychological research on intergroup relations, and critical race and gender studies. The students' voices have been used to show how their experiences in dialogue illustrate the use of the communication processes, which are created by the pedagogy of intergroup dialogue. We have argued that because specific affective and cognitive psychological processes occur during intergroup contact, some fostering positive outcomes and others fostering negative outcomes, these psychological processes play an important role in our framework. We have delineated how the communication processes are expected to address the challenges of negative intergroup interactions and to encourage increased affective positivity and cognitive involvement—our two primary sets of affective and cognitive processes—and how they in turn should foster greater intergroup understanding, positive intergroup relationships, and intergroup action.

In chapter 5, we present evidence from the quantitative analyses of the pre-, post-, and longitudinal-post-survey data on the impact of intergroup dialogue on the measures of the concepts included in the latent constructs in this theoretical model. We also test the model, using structural equation modeling, to assess the fit of our data to this model that involves all of the linkages posited in figure 3.1 between pedagogy, communication processes, psychological processes, and outcomes.

Authored by Biren (Ratnesh) A. Nagda, Patricia Gurin, Nicholas Sorensen, and Kathleen Wong (Lau).

PART II

Studying Intergroup Dialogue: Methods, Effects, and Processes

CHAPTER 4

Studying Intergroup Dialogue: Using Mixed Methods

In the previous two chapters, we described the practice and theoretical models that guided the intergroup dialogue (IGD) courses investigated in this project. The practice model involves an interactive pedagogy implemented across four stages. The theoretical model posits that dialogue pedagogy leads to distinctive communication processes that form the heart of intergroup dialogue. Two of these processes, which we call dialogic, focus on personal sharing of experiences and beliefs and on taking risks by disclosing uncertainties and feelings (engaging self) as well as listening and inquiry about the ideas and experiences of other members of the dialogue (appreciating difference). Two other processes, which we call critical, focus on sharing and reflecting on power and privilege by discussing how socialization and social stratification have operated in their lives (critical reflection) as well as on discerning both commonalities and differences that can be leveraged into collaborative relationships (alliance building). These four processes promote changes that take place within individual participants. Some of these changes involve cognition, specifically increased analytical thinking about society, greater consideration of multiple points of view, more complex thinking, and increased involvement in identity. Other changes involve emotions, including more positive interactions across difference and more positive emotions when such interactions occur. Pedagogy, communication processes, and psychological processes together are expected to produce increased intergroup understanding, empathy, and action—the three sets of predicted effects of intergroup dialogue.

The objective of the multi-university study (MIGR) was to see whether these effects occurred and how the communications that take place among dialogue participants and the psychological processes that take place within the participants might account for the effects. In this chapter, we present the research methods used to address this objective. We needed a research design that would ensure that whatever effects we found could be attributed to participation in a dialogue rather than to changes over an academic term that the students might have undergone had they not been in an intergroup dialogue course. We needed statistically rigorous methods to test for both effects and explanations for them. We also wanted to explore how students participated in dialogue and how they talked and wrote about their dialogue experiences, a goal that called for qualitative methods as well as quantitative methods.

This chapter describes the standardized curriculum that comprised the intervention being assessed in the MIGR project, the research design and methods used to assess effects, and the qualitative materials and analyses used to give a more nuanced understanding of what goes on in intergroup dialogue courses.[1]

RESEARCH DESIGN: STANDARDIZED INTERVENTION

The challenge was how to standardize the curriculum across the institutions to form the experimental intervention. To varying degrees, each of the nine participating institutions already had an IGD program in place. However, because the programs were not using identical curricula, initially we did not have an intervention that could be evaluated. The nine teams of collaborators worked together in face-to-face meetings to develop a uniform curriculum. Those meetings were themselves an IGD because various collaborators had to compromise and at times let go of strongly held commitments to a particular reading or activity or assignment. The collaborators had to share their perspectives and experiences using particular readings, in-class exercises, collective reflection activities, and writing assignments; they had to listen to and learn from each other to eventually agree upon a uniform curriculum comprised of the same content for each of the dialogue sessions, the same readings, the same in-class exercises, the same out-of-class project, and the same final paper assignment. These team meetings, which were crucial in setting a collaborative culture that continued over the five years of the project, helped ensure that all institutions were implementing the curriculum and following uniform research procedures. In addition, the primary investigator (Patricia Gurin) talked monthly with each institution's primary collaborator to further ensure standardization of the intervention and research procedures. The one nonstandard feature was that some institutions were required to use faculty as facilitators, others had to use professional staff, and still others were allowed to use student peer facilitators. A uniform approach to facilitators was not possible, though the project did attempt to implement common training. This institutional variability is a limitation in the study.

A Field Experiment: Dialogues and Control Groups

An experimental design was created to test whether the intervention produced the predicted effects of intergroup dialogue presented in chapter 3. Because students in all nine institutions had to apply and could not automatically enroll, it was possible to conduct a true field experiment across these institutions. Students who applied for either a race-ethnicity or a gender dialogue course at each of the nine institutions were randomly assigned either to an experimental group (the race or gender dialogue course) or to a race or gender wait-list control group. Figure 4.1 shows the research design for the project, showing that students who were randomly assigned to either dialogue classes or to wait-list control groups were administered the same surveys over time.

This research design helped us answer several important questions. First, could the effects discerned in the study be attributed to participation in intergroup dialogue? Randomly assigning applicants to either an experimental or a control group equates both groups for student motivation to take a dialogue course. This feature of the design addresses a specific selectivity question, namely, would students have changed from the beginning to end of the academic term had they not enrolled in an IGD. When studies merely measure students in a particular course at the beginning and end of a course and discern changes over that period, it is not clear whether the changes happened because of the course or because the students changed by virtue of being in college another semester. Randomly assigning students who applied to take a dialogue course to the course or control group means that changes

Figure 4.1   Research Design

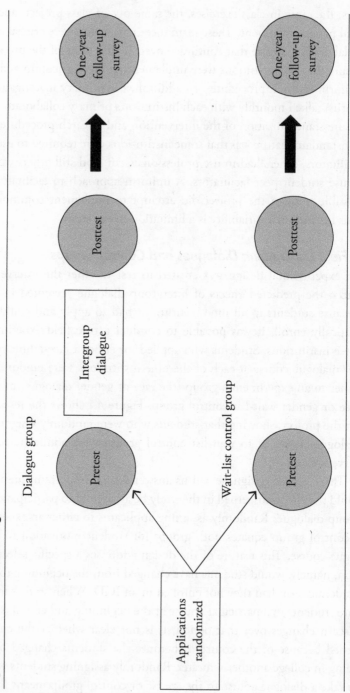

Source: Authors' compilation.

Figure 4.2   Participants

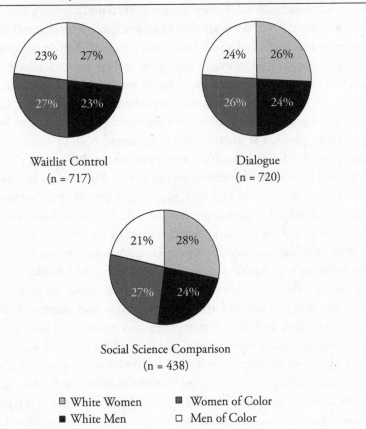

Waitlist Control
(n = 717)

Dialogue
(n = 720)

Social Science Comparison
(n = 438)

☐ White Women   ■ Women of Color
■ White Men   ☐ Men of Color

Source: Authors' compilation.

that were measured in this research project can truly be attributed to participation in the course.

Altogether, the study team conducted fifty-two pairings of dialogue course
groups and control groups across the nine universities to test whether effects
could be attributed to participating in intergroup dialogue. In total, the dialogue (experimental) groups included 720 students, with an average of fourteen (range eight to eighteen) in each group; the control groups included 717
students, with an average of fifteen (range seven to twenty-one) in each
group. A total of 1,437 students participated in the study. Figure 4.2 shows
the breakdown of these groups.

A second question is whether effects of IGD would be sustained over time. As depicted in figure 4.1, both the experimental and control groups were administered surveys at the beginning of an academic term (pretest), the end of that term (posttest), and a year later (post-posttest). This design made it possible to assess immediate effects (pre-post) and longer-term effects (pre-post-post). It is rare in the research literature on intergroup relations, diversity education, and antiracist education to investigate if effects last beyond an immediate and often very short-term intervention or beyond one semester.

A third question is whether effects are found both in race-ethnicity dialogues and gender dialogues. We were interested in this issue of generalizability on the basis of some initial suspicion that dialogue might be effective primarily (or even only) in race dialogues simply because race has been such a persistent but rarely talked about social divide. We decided to include gender dialogues as well as race-ethnicity dialogues to see whether dialogue effects applied to at least one topic other than race. A second reason to include gender dialogues was that all of these nine institutions had developed both gender and race dialogues. Altogether we conducted twenty-six pairings of race-ethnicity dialogue courses and control groups and twenty-six of gender dialogue courses and control groups. In two instances in both parts of the study, one control group served as the control for two dialogues. The same curriculum was developed for both race-ethnicity and gender dialogues, except some readings were specific to one or the other topic areas. The instruments used to assess possible effects were identical for the two types of dialogues except for occasional substitute phrasing referring either to gender group or to racial-ethnic group.

The design also addressed generalizability across students who differed in race-ethnicity and gender. In each pair of dialogues and control groups, the goal was to enroll an equal number of white men, white women, men of color, and women of color. This feature of the design allowed us to assess whether IGD affected both women and men, and both students of color and white students in the two types of dialogue courses. As figure 4.2 demonstrates, by and large this goal was accomplished, roughly equal percentages of each demographic group participating in each condition.

The question might be asked why we did not try to pair white students with students from separate groups of color, or pair students in each of the racial-ethnic groups with one another. The answer is that there were simply not enough students applying to participate in intergroup dialogues from each of the separate racial-ethnic groups to conduct multiple dialogues and control groups involving separate groups of color. We see this as a limitation of the study that could not be avoided given the numbers of various racial-ethnic groups in the dialogue applicant pools at these institutions.

Social Science Comparison Groups

The design also included nonrandomized comparison groups comprised of students enrolled in traditional lecture-discussion social science classes on race and on gender. Although we had no role in what topics were covered and the topics differed somewhat across institutions, all of them covered literature on the social construction of race and of gender, socialization of gender and racial attitudes, and racial-gender inequality. These groups were used to test whether effects of the dialogue courses could be attributed to the method of dialogue above and beyond learning content about race and gender. This design feature provides evidence for the importance of the dialogue method by being able to test whether change over time turned out to be greater for students in the dialogue courses than for those in the social science classes. The test is obviously not as definitive as it would have been had applicants to the dialogue courses been randomly assigned to the social science courses. That was not possible. What was possible was recruiting volunteers from social science classes and randomly selecting individuals from four demographic groups from that volunteer pool to mirror the number and distribution of students in the dialogue and control groups. We collected data from twenty-seven social science comparison groups (fourteen race and thirteen gender), with an average of sixteen students (range six to twenty-two) per group. In one instance, one social science comparison group was paired with two dialogues, making a total of fifteen pairs of race dialogue and comparison groups, and fourteen pairs of gender dialogue and comparison groups. The social science comparisons were conducted the same academic term that the dialogues with which they were paired were conducted. Altogether, 438 students, divided approximately equally across the four demographic groups, participated in the social science comparison component of the study. Figure 4.2 shows that the breakdown of the four demographic groups was approximately equal in all three research groups: dialogue, control, and comparison groups.

MIXED METHODS

This project is a mixed-methods research project. As researchers, we take this to mean that the project purposefully incorporated quantitative and qualitative methodologies for data collection and analyses. Across the nine participating institutions a team of eight quantitative researchers and eight qualitative researchers collaborated from the beginning to develop the theoretical focus for the project, the research questions and the research design. Valerie Caracelli and Jennifer Greene describe the productive tensions that can result from a mixed-method project:

> A mixed method study that combines these two traditions [quantitative and qualitative] would strive for knowledge claims that are grounded in the lives of the participants studied and that also have some generality to other participants and other contexts, that enhance understanding of both the unusual and the typical case, that isolate factors of particular significance while also integrating the whole, that are full of emic meaning at the same time as they offer causal connections of broad significance. (1997, 13)

Our research team's approach was that this project would work with the strengths and limitations of both quantitative and qualitative methodologies. Margarette Sandelowski (2003) examines the extent to which methods are mixed throughout the framing, design, and analysis of the research project. Many mixed-methods projects make quantitative or qualitative the driving methodology and treat the other methodology as an add-on. An example of add-on designs in some so-called mixed-methods projects might be attaching open-ended questions at the end of a quantitative survey, or conducting interviews that are so highly structured that they primarily incorporate quantitative scales, or providing a few descriptive statistics about participants in a primarily qualitative study (Sandelowski 2003).

The research design of this project incorporated theoretically coordinated methodologies that offered opportunities for both quantitative and qualitative analyses. The primary data sources included end-of-semester student papers, semistructured audiotaped interviews, videotaped dialogue sessions, and pre-, post-, and post-posttest quantitative surveys. We began the project with what Alan Bryman calls a process rationale whereby "quantitative research provides an account of structures in social life but qualitative research provides sense of process" (2008, 91). During the project we took an even more integrated approach, using both quantitative data and qualitative data for examining processes that occurred in the dialogues. Chapter 5 presents the quantitative analysis of the processes that were measured by the surveys and were influential in accounting for three sets of outcomes. Chapters 6, 7, and 8 present both qualitative and quantitative analyses of the interviews, student papers, and videos. Thus, as the project developed and our cross-institutional team continued to meet, we developed an evolving mixed-method rationale in which triangulation or mixing methods occurred continually.

Quantitative Assessments

All students in the experimental (dialogue), control, and comparison groups were administered a survey before classes started for the term and another survey at the end of the term. These surveys provide the primary measures for assessing the effects of dialogues (comparing change among the dialogue students with change among both control group students and the comparison group students). A one-year longitudinal follow-up survey of the dialogue and control group students was also included in our analyses of longer-term effects. Results using the survey measures appear in chapter 5. The survey measures are also used in chapter 5 in testing how well our theoretical framework for IGD fit the data, thus answering through quantitative assessments how dialogue produced effects. The surveys covered basic demographic information and measures of all concepts involved in the theoretical framework described in chapter 3. Appendix 1 details all the survey measures used in this book.

Analysis Strategies for the Survey Measures

The analytic approach using the survey measures differed for examining the effect of intergroup dialogue on the outcomes (that is, did it work?) and for examining the processes by which intergroup dialogue fostered these outcomes (that is, how did it work?).

To examine the effects of intergroup dialogue, we used multilevel linear modeling (MLM), which accounts for the nature of the data: that it was hierarchical or nested in the sense that it included multiple time points for each student, multiple students within each group—dialogue, control, or social science comparison.[2] The models used to estimate the effect of IGD also control for important individual differences in the students when the experiment began, including their year in college, exposure to pre-college diversity, and any prior courses focusing on race or gender content. To examine whether the effects of intergroup dialogue differed between race-ethnicity and gender dialogues, we tested whether the treatment effect (the greater change over time among dialogue than among control group students) differed in race and gender dialogues. Similarly, we also tested whether the treatment effect differed for white men and women and men and women of color.

To examine how effects occurred, this study used an analytic approach that allows us to examine many pathways by which students changed over time and thus to provide the most comprehensive picture possible of how intergroup dialogue fosters increased intergroup understanding, intergroup relationships, and commitments to intergroup action. This method (structural equation modeling, SEM[3]) was used to test the theoretical framework we hypothesized in chapter 3 would foster the outcomes of intergroup dialogue.

These two analytic approaches, one for assessing effects and one for assessing processes, are specified more fully in chapter 5, and in greater detail in appendix 2.

Qualitative Assessments in Dialogues

Three types of qualitative materials were collected for the students in the dialogue courses. The 720 final student papers were used to analyze the students' evaluations of their dialogue experiences. In addition, a more intensive qualitative study was conducted in twenty dialogues (ten race and ten gender). In these twenty courses, videotaping was conducted in three sessions and all students were interviewed at the end of the term.

The materials from the final papers, videos, and interviews were used four ways in the project. One was to delve into particular concepts (see chapter 6 on empathy) in our theoretical model, using narrative methods in which students would have opportunities to use their own language to construct meaning. A second was to make connections to specific types of meaningful dialogue interactions, and thus add depth to concepts assessed from the surveys. A third was to illustrate concepts and findings using narratives from the interviews and final papers. The last was to examine in-depth how the students experienced the practice model and to capture how they and the facilitators participated in dialogue. This constellation of qualitative material data analyses provides opportunity for two analytic insights, first, the conceptual development of the theoretical model that emerges from the emic insiders' perspectives and cultural language of dialogue participants (Cresswell 1998; Goodenough 1970; Kitayama and Cohen 2007), and second, a rich and in-depth understanding of the pedagogy as experienced by students.

FINAL PAPERS Students in all fifty-two dialogue courses were given the same final paper assignment, which asked them to write about their hopes and fears at the beginning of the class, their evaluations of the quality of interactions and level of trust that was created in the class, how disagreements were handled, what they had learned about group identity, what intergroup skills they had learned, and how they expected to use those skills after the class ended. They were instructed to use at least six of the course-assigned readings in responding to these topics in their eight- to ten-page papers. The students had signed a consent form that assured them that their papers would be copied, assigned a unique identification number, and used for research purposes independently of the grading of the original papers by facilitators.

The final papers were read and codes were developed by graduate students supervised by a research analyst. The codes reflected the major themes they discerned in the papers. The graduate students were not given the theoretical framework but were asked to be attentive to possible evidence of pedagogy, processes, and outcomes as they read the papers. In sequential applications of the initial codes to additional samples of papers, the research analyst team developed a codebook with twenty-nine codes that were then applied to the 720 final papers from the fifty-two dialogue courses. This aspect of the coding process followed generally accepted qualitative analysis procedures delineated by Bryman (2001).

Coding teams were assigned one-third of these twenty-nine dimensions to code so as to maximize intercoder reliability by each team focusing on a smaller number of dimensions. Training for reliable coding was conducted with each team, and only after each team had achieved reliability agreement of 80 percent or better for the dimensions for which they were responsible was training considered complete. Because the coding of this large number of student papers required three semesters, training up to 80 percent reliability had to be conducted each term. Two graduate student supervisors were stable across the three semesters, as were ten of the forty undergraduate coders. After a training reliability standard had been achieved, ten percent of the papers coded by each team were checked for reliability. The average agreement across the twenty-nine dimensions ranged from 67 percent to 95 percent.

Undergraduate research assistants entered the codes into the NVivo qualitative analysis software program. In addition to categorizing the entire narrative in a student paper by the twenty-nine codes and storing narratives for each code, NVivo provides a count of the number of times each code appeared, which is called a reference in the software, across each student's entire paper. A single reference could be a word, a sentence, or a paragraph—however much content that the coder judged represented that code. The counts for each of the codes could be analyzed quantitatively, like any other numeric measure. Thus, it was possible to use the narrative material from the students' final papers both qualitatively and quantitatively.

INTERVIEWS Students in ten race and ten gender dialogues, one each at eight institutions and two each at the University of Michigan where the IGD program was larger, participated in structured interviews at the end of the term in which the dialogue course was conducted, a total of 248 students. Interviewers, matched for gender and race of the interviewee, were not involved with running the dialogue courses. This was important so that students understood that their instructors were not part of the research project and that the data collected from the students would not be seen by their instructors. Consent forms assured students that their names would not appear on the research materials, which would be stored by a unique identification number. Students were also asked to consent to the project quoting anonymously from their interviews. The interviews were conducted with student dialogue participants at the end of the term after the completion of the dialogue course and submission of their final papers. Interviewers met one on one with each interviewee and used a semistructured protocol. The interviews were recorded and transcribed.

In the interviews, which lasted approximately an hour, students were asked to respond to questions about interactions with students from their own and the other identity group that provided measures of intergroup empathy (see chapter 6), their engagement in the dialogue (see chapter 7), and cognitive and affective processes that were expected to correlate with the measures of engagement and with behaviors observed in the videos conducted when students were interviewed (see chapter 8). Given the number of students interviewed, these topics were introduced with standard questions read by all interviewers with directions for probing responses to these questions. The specific coding procedures used to develop measures from the interviews are described more fully in chapters 6 and 7.

Codes for engagement, empathy, and cognitive-affective processes, like those for the final papers, were developed in an iterative process that began with multiple readings of the interviews, followed by initial codes that were applied, refined multiple times, and eventually used systematically by trained coders. Training coders and checking the reliability of the coded material from the interviews followed the procedures described for training and reliability checking for the final papers.

As was done for the final papers, the qualitative research team used NVivo to analyze the coded material from the interviews. Contrary to some misconceptions, NVivo software does not analyze data in some automatic way. In our study, the qualitative analysts first read a selection of interview transcripts and papers to generate an initial set of codes, using widely agreed-upon approaches of qualitative scholars. Each interview and paper was then manually coded. This coding was then entered into NVivo, which provides a technologically convenient management system to attach codes to data and retrieve coded passages methodically. Participant attributes (race-ethnicity, gender) and attributes of the dialogues (gender or race-ethnicity topic, institution, academic term they were conducted) were entered into the NVivo management system to retrieve narrative material not only by code but also by these attributes for further in-depth coding and refinement of analysis. The team also used NVivo to count the number of times a student addressed each of the coded dimensions across the total paper and across the total interview to assess how interconnected these dimensions were, and to provide narrative examples of each of the dimensions.

Two types of analyses were conducted. One was a qualitative analysis of the themes that eventuated in coded material and, as is evident in chapters 6 and 7, additional in-depth coding of themes that had not been previously coded and that emerged in further reading of a subset of interviews small enough to carry out such qualitative analyses. The second, conducted within NVivo, was a quantitative analysis comparing the average number of times that particular dimensions were coded across the interview. The counts were later entered into SPSS for a statistical analysis of possible differences between race-ethnicity and gender dialogues in what was coded in the final papers and interviews.

VIDEOS   Three sessions of each of the twenty dialogues making up the intensive study of the project were videotaped (one early, one in the middle, and one late in the term). The same session was taped at each of the institutions. The tapes were edited and thirty minutes covering the same structured interactions in each session were coded for six dimensions. First was attentiveness of listening, that is, the degree to which students appeared to listen to what was being said by another participant. Second was speaking initiative, or the degree to which a student responded to others and also initiated conversation. Third was openness, that is, the extent to which students used storytelling and made self-reflective comments, showing awareness of their biases and appreciation for difference. Fourth was inquiry, the extent to which a student made comments showing an attempt to find and create common ground by building a mutual understanding and asking questions of others. Fifth was advancing a perspective, that is, the extent to which a student supported or defended his or her point of view. Sixth was debating, the extent to which a student argued with other dialogue participants, defended his or her perspective in a manner revealing strong emotional attachment to that position and thus tended to polarize an issue rather than seek clarification and understanding. In addition, the facilitators' behavior styles were coded for the manner with which facilitators guided and responded to the participants. Facilitator behaviors were coded for four characteristics. First was advocacy, defined as behaviors in which a facilitator interrupted or talked over participants in support of his or her position, polarized an issue by presenting just one perspective, or disagreed with a participant in an adamant, emotional manner. Second was listening and supporting, defined as behaviors such as nodding, turning to a participant, leaning forward to show support or interest in a student's comments. Third was inquiry, using the same definition as for the students. Fourth was reflection-redirection, defined as behaviors such as repeating, rephrasing, naming something, asking questions that show an attempt to establish what participants believed and how they developed their perspectives from their identities and experiences. Procedures for coding the student and facilitator behaviors are described more fully in chapter 8.

The thirty minutes of each videotape to be coded were standardized across institutions so that the same ten minutes were coded at the beginning of the session (called check-in), ten minutes when the core activity of the session began, and ten minutes when the group as a whole processed what had happened during the dialogue session. The codes were developed and applied to the tapes, minute by minute, by graduate and undergraduate students at the University of Michigan. Two students coded each minute for each dimension, and reliabilities were calculated.

ADDRESSING LIMITATIONS IN PREVIOUS RESEARCH

Although intergroup relations programs now number in the thousands, they have not been extensively evaluated, perhaps because such evaluations are labor intensive and expensive and because the practitioners who conduct them are typically not trained in evaluation research. Nonetheless, a number of evaluations have been conducted. Reviews of these studies indicate that most of these programs are effective (Levy et al. 2004; Paluck and Green 2009; Stephan, Renfro, and Stephan 2004; Stephan and Stephan 2001, 2004), although some programs have been found to have little or no impact on intergroup relations. The most commonly measured outcome in these students is reduction of prejudice, although other attitude-related outcomes such as stereotypes, ethnocentrism, tolerance, respect, and trust have also been examined. However, in the past, few studies examined more than one or two outcome variables and none has included the wide variety of outcomes assessed in this study. Moreover, only a few of the studies conducted in the natural environment rather than in the laboratory have used experimental designs. Only rarely have previous studies examined effects that might last beyond a specific time-limited intervention. These studies have almost never examined the processes involved in bringing about the changes the programs caused. Finally, too few have examined impact on multiple racial-ethnic groups. The Multi-University Intergroup Dialogue Research Study addressed all of these limitations that characterize much of the previous field-based research in intergroup relations and in particular the limitations of previous studies specifically of intergroup dialogue.

Random Assignment: A True Experiment

To our knowledge, no study has been designed using random assignment in field studies of intergroup relations. Some studies have taken advantage of intergroup situations in which institutions have randomly assigned students from different racial-ethnic backgrounds to different situations. For example, studies of roommates have taken advantage of housing policies that use random assignment in some universities. In those studies, it is typically white students who are randomly assigned to live with students of color or with other white students. Only rarely has it been possible, due to small numbers of students of color, to randomly assign them to live either with other students of color or with white students. In contrast, this study was designed from the beginning to use random assignment to create experimental groups and control groups involving both white students and students of color. The failure to use random assignment is notable not only generally in intergroup relations studies but also specifically in previous studies of intergroup dialogue. At best, studies of IGD have depended on pre-post designs with matched comparison groups (Gurin, Nagda, and Lopez 2004; Gurin et al. 1999; Lopez, Gurin, and Nagda 1998). Thus, it is not clear from previous studies whether students equally motivated to take a dialogue course would also have shown similar changes over the course of a semester had they not participated in a dialogue course. The only way to assess that kind of selectivity is to randomly assign equally motivated students to either a control group or a dialogue group. The design of this research addresses this serious limitation.

Perhaps one of the reasons that random assignment is so infrequently used in field studies is that it is difficult to accomplish outside laboratory situations. In fact, the difficulties in the first academic term in which the institutions that were part of this study attempted to carry out random assignment proved daunting. Only two institutions that initially attempted to use random assignment succeeded. The data from the other institutions were discarded and those institutions began afresh and successfully the next term. By the second term, all institutions had learned how to use the uniform procedures for random assignment of applicants to race-ethnicity or gender dialogues (the experimental groups) or to the control groups.

Generalization: Dialogues and Students

Because most previous research on intergroup dialogue has been conducted on one type of dialogue, usually race-ethnicity dialogues, and with no systematic attention to equalizing participants from different demographic backgrounds (Miller and Donner 2000; Nagda, Kim, and Truelove 2004; Nagda and Zúñiga 2003), it was not known whether the effects of dialogue would generalize across race-ethnicity and gender dialogues and across students who differed in race-ethnicity and gender. The design of this project explicitly called for conducting experiments involving race-ethnicity dialogues with race-ethnicity control groups, and conducting gender dialogues with gender control groups, as well as equating the number of women of color, white women, men of color, and white men in all experimental and control groups. The importance of having investigated both race-ethnicity and gender dialogues and assuring equal representation of the four groups of students cannot be overstated. Although dialogue courses and programs are sometimes discussed as though they affect all kinds of applicants, scant evidence for that existed before this investigation. In fact, before this project, it was common in these institutions that race-ethnicity dialogues were conducted primarily with women and gender dialogues primarily with white students simply because more women than men applied for race dialogues, and more white students than students of color applied for gender dialogues.

We show in chapter 5 that the quantitative analyses demonstrate that intergroup dialogue generally had similar effects in both types of dialogues and for students from different demographic groups. This is both surprising and good news. Practitioners of multicultural programs often assert that the dynamics of interaction and learning will differ for different topics and different groups of students. The quantitative analyses of the survey data support a generalized effect of dialogue, whereas the qualitative analyses provide a more nuanced understanding of race-ethnicity and gender dialogues. The use of mixed methods in this project is one of its research strengths.

Longitudinal Effects

To our knowledge, only one study of intergroup dialogue (see Gurin et al. 1999; Gurin, Nagda, and Lopez 2004) followed students beyond the end of the course. Thus, previous research is limited in not knowing whether change that occurs during the dialogue course lasts over time. Assessing longitudinal effects has also been rare in the vast literature on studies of intergroup relations (for how few of the 515 studies they reviewed followed participants over time, see Pettigrew and Tropp 2011). Yet, effects evident immediately after a course (or intervention of any kind or laboratory study) may reflect only transient impact or demand characteristics whereby participants might respond according to how they think teachers of courses, creators of interventions, or designers of laboratory studies want them to respond. The longitudinal feature of this research project is therefore noteworthy for assessing whether immediate effects of dialogue persisted beyond the term. In general, the effects, although smaller than immediately at the end of the dialogue, were still evident a year later (see chapter 5).

Attrition

This project produced an estimable track record of following students who were assigned to the dialogue, control, and comparison groups. We successfully contacted 95 percent of the participants for the posttest administered at the end of the term in which dialogue and comparison courses were offered. A year later we successfully contacted 82 percent of the dialogue and control groups. These follow-up response rates also did not differ for students in the dialogue, control, or nonrandomized social science comparison groups. As discussed in chapter 5, where we present the quantitative results, we dealt with missing data that resulted from attrition using multiple imputation.[4]

REMAINING LIMITATIONS

Some limitations remain. Most important, this project does not answer all the questions raised by the kind of selectivity produced by motivation to be in an intergroup dialogue. It answers whether motivated students would have changed had they not had the dialogue experience but it does not allow generalization to students who have not applied for race-ethnicity or gender dialogues. In addition, in making presentations about the project at various national meetings, we have heard the critique that we are reaching only the already committed "choir." We are always asked whether IGD should be required of all students. The research team does not think that it should both because such a requirement would doubtless influence the dynamics of dialogue courses and because even motivated students need dialogic and critical analysis skills to be effective in intergroup collaborations.

The control condition in this field experiment merely required that those applicants to the dialogue courses not receive the intervention. It would have been useful to have included additional randomized control groups and nonrandomized comparison groups (in addition to the social science comparison groups) to examine the outcomes for students enrolled in other kinds of diversity and social justice courses. Of course, additional types of comparison groups would be most useful if students' enrollment were determined by random assignment.

Another limitation is that an entire curriculum, comprising four stages, many structured activities, and a rich array of readings, forms the intervention in this field experiment. We cannot test what aspects of the curriculum produced effects. The one exception to this limitation is that because of observations in the videos, it was possible to evaluate the influence of facilitator behaviors on student behaviors. To know what curricular features are especially influential, follow-up experiments varying specific features need to be conducted. What we do know from this project is that the curriculum used across the nine universities had broad and significant effects on participants.

A MULTI-UNIVERSITY COLLABORATION OF DIVERSE INVESTIGATORS

The project involved full collaboration of practitioners and researchers from the nine universities. At some institutions, such staff was drawn from both the divisions of academic affairs and the divisions of student affairs; at others, it was drawn from one or the other division. The primary collaborators, one from each institution plus the three co-investigators (the authors of this volume) and three consultants represented both gender and racial-ethnic diversity: eleven women and five men; ten collaborators of color, six white collaborators.

The primary collaborative team developed the standard intervention, as described. In addition, the team developed common, though not identical, approaches for training facilitators, because the status of the facilitators—faculty, professional staff, graduate students, and peer undergraduate students— was the one element that could not be identical across institutions. The team also developed all instruments used in the research: the surveys, final paper assignments, video and survey protocols. The coding procedures, which were developed and eventually carried out at the University of Michigan and the University of Massachusetts, were discussed and refined at the collaborative research workshops with collaborators from all nine universities.

To make this level of collaboration possible, the teams from each university met with the teams from the other universities two times a year, each workshop lasting three or four days. Each participating institution hosted at least one research workshop. In all instances, the project team met with the host university officials so that the hosting institutions would have a broad conception of IGD beyond their campus, and understand its larger context within higher education.

The crucial dimension for successful collaboration was the extent to which each campus provided institutional support for the work. Support included funding for campus teams to participate in the collaboration and to attend the ongoing research workshops. Each institution also committed to continue funding their dialogue programs throughout the project period at least at the level that existed when the research project began.

PRACTICE INFORMING THEORY AND THEORY GUIDING RESEARCH

The project was a multidisciplinary and multirole approach to understanding the outcomes and processes in intergroup dialogue. From the beginning, we paid attention not only to the disciplines that influenced our work but also to the different roles we had in higher education. Our collaborators were trained in social psychology, higher education, social work, communication, or women's studies. Some collaborators were primarily researchers, others were primarily practitioners in student affairs, and still others were practitioner-researchers. The project was guided by the research and practice of intergroup relations in social psychology and the research and practice of diversity and social justice education in higher education, both of which suggested outcomes and processes that are traditionally measured in these fields, as well as outcomes that have received very little attention (see chapter 2). The theoretical framework guiding the research (see chapter 3) was also informed by our practice of intergroup dialogue over the last twenty years, which has combined the insights from social psychology, higher education, group work practices in social work, and women's studies.

Given the rich diversity of disciplines and professional commitments within the team, we intended from the onset of the project to harness the mutuality of practice, theory, and research. We bridged theory, research, and practice two ways. First, we focused on bridging theory to practice. IGD efforts, and many other campus diversity efforts, are informed by Gordon Allport's (1954) specification of conditions for optimal intergroup relations, for example, equal status between groups, cooperation, common goals, and authority sanction. Allport's articulation of these conditions has led to many waves of research on intergroup relations, and it is still widely used as a basis for designing and improving programs in education and community settings (see Stephan and Stephan 2001; Stephan and Vogt 2004). In addition, Gurin and her colleagues (2002), in their documentation of research for the University of Michigan's affirmative action cases, developed a framework for understanding research on diversity in higher education. They specified three aspects of campus diversity: structural (compositional) diversity, curricular diversity, and interactional diversity. They also underscored that structural diversity, although important to increase the likelihood that students will interact across diverse peer groups, is not enough on its own to produce educational benefits of diversity. Students' active engagement with diversity is critical. Both curricular and interactional diversity played important roles in explaining when students engage with diversity. Our work cut across the curricular and interactional realms, and is designed to actualize the theories of intergroup contact and diversity in higher education into practice.

A second approach focused on bridging practice to theory and research. This was perhaps the biggest challenge. Our team shared a concern that the project's educational outcomes needed to be tied specifically to the goals of IGD. From practice, we knew that IGD benefited students beyond merely reducing prejudice (a primary outcome in antiracist studies and studies of intergroup contact) or developing a pluralistic orientation (a primary outcome in studies of diversity in higher education). Thus, we expanded the range of outcomes for this project to include intergroup understanding, intergroup relationships, and intergroup collaboration and action. In addition to guiding the definition of research outcomes, this practice influenced our theoretical framework in other ways. We knew it was important to focus on mechanisms of change, measuring what our practice had revealed to be influential mechanisms for explaining the effects of dialogue. Our practice led us to emphasize communication processes among participants and psychological processes that take place within individuals as the primary mechanisms of change. As practitioners of intergroup dialogue, we believed that the social process of becoming a community of learners committed to both one's own and others' learning was facilitated by the kind of communications that occurred among the participants (Nagda 2006). Ultimately, we crafted a comprehensive theoretical framework that connects the intervention (pedagogy) to the outcomes of dialogue, and specifies a mechanism of change through the communication and psychological processes.

CONCLUSION

In this chapter, we have described a mixed-methods research project that combined a multi-university experiment comprised of fifty-two intergroup dialogue courses and fifty-two wait-list control groups, and an intensive substudy of twenty intergroup dialogue courses that involved three sets of qualitative assessments—students' final papers, interviews of students at the end of the academic term, and videotape recordings of three sessions in each of these courses. We turn now to what we learned from both the experiment (chapter 5) and from the intensive substudy (chapters 6, 7, and 8). We will show that the two sets of methods generally supported each other in demonstrating both the effects of intergroup dialogue and how those effects were produced.

_____

Authored by Patricia Gurin, Kathleen Wong (Lau), Nicholas Sorensen, Biren (Ratnesh) A. Nagda, Ximena Zúñiga, Kelly Maxwell, and Cookie White Stephan.

CHAPTER 5

Effects of Intergroup Dialogue:
A Focus on Processes and Outcomes

In chapters 2 and 3, we delineated the ways in which the critical-dialogic practice model and theoretical framework of intergroup dialogue (IGD) differ from but also integrate some features of other approaches in intergroup relations and approaches to diversity and social justice education. We also described the theoretical concepts and relationships that comprise our framework. In this chapter, we move to two central questions: Did intergroup dialogues have the predicted effects on psychological processes and outcomes? Did the process framework delineated in chapter 3 explain how intergroup dialogue had effects on these processes and outcomes?

EFFECTS OF INTERGROUP DIALOGUE

A true experiment is at the heart of our study of the effects of intergroup dialogue. As described in chapter 4, this experiment involved a comparison between students randomly assigned to participate in an intergroup dialogue course and those randomly selected to be placed on a wait list (and provided with an opportunity to take an intergroup dialogue in the future). The students who participated in the intergroup dialogues constituted the experimental condition, and those on the wait list served as the control condition.

All of the students in the experimental and control groups were given a survey at the beginning of the term when the dialogue course took place and again at the end of the term. In addition, surveys were administered to these students a year later to assess whether the immediate effects of intergroup dialogue were still evident. This pretest/posttest/longitudinal posttest design enabled us to examine whether the intergroup dialogues increased intergroup understanding, relationships, and action, as well as psychological processes, more among the participants than among the control students, who were equally motivated to enroll in IGD courses. For the dialogues to be considered effective, it is necessary not only to demonstrate that the students in the experimental group displayed positive changes from the pretest to the posttest, but also to show that the students in the control group either did not change or changed significantly less than the experimental group during the period. The value of random assignment is that it nearly always means the experimental and the control groups are equivalent to one another before the study begins. In this study, randomization did produce equivalence between the dialogue and control group students at pretest on all but two of the twenty-four multi-item measures discussed in this chapter. Then, if the two groups differ at the end of the experiment, and the experimental group shows greater increases than the control group, there is a high degree of certainty that this difference is due to the effects of the experimental condition.

In this chapter, we first address the effects of intergroup dialogue. Did students randomly assigned to the IGD courses change more than students randomly assigned to the control groups on the psychological processes and on the three sets of outcomes that comprise our theoretical model?

Are the effects of intergroup dialogue found in both race-ethnicity dialogues and gender dialogues?

The study was designed to answer this question by including an equal number of race-ethnicity and gender pairings (twenty-six), for a total of fifty-two. However, for four dialogue and control group pairings (two race-ethnicity and two gender), one wait-list control group served as the control for two dialogues. Because of the long history of the racial divide in the United States and thus the salience of race and ethnicity, as well as the discomfort of talking about race across race, it is possible that the effects of IGD might pertain uniquely to race-ethnicity dialogues. The gender dialogue–control group pairings were included to assess the generality of dialogue effects. Because both race-ethnicity and gender dialogue courses were offered at all participating institutions, we could assess the question of generality at least across these two dialogue topics. Although it would have been useful to examine the effects of other types of dialogue courses (for example, on social class, sexual orientation, religion, domestic-international), this was not possible because they were not offered consistently at the participating institutions.

Do the effects of intergroup dialogue exist for students from groups that differ in relative privilege in society?

To answer this question, an equal number of white men, white women, men of color, and women of color were randomly assigned to both the race-ethnicity and gender dialogues and to the race-ethnicity and gender control groups from those students who applied to take an intergroup dialogue course. As noted in chapter 4, in no institution was the number of students from the various groups of color applying to take intergroup dialogue courses high enough to conduct dialogues by pairing students in each group of color with white students or pairing two groups of color with each other. That inability is a limitation, one necessitated by the applicant pools at the participating institutions.

In our analyses, we take account of the meaning of being a white man or woman and a man or woman of color within a race-ethnicity dialogue and within a gender dialogue. We consider these four groups as being from either more or less privileged groups in the context of a race-ethnicity or gender dialogue. In a gender dialogue, women are considered to have relatively less privilege in society, and men are considered more privileged. In a race-ethnicity dialogue, women and men of color are considered to have relatively less privilege in society, both groups of whites to have more privilege. The relative privilege of white men and women of color did not differ across dialogues because in both, white men represent relatively more privilege and women of color represent relatively less. Thus, we address the issue of demographic differences by examining the differences between the students in more and less privileged groups in both race-ethnicity and gender dialogues.

Do the effects of intergroup dialogue reflect content of the course, or does the pedagogy create effects above and beyond it?

To answer this question, we compared students randomly assigned to the dialogue courses with those enrolled in social science courses covering race-ethnicity or gender content. As described in chapter 4, students in these comparison courses were randomly selected. The comparison classes were conducted at the same time and at the same university as the IGD classes. Like the experimental and control groups, the comparison groups included nearly identical numbers of men of color, women of color, white men, and white women. Most important, the intergroup dialogues and the social science comparison classes shared the same focal content topics. Thus, these comparisons make it possible, within the limits imposed by the lack of random assignment, to address the question of whether it was the content or also the pedagogy of intergroup dialogues that was responsible for their effects.

Are the effects of intergroup dialogue still present a year later?

As noted in chapter 4, including a longitudinal follow-up assessment of students was an important feature of the study's design, and is rare in research on intergroup relations. Comparing change from pretest to eighteen months later for both dialogue and control group students makes it possible to determine whether there is a significant long-term effect.

Are there any negative effects of intergroup dialogue?

The survey questions used to assess the effects of IGD were phrased in both positive and negative directions. In many of the multi-item measures developed from these questions, we reversed coding the negatively phrased questions so that high scores on our scales represented positive effects of dialogue. In addition, to examine possible negative effects of dialogue, we created two multi-item measures from questions focused on negative emotions and negative interactions that may occur during intergroup contact. A negative impact would be evident if there were a greater increase over the academic term in negative emotions and negative interactions among dialogue students than among their control group counterparts.

The Overall Effects of Intergroup Dialogue

To examine the effects of IGD, we used multilevel linear modeling (MLM), which accounts for the nested structure of the data, such as multiple time points for each student, multiple students within each group—dialogue, control, or social science comparison.[1] Specifically, for each psychological process and outcome, we tested whether students in IGD changed significantly more over time than their counterparts in the control group,[2] while controlling for important student-level individual differences at baseline (before the IGD began), including their year in school, exposure to pre-college diversity (in their neighborhoods, high schools, and places of worship), and prior courses that students had taken in college that involved race-ethnicity or gender content. We also examined whether students in the dialogue and the control groups differed at baseline (pretest) on any of the measures presented in appendix A. Specifically, we tested for statistical differences between dialogue group and control group students on twenty-six pretest measures, (twenty-four positive outcomes and two additional measures assessing negative interactions).[3] Across the twenty-six measures, we observed statistically significant differences on only two measures—comfort in communicating across differences and frequency of self-directed action. These findings thus show that randomization was successful. Before students in the dialogue condition had the opportunity to take the course, they did not differ from their counterparts in the control group on twenty-four of twenty-six measures.

In sum, the positive impact of IGD is robust. The impact is demonstrated by consistency and statistical significance across many indicators of effects, by effects that, though smaller, were still reliable a year later, and by effects on nearly all measures in both race-ethnicity and gender dialogues and for students from both more and less privileged groups within race-ethnicity and gender dialogues. The results also support the importance of dialogue pedagogy because on two-thirds of the measures, intergroup dialogue students changed significantly more than students in the social science comparison classes with content focused on race-ethnicity or gender.

EFFECTS OF INTERGROUP DIALOGUE ON PSYCHOLOGICAL PROCESSES AND OUTCOMES

To address the central question about the overall effect of intergroup dialogue, this chapter presents five figures, based on models estimated with MLM, using composite indices of the two sets of psychological processes and the three outcomes in the critical dialogic framework of intergroup dialogue described in chapter 3. Means on the separate multi-item scales that make up these composite measures, with statistical evidence from the MLM models and effect sizes, can be found in appendix B. We calculated effect sizes d for differential change in each measure over time following Stephen Raudenbush and Xiao-Feng Liu (2001; see also Feingold 2009).[4] Other effects of dialogue, summarized in this chapter, are also detailed statistically in appendix B. Appendix A gives information about all the measures, with alphas demonstrating their level of internal consistency.[5] The surveys can be accessed in a guidebook available on the Russell Sage Foundation website.

Effects on Psychological Processes

The critical-dialogic theoretical framework of IGD presented in chapter 3 posits that the distinctive communication processes among intergroup dialogue participants foster psychological processes, both cognitive and affective, within the participants. Did the IGD students increase more in cognitive involvement and in affective positivity than the control group students, as our theoretical framework posits they should?

COGNITIVE INVOLVEMENT   Cognitive involvement is represented by measures of four concepts: liking for complex thinking, analytical thinking about society, consideration of multiple perspectives, and identity involvement (thinking and learning about one's identity). The means for each of these four cognitive measures were averaged to form an index measure of cognitive involvement. The complex thinking measure asked students how well, on a seven-point scale ranging from "not at all like me" to "very much like me," five statements described them. Examples include "I like tasks that require little thought once I've learned them" and "I prefer simple rather than complex explanations for people's behaviors" (both reverse coded). The analytical thinking about society measure also asked students how well four additional statements described them. Examples include "I think a lot about the influence that society has on my behaviors" and "I am fascinated by the complexity of the social institutions that affect people's lives." These two measures were adapted from the need for cognition scale (Cacioppo and Petty 1982) and the attributional complexity scale (Fletcher et al. 1986). The measure of consideration of multiple perspectives assessed tendencies to look at issues from different viewpoints as well as a willingness to consider many sides to an issue. This measure, which is often considered to be a measure of cognitive empathy in the psychology literature on empathy, is the perspective-taking subscale of Mark Davis's (1983) empathy scale. Students were asked how well five additional statements described them. Examples

Figure 5.1   Effects of Participation in Intergroup Dialogue on Cognitive Involvement

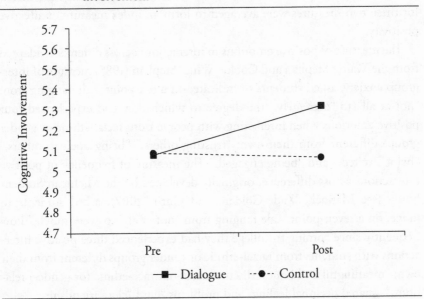

Source: Authors' compilation.

include "I strive to see issues from many points of view" and "I sometimes find it difficult to see things from the other person's point of view." The measure of identity involvement, adapted from measures of cognitive centrality of identity (Gurin and Markus 1989) and collective self-esteem (Luhtanen and Crocker 1992), includes thinking and behaving in ways that allow one to learn about one's identity, either racial-ethnic or gender. Students were asked to agree or disagree with five statements, on a seven-point scale ranging from "strongly disagree" to "strongly agree." Examples include "I think a lot about how my life will be affected by my race-ethnicity (or gender)" and "I have spent time trying to find out more about my racial-ethnic (gender) identity group."

Figure 5.1 shows the effect of intergroup dialogue, relative to the control group, on a composite measure of cognitive involvement. It shows that there was no difference between the dialogue and control groups at pretest, increased cognitive involvement among intergroup dialogue students from pretest to posttest, and no change for the control group students from pretest to posttest. The difference between the two groups at post-test is statistically significant.

AFFECTIVE POSITIVITY Affective positivity is represented by measures of positive emotions and positive interactions with others.[6] Specifically, the means for these two measures were averaged to form an index measure of affective positivity.

The measure of positive emotions in interactions across difference, adapted from the Walter Stephan and Cookie White Stephan (1985) measure of intergroup anxiety, asked students to indicate, on a ten-point scale ranging from "not at all" to "extremely," the degree to which they had experienced four positive emotions when interacting with people from racial-ethnic or gender groups different from their own: "trusting others," "being open to others," "being excited," and "being engaged." The measure of frequency of positive interactions across difference, originally developed by the Michigan Student Study (see Matlock, Wade-Golden, and Gurin 2007), asked students to judge, on a seven-point scale ranging from "not at all" to "very much," how frequently since coming to college they had experienced three positive interactions with students from racial-ethnic or gender groups different from their own: "meaningful and honest discussions about race-ethnic (or gender) relations," "shared personal feelings and problems," and "close friendships."

Figure 5.2 shows the effect of intergroup dialogue, relative to the control group, on the composite measure of affective positivity. It shows the same pattern as for cognitive involvement, namely, that the two groups did not differ at pretest, that dialogue students increased significantly in positivity from pretest to posttest, and the control group students did not. The difference between the two groups at post-test is statistically significant.

In summary, these two figures demonstrate a significant effect of intergroup dialogue on the measures that make up the two sets of psychological processes—cognitive involvement and affective positivity. These are the psychological process measures used later in this chapter in the structural equation model (SEM) test of the critical-dialogic theoretical framework.

Effects on Three Sets of Outcomes

The critical-dialogic theoretical framework of intergroup dialogue presented in chapter 3 includes three sets of outcomes that specifically match IGD goals: intergroup understanding, intergroup relationships, and intergroup action. Thus, to demonstrate a positive impact of IGD, we expected to observe effects of intergroup dialogue on measures relevant to each of these three sets of outcomes. Figures 5.3 through 5.5 display the effects of dialogue relative

Figure 5.2   Effects of Participation in Intergroup Dialogue on Affective Positivity

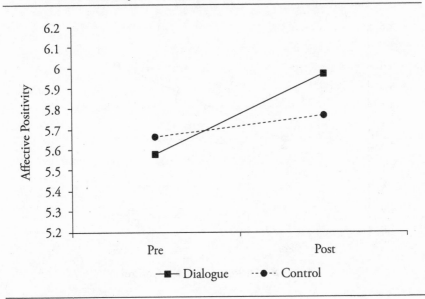

Source: Authors' compilation.

to the control groups on composite measures of these three outcomes. The visual depictions represent composite indices of these three sets of outcomes. Had the data not supported these effects, we would have viewed the impact of intergroup dialogue to have been quite limited.

STRUCTURAL UNDERSTANDING OF INTERGROUP INEQUALITY   IGD courses aim to help students understand how power and privilege are related to various types of inequalities. The main focus for intergroup understanding in the critical-dialogic framework is increasing awareness that inequality exists and that it results, at least in part, from societal structural arrangements. In chapter 3, we explained why understanding the structural causes of inequality is an important outcome of the critical-dialogic model. The many learning activities, readings, and facilitation in the IGD pedagogy, operating through communication and psychological processes, are designed to produce this increased understanding.

Students' beliefs about the causes of racial-ethnic and gender inequalities were measured by survey items developed for the National Election Study at

Figure 5.3 **Effects of Participation in Intergroup Dialogue on Structural Understanding of Inequality**

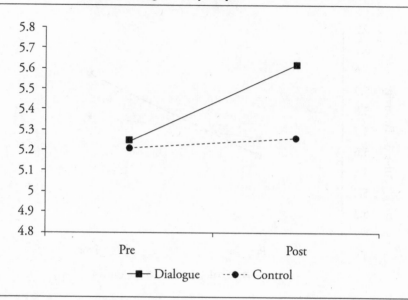

Source: Authors' compilation.

the University of Michigan in 1972 (Gurin, Miller, and Gurin 1980) and subsequently used in national surveys at Michigan's Institute for Social Research. Students were asked how much they agreed, on a seven-point scale ranging from "strongly disagree" to "strongly agree," with four statements attributing racial-ethnic inequalities and another four attributing gender inequalities to structural causes. An example of the racial-ethnic measure was "Unfair hiring and promotion practices help keep many people of color from gaining positions of power." An example of the gender measure was "Discrimination in the workplace still limits the success of many women." Students in both race-ethnicity and gender dialogues were asked to respond to both the racial-ethnic and gender attribution statements. Specifically, although we assessed students' structural understanding of racial and gender inequality separately, the means for these two measures were averaged to form an index measure of their overall structural understanding.

Figure 5.3 shows the effect of IGD, relative to the control group, on the composite measure of structural understanding of inequality. As expected, given random assignment of students to the dialogue courses and to the control group, the two groups did not differ in how much they attributed the causes of gender and racial inequalities to institutional and structural features of society on the pretest measures. They did differ on the posttest composite measure: structural attributions increased for the dialogue students but not for the control students. This difference indicates the significant effect of intergroup dialogue.

Table B.3 shows the effect of dialogue separately for structural attributions for race-ethnic inequalities and for gender inequalities. Dialogue had a significant impact on each. Moreover, the impact on both types of attributions in both race-ethnicity and gender dialogues was significant (see table B.6). This finding is noteworthy because it indicates a generalized effect of dialogue, such that students increase their understanding of structural inequality as it pertains to both gender and race even though their dialogue focuses more heavily on one or the other.

INTERGROUP EMPATHY   As noted in chapter 3, a substantial body of research has documented the important role of empathy generally in intergroup relations and specifically in intergroup dialogue. What is not so clear from previous literature is how intergroup empathy can result from intergroup contact. We hypothesized that IGD would increase intergroup empathy, which, as highlighted in chapter 3, is usually conceived of as emotional empathy. In emotional empathy, people respond emotionally to individuals as they tell their personal stories. In the intergroup dialogue context, these stories often involve students' identities and their experiences as members of identity groups within the context of unequal power relations. Intergroup dialogue emphasizes intergroup empathy as an end in itself because it allows and encourages people from diverse backgrounds who often differ in power and privilege to connect emotionally with each other. Intergroup empathy can function as a dialogue process by fostering other positive intergroup relations outcomes, as shown in our theoretical model in chapter 3.

To measure intergroup empathy students were asked how well, on a seven-point scale ranging from "not at all like me" to "very much like me," eight statements described their feelings in conversations with people from racial-ethnic or gender groups different from their own. Examples include "When people feel frustrated about racial-ethnic stereotypes applied to their group, I

Figure 5.4   Effects of Participation in Intergroup Dialogue on Intergroup Empathy

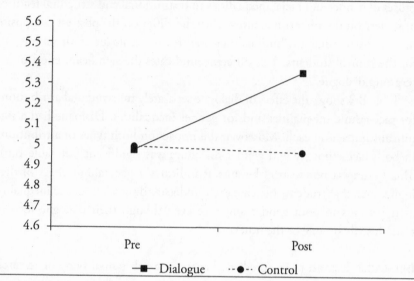

Source: Authors' compilation.

feel some of their frustration too" and "When people feel proud of the accomplishments of someone of their racial-ethnic (gender) group, I feel some of their pride as well."

Figure 5.4 shows the effect of IGD, relative to the control group, on intergroup empathy. Given random assignment of students to the dialogue courses or to the control group, the two groups of students did not differ in intergroup empathy at pretest. They did differ on the posttest measure of intergroup empathy. The dialogue students increased in intergroup empathy from pretest to posttest but the control group students did not. Thus, intergroup dialogue has a significant effect on intergroup empathy.

INTERGROUP COLLABORATION AND ACTION   Most practitioners of intergroup dialogue conceive of it as more than mere talk (Chesler 2001; McCoy and Scully 2002). That is definitely true of the critical-dialogic practice model and theoretical framework that guided this study. In a sense, the ultimate outcome of intergroup dialogue is going beyond mere talk to find ways that people can work together across difference to create a more just society. IGD courses aim to help students grasp the value of collaborative, cross-group action and to gain skills necessary for such collaboration. This goal of IGD also reflects the emphasis from the Association of American Colleges and Universities (2002) on personal and social responsibility as outcomes all college students should achieve.

As described in chapter 2, the last stage of the IGD curriculum covers readings, in-class exercises, and an out-of-class intergroup collaboration project (ICP), which together help students understand what fosters and inhibits intergroup alliances and collaborative action. The ICP is a laboratory for analyzing and making intergroup collaboration effective and gives students the opportunity to practice what they learn from the readings and in-class activities and reflections. Having students practice collaboration reinforces the core emphasis in intergroup dialogue on learning how to build alliances that can make intergroup action both more probable and effective.

To measure action, students were asked both how frequently they acted, on a seven-point scale ranging from "never" to "very often," and how efficacious or confident they felt, on a seven-point scale ranging from "not at all confident" to "extremely confident," about acting to further educate themselves, acting to educate others, and acting collaboratively with others. These frequency and efficacy measures were developed by Biren (Ratnesh) Nagda, Chan-woo Kim, and Yaffa Truelove (2004), and the items for collaborating with others were developed specifically for this study. Acting to educate the self was assessed by four statements: "recognize and challenge the biases that affect my own thinking," "avoid using language that reinforces negative stereotypes," "make efforts to educate myself about other groups," and "make efforts to get to know people from different backgrounds." Acting to educate others was assessed by two statements: "challenge others on derogatory comments" and "reinforce others for behaviors that support cultural diversity." Acting collaboratively was assessed by three statements: "get together with others to challenge discrimination," "participate in a coalition of different groups to address some social issues," and "join a community group or organization that promotes diversity." The students were also asked, using a standard measure in the annual, national surveys of college freshmen conducted by the Cooperative Institutional Research Program (CIRP) at the University of California, Los Angeles, about how important, on a seven-point scale ranging from "not at all important" to "extremely important," five postcollege civic actions would be for them when they graduated from college. Ex-

Figure 5.5   Effects of Participation in Intergroup Dialogue on Action

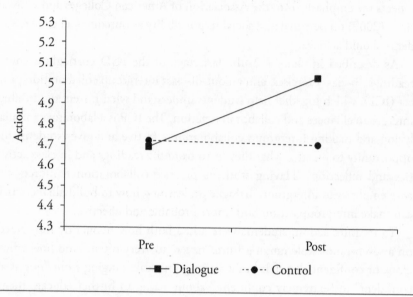

Source: Authors' compilation.

amples include "influencing the political structure by voting, participating in education or get-out-the-vote campaigns" or by "working to correct social and economic inequalities."

Figure 5.5 shows the impact of intergroup dialogue on an index of seven measures including both the frequency and efficacy of actions to educate self, actions to educate others, and intergroup and collaborative actions, as well as the importance of postcollege civic action. Students in the IGD courses increased on the index of action, but those in the control group did not and even decreased slightly (nonsignificantly) over the course of the term.

EFFECTS ON OTHER MEASURES OF OUTCOMES   Other measures of intergroup understanding, intergroup relationships, and intergroup collaboration and action were also included in the study. All but one show essentially the same pattern demonstrated by figures 5.3, 5.4, and 5.5. Tables B.1 through B.5 show the statistics from MLM analyses of effects on these measures as well as those included in the composite indices depicted visually in the figures in this chapter. These tables also show the longitudinal effects derived from the one-year follow-up of both the dialogue and wait-list control students that we discuss later in the chapter.

With respect to intergroup understanding, IGD was expected to reduce students' individual attributions for inequality to such factors as poor work ethic, unwillingness to make sacrifices necessary for success, lack of ability, and lack of effort. Such attributions were measured on a seven-point scale ranging from "strongly disagree" to "strongly agree" for race and gender inequality (Gurin, Miller, and Gurin 1980). As expected, the dialogue students at the end of the term used such explanations less often than at the beginning, but the wait-list control students did not change significantly over time.

Students in intergroup dialogue also became more critical of practices that reflect inequality, as measured on a seven-point scale ranging from "strongly disagree" to "strongly agree" by three statements written for this study: "Racial profiling is a serious problem in our society," "The biases built into the legal and justice systems contribute to the inequality in our country," and "There should be stronger legislation against perpetrators of hate crimes." The dialogue students increased in their critique of inequality but the control group did not change. In addition, the dialogue students more frequently embraced the idea that diversity is an educational benefit, but the control group did not change. Diversity attitudes were measured, again on a seven-point disagree-agree scale, by six statements originally developed by the Michigan Student Study (see Matlock et al. 2007). Examples include "A diverse student body is essential to teaching students the skills they need to succeed and lead in the work environments of the twenty-first century," and "The current focus on diversity undermines the common ties that bind us as a nation (reversed)." The attitudes toward diversity of dialogue students became significantly more positive, whereas those among the wait-list control students showed no significant change.

Turning to intergroup relationships, a second measure of positive relationships concerns motivation to bridge differences. An initial measure developed by Nagda and Ximena Zúñiga (2003) and later modified by Nagda, Kim, and Truelove (2004), bridging differences emphasizes mutuality of learning across difference, as measured on a seven-point scale ranging from "not at all like me" to "very much like me" how well seven statements described them. Examples include "It is important for me to educate others about my racial-ethnic (or gender) group," "I like to learn about racial-ethnic (or gender) groups different from my own," and "Sharing stories and experiences of my racial-ethnic (gender) groups with others matters a lot to me." Our analyses showed the same pattern of effects as we found for intergroup empathy. Dialogue students became more motivated to learn about other social groups and to have other groups learn about their groups, whereas the control students did not shift in such motivation over the course of the term.

Two additional measures of action further support the overall pattern of effects relevant to taking action. The effect of dialogue was significant on four campus-based social justice activities, such as involvement in "groups reflecting other cultural-ethnic backgrounds," and "groups promoting gender awareness and equality," measured on a seven-point scale ranging from "not at all involved" to "very much involved." Finally, the effect of dialogue on self-assessed skills in dealing with conflict was measured on a seven-point scale ranging from "strongly disagree" to "strongly agree" by eight statements written for this study. Examples include "I can help people from different groups use conflict constructively" and "I am usually uncertain how to help people learn from conflicts" (reversed). There was no significant effect of intergroup dialogue at posttest.[7] We show later in this chapter the significant effect one year after the dialogue ended, dialogue students having increased more than control group students in feeling skilled in dealing constructively with conflict.

Summary

The figures in this chapter and tables B.1 through B.5 show remarkably consistent effects of IGD from pretest to posttest across the twenty-four measures of psychological processes and outcomes. Dialogue had a significant impact on twenty of these measures. Thus IGD overall was immediately effective in its aims of increasing cognitive and affective psychological processes as well as the three sets of outcomes—intergroup understanding, intergroup relationships, and intergroup collaboration and action. IGD demonstrated small to moderate effects on the three sets of outcomes. Across all intergroup understanding measures tested, effect sizes averaged 0.19 at posttest, but were notably higher for students' structural understanding for racial-ethnic inequality (0.25), structural understanding of gender inequality (0.28), and their critique of inequality (0.24). Further, effect sizes were higher on average for intergroup relationship measures (0.41) and intergroup action (0.24) at posttest, particularly the frequency of self-directed action (0.47) and intergroup collaboration (0.38) measures. The average effect sizes are within what Howard Bloom and colleagues (2008) consider policy relevant.

GENERALITY OF EFFECTS

Do the effects occur in both race-ethnicity and gender dialogues?

To examine this question, we tested for significant interactions between the dialogue effect on each psychological process outcome measure (time by condition interaction) and the dialogue topic (race-ethnicity versus gender) (time by condition by topic). These analyses are summarized in table B.6. They demonstrate that of the twenty overall significant positive effects of dialogue, only three—critique of inequality, frequency of educating the self, and frequency of educating others—showed effects that differed in race-ethnicity and gender dialogues. On these three measures, effects were significant in both types of dialogues, but the effects were larger in race-ethnicity than in gender dialogues. The results thus demonstrate a remarkably consistent picture of effects across both race-ethnicity and gender dialogues.

Do the effects differ across societal privilege?

Race and gender of the students were controlled by making sure that each dialogue-control group pairing included, as closely as possible, four students from each of the four demographic groups: white women, white men, women of color, and men of color. Of interest in our analyses, however, is whether IGD had greater effects depending on the privilege in society of these four groups. We assessed this possibility by checking for statistical interactions between the dialogue effect on each psychological and outcome measure (time by condition interaction) and the societal privilege of students within race-ethnicity and within gender dialogues (time by condition by societal privilege). In general, we again see a picture of generalized effects, in this case across the students from more and less privileged groups. Of the twenty-four measures in table B.6, interactions between the dialogue effect and more privilege or less privilege status on six measures were statistically or marginally significant. Four of these—frequency of positive interactions, identity involvement, motivation to bridge differences, and anticipated post-college political and civic involvement—showed overall significant effects for all students. The interactions, however, showed that the effects were larger for the more privileged students, specifically, white students in race-ethnicity dialogues and men in gender dialogues. Even on these four measures, however, there was a significant effect of dialogue among the students from the less privileged groups, just smaller than it was among those from the more privileged groups. On the other two measures where the marginal effect differed for the more and less privileged students (comfort in interacting across difference and skills in dealing with conflict), dialogue did not show an overall significant impact. The marginal interaction showed that on these two measures there was an effect for students from relatively more privileged groups.

The few significant interactions involving the effect of dialogue and privileged or less-privileged background should not mask the important conclusion that dialogue was broadly effective for both groups of students.

Do the effects reflect content learning only?

As we explained in chapter 4, we randomly selected students from volunteers in race-ethnicity and gender social science classes that occurred during the same academic terms in which the matched IGD courses were conducted. These students served as matched comparisons for the students in the intergroup dialogue courses. Like their counterparts in the dialogues, students in the comparison groups were drawn as equally as possible from each of the four demographic groups. There were twenty-seven social science comparison groups, fourteen for race-ethnicity and thirteen for gender. These students completed the same pre- and post-survey instruments as those completed by the students who participated in the intergroup dialogues. These groups made it possible to determine whether the dialogue courses produced significantly larger effects than the social science classes on the two sets of psychological processes and the three sets of outcomes measured in the study. If the dialogue students showed greater change than the social science comparison students over the course of the term, the results would support the importance of the dialogue pedagogy above and beyond content, which was similar in both dialogue and social science classes.

The results shown in table B.7 largely supported our expectation that students in the intergroup dialogue groups would show significantly greater change than those in the social science comparison groups. With respect to intergroup understanding, IGD students showed significantly larger increases than social science students on all but one of six measures. The exception concerned individual attributions about racial inequality, on which neither dialogue nor social science students changed over the academic term. Dialogue students also significantly increased more than social science students on both measures of positive intergroup relationships. Students in IGD also showed significantly larger gains than their counterparts in social science courses on all but two of the nine intergroup collaboration and action measures. The exceptions were sense of efficacy in taking action collaboratively with others and increased self-assessed skills in dealing with conflict.

Psychological processes were not consistently more affected by IGD than by the social science courses. Of the seven psychological measures, dialogue students increased more than social science students only on two measures—significantly more on identity involvement and marginally more on consideration of multiple perspectives. With respect to the measures of affective positivity, both IGD and social science students increased over the academic term on frequency of positive interactions and positive emotions, but not differentially. Neither dialogue nor social science students changed in how comfortable they felt in such interactions. With respect to the cognitive involvement measures, as noted, dialogue students increased in identity involvement and consideration of multiple perspectives more than social science students, but neither group changed in complex thinking and thinking about society.[8]

In summary, dialogue students increased more than social science students on two-thirds of the twenty-four measures of possible positive effects, demonstrating that to a large extent the effect of dialogue was not simply from students learning about race-ethnicity and gender content. The value of including social science comparison groups in the study is supported by these findings. The impact of the dialogue courses generally was above and beyond the content that they shared with social science courses on race-ethnicity and gender. Students in dialogue courses learned, as predicted, not only from content but also from a distinctive pedagogy and set of communication processes. Social science classes had positive effects, as they should. It is simply that on a large majority of these measures, IGD courses had larger effects.

LONGITUDINAL EFFECTS

One of the strengths of this study is the longitudinal follow-up post-posttest that the students in the intergroup dialogues and the control group completed one year after the dialogues ended. The response rate (82 percent) for this follow-up survey did not vary by race-ethnicity of the students, condition (dialogue versus control), or topic (race-ethnicity versus gender) of the experiment. The response rate for women (85 percent) was higher than that of men (79 percent). As highlighted earlier, missing data were imputed using multiple imputation (see appendix B) to minimize any bias associated with attrition from the study one year later.

To a remarkable degree, the effect of IGD relative to the control group was still evident in the longitudinal follow-up data on nearly all measures. Of the twenty measures that showed a significant impact of dialogues at time 2, there was still a significant effect of dialogue a year later on eighteen measures. There was a long-term effect on all but positive emotions in interacting across difference and confidence in intergroup collaboration (see tables B.1 through B.5). In addition, of the four measures that did not have an impact of dialogue at time 2, longitudinal analyses showed reliable effects at time 3 on comfort in communication across difference, complex thinking, and skills in dealing with conflict. The longitudinal effect on comfort in communicating across differences is noteworthy because it supports other research on intergroup relationships and intercultural interactions, showing that decreased anxiety, and thus likely increased comfort, may not take place immediately when people interact across difference (Pettigrew and Tropp 2011). It also appears that practicing the skills learned in intergroup dialogue and continuing to interact and collaborate across differences ultimately resulted in greater comfort in intergroup situations. On only one measure, consideration of multiple perspectives, was there no effect at either time 2 or time 3. These results show that dialogue students increased more than control group students from time 1 to time 3 on twenty-one of the twenty-four measures.

That the effect of dialogue still existed a year after the dialogue course ended is important. It counters the possibility that the immediate effects of intergroup dialogue might reflect the possibility that students in the dialogues exhibited demand characteristics, that is, were reporting what they thought facilitators would want them to say. That should not have happened in any case because the data collection in the study was conducted by the research team, not the facilitators. The finding of continued effect a year later is impressive because so few studies of intergroup contact have even assessed long-term effects.

NEGATIVE EFFECTS

The picture our results paint about the impact of IGD courses is overwhelmingly positive. However, a few other results suggest a somewhat more complicated picture with respect to emotional processes. We measured negative emotions—frequency of feeling worried, anxious, tense, or fearful—and negative interactions—frequency of having been put down or made to feel uncomfortable, of having had tense or somewhat hostile interactions, of having had guarded or cautious interactions, and of having felt excluded or ignored when interacting with people from different racial-ethnic or gender groups. What did the results indicate about possible negative effects of intergroup dialogue on these measures?

There was no immediate or long-term effect of intergroup dialogue in either increasing or decreasing negative emotions relative to students in the control groups (see table B.8). In contrast, there was an immediate effect on increasing negative interactions across difference. Such interactions increased significantly more in the dialogue group than in the control over the course of the term. This is not surprising because IGD is designed to move students out of their comfort zones to become aware of inequalities that affect them and their peers. Moreover, learning about privilege and power can sometimes arouse anxiety, guilt, anger, or other negative emotions. The dialogue students stressed in their final papers that before IGD they had rarely interacted across race-ethnicity in any depth and had only minimal understanding of the life experiences of their peers from different racial-ethnic groups. Of course, the students had interacted across gender, but even in that regard they indicated that they rarely, if ever, had substantive conversations about how gendered structures in their schools and communities affected women and men differently. The pedagogy and communication processes of intergroup dialogue are designed to help students address the feelings of being ignorant, uneasy, angry, and even guilty so that they can learn from each other. It is not unexpected, therefore, that there was a greater immediate increase in negative interactions among dialogue than among the control group. The immediately greater increase in negative interactions among dialogue than control group students was especially true of students of color (see table B.6).

What is most important is that the impact of IGD on negative interactions did not last. A year later, the dialogue and control groups did not differ on this measure because negative interactions had dropped among the dialogue students by a year after the dialogue ended to their level at time 1 and to the level of the control students. This suggests that the immediate negative behavioral effects that are reported in studies of intergroup contact (Richeson and Shelton 2007) are not likely to endure for very long. What we see in these results is that IGD involved an immediate negative effect that by the end of the following year was no longer evident, and that over time the effects of dialogue were exclusively positive.

CONCLUSIONS AND DISCUSSION: THE EFFECTS OF INTERGROUP DIALOGUE

The results described in this chapter repeatedly indicate support for the predicted effects of intergroup dialogue. The twenty-four measures of possible positive effects analyzed using MLM (delineated specifically in appendix B) show the following effects:

impressively consistent, small to moderate effects at posttest comparing dialogue students with control group students on twenty of the twenty-four positive outcome and psychological measures

similar immediate effects in both race-ethnicity and gender dialogues on all but two of the twenty measures showing an overall impact of dialogue, and in these two instances the effects were larger in race-ethnicity than in gender dialogues

similar immediate effects for students from groups that differed in societal privilege on all but four of the twenty measures showing an overall impact of dialogue, and in these four instances, effects were larger for groups with more privilege

larger immediate effects for students in dialogue courses than for those in traditional social science classes on two-thirds of the measures

long-term effects comparing dialogue and control students a year later on twenty-one of the twenty-four positive measures

one immediate negative effect (increasing negative interactions), which a year later was no longer a reliable difference

Table 5.1 summarizes these findings, which are detailed in the tables in appendix B. The check marks in the columns indicate a significant effect of intergroup dialogue.

Every year, hundreds of thousands of courses are offered in universities across the country. Few have ever been as rigorously evaluated as intergroup

Table 5.1   Summary of Findings

Measure	End of Course — Effect of Intergroup Dialogue	End of Course — Comparison with Social Science Courses at Posttest	One Year Later — Effect of Intergroup Dialogue
Affective positivity			
Frequency of positive interactions	✓		✓
Positive emotions	✓		
Comfort			✓
Cognitive involvement			
Complexity of thinking			✓
Thinking about society	✓		✓
Consideration of multiple perspectives		✓	
Identity involvement	✓	✓	✓
Intergroup understanding			
Structural race	✓	✓	✓
Structural gender	✓	✓	✓
Individual race	✓		✓
Individual gender	✓	✓	✓
Critique of inequality	✓	✓	✓
Attitudes toward diversity	✓	✓	✓
Intergroup relationships			
Intergroup empathy	✓	✓	✓
Motivation to bridge differences	✓	✓	✓
Intergroup action			
Frequency of self-directed action	✓	✓	✓
Frequency of other-directed action	✓	✓	✓
Frequency of intergroup collaboration	✓	✓	✓
Confidence in self-directed action	✓	✓	✓
Confidence in other-directed action	✓	✓	✓
Confidence in intergroup collaboration	✓		
Postcollege involvement	✓	✓	✓
Involvement in social justice activities	✓	✓	✓
Skills in dealing with conflict			✓
Negative interactions			
Frequency of negative interactions	✓	✓	
Negative emotions		✓	

Source: Authors' compilation.

dialogue in this study. Almost none have been subjected to experimental tests employing random assignment. Nor are there many examples of the assessment of long-term effects of classes, or comparisons of their effects with other comparable classes. Even in the vast literature on experimental effects of intergroup contact, the long-term effects have rarely been assessed. This study has done all of these things. It thus provides more conclusive data about the effectiveness of a curriculum about diversity and justice within universities than all but a few of the other hundreds of thousands of courses offered in American universities.

The results of our study are impressive because of their consistency and because of the conservative statistical methods we used to test effects. Five findings over the course of a term are conclusive. One, students who participated in IGDs developed more insight into how members of other groups perceive the world. Two, they became more empathic with the feelings and concerns of people who differ from them and more thoughtful about the structural underpinnings of inequality. Three, they had more positive relations with members of other social groups and showed greater understanding of their own social identities. Four, they increased in their motivation to reach out to other social groups and work with them. Five, they placed a greater value on diversity, took more steps to promote social justice, and became more committed to taking social justice actions in the future.

Several of the effects demonstrate that intergroup dialogue had the type of consistent impact on motivations, cognitions, and behaviors known to help reduce racial and ethnic prejudice (Pettigrew and Tropp 2011). Related literature shows that intergroup contact reduces prejudice three ways. One, it enhances knowledge about other groups, which in this study is reflected in long-term effects on complex thinking and analytical thinking about society. Two, it reduces anxiety about intergroup contact, which is reflected by long-term effects on positive interactions across difference and increased comfort in communicating across differences. Three, it increases intergroup empathy. The literature shows that the effects of intergroup contact on prejudice are enhanced when the contact occurs with the support of relevant authority figures, is cooperative, involves equal status among the participants, and allows people to get to know one another as individuals. As noted in chapter 2, intergroup dialogues have all of these qualities and thus should and did help to produce beneficial effects.

The significant effect on complex thinking a year later and the significant effect on analytical thinking about society immediately and marginally a year later also deserve special emphasis. These measures were derived from widely used measures of need for cognition and attributional complexity, which were designed to assess a general preference for complex rather than simple tasks or explanations for human behavior. Thus, being involved in IGDs led students to prefer a more complex understanding of themselves and the world around them. These effects would be important in any university course and show the power of IGDs to affect critical thinking more generally than simply in the domain of intergroup relations. Of particular relevance to this study, and noted in chapter 3, recent research indicates that high levels of attributional complexity are associated with lower levels of racism and stereo-typing (Schaller et al. 1995; Tam, Au, and Leung 2008).

The significant increase in identity involvement, another part of cognitive involvement, challenges what has been a standard view in social psychology, namely, that salient social identities will have negative implications for inter-group relations and that they should be de-emphasized in intergroup contact (for overviews of the standard view, see Gaertner and Dovidio 2000; Stephan and Stephan 2001). We described that view in chapter 2 and presented inter-group dialogue as a contrary approach that provides a rationale for keeping group identities salient during intergroup relations. We hypothesized that increased identity engagement would have positive implications for inter-group relationships, understanding, and action because thinking about one's group identity and its tie to group-based perspectives can lead to understanding that the same connection exists for members of other groups as well. The results in the SEM analysis given later in this chapter testing our theoretical framework support the hypothesized positive role for identity engagement. They demonstrate that the impact of intergroup dialogue in increasing identity engagement had positive rather than damaging implications for all three sets of outcomes in this study (for evidence of the positive role of identity engagement for additional intergroup outcomes measured in this study, see Rodriguez, Gurin, and Sorensen 2010).

The results showing that IGD increased understanding of group-based in-equalities are noteworthy because, as highlighted in chapter 3, most members of all groups, except African Americans, do not explain racial inequalities in structural terms (measured in national surveys as caused by racial discrimination). The problem with failing to appreciate the structural causes of various dimensions of inequalities in the United States, besides being inaccurate, is that it leads people to be disinclined to support policies that would reduce these types of inequality (Bobo 2011). Coming to understand structural impediments that affect some groups more than others—such factors such as poor education, less access to health and nutrition, less access to healthy foods, lower access to loans, and institutional barriers such as requiring credentials that some members of minority groups and poor people cannot obtain as easily as other groups—can lead people to advocate social changes to eliminate these problems (Bullock, Willams, and Limbert 2003; Hughes and Tuch 2000). Although questioning the legitimacy of the extensiveness of inequality is important for all groups of Americans, Patricia Gurin, Shirley Hatchett, and James Jackson (1989) found in a national study of African Americans some years ago that questioning the legitimacy of inequality was one of the most important social psychological resources that led this demographic to participate in both electoral and nonelectoral political activities. Recent studies of the motivation to participate in collective action confirm that questioning the legitimacy of inequality is one of the most important motivations for action (Louis 2009; Ellemers and Barreto 2009), especially among people in low-status groups but also among people in high-status groups to support actions and policies on behalf of low-status groups (Iyer and Ryan 2009). Research on intergroup contact also demonstrates that questioning the legitimacy of inequality is critical to creating more effective intergroup interaction because members of both advantaged and disadvantaged groups are more willing to engage in communication about group-based power differences when a critical lens is provided for considering inequality (Saguy, Dovidio, and Pratto 2008).

The effect of IGD in increasing students' motivation to bridge difference also deserves special note. Although intergroup empathy rather than motivation to bridge differences was selected in this chapter as a primary criterion of dialogue's impact on intergroup relationships, we just as easily could have selected motivation to bridge difference. We have shown in this chapter that dialogue students became more motivated to learn about other groups at the same time that they became more motivated to educate others about their own groups. The control group students did not become more motivated to bridge differences. This reciprocal process of learning about others and providing ways for others to learn about one's group captures much of what goes on in intergroup dialogue. In this sense, motivation to bridge differences, like intergroup empathy, is both a process and an outcome. Previous research has demonstrated its impact on students' confidence in taking self- and other-directed actions (Nagda, Kim, and Truelove 2004). The results in this chapter, which demonstrate that dialogue was successful in enhancing the motivation to bridge differences and that this effect was still evident a year later, affirm the importance of reciprocal learning about groups that both our practice model and theoretical framework emphasize. Our focus on bridging differences is in line with emerging research on intergroup forgiveness and reconciliation showing that reciprocal self-disclosure and empathy are important processes for improving intergroup relationships beyond simply preventing prejudice (Hewstone et al. 2006; Nadler and Schnabel 2011).

Finally, these results resoundingly indicate that IGD is more than mere talk. Students in both race-ethnicity and gender dialogues and those from both more and less privileged groups increased in their frequency of educating themselves, educating others, collaborating with others, and stressing the importance of postcollege civic engagement more than the control students, as well as more than social science students.

TESTING THE THEORETICAL FRAMEWORK: HOW DIALOGUE PRODUCES EFFECTS

Having established that IGD works—that it is effective in increasing intergroup understanding, intergroup relationships, and intergroup collaboration and action—a next question is how intergroup dialogue works. To address this question, we test the theoretical process model outlined in chapter 3 for how the pedagogical features, communication processes, and psychological processes are expected to foster the outcomes of interest. Specifically, using only the students in the dialogue courses (720), we use structural equation modeling (SEM) with latent constructs to simultaneously test two questions. First, we examine how the two primary active ingredients of intergroup dialogue, the pedagogical features and the communication processes, foster the psychological processes and through them the three sets of outcomes: intergroup understanding, intergroup relationships, and intergroup collaboration and action. The latent constructs we use for psychological processes and outcomes are the same ones highlighted in figures 5.1 through 5.5. We also use latent constructs for the pedagogy features and communication processes not discussed in this chapter. These features and processes were assessed only at posttest for students who took intergroup dialogue, because the measures required students to reflect on both the frequency and importance of these processes within their intergroup dialogue courses. Given that these items focused on what happened during the course, they could not be assessed on the pretest or for students in the wait-list control group. Specifically, we are interested in the SEM analysis in the impact of pedagogy and communication processes that took place during the dialogues, and how the increases in the psychological processes and outcomes over the course of the term predict where students ended up on the three major outcomes one year later.

Analysis of the Critical-Dialogic Theoretical Framework

The structural equation model includes six latent constructs: dialogue pedagogy, communication processes, two psychological process constructs (affective positivity, cognitive involvement) and three outcomes (structural understanding of inequality, intergroup empathy, and intergroup action.

To measure the three components of IGD pedagogy described in chapter 2, students rated at the end of the term (posttest only) the extent to which content learning and structured interaction contributed to their learning, as well as the effectiveness of their facilitators. Content learning was assessed with three items: journals-reflection papers, other written assignments, and assigned readings. Structured interaction was assessed with five items, which included ground rules for discussion, a diverse group of students, and collaborative projects with other students. The effectiveness of facilitation was assessed with eleven items, which included creating an inclusive climate, modeling good communication skills, helping clarify misunderstandings, and encouraging us to continue discussion when it became uncomfortable.

To measure the four components of communication processes described in chapter 3, students rated at the end of the term (posttest only) the frequency with which engaging self, appreciating difference, critical reflection, and alliance building took place within their dialogue course. Engaging self was assessed with five items, which included sharing views and experiences and speaking openly without feeling judged. Appreciating difference was assessed with four items, which included hearing different points of view and learning from each other. Critical reflection was assessed with four items, which included understanding how privilege and oppression affect our lives and examining the sources of my biases and assumptions. Finally, alliance building was assessed with seven items, which included sharing ways to collaborate with other groups to take action and understanding other students' passion about social issues.

Cognitive involvement includes indicators of pre-post change (residual scores) for the four cognitive involvement psychological processes described earlier in this chapter: complex thinking, analytic thinking about society, consideration of multiple perspectives, and identity involvement. Similarly, affective positivity includes indicators of pre-post change (residual scores) for the two affective positivity psychological processes described earlier: positive interactions with members of other groups and positive emotions in an intergroup setting.

Structural understanding of inequality includes two indicators, specifically structural understanding of racial-ethnic inequality and structural understanding of gender inequality. Because intergroup empathy includes only one measure, eight individual items served as indicators rather than composites of multiple subscales. Intergroup action similarly includes indicators described earlier—efficacy and frequency in taking self-oriented action, other-oriented action and collaborative action as well commitment to taking action postcollege directed toward alleviating inequalities. Indicators of each measure of pre-post change are residual scores whereas indicators for outcomes at one-year follow-up are raw means of each subscale or individual item scores (for empathy) one year after the dialogue ended. Latent constructs were each verified with reliability, factor, and confirmatory factor analyses and do not include correlated error terms between indicators within a latent construct to increase the replicability of the structural parameters (that is, minimize over fitting) while providing a more conservative test of the hypothesized model.

To test the proposed theoretical model, we tested all possible direct pathways to pre-post change in each of the three outcomes. For example, the pedagogical features can predict increases in each of the outcomes directly or indirectly (through communication processes and through the two psychological processes). Thus, indirect pathways to pre-post change in the outcomes were not forced but rather emerged after controlling for possible direct pathways.[9] However, to examine whether pre-post change in each outcome predicts where students ended up on each outcome a year later, only three direct pathways were included for each outcome at one-year follow-up: the measure of pre-post change for that outcome, the latent construct of intergroup pedagogy, and the latent construct of communication processes. Given the prominent role of pedagogy and communication processes in IGD, we were interested in testing whether pedagogy and communication processes during the dialogue courses had lasting direct effects on the outcomes one year later. Of course, we expected that both would have indirect effects through changes in outcomes at the end of the dialogue courses. In addition, we wanted to know whether these unique features of intergroup dialogue might also have direct effects on the three sets of outcomes a year later. In the results, only significant pathways are reported.

We used a maximum likelihood (ML) estimation procedure to estimate the specified model based on a variance-covariance matrix (for greater detail on the SEM procedures, see appendix B). The variance-covariance matrix was calculated from a dataset where missing data at posttest and at one-year follow-up were multiply imputed.[10] Given that participants were nested within dialogue groups, the findings presented were also tested controlling for dialogue group means. No changes in the direction or significance of parameters were found, suggesting that the individual processes that are presented cannot be attributed to dialogue group effects. Acceptable model fit was indicated by a root mean squared error (RMSEA) less than .06, χ^2/df ratio less than 3.00 and .85 or higher for the goodness of fit (GFI), Tucker Lewis (TLI), and comparative fit (CFI) indexes.

Results

The theoretical framework outlined in chapter 3 posits that the pedagogical features of intergroup dialogue foster critical-dialogic communication processes, which together indirectly promote increases in the three outcomes—structural understanding, intergroup empathy, and intergroup action—between the beginning (time 1) and end of the dialogue course (time 2). These are increases at posttest via increases in psychological processes focused on cognitive involvement and affective positivity. Using a conservative analytic approach, we find strong evidence supporting the hypothesized process model (for a diagram and indices of model fit, see figure 5.6). Direct and indirect effects are presented in tables 5.2 and 5.3.

The results also show that increases in each of the three outcomes over the course of the dialogue predicted where students ended up one year later on

Figure 5.6   Structural Equation Model Test of a Process Model for Intergroup Dialogue

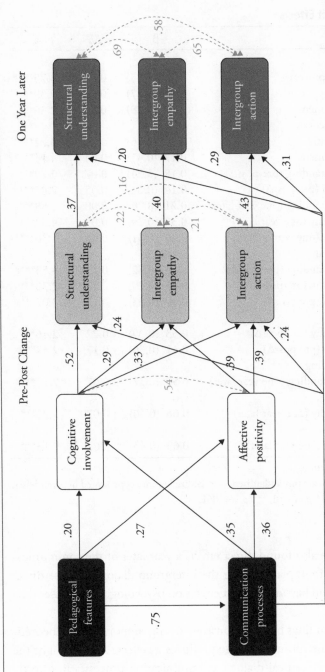

Source: Authors' compilation.

Note: RMSEA < .05, GFI = .87, TLI = .89, CFI = .90, χ²/df = 2.75. Estimates are standardized (or correlations in light gray). Only significant pathways are presented. Rounded rectangles represent latent variables, each containing multiple indicators. Dashed lines represent correlated error terms. The model estimated all possible direct pathways from latent variables presented earlier in the model (to the left) to latent variables presented later in the model (to the right), with the exception of outcomes at one-year follow-up. Because the theoretical model did not hypothesize direct relationships between the cognitive and affective mediators (cognitive involvement, affective positivity) and outcomes one year later, we tested only the direct effects of pre-post change in each outcome over the course of the dialogue on where students end up one year later, and direct effects of the IGD pedagogical features and communication processes on these longer-term outcomes.

Table 5.2   Direct Effects

	β	SE	Z
Pedagogical features			
communication processes	0.77 (0.75)	0.06	13.75****
affective positivity	0.16 (0.27)	0.07	2.38**
cognitive involvement	0.10 (0.20)	0.04	2.36**
Communication processes			
affective positivity	0.20 (0.36)	0.06	3.22****
cognitive involvement	0.17 (0.35)	0.04	4.14****
structural understanding (pre-postΔ)	0.18 (0.24)	0.07	2.70***
intergroup action (pre-postΔ)	0.14 (0.24)	0.05	2.87***
structural understanding (one year later)	0.21 (0.20)	0.08	2.58***
intergroup empathy (one year later)	0.38 (0.29)	0.09	4.32****
intergroup action (one year later)	0.26 (0.31)	0.06	4.36****
Cognitive involvement			
structural understanding (pre-postΔ)	0.78 (0.52)	0.17	4.53****
intergroup empathy (pre-postΔ)	0.45 (0.29)	0.17	2.70***
intergroup action (pre-postΔ)	0.39 (0.33)	0.13	3.07***
Affective positivity			
intergroup empathy (pre-postΔ)	0.53 (0.39)	0.22	2.46**
intergroup action (pre-postΔ)	0.41 (0.39)	0.17	2.47**
Structural understanding			
structural understanding (one year later)	0.50 (0.37)	0.07	7.15****
Intergroup empathy			
intergroup empathy (one year later)	0.66 (0.40)	0.07	9.23****
Intergroup action			
intergroup action (one year later)	0.63 (0.43)	0.07	9.13****

Source: Authors' compilation.

Note: Reported estimates are unstandardized; standardized estimates presented in parentheses.
$*p$ = .10, $**p$ = .05, $***p$ = .01, $****p$ = .001.

those outcomes. We also found direct effects a year later of the communication processes that took place during the intergroup dialogue. These direct effects were above and beyond indirect effects on psychological processes during the IGD course.

Together, these findings both demonstrate strong support for our theoretical model for how intergroup dialogue produces its effects and highlight the prominent role of the critical-dialogic communication processes in directly

Table 5.3   Indirect Effects

	β	SE	95% CI
Pedagogical features			
cognitive involvement	0.13 (0.26)	0.04	(0.07, 0.21)****
affective positivity	0.16 (0.27)	0.05	(0.06, 0.27)***
structural understanding (pre-postΔ)	0.32 (0.40)	0.07	(0.18, 0.47)***
intergroup empathy (pre-postΔ)	0.33 (0.42)	0.08	(0.21, 0.51)****
intergroup action (pre-postΔ)	0.33 (0.54)	0.05	(0.24, 0.46)***
structural understanding (one year later)	0.27 (0.26)	0.07	(0.14, 0.41)****
intergroup empathy (one year later)	0.49 (0.37)	0.09	(0.34, 0.68)****
intergroup action (one year later)	0.36 (0.40)	0.06	(0.26, 0.49)****
Communication processes			
structural understanding (pre-postΔ)	0.13 (0.17)	0.05	(0.04, 0.22)**
intergroup empathy (pre-postΔ)	0.19 (0.24)	0.07	(0.10, 0.33)****
intergroup action (pre-postΔ)	0.15 (0.25)	0.05	(0.08, 0.26)****
structural understanding (one year later)	0.16 (0.15)	0.04	(0.09, 0.25)****
intergroup empathy (one year later)	0.17 (0.13)	0.04	(0.09, 0.26)****
intergroup action (one year later)	0.18 (0.21)	0.04	(0.12, 0.27)****
Cognitive involvement			
structural understanding (one year later)	0.39 (0.19)	0.14	(0.18, 0.69)***
intergroup empathy (one year later)	0.30 (0.12)	0.19	(–0.02, 0.57)*
intergroup action (one year later)	0.25 (0.14)	0.14	(–0.01, 0.43)*
Affective positivity			
intergroup empathy (one year later)	0.35 (0.16)	0.27	(0.13, 0.96)***
intergroup action (one year later)	0.26 (0.17)	0.19	(0.09, 0.70)***

Source: Authors' compilation.

Note: Reported estimates are unstandardized; standardized estimates presented in parentheses.
*$p <$/$= .10$, **$p <$/$= .05$, ***$p <$/$= .01$, ****$p <$/$= .001$

and indirectly affecting the change over the course of the term and where students ended up a year later.

We turn now to the qualitative material—interviews, final papers, and videotapes—collected in the qualitative part of the study to examine empathy, engagement, and both student and facilitator behaviors.

Authored by Nicholas Sorensen, Patricia Gurin, Biren (Ratnesh) A. Nagda, Walter G. Stephan, Richard Gonzalez, Gretchen Lopez, and Jaclyn Rodriguez.

CHAPTER 6

Empathy in Intergroup Dialogues

In this chapter, we focus on empathy because it is such a vital component of intergroup relations. Empathy is viewed by many as the foundation of social life (see the discussion of empathy in chapter 3), and has always been an important goal of intergroup dialogue (IGD). As discussed in chapters 3 and 5, many studies have shown that empathy is linked to desirable outcomes such as decreased prejudice, fear, and anger toward out-groups, as well as increased intergroup contact and positive emotions toward out-groups (Pettigrew and Troop 2008, 2011; Stephan and Finlay 1999). In chapter 5, our survey data demonstrated that intergroup dialogues increased empathy. As predicted in the theoretical framework, these data also showed that empathy was fostered by both the communication processes and psychological processes, which were fostered by the pedagogical features of the dialogues. In this chapter, we take a mixed-methods approach to examining empathy in the interviews and the students' final papers to understand in a more nuanced way how students experienced and expressed empathy in IGD. Interview material is used in all examples of empathy presented in this chapter; material from the final papers is sometimes used to supplement how a particular student experienced empathy.

Empathy occurs in dialogues when individuals respond to the experiences of members of other social groups by trying to understand their perspectives (cognitive empathy) or by feeling what they feel or responding emotionally to their experiences (emotional intergroup empathy). In our quantitative analyses in chapter 5, we used a survey measure that focused on emotional empathy. In this chapter, we also include cognitive empathy. Most of the examples in this chapter represent empathy being expressed across race-ethnicity in the race-ethnicity dialogues or across gender in the gender dialogues. A few examples reflect empathy for dialogue members within a student's racial-ethnic or gender identity group (that is, intragroup empathy). However, because these few instances of intragroup empathy arose in an intergroup context, we include them in the analysis.

In this chapter, we first describe the mixed-methods approach used in analyzing the qualitative materials. This approach began with qualitative analysts, later included quantitative analysts, and then involved both of them in developing the framework presented in this chapter. Both teams included researchers and practitioners.

QUALITATIVE APPROACH IN A MIXED METHODS STUDY

In this chapter, we use data from the interviews as the primary source to explore empathy. We also use the final papers to supplement what we learned from the interviews. Both data sources are retrospective. They capture how the students made sense of their experiences in the dialogues in somewhat different ways. The interviews were designed to elicit spontaneous responses on pedagogical elements and communicative exchanges in the dialogues. The papers provide more reflective responses that capture how the students evaluated their curricular readings, the dialogue experience over the arc of the course, and their own learning. In all the examples, we use pseudonyms.

We describe in detail two phases of coding and analyzing these data, first by the qualitative research team and then by both the qualitative and quantitative teams working together. We do this because it is rare for mixed methods to be used to the extent involved in this analysis of empathy.

Phase I. Coding and Initial Analysis of Empathy in the Interviews and Papers

To reduce the number of transcripts, the qualitative team selected a subset of dialogues on the basis of impact scores. Impact was determined by a score given by the interview coders at the end of each interview. These scores ranged on a seven-point scale from negative impact, representing the coder's evaluation of the student having less insight and understanding than before taking the course, to very high positive impact based on the student using terms such as "a transformational experience" or having had impressive new insights about themselves and others. The individual scores were averaged to give each dialogue a group score. To have a range of dialogues represented in the subset, the two highest scoring groups from the race and the gender dialogues were selected, along with the lowest scoring group and one moderate impact group from each type of dialogue.

This chapter presents excerpts from the interviews used in our analyses of those four race and four gender dialogues. The findings from this smaller set of dialogues were checked using all twenty dialogues in the intensive study. Using a grounded theory approach to search for emergent themes, the analysts found two types of empathy. The first focused on how students expressed empathy for a specific individual or group within the dialogue. Because this type invariably included some reference to interpersonal or intergroup relationships, we labeled it relational empathy. The second type included this relational element but also displayed a recognition of the structural positions of that individual or group in relation to power, privilege, and inequality in the wider society. We labeled this critical empathy. In an earlier paper, Biren (Ratnesh) Nagda (2006) identified two closely related forms of empathy as dialogic empathy and critical empathy. Our use of the term relational empathy rather than dialogic empathy highlights the importance of relationships as a source of empathy.

Phase II. Mixing of Analytic Methods

The qualitative analysts shared their initial findings with the quantitative researchers on the research team. Both teams then worked together to refine the distinction between relational and critical empathy that had emerged in the qualitative team's analyses. The two groups of analysts agreed that the emergent themes of relational empathy and critical empathy fit with the overall critical-dialogic framework described in chapters 2 and 3.

EXAMINING RELATIONAL AND CRITICAL EMPATHY

Relational empathy in this chapter is either a cognitive or an emotional response by a participant in the dialogue group to a member of a social identity group. When the response is emotional, the empathizer may be feeling the same emotions (such as happiness, pride, anger) that the other person feels, or may be responding with personal emotions (such as compassion) to that person's situation (compare Stephan and Finlay 1999). When the response is cognitive, the empathizer is taking the perspective of another participant. That is, he or she is trying to see the world from another's point of view. The important point is that relational empathy is directed toward a specific group member or group without seeming to recognize how that person or group is located in and affected by a particular structural position in society. Critical empathy includes an acknowledgement of the other person's or group's position in a system of power and privilege, and thus that the individual or group is representative of a structural phenomenon rather than an idiosyncratic one (DeStigter 1999; Nagda 2006). In some instances, critical empathy also included an acknowledgement by the empathizer that he or she has a place in that system of power and privilege. Nearly all of the incidents of empathy—both the relational and critical ones—were drawn from the interviews or the final papers when students described a story shared by another student in the dialogue. Storytelling proved to be a crucial source of empathy in both the race-ethnicity and gender dialogues.

These two types of empathy, which are used throughout this chapter, emerged from the initial analysis conducted by the qualitative analysts. They were not a priori concepts laid upon the qualitative data. As will be evident, the distinction between relational and critical empathy is sometimes patently clear and sometimes more ambiguous—a somewhat fuzzy boundary. If the coders thought that a particular example was ambiguous with respect to this distinction, it was coded as relational empathy. For instance, if a student used words such as racism or sexism or stereotypes but did not show an understanding of the structural factors implied by these terms, the example was coded only as relational empathy.

Next, we present the analysis and the excerpts from the interviews and final papers that demonstrate relational and critical empathy in the race-ethnicity dialogues, followed by analysis and excerpts of these types of empathy from gender dialogues. First relational empathy, then critical empathy examples are detailed.

RELATIONAL AND CRITICAL EMPATHY IN RACE-ETHNICITY DIALOGUES

As we have noted, most of the incidents of empathy coded in the interviews and final papers appeared when students described a story told by another student in the dialogue class. Across the four race dialogues used in the qualitative analysis for this chapter, sixteen stories were recalled and reacted to by more than one student. We labeled these signature stories. These seem to have resonated in the dialogue and proved especially valuable in analyzing empathy. Another thirty-five stories were unique, that is, reported by only one student.

Relational Empathy

When talking about experiences coded as relational empathy, students in the race-ethnicity dialogues tended to focus on a particular individual's or group's story. One account from Lily, a woman of Asian background, is representative of the students who displayed relational empathy. She talked about trying to understand the experience of Susan, a white woman, who felt out of place at a concert where the audience was predominantly African American.

> [Susan] mentioned how over the weekend she had gone to a hip hop concert. The whole time she was there she had an awesome time. She's very much into hip hop and she loves that culture. But she was one of very few white students at the concert, and she said that it made her feel like she didn't belong there. It made her feel like, "Ok, what is the white girl doing here." . . . And she also started crying in the dialogue because that was something I think that she struggled with a lot because she wanted to go to these events, she wanted to do these things but she always felt it's not somewhere that she should be going. . . . It was very moving to hear Susan and I really wanted to understand what she thought and felt. (Woman of color, race-ethnicity dialogue)

Lily tried to see things from Susan's perspective; she specifically attended to the tension between Susan's interests and her feeling that she might not belong at the concert. Lily noted that she could not completely understand Susan's experience, saying, "I'm Asian and there are times when I go to events that are predominantly African American, and I'm the only Asian there or nonblack person there but I don't ever feel like I'm targeted or feel like I shouldn't belong there." Despite this difference, she found Susan's story very moving, indicating she was experiencing empathy. This example was judged to be relational empathy because Lily did not connect Susan's story to broader social phenomena such as normative pressures and expectations associated with cultural spaces.

An analysis of Lily's final paper revealed another account of relational empathy in which she described an unexpected disagreement with an African American male student, Curtis. Lily viewed him as open-minded and committed to social justice. He had previously shared that he was a "black man who wants to see empowerment of the black race." In this episode, Curtis explained his opposition to interracial dating. Lily reported being surprised because she thought his position was inconsistent with his expressed commitment to equality and social justice. Lily, who supported interracial dating, said she wanted to understand Curtis' experience of feeling "betrayed by his 'people' when black men or women date outside of their race." She explained that Curtis raised her level of awareness about the complexity of identity and interracial dating, especially "how people who shared her commitment to social justice could still disagree with her about interracial dating." She further stated that she needed to learn to listen better to understand perspectives different from her own, and that she learned that "being open-minded also does not always mean that everyone will agree about something." This was an important step for Lily, although she arrived at this conclusion without analyzing why she and Curtis, two students of color whose positions differ in a racial-ethnic stratification system and whose racial-ethnic groups have greatly different rates of interracial marriage, might have differing perspectives on interracial dating. Nor did she use her awareness of this disagreement with Curtis to critically analyze her position. She seemed primarily focused on understanding Curtis as an individual whose perspective differed from hers. That is the essence of relational empathy.

In both instances involving the stories of Susan and Curtis, Lily displayed relational empathy because she did not seem to connect Susan's and Curtis's stories to broader structural issues that hip hop and interracial dating often involve.

Nicole, a white woman, related several accounts involving relational empathy in her interviews and in her final paper. We focus on two, both demonstrating an emotional basis of relational empathy. In the interview, Nicole described a story that an African American male, Terrence, shared about a childhood experience. Terrence's story shocked her, and she said that it "definitely had an impact on me."

One of the students in the class, he's a black male, and part of his story is that when he was little and playing out in the yard with his cousin, one of their neighbors who was white went out and started playing with them. Then the white child's mother came out and told him that he couldn't play with my classmate and his cousin. She didn't explicitly say, "You can't play with them because they are black," but my classmate said he could definitely see that was what was going on. The white child played with kids in the neighborhood who were white. That story definitely had an impact on me. In my upbringing, I just can't ever see my parents doing that, and it shocked me that someone would actually stop their kid from playing because of race. I felt for him, going through that when he was little. (White woman, race-ethnicity dialogue)

Nicole understood that race was involved in Terrance's story and to this extent recognized that racial stratification lay behind the white mother's admonishment to her son. It did not qualify as critical empathy, however, because Nicole did not amplify her understanding of race but instead seemed primarily affected by this one student's story.

In her final paper, Nicole described an incident involving her ICP group in which she felt empathy for Ryan, another African American classmate:

My ICP group was made up of four very different people. I did not notice that race was an issue within our group . . . but I was shocked when one of my group members, a man of color, a black male, said that he worked extra hard so that the other group members would not think he was "the lazy black kid." He came early to every meeting and seemed to go above and beyond with all of the work that he did. I felt bad that a man of color sensed he had to prove himself to the rest of the group. . . . He felt that he had something to prove because other members of his group would have stereotypes of black students.

Nicole's use of the word *stereotypes* in referring to Ryan's story indicates some understanding of the structural foundations for his story. However, it was primarily relational empathy because Nicole did not amplify how Ryan's story reflected a common problem stemming from structurally created and reinforced stereotypes.

Critical Empathy

In the critical empathy accounts, students displayed empathy toward a particular individual or group, just as they did in the examples of relational empathy, but they also showed a clear recognition that privilege affects groups of people differently. Sometimes the students also could see that they, too, were part of a system of power and privilege, and thus that their connection with the storyteller was structural as well as personal.

Alex, a white man, provided an example of critical empathy. In his interview, Alex described how a particular story told by Bryan, a black man, caused him to feel angry about the injustice Bryan had experienced at the hands of police. Bryan's experience affected Alex because it was not something Alex had experienced. This is another example of intergroup empathy through dissimilarity, where the participant initially experienced the shock of learning about a drastically dissimilar experience of someone from another group.

> We were kind of continuing along talking about experiences of racism that we had seen and [Bryan] was talking about how he had been walking with some of his friends through a neighborhood and a police car eventually pulled up behind them. The police officer came out and searched him and was just being extremely rude and didn't really have any reasons other than the fact that they were black. The officer was grabbing him inappropriately and just not doing his job right. So that was not something I've experienced before, a first-hand account of blatant racism. I was angry just thinking about the reality of police harassment. . . . It comes up in the news every once in a while but it's never a big deal. I feel like people can just change the channel and move on. So I was upset that it happens and that there's not really much knowledge about that. A lot of people still think that racism ended with the civil rights movement or that it's just not a big deal. And I felt empathy for him that he had to go through that. I just felt like I understood him better because he had really experienced this and was still trying to change things. He didn't give up after that, he wasn't just like, "Oh, this is how the world is." He had the strength to keep going and that was just one of his stories. He had a lot of other stories. Yeah, it was powerful that he had that strength and made me want to keep going and fight more. There was a little bit of guilt in there that I've experienced since I first started learning about racism. (White man, race-ethnicity dialogue)

This example represents critical empathy because Alex alluded to systematic police harassment as a form of racism. Alex also mentioned feeling "a little bit of guilt" and being upset by the racism experienced by Bryan which are indicators of relational empathy.

Critical intergroup empathy is also seen as Lucinda, a Latina, shared how she tried to make sense of the emotional empathy she experienced when she listened to the difficulties white students revealed in acknowledging their white privilege. She did not reference a particular story or a particular person, but referred to a social identity group as the target of her empathic feelings. Her critical empathy has a very ambivalent quality.

> I didn't grasp [the concept of white privilege] and then hearing [the white people in the dialogue] talk it was like hearing somebody own up to a murder or something bad, and it's very uncomfortable . . . and then you automatically want to . . . blame them. . . . I saw they had a lot of shame. . . . I felt uncomfortable because I was like, "Why should they feel shame when it's not their fault?" But then at the same time, I realized that it was their fault. They don't necessarily cause their own privilege but they are happy to take advantage of it. And usually they don't even see that they have privileges that come simply from being white in this society. (Woman of color, race-ethnicity dialogue)

Lucinda shared her emotional ambivalence in reaction to the white students' display of shame. She felt discomfort, which led her to consider excusing the white students in her dialogue from blame. Then she argued that whites do have some responsibility—that "it was their fault . . . because they are happy to take advantage of it [privilege]."

Although her interview portrays Lucinda wrestling with the concept of privilege and how empathic she was with the struggles of white people, her paper exhibits an even more emphatic tone that supports the classification of her intergroup empathy as critical in nature. She explored how whites and people of color consider the issue of subordinate and privileged societal positions differently.

> Students of color could identify as subordinates on account of their experiences, which dealt with different forms of oppression, ranging from racial profiling by police officers to in-class discrimination by teachers and students. White students do not share in those experiences and therefore cannot accept the fact that they happen and represent white privilege. (Woman of color, race-ethnicity dialogue)

Lucinda's critical empathy included relational elements, as critical empathy always does. She felt uncomfortable for whites who have to deal with the complexities that white privilege evokes for them. Lucinda's critical empathy involved seeing these complexities in structural ways, including that the different perspectives on privilege expressed by white students and students of color derived from their systematically different life experiences. She understood their perspectives within the framework of structural inequality.

In the next example, Dustin, a white male, showed critical empathy toward a specific white student. He described being afforded the opportunity to express compassionate feelings for Elaine, a white woman who shifted from denial and intellectualization about racism to tears as she began to recognize how she was implicated in structures of inequality.

A young woman in the group I was constantly frustrated with was [Elaine]; it was her lack of understanding of how other people are treated and what's happening with this entire institutionalized internalized system just constantly caught me off guard. . . . I was really trying to identify with her and be compassionate. . . . One instance was when she talked about working at a restaurant as a server, saying, "When I serve the patrons of color I have to be really nice and make sure that they are all set up. I take extra care of them because I am worried that I'm going to offend them." Everyone is like, "Yeah, I understand." She said, "It's like I have to lower myself down to their level in order to make sure they are okay." And just then the room went silent and she kept going. And she's like "whoa, what?" The facilitator, asked, "Do you know what you said?" "No," she didn't. The facilitator said, "down to their level." Suddenly [Elaine's] stance toward race as something that is intellectualized just came crashing down . . . and tears were spilled. . . . It was [not] anything anyone can ever forget—to have that realization that it's not just a system but it's working through us and here it is. . . . If that's the person she truly is, someone who cares enough to really cry over it and feel as though this is something that needs to change, then that's someone I can work with. (White man, race-ethnicity dialogue)

Initially Dustin tried to empathize with Elaine and had difficulty in doing so. But he went on to display critical empathy when he focused on how the institutionalized system of racism operates through individuals and, with increased empathy for Elaine, felt that he could work with her.

John, a Latino, also demonstrated critical empathy toward a white student, Steven, who stood up against racism. John felt a connection to Steven and was affected by his story. John seems to have viewed Steven as someone who understood that racism and color blindness are features of the racial social structure.

> I remember [Steven] mentioned how he worked in a sporting goods place, along with an older white worker and a Mexican worker who cleaned and did the labor work. One day another white male came in and said, "Shouldn't these Mexicans go back where they came from?" The older male worker agreed and nodded to Steven, waiting for him to agree, too. Steven told him, "No, I don't believe that, that's wrong." [When I heard Steven's story,] I was angry, just distraught, kind of disappointed—really not surprised because even though racism has gradually decreased, it still occurs no matter what you think. You may think it's over, you can try to be color blind, but it's there. And I was glad Steven spoke up because not everybody would have. Some people would be color blind in the situation and oblivious to what's happening. I felt for how Steven dealt with the situation. (Man of color, race-ethnicity dialogue)

The relational aspect of empathy was present in John's connection and positive feelings for Steven because he spoke up against the older white man, but also in his anger and distress with the continued existence of racism. The critical aspect of empathy was evident in John's understanding that the racism in Steven's story involved color blindness that can keep people from understanding how racism works in society.

In his paper, John showed another example of critical empathy, in this instance toward an African American narrator in an assigned reading. Throughout the final papers, students consistently referenced specific readings and authors as sources of perspectives and experiences that helped them empathize relationally and critically (for a discussion of the concept of narrative fiction in textual engagement and reader empathy, and thus how readings can provide new perspectives in dialogue, see Nussbaum 1996). John described that the narrator in the reading was walking by a white woman who glanced back a couple of times before she began to run, apparently because she thought the narrator was a mugger, a rapist, or something worse. The narrator in the reading described how this incident made him feel because he, as an African American man, could never imagine hurting anyone. John's relational empathy with the narrator is based on a shared experience of feeling judged based on a stereotype. He explained, "As in this story, I have felt this way, that I was being judged with no real evidence of my character, morals, and personality." Then he moved to a more critical kind of empathy by suggesting that racial stereotypes made it impossible for the African American male narrator to be judged for who he really is: "I understand that the world can be an ignorant place at times and that racism still exists. . . . Racism plays a big part in racial relationships." In these examples, John displayed critical empathy toward a white student and a black narrator in two accounts that situate them and him within a social structure characterized by color blindness and racism.

In summary, empathy was expressed in both relational and critical ways in these accounts from the four race-ethnicity dialogues used in the intensive analysis. Relational and critical empathy most often occurred in response to stories students from the other identity group told in the dialogue. The students often noted the dissimilarity between their experiences and those of the storyteller. In some cases, the students responded with empathy to stories told by members of their identity group and in these cases noted both similarities and dissimilarities.

RELATIONAL AND CRITICAL EMPATHY IN GENDER DIALOGUES

We turn now to the analysis of empathy in the gender dialogues. The examples reported here come from students in the four gender dialogues used in our intensive analysis. Across the dialogues, fourteen stories were signature (mentioned by more than one student) and thirty-one were unique (related by only one student).

Relational Empathy

Most of the accounts in the gender dialogues involved relational empathy in response to another individual's or group's story. Although some of them included terms such as sexual abuse, gender norms, rape, stereotypes, or body image that allude to issues with structural underpinnings, most of these stories were told with only minimal recognition of the generality of the gender-based problems such terms connote.

Brittany, a white woman, provided an example of relational empathy.

It was actually the male facilitator and he just talked about how when he was in high school, he was that stereotypical jock who just would whatever, play girls and all his friends they would just be the stereotypical male chauvinist pigs. I forget what turned him, but that now he looks back on that, he is just totally ashamed and has made a complete turnaround. And it was just really inspiring because I feel like so many guys have the opportunity to do that but won't take it. They'll just be stuck in this mindset and so it was really good to hear that he actually stepped outside that box. (White woman, gender dialogue)

Brittany displayed relational empathy when she said she found his story of shame regarding his high school years of being a stereotypical jock "really inspiring" and was happy that he had made "that turn-around." Although Brittany referred to gender stereotypes, she seemed to treat stereotypes as a personal quality that individual men can accept or reject, rather than as cultural conceptions that are embedded in socially structured relationships between men and women. An analysis of Brittany's final paper data found similar relational empathy.

Josie, an African American woman, exhibited relational empathy that was both cognitive and emotional in response to a story that Al, an African American man, told about his sister's rape. Cognitively she relied heavily on perspective taking and active listening to connect with Al. Josie also reacted to Al's story emotionally, although she did not label any specific emotions that she felt in connecting with Al's experience:

Al just started off with, "You know I'm a football player. Everyone sees me this way and attaches the male stereotype—being macho, being kind of a dick to people about things, and kind of degrading women." And he's like, "I hate it because my sister was raped and I was personally always told to take care of her, to protect her. I went away to college. The first year, I get a phone call from her saying she was raped and I was so angry. I didn't know what to do." And he was talking about how he wanted to just find the guy and kill him. Then he said sometimes it's really awful because he's so close with his sister that when he's on this football team, which is a totally different group of people, how conflicted he is; and sometimes he's like, "I don't even have fun." He's like, "I have to listen to these guys and some of these guys are the typical guys that I would never want my sister to be near." And he's like, "But I engage in this lifestyle because I like football. But sometimes it's just not fun." I remember he almost started crying after he talked about his sister being raped. I mean that was real impacting to me to listen to a story like that. . . . Emotionally I felt very . . . I don't know, I guess empathetic. I really felt like, "Wow, I'd want a brother like Al, you know that felt really protective of me." I really felt for him and I put myself in his shoes. I was like, "Wow, I can't even imagine what it'd be like to be a male and feel this way on a football team, and have a sister that this happened to and feel that angry—to want to kill someone. I guess it was empathy. I was just trying to feel what he felt. (Woman of color, gender dialogue)

Josie actively listened as she tried to put herself in Al's shoes, yet she recognized that she couldn't "even imagine what's it be like to be a male" who had this happen. She intentionally tried to understand Al. Her use of *I* as she recounted the story further indicated her attempt to imagine herself in Al's experience—to see this incident from his unique vantage point. Although she gained insight into his feelings and linked them to masculine stereotypes, she did little to critically evaluate these gendered stereotypes or comment on violence as a broader phenomenon in gendered relationships.

In alignment with her interview, in her final paper Josie expressed relational empathy collectively for the men in her dialogue. "With the form of the class, talking without raising hands, I can understand the frustration the men had with women constantly interrupting each other and never getting that 'break' of silence for the men to share." Josie felt connected to the men in her dialogue and cognitively understood their frustration, yet in this particular example she did not contextualize the gender dynamics in the dialogue group within a larger framework of power and privilege. Her relational empathy reflected how students may use perspective taking to understand the feelings and experiences of members of the other group in the dialogue and not move further to make a critical connection beyond specific individuals.

Vincent, an African American man, expressed relational empathy toward Claire, a white woman who told of being negatively affected by comments about her body made by her male friends. Claire's story had an emotional impact on Vincent. It was so dissimilar from his experience that he said it "really opened my eyes."

[Claire] said that she hung around with lots of guys instead of females for whatever particular reason that may be, and she said that they always used to joke around with her and make fat jokes towards her and then she developed an eating disorder. It really opened my eyes to how much what you say affects somebody. And I just really sympathized for her because I know these kids probably were just kidding and didn't want to do that because obviously they were her friends. Things like that happen every day and it just made me realize that you need to watch what you say to people even if it is in a joking fashion. So that was probably the story that hit me the most. (Man of color, gender dialogue)

Vincent's active listening and interest in Claire's feelings prompted his realization about the power of words. Although moved by and connected to her story, he did not place this incident of put-downs into the context of power. Putting others down, sometimes subtly or through jokes, is one of the ways that dominant groups maintain their privilege without awareness that their behaviors have that intent or consequence (Apfelbaum 1979; see also the discussion of micro-aggressions in chapter 9). An analysis of Vincent's final paper data found similar relational empathy.

Robert, a white man, empathized with Rosalie, a white woman, when she recounted being physically abused by her brother when she was much younger.

I was like wow, wow. I was really surprised that she was so willing and about to talk about it. It hurt. I felt for her and what she has gone through. . . . At first it made me uncomfortable because I am not used to stories like that, which makes me think I have a whole bunch of shallow relationships with my friends. I do have strong conversations with the people I am closest to but those conversations never get easier for me. I was empathizing with her. Just the fact that abuse of women exists. Like I knew it existed but I just had never met anybody who experienced it firsthand. Like I was amazed that it's really true, not just on *Law and Order* and all that stuff. I'm disgusted that it happens. (White man, gender dialogue)

Robert conveyed a high level of discomfort in hearing a personal abuse story and at the same time he was able to feel for Rosalie. It appears that Robert understood that Rosalie is not alone in experiencing physical abuse, but he did not indicate how it happens or how physical violence, including rape, reflect the differential power of women and men. An analysis of Robert's final paper data found similar relational empathy.

These examples, which were classified as primarily relational, display some references to structural issues, but did not explore these issues in any detail. They do indicate that dialogues were successful in helping students connect across groups, even if these examples primarily focused on individual group members.

Critical Empathy

Some students in the gender dialogues also exhibited critical empathy, though it was less common than in the race dialogues. Deanna, a white woman, displayed critical empathy toward Trina, a woman of color, who was wrestling with issues of privilege. Deanna's empathic connection with Trina helped her grasp that the societal issue of privilege was broader than Trina's specific experience. Deanna began to consider whether her own problems were at least somewhat socially structured and not totally unique to her.

> Trina identified as bisexual and Asian. She just seemed really, really, really thoughtful. . . . She had an impact on me. . . . I mean, just like what I said: her background. I think her dad had a really big impact on her as a very stereotypical male figure. In a lot of ways she has a targeted identity because she's a girl, Asian, and sort of bisexual. But I know that she also, like I am, is from the middle to upper middle class. She has money so I think her economic privileges produce a controversy within her. You know, she feels oppressed in some ways but privileged in others. I just felt like I could relate to her. . . . She could see how her situation involved gender oppression and class privilege. It was like, "Oh maybe I actually am experiencing that too," because I never thought about my own problems in that way. I figured my problems were just my problems. . . . I never really thought about it in the way that she presented it. And that made me feel sort of sad, actually. Confused. And then also very curious to see if I could, how I could sort of figure that out within myself. (White woman, gender dialogue)

Deanna understood that Trina has the multiple identities of female, Asian, bisexual, and upper middle class, and that Trina's experience of being a bisexual woman of Asian background was intertwined with what it meant to Trina to have class privilege. Recognizing multiple identities, an aspect of critical analysis, helped Deanna question her relationship to class privilege, something she had previously not associated with her identity. In both ways, Deanna was grasping how intersecting identities are embedded in social structure and thinking about her relationship to privilege.

Another example of critical empathy was evident in the response of Derek, a heterosexual man of color, on hearing about the exclusionary experiences of Jeffrey, a gay man of color. Jeffrey spoke about how harshly gays were treated in Montana where he had grown up.

> He came out when he was thirteen or fourteen years old. And he came out big because he was writing stories for the local newspaper, and it was a story of direct blatant discrimination against him. It really, really impacted me because I can't believe these things are still happening in the United States where we claim we're for equal rights. We have the Constitution; we have the Bill of Rights; yet, we just claim so many things but then we don't accept certain groups. . . . I just couldn't even grasp that I would have to, if I were gay, think about where I'm going . . . how people are going to look at me, how they're going to treat me. And I think that really impacted me on a whole different level. I felt a lot of anger, there was a lot of sadness. I mean you couldn't help but feel sorry because this stuff is really happening and I was really angry just because I can't believe it is happening. I was more in shock I guess. And it was like anger/shock just because something like that, in my personal opinion, shouldn't be happening in our society. (Man of color, gender dialogue)

An emotional connection with Jeffrey, involving anger, sadness, and shock, led Derek to a broader understanding of oppression against gays. Derek's empathy was both emotional and cognitive. He tried to understand Jeffrey's situation and felt sadness for him, but also generalized beyond Jeffrey, feeling anger towards an exclusionary social system. Derek expressed shock, stating as a heterosexual he could not "even imagine" what Jeffrey had experienced as a gay man. Derek seemed connected to Jeffrey not through their common identities and experiences as men of color but through society's different treatment of them as heterosexual and gay men. Intersecting identities played a role in Derek's understanding that gender identity becomes more complicated when a gay sexual orientation is an intrinsic aspect of it.

In his final paper, Derek drew similar connections between oppression based on gender and sexual orientation and expressed critical empathy for gays, lesbians, bisexuals, and women in general.

I believe that the most striking fact that was presented to me in the web of oppression was the fact that today in thirty-three states it's legal for your company to fire you for being gay, lesbian, or bisexual. And in forty-two states, you can be fired for being transgender. This is very surprising and disturbing because to me this is very unfair and seems to be outdated and should not be part of the laws of our society. . . . The fact that I've been in this class has allowed me to think and see the woman side of gender. In the *Web of Oppression*, I realized that there are more genders that exist and I must also challenge myself in thinking about all genders. Also I have become aware that my male privilege is very present through many of our institutions such as the media, economy, and athletics. I have a whole new feeling toward the complicated oppressions that some other men and many women have to deal with. (Man of color, gender dialogue)

Although Derek highlighted the role of law in creating and sustaining inequality, he expanded his thinking to include other social institutions such as the media, and he saw that his male privilege was afforded by the gender structure of these institutions. He also articulated the need to think beyond the gender binary to be truly inclusive and socially just.

In summary, in the gender dialogues students seemed to express relational empathy with a specific individual or group more often than critically recognizing that the recipient of empathy was prototypic of broader social phenomena.

LEARNING ABOUT RELATIONAL AND CRITICAL EMPATHY FROM MIXED METHODS

In phase 2 of our mixed-method analysis of empathy, we found a thematic difference between race and gender dialogues: relational empathy was more evident in gender than in race-ethnicity dialogues, and critical empathy in race-ethnicity than in gender dialogues. This finding seems to contradict the conclusion in chapter 5 that intergroup dialogue had similar effects on empathy in both race-ethnicity and gender dialogues, and that the processes by which empathy was increased were similar in both types of dialogues as well. The distinction revealed in the mixed method analysis of empathy in the interviews was not evident in the survey analysis of empathy.

In the third phase of our analyses, we sought to answer two questions about the relative emphasis on these two types of empathy in race-ethnicity and gender dialogues: Does the relatively greater display of critical empathy in race-ethnicity dialogues, and the relatively greater display of relational empathy in gender dialogues in the examples in this chapter extend to all the participants in the four race and gender dialogues used in analyzing empathy? Does this difference in empathy apply beyond these eight dialogues to all twenty dialogues in the intensive qualitative study?

The answer to the first question derives from a qualitative analysis in which the coders read all the transcripts from the four race and four gender dialogues. The reading and analysis of those transcripts were what initially revealed that the theme of power and privilege was more evident in the data from race-ethnicity dialogues, whereas the relational theme was more evident in the data from the gender dialogues. The coding of all transcripts from the eight dialogues we used in phase 3 of the analyses supports the conclusion we drew from the examples presented earlier in this chapter. In fact, the analysis of the coded transcripts from all eight dialogues demonstrated an even more pronounced difference between race-ethnicity and gender dialogues. In the four gender dialogues, the ratio of relational empathy to critical empathy was nine to one, but in the four race dialogues it was even.

The answer to the second question required systematic coding of the remaining twelve dialogues that the qualitative team did not use. The twelve were coded using the distinction between relational and critical empathy. Again, relational empathy was coded when one of those passages referred only to empathy with a specific person (or group) in the dialogue, and critical empathy was coded when the reference also recognized the other person's position in a system of power and privilege.

The frequencies that NVivo provided of relational and critical empathy from the entire set of twenty dialogues (the eight that the team analyzed to answer question 1 and the additional twelve) were exported into SPSS. Analysis of variance was conducted to determine whether relational and critical empathy differed in race-ethnicity and gender dialogues, and whether the four types of students (white men, white women, women of color, and men of color) differed in the frequency with which they expressed relational and critical empathy within race-ethnicity and gender dialogues or across the two types of dialogues.

These analyses showed that the four types of students did not differ in the expression of relational and critical empathy (F for relational empathy = 1.33, for critical empathy = .51). This lack of difference was found across the two

Figure 6.1   Counts of Empathy in Race-Ethnicity and Gender Dialogues

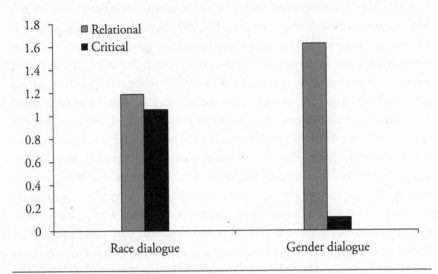

Source: Authors' calculations.

types of dialogues and within each of them. The analyses did display a significant difference between race-ethnicity and gender dialogues with respect to
relational empathy ($F = 7.34$, $p < .01$) and a highly significant difference with
respect to critical empathy ($F = 58.06$, $p < .000$).

Figure 6.1 shows the average number of times that individuals in race-
ethnicity dialogues and gender dialogues displayed relational and critical empathy in their interviews. The difference is striking. The average scores for
individuals in the two types of dialogues range from 0 to close to 2. The average for both relational and critical empathy was slightly over 1 in the race-
ethnicity dialogues, whereas the average was 1.7 for relational empathy but
close to 0 for critical empathy in the gender dialogues. Thus the students in
the race-ethnicity dialogues expressed the two types of empathy fairly equally,
but relational empathy predominated in the gender dialogues. Relational empathy was found in gender dialogues more frequently than in race-ethnicity
dialogues, and critical empathy was found in race-ethnicity dialogues more
frequently than in gender dialogues.

What might explain the different emphases on relational and critical empathy in race-ethnicity and gender dialogues? One explanation lies in the

nature of the content of the stories told in the dialogues. The gender stories were often about specific interpersonal relationships: a male wanting to protect his sister from rape but failing to do it, a woman struggling with her body image and being teased by male friends, physical abuse, a male facilitator who overcame sexist attitudes and behaviors, gendered communication styles within the dialogue, and appropriate sexual behavior for men and women. Of course, these stories could have been interpreted by the students using culture, structure, power, and privilege. Sexual abuse and rape could have been seen and discussed in terms of power. Instead, the accounts the students told were almost entirely restricted to what happened in one person's life. In contrast, stories related in race dialogues more frequently added something about structural factors and differential treatment that went beyond that specific person. Some accounts mentioned the storyteller's immigrant status or referred to racial profiling and to racial harassment at work. Such stories evoked racial issues as general phenomena and were more easily interpreted structurally in terms of power and privilege. Thus it is not surprising based on the content of the stories that empathy was expressed as both relational and critical in the race dialogues and almost exclusively as relational in the gender dialogues. The content the listeners had available was simply more interpersonal in the gender dialogues and more explicitly societal and structural in the race dialogues. Of course, to some extent that begs the question because something socially significant must explain why the content of the stories told by students differed in the two types of dialogues.

To be sure, students in the gender dialogues did talk and write about gender norms. They demonstrated that they know that different standards for sexual behavior exist for men and women. They knew there are different physical standards of beauty and prowess for men and women. Still, they used the terms gender *norms* or *gender socialization* without examining those terms. Dialogue facilitators frequently said that students talk about gender norms as "just the way things are," as standards that have been so much a part of their lives for so long that they are taken for granted. Facilitators also noted that these students believed that there is more racial-ethnic discrimination and inequality than there is for gender, and so it doesn't occur to them to interpret gender inequality and injustice in structural terms.

Another possibility for the predominance of relational empathy in the gender dialogues is the tendency of men and women to avoid what can disrupt or threaten intimate relationships across gender. Faye Crosby (1984) notes that when perceptions of discrimination require a painful recognition of inequality or injustice in personal, intimate relationships, people tend to deny or ignore the existence of discrimination. Intimacy characterizes the relationships between men and women more than relationships across other social categories (Rudman and Glick 2008). This fairly unique intimacy across dominance/subordination in the case of gender relationships is a major reason that gender consciousness is more difficult to develop than either race or class consciousness (Gurin, Miller, and Gurin 1980). It can be painful for a woman to see inequality in her ongoing relationships with a male partner or with her father or brothers within the family. Even if she recognizes inequality, it may be less threatening to interpret it as the result of the personalities of particular men than to see gender relationships as generally shaped by wider societal forces that are likely to determine her future relationships as well. It can be painful as well for a man to recognize gendered patterns of interaction and his role in sustaining those patterns in his long-term relationships with a female partner or his sisters or mother. This is not to discount the pain and difficulty involved in recognizing any kind of inequality in personal relationships across social groups, but cross-race-ethnic relationships are less often embedded in the level of intimacy common for gender relationships.

In contrast, students in the race-ethnicity dialogues less often have close personal ties and intimate relationships across race-ethnicity. Even today, most college students come to college from racially segregated neighborhoods and high schools (Orfield, Eaton, and the Harvard Project on School Desegregation 1996; Orfield and Lee 2006). Residential segregation by race, ethnicity, class, and rural-urban region not only helps determine levels of intimacy in intergroup relationships but also helps shape students' assumptions about commonalities and differences. Because of racial residential separation, most students arrive at race-ethnicity dialogues knowing that they lack knowledge of how students in the other group view race-ethnicity or its impact on their experiences. They don't assume that they already understand how race works differently for or among groups of color and for white students. They come to race-ethnicity dialogues believing that they have a lot to learn. In contrast, students come to gender dialogues believing that they know how gender works. It is harder for them to see gender as a distinction they need to probe and understand at a deeper level because women and men interact all the time, often in intimate ways. Thus, although they acknowledge gender norms and understand that their lives have been affected by socialization into a gender-based system, their close interactions across gender and familiarity with each other seem to mitigate against a critical analysis of gender inequalities.

Difficulty in recognizing gender-based inequalities and attributing them to structural factors (schools, religious practices, media, and the marketplace through commodification of sexuality) may also derive from the postfeminist belief among many young people today that men and women have already achieved equality (Nedeau 2008). Deanna displayed this belief when she wrote that "sexism seemed like a thing of the past, something my grandmother had to face, and maybe even my mom—but I wasn't a victim of sexism!" Dialoguing across differences in power and privilege is exceedingly challenging when the less privileged group does not see itself as unequal. This does not mean that young women and men are unconcerned about gender inequality. The facilitators in the dialogues emphasized, however, that both women and men seem to resist a broader analysis of societally based inequalities, because such an analysis requires them to imagine that many personal gender-based relationships, including ones they may form in the future, are apt to be affected by issues of power and privilege. Scholars writing about the perspectives and beliefs of what is often called the postfeminist generation stress this disjuncture between awareness of and reaction to inequalities in personal relationships and in the broader social world (Baumgardner and Richards 2000; Walker 1995).

But why did we see practically no evidence of dialogue having a different impact on empathy in race-ethnicity and gender dialogues in the quantitative analysis of the surveys? Relative to the survey questions, the openness of the interviews and paper assignments invited storytelling, which proved to be a rich source for creating empathy. Surveys do not allow storytelling. Whereas the quantitative measure gave a picture of the extent of emotional empathy and its change over time, the qualitative measures provide access to more naturalistic expressions and conceptions of empathy. As a result, the coders were able to identify a distinction between relational and critical empathy, thus validating the value of using mixed methods in both data collection and analysis.

The statistical analysis also addressed whether levels of empathy differed among women of color, men of color, white women, and white men. It shows that the four groups did not differ in the frequency of their expression of critical and relational empathy. This finding complements rather than contradicts conclusions from the quantitative analysis of the survey data in chapter 5. Why, we might ask, does intergroup dialogue have equivalent impact on empathy among these four types of students whose identities and experiences differ? Students from both more privileged and less privileged social positions and experiences face challenges in learning how privilege and group-based inequalities operate in society, and how they might form coalitions to work for a more just society through alliance building. Their challenges are not identical, but all these students come to dialogue with stereotypes and assumptions that the curriculum and communications within dialogue directly undermine. Students learn more complex and nuanced understandings of privilege, inequality, and social action. Students from all backgrounds face a huge challenge of imagining what the experiences of those from other backgrounds may have been, and thus how they can make empathic leaps. At the same time, they face a challenge of knowing they should not, indeed cannot, conclude that everyone is the same.

The comparability of dialogue impact and of emphasis on relational and critical empathy across the four types of students raises the question of who empathizes with whom. That is, who are the targets of empathy? Is empathy from members of more privileged groups to less privileged groups more frequent than the reverse? Before this study, that question received little attention (but see Sorensen et al. 2010). Some critics of IGD suggest that students from less privileged groups are not likely to feel empathy for those from more privileged groups, and moreover, these critics argue that they shouldn't (see discussion of this criticism in chapter 9). One reason offered by critics is that empathy for the more privileged would likely undercut the development of solidarity and political consciousness critical to collective action within the less privileged group (Gorski 2008). In our critical-dialogic model of IGDe, we argue instead that mutuality of empathy is both possible and useful for motivating action, especially action that depends on coalitions and intergroup collaboration (see Nagda 2006; Nagda, Kim, and Truelove 2004).

What did we learn about the directionality of empathy expressed between more and less privileged groups in our analysis of the interviews and student papers? A code was developed for directionality of empathy for each instance of empathy. An analysis of the coded data indicated that approximately the same percentage of empathy was directed from white students to students of color (67 percent) as from students of color to white students (70 percent) in race-ethnicity dialogues. Likewise, approximately the same percentage of empathy was directed from men to women (67 percent) as from women to men (71 percent) in gender dialogues. The remaining incidents of empathy were expressed to in-group members. This pattern indicates that the dialogues were effective in fostering empathy from and toward members of both more and less privileged groups.

These findings on directionality of empathy expression revealed in the qualitative analysis further confirm the value of mixed methods. It was not possible to discern in the quantitative analysis of the survey measures to what group students were expressing empathy. But it was possible to do so in the qualitative study.

THE POWER OF STORIES: COMMUNICATION PROCESSES AND EMPATHY

In the interviews and papers, it is obvious that the students experienced empathy when they listened to a story told by another dialogue participant. In this section, we explore the role storytelling played in promoting empathy in intergroup dialogues. In the interviews and papers, students were neither asked nor prompted to think of stories they heard in the dialogues. The stories in which empathy emerged were told in different parts of interviews and papers in response to questions about interaction, learning, identity, and emotions.

Storytelling, which includes sharing, listening, and making meaning of these stories together, is part of the intergroup dialogue pedagogy. Be it the individual stories of socialization that students share in the testimonials, or the group stories shared and listened to in caucus groups and fishbowls, or the related stories people discover in discussing the impact of controversial issues on individuals and groups in the hot topics sessions, stories in intergroup dialogue bring individual experiences into public dialogue and provide a way for students to gain social knowledge. Facilitators help students connect with each other to explore the impact of the stories and to make collective meaning of them. Students often described to the interviewer vivid details about the emotions a fellow student displayed in telling a story and about the emotional and cognitive empathy they experienced themselves in listening to a story. They framed their personal growth in IGDs in terms of their increased abilities to listen to and learn from the experiences and emotions of other students. They appreciated their empathic connections with their peers as valid sources of knowledge, in some cases elevating this knowledge above what they may have learned in social science classes or from the news media.

Students' accounts of the power of stories in their learning also give us a more nuanced understanding of the role of the four communication processes central to the critical-dialogic model of IGD—engaging self, appreciating difference, critical reflection, and alliance building (Nagda 2006). Together, the four processes help students achieve meaning from the stories. We emphasize the role of storytelling and communication processes in promoting empathy in part because these aspects of IGD differentiate it from traditional classrooms. Storytelling necessarily involves engaging self by sharing one's experiences among others who are expected to do the same. Students told the interviewers about becoming ready to take risks to reveal their ignorance, uncertainty, and fears when others took such risks in telling their stories. They felt a sense of courage. A woman of color in a gender dialogue we quoted in chapter 3 expands the impact of the care and trust developed in the group on her own courage: "I realize now that it is not possible to grow as a person without taking some risks. I took risks by sharing personal experiences, sharing my emotions, and standing up for my beliefs." Like this student, others gained confidence by telling their stories and having classmates listen to them and validate their importance. They also gained confidence by listening to the stories of others and seeing the experiences of others validated instead of demeaned or disputed.

Reading the students' narratives about the importance of telling their stories and listening to others' stories, we saw another level of courage and engaging self emerge. That is, in the public dialogue space, students felt courageous enough to revise their previously held perspectives. In addition to sharing their stories with others, they rethought or revised their perspectives. For example, Lily quoted earlier, shared how she had to revise her thinking after the conversation with Curtis about interracial dating. Whereas previously she had assumed that their shared social justice commitment meant that they would also agree on interracial dating, she realized that "being open minded does not always mean that everyone will agree about something." Similarly, John at first showed relational empathy with another student in his dialogue because both of them were judged and stereotyped with "no real evidence of my character, morals, and personality." Then through collective dialogue, John realized that his experience was different because of racism and the impact of racial stereotypes on African American men. Through storytelling, engaging self is seen more holistically by capturing the internal cognitive and emotional processes that occur when students share their own stories.

We believe that the power of stories, especially sharing stories, is affirmed and strengthened by others' listening to the stories. Students learned by listening to stories that often required an empathic leap across dissimilarity in backgrounds and experiences. Storytelling thus provides a path for the process of appreciating difference. Often listeners reacted to the stories of the other students as unexpected and surprising. This response was evident, for example, when Nicole, a white woman, recounted the childhood experiences of Terrance, an African American man who as a child had been excluded by white parents from playing with their children. Nicole said that she couldn't imagine her parents doing such a thing. Other students, reacting to stories involving dissimilarity, also reported being surprised, sometimes even shocked. Some used the word *wow* or other expressive emotional words in their interviews. In a race-ethnicity dialogue, for example, Alex compared the knowledge he acquired about police harassment from hearing Bryan's story to what people learn from the media, and stated that he was "angry just thinking about the reality of police harassment." Appreciating difference was more than distant knowing about others; it also involved feeling others' realities.

Although dissimilarities were often expected because of the differences in the identities between the student and the storyteller, some stories related by members of the students' own identity group were unexpected. Listening helped students recognize the complexity in stories of peers who shared their identities. Derek, for example, expected similarity between himself and Jeffery as two African American men. Derek was deeply affected when his expectation of similarity gave way to appreciating the difference in how they had been treated because of their difference in sexual orientations. Being attuned to difference parallels Martha Nussbaum's (2001) suggestion that in the process of empathizing, "one must be aware of one's own qualitative difference" from the other person (328). According to Nussbaum, empathy requires dual attention in which one imagines what it is like to be in the other person's place, and at the same time understands that one is not. These two layers of empathizing, when considered through a critical lens of structural inequality and collective empowerment, involve critical reflection of difference and alliance building. The first layer, which stimulates critical reflection, is listening to stories and recognizing that the storyteller has a different social position and different experiences. That recognition helps students grasp how societal structures have influenced their classmates, and though they may not have shared the same experiences or social locations, they can imagine and feel how those experiences have affected their fellow students.

Critical reflection involved understanding the experiences of other students in more complex ways. In many instances, students also grasped that privileges attached to social locations have affected them as well. We found many instances in which the power of stories applied across lines of privilege, helping students understand what privilege means. Listening to stories helped them see that societal norms not only affect women but also restrict men's emotional expression, and that racism has intellectual and emotional costs for white students as well as for students of color. The students marveled at the complexity of the knowledge they acquired about group identity through intersectionality, for example, that the gender or race of a fellow student had to be understood in relationship to the student's other identities and in relationship to their own gender or race, and that in both instances those identities meant something different when their interconnections with other identities were made transparent. They gained complex knowledge through the power of stories that fostered empathic experiences in the dialogue. Thus, critical reflection and empathy together enabled students to examine their positions in relation to others, to perceive differences within similarities, and to grasp in a compelling way that social structure affects people with both more and less privilege, albeit affecting them differently.

The second layer of empathizing that Nussbaum addresses is imagining—being in someone else's place and emotionally connecting across difference. Students noted the great difficulty of empathic imagination required to place oneself in the role of another person yet avoid the trap of thinking we are all the same. They sometimes said that they could not imagine having similar, unjust experiences. Yet they connected emotionally. Emotional empathy often occurred during the collective critical reflection phase of intergroup dialogue when the students together made sense of the stories shared in that session. The students stretched their imaginations, comparing the experiences of other students with their relatively more benign or more challenging experiences. In this process of critical reflection, emotions such as moral indignation, distress, sorrow, and righteous anger often arose (Hoffman 2000). It was in these emotional empathic connections that alliance building began to unfold. Students who listened to stories of racial profiling, sexual abuse of women, and harassment and violence toward gay people wondered how they had known about these injustices but did not "really know them" until they heard a story from a fellow student in dialogue. They became motivated to do something together to attack injustice. It was not simply hearing the stories of injustice that stimulated that motivation, but also experiencing emotions as they listened. Derek expressed disbelief and anger when he listened to Jeffrey's story of being gay.

> I just couldn't even grasp that I would have to, if I were gay, think about where I'm going . . . how people are going to look at me, how they're going to treat me. And I think that really impacted me on a whole different level. I felt a lot of anger, there was a lot of sadness. . . . I was really angry just because I can't believe it is happening. (Man of color, gender dialogue)

Expression of similar emotions, while continuing to appreciate qualitative differences in experiences and having the space to share their own stories, prompted possibilities for building alliances. The parallel emotions were also important for the storytellers in that their emotions could be validated or at least reflected in others and not discounted.

The power of stories resonates through all of the students' narratives in the interviews and their final papers, especially when they reflected on the learning through cognitive and emotional connections to others. Sharing stories and listening to others' stories, as the students' narratives show, is not simply for the sake of knowing different experiences. They have to do specifically with becoming more complex thinkers and more attuned to their own and others' feelings. This active cognitive and emotional engagement is evident in all four of the communication processes that storytelling fosters. A man of color in a race-ethnicity dialogue we quoted earlier in chapter 3 captures, in summary, the connection between storytelling, communication processes, and empathy:

> As time went on, we were able to open up to each other and reveal ourselves to each other by sharing personal stories, experiences and examples from our lives. I felt that the feelings and perspectives that we shared with each other were genuine and that we developed a sense of trust that allowed us to share our personal accounts with the group. The trust and sharing were essential in

developing empathy for each other. We were also able to challenge the thinking of others and our own method of thinking which enabled us to ask other group members difficult questions and work through disagreements and conflicts. (Man of color, race-ethnicity dialogue)

CONCLUSION

In summary, the findings in this chapter illuminate how empathy is experienced and manifested during IGDs. The mixed methods analysis revealed a distinction between relational and critical empathy not evident in the survey analysis. Both types of empathy involved emotional or cognitive connections with specific individuals or groups, but critical empathy more than relational involved an understanding of the broader implications of that experience in relation to a system of power and privilege. The dialogues create a climate in which these two types of empathy are directed toward members of the other identity group as well as of their own. Both types have the power to transform relations between identity groups because they provide insights into the out-group as well as the in-group, and they deepen the understanding between them.

Empathy in intergroup dialogues is the culmination of a process outlined in our theoretical framework, that is, the pedagogical features of the dialogues involve storytelling, which engenders communication processes and psychological processes that foster empathy. Empathy most frequently emerged when participants listened and reflected on the stories presented by others. Storytelling, which the curriculum of intergroup dialogues is designed to promote, draws participants into the experiences and world views of their classmates and turns abstract issues such as racism, sexism, discrimination, and prejudice into personal issues that concern people they care about. The participants become engaged in the stories and larger social issues that relate to the stories, come to a new appreciation of the differences between groups, critically evaluate those differences, and are motivated to collaborate with other students in the interests of social justice. However, as the excerpts and analysis show, empathy is not a smooth, clean process in which participants come to a quick appreciation of perspectives, relational differences, and world views. Participants experienced frustration, surprise, anger, and sadness as they heard stories and accounts of discrimination, hurt, and privilege that they did not anticipate or had no basis of shared history to comprehend.

Empathy is emergent, complicated, and on the surface is not simply a person communicating a story and a receiver listening to that story and making comparisons. It involves listening and cognitive and emotional processing of what is heard (see discussion of active processing in chapter 7). This finding is an important insight for facilitators of intergroup dialogues, who need to recognize that empathy often does not entirely look like nor sound like appreciation or connection. Empathy may at times entail denial of shared experiences, incredulousness at disparate experiences, and self-doubt about how one's experiences reflect reality for all groups. Facilitators need to help participants stay present in the dialogue and stay in self-reflection rather than move to promote mutual understanding prematurely.

The evidence presented here demonstrates that IGDs lead to similar degrees and quality of relational and critical empathy in both genders and in both whites and people of color. This result indicates that dialogues draw all types of participants into empathic relationships with members of the other group and their own group. Finally, evidence indicates that race-ethnic dialogues lead to an equal emphasis on relational and critical empathy, whereas gender dialogues lead to more relational than critical empathy, most likely because participants have such long personal histories of close relations between women and men to draw on when telling stories in the dialogues.

In this chapter, we drew a distinction revealed in our mixed-method analyses between two types of empathy: relational empathy focused personally on a particular individual; critical empathy also focused on an individual but recognized him or her as an exemplar of common group-based, societal experience. Intimacy of relationships, which more frequently characterizes intergroup experiences involving gender than of race-ethnicity, appears to diminish students' expression of critical empathy. It is simply more difficult to recognize how social structure is implicated in the experiences of others with whom one has close, intimate connections. Facilitators therefore face a special challenge, which we discuss further in chapter 9, in guiding students in gender dialogues to perceive and analyze stories told by others as representative of broad societal arrangements and are not merely idiosyncratic to a particular individual.

Authored by Kathleen Wong (Lau), Patricia Gurin, Biren (Ratnesh) A. Nagda, Amy Carpenter Ford, Walter G. Stephan, Kelly Maxwell, Rosie Perez, and Carmen McCallum.

CHAPTER 7

Engagement in Intergroup Dialogue: Listening, Speaking, and Active Thinking

I would say that as people started sharing more personal experiences, it made me feel that, wow, this person really trusts the group to even share stuff like that, and maybe I can do it too, and so I kind of dipped my toes in the water and so I just eventually had my whole body in the water. (Woman of color, race-ethnicity dialogue)

Well, I wouldn't say there was ever a time I didn't feel engaged, they're really good about always making everyone get to say their piece . . . it's not like I spent too much time talking, I always, I spent a lot of time listening and that was important to be engaged in class and knowing that you need to listen to learn, not just talk. (White woman, race-ethnicity dialogue)

I had a huge problem with communication in terms of opening up myself, but with this class I was able to overcome that fear. . . . I had no problem with raising my hand or just jumping into a conversation and letting people know how I felt . . . which was like, wow, coming from someone who would never talk in class or talk to the TA personally after class to openly speaking in class, that was a big change and it felt too, it was a boost of confidence which is great. (Man of color, gender dialogue)

In the beginning when I thought about social identity, I just thought about how I developed my own male identity in terms of gender and I just kept thinking about how I played sports, you know, and that sort of creates male bonds for me and my friends. That was sort of how I developed it. Through the dialogue I started thinking more about my role as a male in society and how my role as a male affects the opportunities that females have too and not just me as a male but my role in society and things like that. I started to realize that as a male I have the power to influence sexism as well and not just think about my own gender. (White man, gender dialogue)

These statements are drawn from students describing their meaningful learning in intergroup dialogues (IGD). Based on interviews after the end of the IGD courses, these examples illustrate that students were moved to listen, speak, and think in race-ethnicity and gender intergroup dialogues. This chapter examines the three types of engagement that emerged from an analysis of the full set of 248 interviews. These were then explored in greater depth through a systematic and grounded analysis of a smaller sample of forty interview transcripts.

For these analyses, we defined engagement in the dialogues as a process that involved the students devoting their attention to, and personally responding to, events during the dialogues. Our goals were to explore the types of engagement that students in the dialogues described and identify the factors that appear to foster engagement. Although it is clear that the three forms of engagement we discovered and examined—listening, speaking, and active thinking—are interconnected, circular, and mutually enhancing, we examined each type separately to more fully understand why the unique pedagogical approach and curriculum of IGD appear to encourage participants to speak, listen, and try to understand both the content and the experience of intergroup dialogue.

The qualitative approach to understanding listening, speaking, and active thinking engagement presented in this chapter further informs the theoretical and empirical findings presented in previous chapters. Chapter 3 posits that the pedagogical features of intergroup dialogues foster critical-dialogic communication processes that in turn activate psychological processes that ultimately determine the outcomes of dialogues. Chapter 5 presents evidence from the quantitative analyses indicating that the degree to which students felt that the pedagogical features of the dialogues (such as readings, structured activities, journals, and reflection papers) contributed to what they learned in the dialogues and was closely related to communication processes such as appreciating differences, critical reflection, self-engagement, and building alliances across group lines.

These communication processes were linked to cognitive involvement in the dialogues (complex thinking, analytical thinking about society, consideration of multiple perspectives, and identity involvement), and to affective processes (positive emotions in interactions across differences and positive interactions across differences). Cognitive involvement and affective processes, in turn, were related to increases in understanding the structural causes of inequality, intergroup empathy, and intergroup action—all of which were still present a year after the dialogues ended. As these chapters suggest, engagement in the dialogues is central to the communication processes, particularly to participants' ability to listen and speak in the group and to their capacity to make meaning from what they hear, say, and feel while in dialogue. In this chapter, we explore these types of engagement through an analysis of students' descriptions of their learning in dialogue. The students' words provide important insights into the dynamics of the communication and cognitive processes that link the pedagogical approach employed in the dialogues and the outcomes of the dialogues.

We primarily used the qualitative method of grounded theory (Strauss and Corbin 1990; Charmaz 2006). We were interested in allowing the data itself to suggest research questions, categories, and connections, and we used the students' words to inform our conceptualization and understanding of engagement in IGD. We paid close attention to how participants framed their experiences and the moments of learning, challenge, and interaction they cited as important. We also analyzed how participants "made meaning" of these experiences as they reflected on them during the interviews. Although the IGD pedagogy and goals provided some ideas at the outset about types of engagement that might be present in the interviews, the importance of listening, speaking, and active thinking as forms of engagement in IGDs was both suggested and supported by the interview data.

Our further exploration of these three types of engagement led us to pose a series of questions about engagement: What were the elements of the IGD curriculum that particularly fostered speaking, listening, and active thinking?

When did participants listen attentively, why, and to whom? Why did participants choose to speak in the dialogues? What kinds of learning insights reflect active thinking engagement?

A MIXED-METHODS APPROACH TO UNDERSTANDING ENGAGEMENT

A multistage process and multimethod approach were used to examine processes of engagement in the interview data. In the first stage of the analysis, transcripts from 248 postdialogue interviews were coded by a trained team of coders. These interviews were conducted with participants in a subset of ten race-ethnicity dialogues and ten gender dialogues selected from among the fifty-two dialogues in the overall project. Both inductive and deductive approaches were used to identify the various types of engagement the participants described. The deductive approach focused on the core elements of engagement reflected in the IGD curriculum and concepts referenced in the theoretical model (that is, pedagogical features, active listening, speaking, critical reflection). The research team looked for evidence of what we referred to at the time as listening, speaking, and critical reflection engagement looked like from the perspectives of the students so that we could develop coding structures that would effectively capture these types of engagement. At the same time, in a more inductive inquiry, the research team read for other engagement themes that emerged from the students' descriptions. These themes, in particular, our discovery of an expanded construction of the critical reflection concept to encompass other forms of reflection, analysis, and insight emerged as additional examples of students' engagement. Coders identified these examples and the research team met together to determine whether these examples were reflective of engagement and how they might be categorized into additional engagement codes. Once the categories were established, the team coded all 248 interviews using NVivo,[1] a qualitative software program that also supports quantitative analysis of qualitative findings.

The quantitative findings reported in this chapter include the frequencies for each type of engagement produced by this initial coding. These findings include comparisons of the frequency of these types of engagement by participants' social identities (women of color, men of color, white women, white men) and type of dialogue (race-ethnicity or gender). However, most of the findings reported in this chapter emerged from a more detailed and in-depth coding conducted in the next two stages of analysis.

The second stage used separate transcripts of sections of the data in the interviews that had been coded as listening engagement, speaking engagement, and active thinking engagement in the original coding to explore elements and themes for each type of engagement. From this more in-depth analysis of each type of engagement, grounded theories were articulated and detailed coding structures were developed for use in the next stage of analysis.

The final stage of analysis involved selecting forty interview transcripts and recoding them using the more detailed coding structures developed in the second stage. This smaller sample was created by randomly selecting one student from each social identity group (women of color, men of color, white women, and white men) from each of the ten dialogue classes to produce a sample with equal numbers of participants from each of the social identity groups represented in each dialogue, from different regions of the country, from varying social and economic class backgrounds, and from different hosting institutions. This round of analysis allowed us to examine our initial findings in more detail and also helped us recontextualize the three engagement processes by examining them in the context of the entire interview rather than as isolated sections of coded data. We also used the software program NVivo to code and analyze data from the sample.

OVERVIEW AND INITIAL FINDINGS

The curriculum and pedagogy of IGD, especially the specific structured activities described in chapter 2, are designed to encourage students to speak, to listen, and to think and reflect, so it is not surprising that these three forms of engagement were evident throughout the interviews. The frequency with which these forms of engagement were evident in the interviews, however, is impressive. Table 7.1 shows the percentage of interviews for which at least one example of each of these codes was present in the initial coding. Ninety-six percent of the students described engaged listening, 72 percent described speaking, and 99 percent described active thinking. These findings confirm the ways IGD aims to foster engagement among students. Table 7.1 also reports the average number of instances of each type of engagement within each social identity group and across the two types of dialogues, and results of statistical tests conducted to see whether these groups differed in how frequently students mentioned the three types of engagement to the interviewers.

Table 7.1   Frequency of Speaking, Listening, and Active Thinking Codes per Interview (N = 248)

Engagement Code	Speaking	Listening	Active Thinking
Number of interviews with at least one instance of each type of engagement	178	239	247
Percentage of participants with at least one instance (race-ethnicity and gender dialogue)	72	96	99
Average number of references per participant	1.52	3.57	8.35
Average number of instances by demographic group			
Women of color (n = 66)	1.74	3.86	8.88
White women (n = 57)	1.25	3.88	8.77
Men of color (n = 58)	2.02**	3.22	8.21
White men (n = 48)	1.15	3.48	8.73
Average number of instances by topic of dialogue			
Race-ethnicity dialogues	1.52	3.45	8.95
Gender dialogues	1.53	3.70	8.17

Source: Authors' calculations.

**Statistically significant difference from other groups at $p < .01$. This was the only significant difference among the four groups.

The students in race and gender dialogues did not differ in the frequency with which they described these types of engagement. Although men of color had a higher frequency of speaking than women of color, white women, and white men, listening and active thinking were coded at similar levels across the four groups. These results show that, for the most part, individuals from all four groups reported similar frequencies of these three types of engagement.

In the following section, we take a closer look at each type of engagement. Although we analyzed listening, speaking, and active thinking as distinct forms of engagement, it is important to keep in mind that these work in concert with each other. Listening would not be possible if no one spoke, and both listening and speaking provide the material for active thinking. We return to the idea that these forms of engagement are interconnected in the discussion section that follows, but believe there is value in examining each type of engagement separately first to more fully understand how and why they are central to the dialogue experience.

LISTENING ENGAGEMENT

A number of writers have emphasized the importance of listening in various dialogical practices (Chasin et al. 1996; Ellinor and Gerard 1998; Isaacs 1999; Zúñiga, Nagda, and Sevig 2002). These authors distinguish between simply hearing other people's words and the more engaged and active process of taking in and trying to understand the meaning of what is being said. According to William Isaacs, this "profound capacity to listen" requires that "we not only hear the words, but also embrace, accept, and gradually let go of our inner clamoring" (1999, 83–84). Fostering listening is also an important part of IGD's pedagogy and curriculum, which provides opportunities to practice active listening skills and to both listen to and speak with members of one's own and other social identity groups (Zúñiga et al. 2007).

Research on learning outcomes in IGD suggests that participants do take in, reflect on, and apply perspectives and information from their dialogue group (Nagda 2006; Sorensen et al. 2009; Zúñiga et al. 2012). These findings affirm that listening is an essential part of dialogue. Numerous examples from the interview data described in this chapter also highlight the importance of listening in IGD. A student who participated in a race-ethnicity dialogue, for example, observed that listening is a necessary part of communication in dialogue.

> I think I really learned through listening. I mean, I really learned through dia-
> logue that [by] listening I can learn a lot, and I think that really helped with
> communication. . . . I guess I just learned that through dialogue and honest
> discussion, it could be a very comfortable experience working with students of
> every color . . . like, people in the group were completely different from me
> but I always found something that I could relate to them on some level and
> that was a skill that was important. (White woman, race-ethnicity dialogue)

Reading comments such as this affirmed our initial interest in understanding how, why, and when listening occurs in IGDs. We coded the interview data for *listening engagement* when a participant listened to something said in their dialogue that engaged them enough to be able to remember significant details about what was said and describe them to an interviewer after the

IGD course was over. In coding the data, we tried to include a large enough section of the interview transcripts to be able to gather additional information about who was speaking, the context of what was being said, and what the participant felt or thought about what he or she had heard. For example, a woman of color in a gender group described not only what she recalled listening to, but also how she tried to understand the other person's experience, even though it was different from her own.

> I remember one particular story . . . when [a male participant in the group] was in grade school, somebody had called him gay. So he kind of like, he had to stop and think about it for a while and kind of interpret that and make sense of it: "Why is he calling me gay, why? Did I do something, did I say something?" So that kind of made me think how people take in what they're given. So it was kind of different because I would never think somebody would even take it like that. I would think, well, I'm not gay so then don't refer me to that. So I guess it did make an impact, because he looked at a different concept in a completely different way. (Woman of color, gender dialogue)

In our analysis of the data, we found that participants recalled and described listening most often in response to or in the context of specific curricular activities, in reaction to specific speakers, and in relationship to specific topics. These three areas of findings are the focus of this section. Although we also coded for and analyzed consequences of listening (see Zúñiga et al. 2012), what students did with what they heard—how they reacted emotionally and cognitively and how they made meaning of what they heard—will be addressed later.

Curricular Context

Intergroup dialogues have a planned, intentionally sequenced curriculum with specific goals and activities for each meeting. Three of the activities—the testimonial activity, the caucus group and fishbowl activities, and the hot topics sessions (all described in chapter 2)—appear to be particularly important in stimulating listening.

The testimonial activity was most frequently associated with listening engagement. This activity takes place in the third dialogue session and requires participants to write about their raced and gendered life experiences before sharing some of these experiences in the group. For example, a white woman in a race-ethnicity dialogue might speak about her experiences as a woman and her experiences as a white person, two identities representing a disadvantaged and an advantaged social group, respectively. It is not surprising that this activity was associated with listening engagement, because it provides participants with an opportunity to listen, without interruption to others' experiences with race, gender and other salient social identities. Through this process, participants often found their assumptions and stereotypes about people challenged, both across and within identity groups. Participants' comments about this activity indicate that they were often surprised by how open and honest the sharing was, and many believed this set the tone for the sharing that occurred later in the dialogue. One participant described his responses to the testimonials of the women in his group in this way.

> Just hearing the story of how harsh some people's upbringings were, like it really kind of struck home with me: "wow, people do have like deep stories, or deeper than you'd actually know." Because in college, it's a lot of times you just come to class and kind of see people and don't really know too much about them, maybe their name and where they're from. But hearing testimonials from some of the girls . . . makes you kind of realize some of their background and makes you kind of feel for them and respect a lot more of like how they got to where they are now. (Man of color, gender dialogue)

The caucus groups and fishbowl sessions were the second most often mentioned curricular activities associated with listening engagement. These sequential activities involve participants meeting separately with others in their social identity or caucus group (as defined by the focus of the dialogue) and then returning to the larger group to participate in a fishbowl in which each group, in turn, discusses what they had said in their caucus group in a smaller circle as members of the other caucus group sit in a larger circle around them and simply listen. One participant recalled these activities.

> I remember one activity, it was called the fishbowl activity or the caucus group . . . we were in one group in one room and the rest of the people were in a different group in another room, and we were just to discuss experiences in our lives. Like did we encounter racism and how did that make us feel and how do we feel that we should handle it? And we more or less bonded over our experiences in the caucus group. And then . . . we came back all together and we [shared] what we talked about in the separate groups. . . . We [the people of color group] were really open about talking and sharing our experiences with

racism and inequality. And then after that we switched roles so the [people of color] group was on the outside and the white people were on the inside. It was really hard for them. They . . . were like the opposite of us, they were closed off, they didn't want to talk about it, they were kind of standoffish. . . . That made me feel really engaged, though I wasn't saying anything, I was just purely listening to them. (Man of color, race-ethnicity dialogue)

The hot topics sessions were the third most frequently mentioned curricular activity associated with engaged listening. During these sessions, which are scheduled halfway through the course, participants engage in three sessions of open dialogue about controversial topics related to the focus of the dialogue, race-ethnicity or gender. The topics are chosen by the group. Participants prepare for sessions ahead of time by reading related articles, then discuss the topic, and then reflect on their dialogue. Dialogue participants often chose topics such as affirmative action, immigration, and sexual assault. One of the goals of the hot topics sessions is to attempt, after several weeks of preparation, to engage in meaningful dialogue and explore difficult questions instead of arguing and debating about contentious issues. Hot topics emerged as important stimuli for listening because they touched on topics of interest to the students and provided opportunities to practice the dialogic skills, including listening, they had discussed earlier in the dialogue. One student described his experience of listening during a hot topics session this way.

Well I just tried to listen to what other people had to say and not necessarily change their views or change my views, just to digest what they were saying and put it on a bigger scale of what it meant. And then just take it from every side and see like where I fell on that and if I felt I wanted to switch over. (White man, race-ethnicity dialogue)

Note how the student describes how he used the skill of active listening during this dialogue session, listening to every perspective and keeping open the possibility that his views might be changed based on what he heard.

Reactions to Speakers

In addition to being fostered by specific curricular activities, engaged listening was also prompted by participants' cognitive or emotional reactions to what a specific speaker or group of speakers said or to specific characteristics of the speakers. About half of the participants mentioned that they had listened carefully to what someone in the dialogue was saying because they could identify with them in some way, because they disagreed with or were unable to relate to what was being said, or because they were struck by how different the experiences or views being shared by the speaker were from their own. Of these, participants in the sample most often described listening to a story, idea, or experience that they either strongly identified with or that helped them understand or empathize with someone else's experience or perception (on the role of storytelling and listening to stories in expression of empathy in IGDs, see chapter 6). For example, several women participating in gender dialogues described listening to other women in their group as they shared their experiences of being molested, an experience they could understand and relate to.

Participants also described listening to speakers who had different views or perspectives, speakers who said things that upset the listener, and speakers who said things that led to conflict in the group. For instance, a woman of color in a race-ethnicity dialogue described in detail a large group discussion about affirmative action that elicited intense disagreement and conflict in the group during one of the hot topics sessions. She not only had a strong reaction to the topic itself, but also reacted to how other students were participating in the discussion and paid close attention to what others in the groups were communicating.

> Some kids were looking around like this is ridiculous, some kids were confused, some kids were scared to say something. People were arguing . . . and it just kept getting bigger and bigger. . . . People kept referring to their schools like "my school's like this" and "my school's like that" . . . and one Latino kid was saying how he didn't have any opportunities at his school . . . and he is, "like it should be based on socioeconomic status." (Woman of color, race-ethnicity dialogue)

As this narrative suggests, conflict and disagreement, how certain speakers express themselves, the group dynamics, or what a speaker or speakers said may have made this and other conversations particularly memorable for the participant over and above the topic at the time. We see in chapter 8 that student behaviors observed in videotapes confirm that students spoke by advancing and defending their positions, rather than listening to others or asking questions of others, more during the hot topics sessions than in any other session. Although the goal in intergroup dialogue is to help students learn how to talk about controversial topics in dialogic ways rather than merely to argue, debate, and defend their positions as they tend to do in ordinary discourse, this study shows that hot topics sessions accomplished that goal only minimally.

Topics of Conversation

It is clear from many of the examples that certain topics of conversation seem to have stimulated listening engagement among participants. In fact, when participants described moments of listening engagement, they provided more information about the topic of conversation than any other aspect of what they recalled. Not surprisingly, most of the topics that participants mentioned reflected the focus of the two kinds of dialogues, that is, most topics were race related or gender related, and only a small number of other-related topics were mentioned. Participants in race-ethnicity dialogues mostly described listening to discussions about topics related to race and ethnicity, whereas participants in gender dialogues most often described listening to topics related to gender. However, participants in gender dialogues described listening to more "other" topics (those not related to the main focus of the dialogue) than participants in race-ethnicity dialogues did.

RACE-RELATED TOPICS   More than a third of the race-related topics participants described focus on some aspect of racism, including individual experiences, systemic racism, and race-related privilege. Several themes emerged in our analysis of how topics related to race- or ethnicity-based oppression and privilege were talked about in the interviews. One important theme was that firsthand stories seem to have helped all participants accept the fact that racism is still a huge problem. Participants recalled listening to personal experiences of racism that included being discriminated against, racially profiled, or tracked into certain academic majors and courses. One conversation that most of the participants in a particular race-ethnicity dialogue recalled illustrated how two students of color, a black man and an Asian woman, were affected differently by the racism of the same academic advisor at their university. Hearing how the black student was registered into remedial classes and the Asian student was registered into honors classes, without regard to their interests and abilities, was a particularly powerful example for the students in this dialogue. Although other participants also described examples of how certain white people still treat people of color badly (individual acts of racism), other interviewees suggested that these stories helped them to understand what was meant by racism as a system of inequality.

The second most commonly mentioned set of topics related to race-ethnicity focused on the problematic and socially constructed nature of racial categories, racial identities, and racial stereotypes. Most of the topics participants reported listening to in this category focused on within-group and across-group differences rather than similarities. For example, some participants recalled conversations about the difficulties and advantages of creating a group of students of color that combined together students from different racial-ethnic identity groups (such as black, Latino, Asian American). Other within-group differences discussed by people of color included differences based on gender, social-economic class, where they grew up (including the racial-ethnic mix of their schools and neighborhoods), first language, and immigration-citizenship status. Participants also recalled that conversations about differences among white people tended to focus on differences in socioeconomic class.

Across-group differences noted or reflected on by people of color included the idea that people of color speak two cultural languages, whereas white people speak only one; the observation that white people and people of color may have very different understandings of economic disadvantage; and the discovery that some white people actually care about racism and may engage in behaviors previously not understood by people of color as attempts to compensate for racism.

GENDER-RELATED TOPICS The most frequently mentioned set of gender-related topics focused on issues related to gender roles, gender stereotypes, and their effects on both women and men. For example, participants recalled stories about the effects of sex role socialization on both women and men, the effects of violent and distorted media images and of impossible standards of physical perfection that particularly target women, and what women and men are really "like." As with race-related topics, participants described listening much more often to conversations about difference rather than discussions about similarities. Unlike participants in race-ethnicity dialogues, however, participants in gender groups often spoke of the apparent differences between women and men as though they were natural or inevitable rather than socially constructed.

The second most frequently mentioned set of gender-related topics focused on aspects of sexism, including gender oppression as a systemic issue, instances of sexist behavior, and gender-based privilege. Examples of sexism mostly involved stories about things participants had observed or experienced outside the group, but some participants also described hearing people within the group express sexist beliefs. For example, a white woman in a gender dialogue described her experience in a discussion about women in government and the military in which some people in the group agreed with statements justifying discrimination against women in these institutions. Although she disagreed, she said, "I took a step back and was ready to listen at least, and hear why it was that they felt that way." In addition to discussing what they had learned about gender inequalities, a number of participants said that they had gained a greater understanding of how women feel unsafe in the world, either because of the threat of sexual assault or because they were the only female in traditionally male-dominated fields or mostly male gatherings. One man of color in a gender dialogue, who compared his experience as a self-identified Asian male to the experience of another student, an Asian woman, noted, "I never noticed how difficult it may be for someone that would be the only female, or one of the only females, in the class."

Finally, one topic area was often mentioned in relationship to gender: sexual assault. This issue was often discussed during hot topics sessions, but related issues (including sexual abuse) also came up in conversations at other points in the dialogues (particularly testimonials) and in dialogues where sexual assault was not selected as a hot topic. Because no single hot topic stood out clearly for race-ethnicity dialogues, it appears that conversations about rape and sexual abuse may trigger listening engagement regardless of whether they are associated with a specific curricular context.

Listening Engagement Summary

This pattern of findings supports the idea that listening is at the heart of dialogue (Isaacs 1999, 83). In addition to finding evidence of listening engagement in almost every postdialogue interview, participants provided many rich examples that shed light on when, why, and to whom participants in IGD listen. Certain topics, reactions to speakers, and the IGD curriculum itself all appear to foster listening. The importance of listening was under-lined by the participants themselves. In the words of one,

> the active listening thing was huge for me. If there's one thing that I'm going to take with me for the rest of my life out of this class, it's that concept. Every time I'm in a conversation with anybody, with people from my own group, different groups, whoever it is, and I'm not paying attention to them, the word active listening just pops in. It just pops in. I say that I've got to pay attention to these people because they've got their own opinions and I've got to take them, even if I disagree with them. Their first sentence might be something I completely disagree with, but I've got to let them finish. If you don't listen to people and don't remember anything they're saying just because you disagree with them, you're not going to get very far. (White man, gender group)

SPEAKING ENGAGEMENT

Developing the capacity to speak across lines of difference to address taboo or controversial topics can be particularly challenging for college students not accustomed to participating in small face to face classroom conversations with diverse peers (Tatum 1997, 2007; Zúñiga et al. 2012). "To speak your voice is perhaps one of the most challenging aspects of genuine dialogue. Speaking your voice has to do with revealing what is true for you regardless of other influences that might be brought to bear" (Isaacs 1999, 159). The type of honest, in-the-moment speaking required in dialogue is often new for many students and can feel quite risky to them. Students are encouraged to find a voice that is true for them, and engage in courageous speech, not sim-ply a rehash of what has been said or written before (Isaacs 1999). In addi-tion, participants must speak in the moment, as opposed to planning what they will say. As Isaacs would suggest, using this voice requires the courage to express the unknown, to confront one's lack of understanding. In using this authentic voice, participants may shift their lived experience into knowledge, which can be transformational for both the individual and the institution.

Participant interview responses were coded as speaking engagement when a student reported and described times she or he was verbally active in the dialogue. All incidents of speaking that provided enough specific information to indicate the substance of what the participant said and a sense of the par-ticipant's motives for speaking were coded. Although the frequency data summarized in table 7.1 suggest that speaking engagement occurred less frequently (an average of 1.5 instances per interview) than listening (an average of 3.5), these differences most likely occurred because for every person who was speaking at any given moment, eleven or more might have been listening. In addition, there were more questions in the interview protocol likely to elicit descriptions of instances of listening than speaking (for example, was there a time when someone from the same or a different identity group shared something that had an impact on you?).

The curricular contexts and topics of conversation associated with speaking engagement and listening engagement are similar, but not identical. For example, speaking, like listening, was frequently associated with specific activities included in the IGD curriculum. However, the hot topics sessions were more commonly associated with speaking engagement, while the testimonial activity was the most common curricular context for listening engagement. This may be because this in-the-moment speaking in the large group dialogue was more memorable for students than speaking in the testimonial activity, which is required for all dialogue participants. As might be expected, participants who spoke and participants who listened also referred to the same topics of conversation. For example, although participants did not always provide enough detail to help identify the specific topics in every section of the data coded for speaking engagement, many of the topics described, such as affirmative action, sexual assault, immigration, and abortion, were the hot topics selections for particular dialogues. Others were topics that came up in other parts of the dialogue curriculum, such as offensive language and white privilege. Despite these similarities, we do not have enough information to compare topics of conversation associated with listening and topics associated with speaking because our grounded analysis of the speaking engagement dataset did not highlight topics of conversation as a major category of analysis for speaking engagement.

What did emerge very clearly in the analysis was that in the sections of the interviews when participants recalled speaking, they often reflected on their internal motives for doing so. Understanding these motives became an important part of our exploration. We identified seven distinct motives. The first five—to share, question, educate, challenge, and defend—reflect the various ways participants communicated their perspectives and their desires to understand each other. The last two—to remark on group process and to facilitate—demonstrate participants' efforts to engage in dialogic skills. Here we focus on providing more in-depth understanding of the three most frequently displayed motives for speaking: to share, to challenge, and to educate.

Speaking to Share

The most commonly identified motive for speaking was to share either personal stories and experiences or thoughts and opinions on a topic. Almost two-thirds of the participants in the forty-interview sample described this kind of motive for speaking. For example, a white woman in a race-ethnicity dialogue said,

> I think probably the most I was ever engaged would be the time we did testimonials. That was really powerful. I was very interested in what everyone had to say and I was very, I was very willing to get my testimonial across well too. . . . When I told my testimonial, I talked about working at a camp for Native American kids. And I was one of the only white people that worked there, and there was really—like I shouldn't have the job because I'm not Native American, and the kids don't have to listen to me because I'm white. . . . So I was just really engaged because I got to tell my story, which I think is really powerful. But listening to everyone else's was too. (White woman, race-ethnicity dialogue)

This statement demonstrates the ways in which participants become engaged by having the opportunity to both listen to others' stories and share their personal stories and experiences.

In addition, a number of participants said that hearing other participants make themselves vulnerable and engage in high-risk sharing made them more willing to do the same themselves. The feeling expressed was "if they can do it, so can I."

Speaking to Challenge

Speaking to challenge others was mentioned by about a quarter of the participants in the subset of forty interviews. Participants challenged members of their own as well as the other social identity group. Usually participants would speak to challenge someone after listening to what they said about a specific emotionally charged topic. In these instances, they reported hearing opinions that hurt, offended, or angered them, although they often stated that the speaker was operating out of ignorance. Participants captured this feeling with phrases such as "that fired me up" or "that was like a pierce through the heart." In her interview, a white woman in a gender dialogue described challenging a man in the group.

> [He] went into this spiel about how in a rape scenario, the rapist is the real victim because the rapist is not able to recover from the rape. And I was pissed, you know, I'm not one to hold my tongue, I was right there, "please don't sit in a room surrounded by women and tell me that a rapist is the real victim in a rape. I don't think so." (White woman, gender dialogue)

This statement also illustrates an additional factor that was sometimes present when the students spoke, but seemed to be particularly salient for speaking to challenge—speaking as an immediate, perhaps emotionally charged reaction. This kind of speaking isn't the result of ruminating and planning what one will say, but a response triggered in the moment by what the speaker has heard.

In addition to challenging individuals in the group, some participants spoke to challenge the group as a whole. For example, a man of color in a gender dialogue said,

> We were talking about misogyny in the music industry, more specifically in the hip hop industry . . . and the moment we started talking, everybody got a little lit up, which was great and . . . it was contradictory, conflict was created, a lot of confrontation where people believed that it is really misogynistic . . . like a lot of women say that, "Oh we want to take these lyrics away, we want to be able to have a nongender-biased type of vocabulary in the music industry." And I said, "that's true but at the same time as much as you want that to stop, you persist in it." And someone gave the example where they said, "Oh we refer to, when I talk to my girls, I say 'hey ho,'" that's an example. Like how are you going to ask us for a change when you yourself are persisting in the vo-cabulary that you don't want? So from then on it was like I really was, I was attentive and I really wanted to offer more because I knew much more. (Man of color, gender dialogue)

This statement illustrates that speaking up can also help the speaker iden-tify particular strengths or ways that the participant can contribute to the group. For example, this participant said that after he spoke up, he spoke up more because he "knew a lot" and realized he could contribute.

Although speaking to challenge can be empowering, it often comes from feeling hurt or angry, which is why these incidents might have been particularly memorable. This type of speaking was new to many participants and sometimes put their relationships at risk, which often created anxiety during the early sessions of the dialogue.

Speaking to Educate

Almost a quarter of the participants in the sample reported speaking to educate the group or particular members of the group by sharing information. Typically, interviewees described engaging in this type of speaking when they perceived that others in the group did not know the basic facts on a topic about which they did. This motive for speaking usually came into play in response to others' statements about a specific topic, such as women in politics, sexual assault, or affirmative action. For example, a woman of color in a race-ethnicity dialogue explained,

> In the black community here we have so many different discussions and information sessions regarding affirmative action, so we know a lot about what it is and what it does and what the effects of it are. But a lot of the majority students, or the white students, really didn't know what it was about. None of the white females even knew that affirmative action affected them at all and none of the white males knew anything about it either. So during that discussion, I was just generally trying to inform people. . . . I just wanted to let everybody know it affects everybody. (Woman of color, race-ethnicity dialogue)

Participants also described speaking in order to educate people from their own identity group. For example, one Latina shared the following reaction after hearing another Latina in the race-ethnicity dialogue use the word *Spanish*.

> It was just like, it was kind of a shock because I wouldn't expect someone from the same group as me to make that error because it's very offensive to people who have been liberated from Spain after all those years of colonization. And it was just like, I don't know how to explain it, it was kind of like this fiery feeling, like an impulse, that I had to say something, like it was something that I

couldn't just let slip by. And so I didn't yell at her or anything, but I told her, "Ok it's not Spanish, it's either Latino. . . ." I told her what I just said to you. . . . So I wanted definitely to bring that issue up because I don't want other students to accept her comment and then learn something wrong. (Woman of color, race-ethnicity dialogue)

Although this woman of color was speaking to correct a member of her own group, she was also cognizant of getting the information across to other people in the group.

Speaking Engagement Summary

Although students described moments of speaking engagement less frequently than either listening or active thinking engagement, almost three-quarters of all interviews included at least one example of speaking engagement. Similar to listening engagement, speaking engagement is associated with specific curricular activities of dialogue. However, the patterns of frequency are different. Speaking engagement was more often associated with curricular contexts where speaking occurred more "in the moment" (as happens in hot topics) as opposed to in planned speaking opportunities (testimonials), suggesting that the instances when a student speaks in immediate response to something that occurs in dialogue are particularly memorable to them.

The motivations for students to speak are also identified. Students describe seven distinct motivations, the most common being to share their experiences or perspectives, to challenge something that has been said, and to educate others. These varied motivations provide insight into the complex process of fostering speaking engagement in dialogue.

ACTIVE THINKING ENGAGEMENT

The examples provided in our discussions about listening and speaking engagement demonstrate that both listening and speaking often stimulate active thinking engagement. The student quotes suggest active thinking when they said, "something I don't normally think about," "like to digest . . . put on a bigger scale of what it meant," "I never thought," "it came as a complete shock for me. . . . I was completely wrong there," "I can't believe we kind of had that parallel story," and "kind of a shock." These phrases suggest that as participants heard and responded to new information provided through others' stories, course content, and activities, they were led to reflect on what they knew and how they understood themselves and the larger world.

Active thinking engagement occurred when participants were engaged in cognitive processing and meaning-making through dialogue. It involved both analysis and self-reflection. The experiential and relational nature of intergroup dialogue and the focus on listening and speaking are intended to help students integrate their experiences in class and outside class in a way that leads to insights and furthers their cognitive development (Evans, Forney, and Guido-DiBrito 1998; King and Shuford 1996; Love and Guthrie 1999). We defined active thinking engagement as those instances in the interviews when students demonstrate that they are actively sorting out information or when they report coming to new realizations as a result of their participation in the dialogue.

Active thinking engagement is a core learning goal for IGD, and listening and speaking engagement are important stimuli for facilitating or triggering it. This excerpt from an interview with a woman of color who participated in a gender dialogue illustrates both what we mean by active thinking and the relationship among listening, speaking, and active thinking engagement. Here she describes an instance when the personal story of one of the male participants had an impact on her.

As soon as we [the women] came in, this guy was telling a story [of] how he was at work . . . I mean he just seemed like a really nice guy at the time. He started talking about how his boss was telling [him] to do all this stuff. Well, it's work and that's what bosses do, they tell you to do stuff. But this particular boss happened to be a woman and he was just really offended. He felt like she was nagging him. He felt like . . . she's always telling him what to do and he was really sad that this woman was telling him what to do. And I was like, oh my gosh, I've never actually heard anyone say that to me before, or in front of me. He wasn't saying it to me obviously, but about a woman . . . I've never actually heard it.

It was a little shocking and I kind of realized it's hard for people to overcome these stereotypes and gender inequalities. And this guy in the end said [he was] really trying to fight that. The last day he told us that he's really trying. . . . And that really impacted me. The fact that after we talked . . . he thought about it and [that] something I said to him impacted him. I just didn't even think that was possible. (Woman of color, gender dialogue)

Her description of this incident and its follow-up illustrates how listening, speaking, and active thinking engagement are intertwined. In fact, this excerpt was coded for listening engagement (she heard a male participant in a gender dialogue speak disparagingly about his female boss) and for active thinking (she had a new realization about stereotypes and gender inequalities). Note how she also referred to having spoken with him about his comments and how he later told her that what she had said to him had an impact on him. In the exchange with him, she realized something about herself that she hadn't thought was possible—that her words had the power to move someone else. This woman's story illustrates how listening and speaking can work in concert to trigger active thinking in the forms of analysis, awareness, and understanding.

The analyses of the 248 interviews demonstrated that virtually all students described multiple instances of active thinking engagement (see table 7.1). The analysis also indicated that these instances of active thinking engagement were fairly evenly divided between instances of critical reflection (when they used social justice language such as power, privilege, discrimination, oppression, stereotypes, and supremacy to indicate an awareness of self or societal components or structures of inequality) and general active thinking (when they mentioned instances of analysis, reflection, or awareness but did not refer explicitly to social justice issues or language).

In the closer analysis of the forty interviews, we focused on developing a more detailed understanding of what active thinking looks like in dialogue, identifying the types of active thinking engagement that students most often described. This deeper understanding of the characteristics of active thinking engagement is important because it offers insights into the extent to which students' cognitive development reflects the goals of IGD. That is, do the types of understanding students developed reflect the central content and relational learning objectives for IGD?

Our analysis of the subthemes and patterns associated with active thinking engagement led us to a further clarification of the active thinking construct as it is demonstrated in these interviews. Cognitive development (or active thinking development) is both a process (as one sorts information, grapples with understanding, works to develop meaning) and an outcome (when one comes to a new awareness, a deeper analysis of a problem, a synthesized perspective on a social issue). In our analysis, we found evidence of a similar distinction: *active processing* (when students demonstrated the process of working to make meaning of what they were hearing and experiencing in dialogue) and *active insights* (when students described an outcome of that process). What follows is a description of active processing and, after it, a description of the six types of active insights that serve as outcomes of that process.

Active Processing

Active processing refers to the complex cognitive processes through which students ultimately create meaning from new information and experiences. It was coded when participants were clearly demonstrating active thinking, but were still trying to sort out or to make sense of information or their feelings related to something that took place in the dialogue (for example, what other people were saying, group dynamics, a topic, a feeling, and so on). In active processing, participants were attempting to form an insight or a clear under-standing, but had not yet been able to do so. These responses were often messy or unclear and often included conflicting pieces of information or ideas.

In this example, a white woman who identified as Jewish discussed what it was like to be a Jewish person in the race-ethnicity dialogue.

> I don't know. It was [pause] like I said before, I just kept feeling like I was torn in between two groups and a lot of times they kind of told us to separate: the white people go here and talk to themselves and then the people of color go here. A lot of times I would always go to the white group just because I mean, I'm not a person of color. But at the same time I felt like I didn't really belong there, and a lot of times the conversation that went on was something that I didn't agree with. So it was just hard, and obviously I knew that there would be so many other topics that I wouldn't have anything to say if I was in the people of color group. So it was just kind of confusing for me. Like I kept having to figure out what I was. (White woman, race-ethnicity dialogue)

The dialogues often exposed students to completely different world views and experiences that they sometimes found surprising, disrupting, and even shocking. This statement is characteristic of many of the instances of active processing because it shows the woman juxtaposing various positions, obser-vations, and experiences as she was struggling to make sense of the internal contradictions these varying positions created. Also, as is true in this case, there was often a rambling sense to the active processing examples, reflecting students' confusion and disequilibrium as they worked to take in new information and new realities and make sense of them. The students' emotions were also often evident.

More than one-third of the interviews had at least one example of active processing, which is lower than the proportion of interviews that provide an example of active insights. The lower frequency of examples of students' active processing may be the result of a unique feature of dialogues. At the end of each class session, facilitators invited students to reflect, sometimes privately in five-minute reflection papers or in dyads and sometimes collectively, about what they had learned in that session, what dynamics had been evident during the dialogue, and what they would need to do in the next dialogue to maximize learning for everyone. These opportunities for reflection promoted the type of active insights reported in the interviews. It is also possible that because the interviews were conducted at the end of the semester, the participants were likely to have worked through their dialogue experiences and achieved insights into them and reported those insights rather than the process of achieving them.

Active Insights

Active insights were coded when participants actually landed somewhere, that is, they reported understanding something on a deeper level than they had previously or coming to a conclusion or a realization. In a number of cases, these kinds of insights were the outcomes of active processing. Intergroup dialogues are designed to create a wide range of opportunities for active insights. These insights ranged in level of cognitive sophistication from acquiring new knowledge to an enhanced awareness of the role of structural and systemic factors in creating societal inequalities. Six forms of active insights are described here, from most to least frequently present in the students' interviews. Overall, however, the insights described here were prevalent throughout the interviews; with the exception of one type of active insight, two-thirds or more of these interviews provided at least one example of each type.

The most common cluster of insights reflected participants' increased awareness or understanding of themselves. Self-awareness insights consist of the ways in which the participants' experiences in IGD affected their understanding of themselves and their development. Participants described three main types of self-awareness insights in the interviews: awareness of their biases and assumptions, awareness of the development of their identities and sense of self, and awareness of the impact that power and privilege had on them.

For example, one participant described how he developed insights into his identity.

I was actually able to really look inside myself personally, really get a sense of who I am. We had this exercise that was the wheel, where you had the personal wheel and then you had the social wheel; you had to differentiate them both in how you perceive yourself and how society perceives you. And, you know, I figured that would take me a quick ten minutes but that exercise actually took me an hour, because I had to really reflect on who I'm surrounded by but at the same time who I identify myself with and who do I really see myself as being. So it was really a question of boiling it down to what my identity is. So I realized I really had to come forward and say, "Hey I'm a black man in this male dominated society." So it really opened me up and I was willing to give out a lot of feelings and emotions that I had inside to the class, which was really cool. (Man of color, gender dialogue)

This student goes on later in the interview to say more about realizing his privilege as a man in a male-dominated society, something he had not realized or acknowledged before. As this example illustrates, IGD provides a powerful opportunity for participants to reassess and reevaluate themselves and their place in the world.

Second, insights into the students' social identity groups also occurred frequently in the interviews. These types of insights had two broad themes: insights about differences in experiences and perspectives that existed within their own identity groups, and insights about commonalities within their own groups—especially feeling more connected to and having more in common with others in their own groups than they had previously felt.

This participant described how the dialogue experience affected her sense of commonality with other women.

I never . . . thought of myself as a female, just about my own identity. And then a lot of times just because I tend not to fall into normal female stereotypes, I always feel like I can't relate to other females as easily. But being in this dialogue group and really talking about gender issues, I realized how much more I relate to other females and certain issues. When we talked about it, you would see it would be like the males felt one way and the females felt another way, and having that sort of camaraderie is something I never felt before the dialogue. (Woman of color, gender dialogue)

Third, because the dialogues provided many new opportunities to learn about the experiences and perspectives of students in other groups, participants often described insights they had gained. These included realizing the complexity within the other group, the differences between the two groups, and what the two groups had in common.

In this example, this woman of color was surprised by the effort a white woman had made not to appear racist, which provided insights into the variety of perspectives among whites.

And here the [facilitators] told us to write on index cards what we wished we could talk about or what something, like a fear we have or a problem we have. One of the white students wrote that she feels like she overcompensates. And so I never thought that white people actually tried to even compensate a little bit, you know I just thought since they are the privileged group, if they don't accept they have privilege, they just live their daily lives and just try to empower themselves more and more each day. But when she spoke, she talked about how she's a cash register, works at a cash register, and when she gives change to black people, she always tries to make sure that she touches their hands to prove, to show that she's not afraid to touch their hands. And so just thinking about [that] wow, you know she's going through all this trouble just to not come across as a racist, like it means that much to her to not be a racist you know. And so I found that to be really interesting. (Woman of color, race-ethnicity dialogue)

A fourth type concerned insights into dialogue group dynamics. Participants demonstrated the capacity to identify, describe, and analyze group dynamics, which at times led to an analysis of broader intergroup dynamics issues. In the following example, the participant described an incident where a woman was upset by something that had happened in the dialogue.

So another instance is a young lady . . . informed the class that she felt attacked because she felt that someone had cut her off when she was speaking and I remember the other person being of the opposite color. . . . and so it made, it gave an emotional air to the class. (Man of color, race-ethnicity dialogue)

This participant demonstrated an awareness of the role another participant played within the group and how her behavior affected the group climate. He included in his analysis of the group dynamics an awareness of how social identities can contribute to or affect those group dynamics.

Fifth, course content insights included participant comments that focused on having learned something new and having achieved a better understanding of key concepts such as power, privilege, inequality, identity, commonalities, and differences through readings and in-class exercises. In the example that follows, the participant described the impact that the dialogue's focus on power, privilege, and oppression had on her.

> I guess it affected my thinking in the way that it just made me more aware and made me more open to, just increased my awareness and my knowledge about all the different power, privileges, and oppression. Just reading the web of oppression, a lot of cards on it, and just talking about male dominance in society on more than one occasion . . . it made me more aware of it. It just kind of made me realize there is a lot of oppression going on. There is definitely a male privilege that is continuing to grow. . . . As you think about oppression, you think about slavery and you think, "Well we're not there right now, but just thinking about how we still have such a long way to go in terms of bringing equality amongst all humans." (White woman, gender dialogue)

Here, the student acknowledges new facts and a deeper awareness of the information related to dialogues topics. Although this type of insight is less complex or sophisticated than other forms, it does represent an understanding and acceptance of new information or perspectives.

Sixth, about half of the participants in the forty interviews analyzed demonstrated at least one example of critical analysis insights. Critical analysis insights refer to instances in which participants demonstrated complex analytical approaches to inequality, going beyond individual-level analyses to sociocultural, systemic, or other multilayered analyses. These critical analysis insights represent the deeper and more complex cognitive outcomes that IGD pedagogy is specifically designed to achieve.

In this example of critical analysis insights, a woman of color in a race-ethnicity dialogue demonstrated complexity in how she thought about race.

We shouldn't focus on thinking of people in race in simple ways because Puerto Rican is what I am, not who I am. And that was something a speaker once told me and I don't think people should try to make their identity who they are, like it's a part of who you are but not the whole person that you are. And if we just think that this race or this ethnicity is who we are, then we're like forgetting the rest of ourselves, you know because . . . if people get so consumed like they, what's that word, I'm trying to remember, they internalize different types of stereotypes and they're like, "Ok since I'm black, I have to listen to hip hop, since I'm Hispanic, I need a [inaudible]" and it shouldn't be that way. It should be if you are black and you don't like hip hop, you have the right to not like hip hop. I know people, like in high school, if you were a black student and you didn't like hip hop, they'd be, "Oh, he's like an Oreo, black on the outside and white on the inside" or something like that. And you know, we shouldn't be thinking that way because everyone is an individual, you know they're not, race shouldn't make who they are. (Woman of color, race-ethnicity dialogue)

This participant juxtaposed the impact of societal influences (specifically stereotypes) with how people judge each other and the expectations everyone has for themselves. She acknowledged the powerful role of systemic stereotypes and systemic privilege, yet also noted the importance of one's individuality. Her reference to internalized stereotypes indicated her ability to use IGD content and apply it to her understanding of the complexities of social forces and its effect on identities and interactions with each other. She acknowledged the need for a nuanced approach that accounts for both individual differences and societal influences. This capacity to go back and forth across multiple levels of analysis is characteristic of many examples of critical analysis insight.

In another example, a participant demonstrated that he was able to apply what he had learned about gender inequalities to the field of finance as he responded to a question about how power and privilege had affected his life.

It started getting me thinking about it in my field that I'm going into. I go to these presentations, right? Every time it's pretty standard that there's a female who might have been an entry level analyst or something but then they move her into human resources. It's always a female that gives a presentation welcoming everybody. Every human resources person is a female. There are females that are in finance but it's a very male-dominated industry. As I was going through this class, I started noticing in business that it was always a woman that would come out and introduce the company to all the people at the presentations. . . . . I don't know if that's a negative. I think the companies are moving toward a less oppressive gendered environment than in the past so I don't know if they are just trying to find roles for females. They are still not giving them the primary roles all the time. The job that I'm going to have is I'm working with three other guys in a small group in finance. It's a weird environment. Finance is a very . . . I went through a lot of interviews. I'd say one-tenth of the people who interviewed me for finance jobs were female. [The male domination in finance has] a lot of historical oppression associated with it, dating back to a long, long time. (White man, gender dialogue)

This individual took the concepts of systemic discrimination and privilege discussed in the dialogue and applied them to the world of finance to which he was headed. He also saw how his own privilege affects others and was able to connect theoretical systemic constructs to his life, developing an emerging critique of his profession and society more broadly.

Active Thinking Summary

Active thinking engagement is a vital component of dialogue that is facilitated by, and helps facilitate, listening and speaking engagement. It is difficult to assess the cognitive processing involved in active thinking or the individual insights achieved through active thinking with quantitative methods. Our use of qualitative methods enabled us to examine both processing and insights in some detail. The active thinking results described here illustrate how participants in IGD were stimulated to engage in an array of different types of active thinking.

Active thinking involved two phases: active processing and active insights. We found that students often struggled to process what was happening and what they were learning in the dialogues and this struggle sometimes led directly to important insights on the nature of relations between social identity groups. These active insights fell into six categories that directly reflect core constructs emphasized in the IGD curriculum: insights about self, within group, across group, core content, group dynamics, and structural or multi-level insights.

CONCLUSION

In the research described in this chapter, a qualitative approach was employed to delve deeper into both how, when, and why students in intergroup dialogue listened and spoke, and the types of active thinking the dialogues fostered. Our qualitative analyses provided compelling evidence of the dynamic nature of the dialogue learning environment and the high level of engagement in dialogue the participants experienced. In the vast majority of the interviews, participants gave evidence of having been engaged through listening, speaking, and active thinking. In addition, our analyses revealed that the levels of listening, speaking, and active insights were nearly equal for participants in race and gender dialogues and for participants from various racial-ethnic and gender backgrounds. Thus, IGD was successful in encouraging students from all four social identity groups to become actively engaged in the dialogues.

These three types of engagement are connected to the communication and psychological processes measured in the quantitative analyses used to examine the theoretical framework guiding the study. Listening is part of the communication process of appreciating difference, which includes hearing others' personal stories, asking questions, and learning from others. Speaking is related to the process of engaging self, that is, sharing views and speaking without feeling judged. Active processing is part of cognitive involvement and thinking more complexly about people's behaviors and societal influences on behaviors. Active insights parallel dimensions of critical reflection—which includes examining biases, understanding how power and privilege affect individual and social life, and reconsidering opinions in relation to others' experiences in dialogue—as well as identity engagement—understanding social identities.

Despite differences in the frequencies across listening and speaking engagement, some of the factors that promote listening and speaking were strikingly similar. Many of the curricular activities that encouraged sharing of perspectives and experiences and opportunities to hear others' perspectives and experiences stimulated both listening and speaking. Peer behavior mattered too, particularly speaker behaviors or statements that compelled deeper listening or a spoken response. Finally, the content of the dialogues played an important role. Certain topics, personal stories, and assertions stimulated active listening as well as participants' desire to "jump in" and educate, share, or challenge. The associations of listening and speaking engagement with features of the curriculum—specific activities, speaker characteristics, topics of conversation—and the range of motivations associated with students taking the initiative to speak provide compelling evidence of the role that the pedagogical approach in the dialogues played in prompting the students to listen and speak.

Active thinking is a specific type of focused cognitive processing that occurs in IGD. Participants were able to describe many instances when they were engaged this way. The information participants focused on and the types of experiences they processed were quite varied. Incidents of active thinking were shaped by what the participants were learning in the dialogues, as well as by the perspectives and knowledge the participants brought with them into the IGD experience. The active insights the students displayed in the interviews indicate that the dialogues helped students think deeply about the complex issues associated with race-ethnicity and gender.

Our examination of the qualitative data not only helps us understand the importance and nature of engagement in IGDs, but also offers additional support for the theories and findings described in earlier chapters of this book. The data contributes to our understanding of how students enact the communication and psychological processes described in chapter 3.

Another valuable contribution from these qualitative analyses of the interview data concerns the nature of active thinking. Two important cognitive processes were involved. One was active processing, in which students appeared to have been trying to figure out information or meaning. The other was active insights, in which students reported that they had learned something new or understood something on a deeper level than they had before. We learned that students talked about gaining insights into themselves (their biases and assumptions, how they were developing over time, and how power and privilege affected them personally), and insights into their identity group and the other (both how they were similar and how they differed). This finding strongly supports a major premise of IGD, that being involved in understanding one's identity actually promotes, rather than threatens, a capacity to be involved in understanding other identity groups. In addition, the students also reported gaining insights into group dynamics and the structural dynamics of their society. The kinds of insights they achieved richly depict how both critical reflection and cognitive involvement are developed.

Our findings also contribute to the literature in higher education, social psychology, and intergroup dialogue-communication on the multiple meanings of engagement (Werkmeister Rozas, Zúñiga, and Stassen 2008). This literature approaches the concept of engagement using a variety of lenses and describes a range of individual and interrelational characteristics as key aspects of student engagement. Our analyses demonstrate the important role that speaking, listening, and active thinking play in student engagement. Researchers on this project who previously had been IGD facilitators were particularly impressed by the importance of listening and active thinking, which are not as obvious as speaking engagement in the classroom setting. Given the important role of listening and active thinking, the curriculum of IGDs and the training of facilitators both need to address specific ways that these less visible types of engagement can be encouraged.

Finally, the key role that the participants played in enhancing their own and each other's engagement in learning should be noted. Throughout our analyses, it was apparent that other students' stories and actions had a profound impact on the participants' willingness to listen and speak, as well as to think actively about the dialogue. The participants also realized that the participation of all of the students in the class, including their own, mattered. John Tagg eloquently describes the characteristics of an engaged learner.

> [A learner who] is seeking to connect new knowledge and his or her existing body of ideas is approaching learning at a different level than the learner who is simply picking up bits of information for a test. In a deep approach to learning, the learner is the agent, an agent in motion, moving through, using, and shaping the object of learning. (2003, 70)

The findings presented in this chapter illustrate what engaged learning looks like in practice. Students, through their narratives, demonstrated that they were agents in motion, facilitating and shaping their own and each other's development and learning.

Next, we turn in chapter 8 to observations of both students and facilitators that provide further understanding of how they engaged in the dialogue.

Authored by Martha Stassen, Ximena Zúñiga, Molly Keehn, Jane Mildred, Keri DeJong, and Rani Varghese.

CHAPTER 8

Observations of Students and Facilitators: A Lens into the Practice Model of Intergroup Dialogue

Chapter 7 analyzed data from interviews of students about their intergroup dialogue (IGD) experiences and revealed ways in which students recalled their engagement in IGDs—listening, speaking, and active thinking. In this chapter, we complement the interview data with videotape data of student and facilitator participation in three sessions of ten race-ethnicity dialogues and ten gender dialogues.

The material in this chapter extends the analyses and findings from chapter 7 in two important ways made possible by videotaping the dialogues. One, we explicate what students were saying when they spoke in dialogue. We learned a great deal in chapter 7 about what encouraged students to listen and speak. From the videotapes it was also possible to code for the extent to which their speaking engagement represented dialogic rather than nondialogic communication. Their communications involved openness, represented by sharing stories with each other; they also involved inquiry, represented by asking each other questions and probing ideas of others in order to find mutual understanding. These are dialogic behaviors that, according to the practice model, should occur in intergroup dialogue. However, the videotapes also revealed that the students displayed two nondialogic behaviors. They debated with each other and advanced and defended their perspectives, much as students do in traditional discussion classes. Thus this chapter adds to chapter 7's depiction of speaking engagement, and most importantly demonstrates the particular features of dialogue pedagogy that fostered dialogic and nondialogic student behaviors. Two, this chapter provides a picture of how facilitators participated in IGDs. One of the limitations of the interview protocol was that it did not ask questions about the facilitators, and thus facilitation was not one of the foci in chapter 7. Because both student and facilitator behaviors were observed and coded from the videotapes, we were able to see how facilitator behaviors related to student behaviors. In this chapter, we show that facilitators, as well as specific features of the curriculum, were influential in students speaking in dialogic rather than nondialogic ways. These two chapters thus complement each other; they together provide a lens into the practice model of IGD through the students' interview accounts of speaking, listening, and active thinking and through their behaviors as observed in the videotaped sessions.

VIDEOTAPING: OBSERVING BEHAVIORS IN INTERGROUP DIALOGUE

Two primary research questions guided our coding and analysis of the videotapes. What did the behavioral data reveal about interactions within intergroup dialogues? Did the observed behaviors support what the practice model (described in chapter 2) posits should happen in IGDs? Specifically, we wanted to know whether the behaviors observed and coded from the videotapes support the distinctions we have drawn throughout this volume between dialogue, debate, and discussion, and whether they reflect the four communication processes that, according to our theoretical framework, IGD pedagogy should produce.

Overview

Videotaping was conducted in the twenty IGDs (ten race-ethnicity and ten gender courses) that comprised the intensive substudy of the multi-university study. Each university carried out the videotaping for one race-ethnicity course and one gender course, with the exception of the University of Michigan, which was able to videotape two of each of the courses because it had a larger IGD program and greater research capacity. At each institution, the same curricular sessions were videotaped on the same three occasions over the span of an academic term. These three sessions were chosen for videotaping because the pedagogy involved in these sessions—content, structured activities, and facilitation—addressed the main curricular goals of stages 2 (exploring differences and commonalities of experience) and 3 (exploring and dialoguing about hot topics). They were also selected because they took place across the academic term, the first session fairly early, the second in the middle, and the third nearer the end of the term. These sessions cannot be used to represent group development across the term, however, because the goals and activities differed in each.

The first videotaping was carried out during the session that focused on learning about social identities. The goal was to help students recognize and analyze their lives through the lenses of race, gender, and other social identities. To remind the reader, the social identity activity (described in chapter 2) began by asking the students to fill out a template asking which social identities (race, ethnicity, gender, class, age, sexual orientation, national origin, religion, ability, and others) were most and least influential in their lives, which they thought about the most and least, which gave them societal privileges, and which they would like to learn about more. The students then shared their responses to the social identity template with each other to explore similarities and differences in their various social identities. This activity and the readings assigned for this session together helped them understand the concept of social identity and build relationships with each other.

The second videotaping took place during the session in which students returned to the whole dialogue group after having been separated during the previous session in caucus-affinity groups. To remind the reader, caucus-affinity groups brought together all students of color and, separately, all white students in a race dialogue; it also brought together all women and separately all men in a gender dialogue to explore concerns and issues that might not have been aired in the intergroup sessions. In the videotaped session, the students had come back together to participate in an activity (described in chapter 2) called fishbowls, that built on their learning from the previous caucus-affinity group session. In the fishbowl activity, each identity group sequentially shared what had happened in their caucus group dialogue, what they had learned, and what they felt was important for the other group to know. As one group was sharing, the responsibility of members of the other group, seated outside the fishbowl, was to listen and then reflect on what they had heard. Then the exercise was repeated, switching the group in the fishbowl and the group on the perimeter. After both groups had a chance to listen and speak, open dialogue was facilitated in which participants compared and contrasted their experiences, asked each other questions, and connected their observations to examples on campus or the larger society. The goal of this exercise is for students to understand that social identities are embedded in structures of power and privilege, and to recognize and analyze how the different identity experiences of the two groups in the dialogue are related to each group's position in the societal social structure.

The third videotaped session occurred during stage 3, in which students engaged in an activity described (in chapter 2) as hot topics. During this activity, students had a dialogue about social issues of particular importance in racial-ethnic or gender relations. Facilitators worked to surface divergent perspectives among students so as to foster deeper understanding of their underlying assumptions and to work through differences and disagreements. The content in the session highlighted an institutional influence on gender (or race-ethnicity) disparities. For example, the gender session explored how the media projects gender and gender relationships in ways that objectify one or another gender and that reinforce gender stereotypes. The race-ethnicity session explored how systematic differences in school quality attended by students of different racial-ethnic backgrounds contribute to racial-ethnic disparities in educational attainments, income, and wealth. Facilitators had asked students to bring examples from their daily visual environments—images and words—that address this particular topic. In the session, students participated in an exercise called the gallery walk (described in chapter 2) in which they posted the visual items on a wall to simulate a gallery. In this activity, students and facilitators walked around the room in silence, looking at the various images and words, and individually reflecting on what the images and words conveyed, what they meant to them, and what emotions the images and words evoked. Later, students shared their initial reactions to the gallery experience in the larger group. Facilitators encouraged participants to examine how and why they were thinking and feeling similarly and differently about this experience. They asked students to think about how the images influenced their everyday thoughts, feelings, and behaviors. They also asked students to think critically about the influence of media, culture, and other institutional practices in creating images that reinforce stereotypes and inequalities.

Procedures

Each dialogue had one videographer, one sound technician, and the Multi-University Intergroup Dialogue Research (MIGR) collaborator who served as the video supervisor. Although it would have been desirable to use two videographers, the budget for the project did not permit it. The two facilitators for the dialogue course also played important roles in each videotaping session. Each of these individuals was provided with verbal guidance and written instructions on how to carry out their roles well in advance of the first, and again at the time of each session.

During each session, the MIGR collaborators at each institution helped the videographer and sound technician set up before the start of class, and reiterated the written instructions they had received when contracted for the videotaping. These instructions involved setting up the video equipment on the outside of a horseshoe shaped semicircle, and to videotape, record sound, and monitor their equipment as noninvasively as possible. The videographer was instructed to use a tripod to swivel the video camera to focus on whoever was speaking as well as on the two to three individuals sitting to either side of the speaker. The videographer was asked to follow these instructions regardless of whether the speaker was a student or a facilitator.

The two dialogue facilitators filled out a seating chart, noting each participant's and facilitator's name, and one or two unique items of clothing that each person was wearing (for example, "a white tank top and navy blue baseball cap"). These forms were made into digital seating charts that listed only the participant's study ID, gender, and clothing descriptions. The videocoders relied on these seating charts to code individual student and the facilitator behaviors. Each coding decision was recorded in a dataset noting video session, the activity underway when a behavior was coded, and the minute within the activity being coded, along with the participant's and the facilitator's study ID, seating position, gender, and unique clothing descriptions.

Coding

Approximately thirty minutes were coded from each full two- to three-hour dialogue session. It was unrealistic both financially and operationally to code the tapes of each entire hour session. The coding focused on three of the standard sets of activities that took place within each dialogue class session (for the session guide, see chapter 2). Coding began when each of these activities began and continued for approximately ten minutes. The three activities were as follows:

Activity 1. The main class activity itself (for example, the social identity wheel, the fishbowl, and the gallery walk activities in sessions 1, 2, and 3)

Activity 2. Collective reflection and dialogue on learning specifically from the activity

Activity 3. Collective reflection on dialogue (learning from the entire dialogue session, what is called dialogue about the dialogue)

Coding was done in one-minute periods, a decision informed by the kinds of data that could be collected from the videos and would contribute insights into the practice model of IGD.

To ensure diverse perspectives in the coding process, coders were selected from diverse backgrounds, including men and women, students from varied racial-ethnic backgrounds, and both undergraduate and graduate students. Separate coding teams coded each video for one of the scales. Thus, two coders independently coded all the minutes in a video for attentiveness of listening; another two coders independently coded the same minutes for speaking initiative, openness, and inquiry; another two coded advancing a perspective; and still another two coded debating behaviors. Once a coder-in-training was able to achieve independent agreement levels of above 75 percent with more experienced coders both on random coding assignments, and on a coding assignment given to all coders (to assess levels of agreement between every possible coding pair), they were permitted to begin formal coding.

Analyses of intercoder reliability conducted after the completion of the study indicate that average agreement across all videos varied by coding pair and by scale. The average agreement between coding pairs for moderate to high attentiveness was 80 percent. The average agreement for speaking initiative, inquiry, openness, advancing a perspective, and debate (all levels) was 78 percent.

The behaviors of both students and facilitators were coded. Each student and facilitator either met or failed to meet the following two criteria for being coded within each minute of observation: whether he or she spoke or did not speak, whether he or she was in the picture. To remind the reader, the videographer focused on a speaker and on the two to three individuals nearby. Proximity to the focal speaker during that minute determined whether a non-speaker was in the picture and thus was coded. These procedures mean that for each minute each person was marked as codable—by speaking or by simply being in the picture in a given minute—or not codable for each videocoding scale. When students were deemed to be codable within a given minute, those who were not speaking were coded for attentiveness of listening to others, and those who were speaking were coded for five scales: speaking initiative, openness, inquiry, advancing a perspective, and debate. Thus, this chapter primarily provides information about speaking engagement. Turning to the facilitators, if one or both were codable for a given minute, the facilitator pair was coded for four behaviors: listening and support, reflection and redirection, inquiry, and advocacy. Presentation in this chapter of the facilitator behaviors represents an average of the pair on these four behaviors.

Videotaping Analytic Methods

Turning to selection of methods of analysis, standard linear regression models assume that each observation is independent. To avoid violating the assumption of independence, all of the ratings for a scale measured across the three video sessions for an individual are aggregated into a single mean, for example, one mean for the attentiveness score. This method is useful for making large-scale comparisons, such as between the mean levels of attentiveness during either the three sessions or the three activities. We report aggregated frequency percentages, which represent the proportion of one-minute coding intervals during which an individual was found to engage in a particular level of nonverbal behavior, such as student attentiveness, or a distinct verbal behavior, such as student initiative in speaking, debating, advancing a perspective, openness, or inquiry. In addition to aggregated frequencies, we also report linear mixed effects, which provide a few advantages over aggregated frequencies.[1]

STUDENT BEHAVIORS IN INTERGROUP DIALOGUE

Developing the student behavior scales to be applied to each minute of observation was done over a year and a half. The research team, led by Elizabeth Meier and composed of undergraduate and graduate students at the University of Michigan, conducted literature reviews, and sequentially developed, applied, and fine-tuned pilot scales. When enough reliability had been achieved and it was felt that the observations of the videotapes had been fairly exhaustively captured, scale development was concluded.

Behavior Scales

Six scales, one coded from observations of nonverbal behaviors and five coded based solely on verbal behaviors, provide a picture of student interaction in IGDs. We turn first to the scale, which was based on nonverbal behaviors.

ATTENTIVENESS IN LISTENING The student attentiveness scale was based on nonverbal behaviors students displayed when the camera focused on a person near them who was speaking. This measure thus concerns how attentively these students sitting near the speaking student appeared to listen to the speaking student. A student's behavior was coded as low attentiveness if she or he were texting, doodling, talking with another student, passing a note to another student, or was sleeping or was slumped in a chair, perhaps with hat drawn over his or her face. Low attentiveness may be thought of as being disengaged with what was happening in the dialogue. Moderate to high attentiveness was coded when the student leaned forward, turned toward the speaker, or showed facial gestures such as smiling, indicating that she or he was listening (and also did not display any of the disengaged behaviors).

To qualify to be coded for one or more of the other five scales, the individual had to speak. This means that these measures concern how frequently across the videotapes each student spoke showing low or high initiative and how often he or she demonstrated openness, inquiry, advancing a perspective, and debate when she or he was the focus of the video camera.

INITIATIVE IN SPEAKING Low initiative was indicated when a student merely responded to another student. Usually such responses were delivered with either low or moderate enthusiasm. Moderate to high initiative was indicated when a student spoke to the class as a whole or commented on what another student had said in a way that produced additional dialogue within the group. Such responses were delivered enthusiastically.

OPENNESS IN SHARING The student openness scale measures the extent to which a student engaged in self-reflection and storytelling within a codable minute. When openness was coded, the students were typically telling stories about themselves or other people, and they also usually displayed some kind of reflection about its meaning to them. To be coded as moderate to high openness (which was the level presented in this chapter because of its acceptable intercoder reliability), the students had to show at least one of three criteria: self-reflection about the meaning of the story or perspective; awareness that it had a personal impact; and how she or he came to understand its impact. If the student told a story about someone other than her- or himself, it had to be true (not fictional or hypothetical), and she or he needed to mention how he or she or the individual in the story was personally affected. The openness score was the number of codable minutes that the student displayed moderate to high openness.

INQUIRY The student inquiry scale measures the extent to which students attempted to find or create mutual understanding of how they and others developed their perspectives and identities. Students usually demonstrated inquiry through asking questions, but inquiry was also coded when students probed the meaning of something another student had shared. To qualify for moderate to high inquiry scale, interactions with other participants had to be expressed respectfully and to appear to be focused on clarifying and understanding, rather than opposing, another participant's perspective. The inquiry score was the number of codable minutes that the student displayed moderate to high inquiry.

ADVANCING A PERSPECTIVE Advancing a perspective was coded when the participant spoke supporting or defending his or her position or viewpoint. This could have been done in a detached way, such as when someone is making an abstract argument in support of a perspective, or in a more animated but moderate way. To qualify for this scale, a student could not interrupt or talk over others, or show strong emotion while advocating a position, as this would have qualified her or him for debate. Advancing a perspective is the kind of student behavior that can, and usually does, occur in discussion classes when students, eager to express themselves, support, or defend their perspectives or wait for another student to stop talking to offer their perspectives. Discussion tends to involve a series of individual monologues rather than students collectively probing and developing each other's ideas with a goal of understanding each other. The score for advancing of one's perspective was the number of codable minutes that the student displayed it moderately or highly.

DEBATING The debating scale measures the extent to which a student argued with other dialogue participants, defended his or her perspective in a manner revealing strong emotional attachment to that position and thus tended to polarize an issue instead of seeking clarification and understanding. For example, a participant was coded for debating when she or he interrupted and talked over another participant or argued for only one side of an issue. The score for debating was the number of codable minutes that the student displayed moderate to high.

FREQUENCIES OF STUDENT BEHAVIORS

Looking first at the percentage of codable minutes that students displayed low attentiveness, or moderate to high attentiveness, we learned that attentiveness was widespread. Overall, 99 percent of the codable minutes that students were in the picture (but not speaking) showed moderate to high attentiveness. Low attentiveness (disengagement) was practically nonexistent. Students who spoke were also generally engaged in that three-quarters of the codable speaking minutes involved moderate to high initiative. They were speaking to the class as a whole or commenting on what another student had said in a manner that produced additional dialogue rather than simply responding to another student in a manner that did not lead to further dialogue.

Together, these two measures of level of listening and speaking complement what was learned in chapter 7 in that these behavioral observations also indicate that students were engaged in the dialogue. Practically none of the behaviors indicated disengagement, and a large portion of speaking showed considerable initiative.

The other four scales tell us what the students spoke about and thus extend what was learned in chapter 7 about speaking. Figure 8.1 shows the percentages of codable minutes in which students showed moderate to high levels of openness, inquiry, advancing a perspective, or debate. The figure shows that the most frequent speaking behavior was openness (41 percent), followed by advancing a perspective (32 percent), debate (18 percent), and then inquiry (16 percent). These percentages add to slightly more than one hundred because occasionally more than one was coded at moderate or high levels in a codable minute.

Figure 8.1   Types of Student Communications Observed

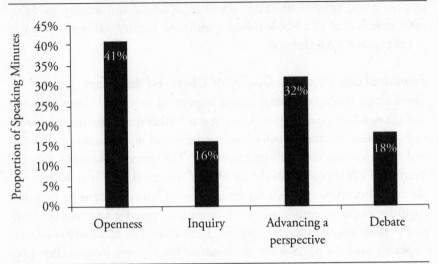

Source: Authors' calculations.

Openness and inquiry, the two behaviors that represent dialogic communication, together constituted 57 percent of all codable speaking minutes. Although that seems to support the practice model of IGD, inquiry was observed less often than desired and expected. The relatively low frequency of inquiry raises an important practice implication that we discuss in chapter 9, where we take up improvements in IGD or its use in other types of classrooms.

Turning to nondialogic behaviors, debate occurred more frequently than ideal in IGD, and advancing a perspective was the second most frequent student behavior. Although advancing a perspective did not rise to the level of debate, it is a behavior more characteristic of discussion in which students serially present or defend their perspectives.

Openness and Inquiry: Distinctive Processes and Behaviors

Openness and inquiry best represent the kinds of communications that IGD tries to promote. These two student behaviors align with the four communication processes that define the essence of intergroup dialogue. Openness is analogous to the communication process of engaging self. When the story or self-reflection included something about power or privilege, openness is also analogous to critical reflection. Inquiry, which included questioning others or trying to find mutual understanding, is analogous to both appreciating difference and alliance building. Together, openness and inquiry made up more than half of all codable minutes, although inquiry was not as frequent as the practice model expects.

Emotional and Empathic Quality of Observed Behaviors

The dialogic quality of openness and inquiry, as well as speaking initiative, and the nondialogic quality of debating was further demonstrated by correlations between the student behavioral measures and the measures of emotions and empathy from the students' interviews. The interview measures were derived from NVivo counts of the number of references a student made across the entire interview to emotions, the emotions of other dialogue participants, cognitive empathy, emotional empathy, critical empathy, and relational empathy (all described fully in chapter 6). These counts for each individual were imported into the SPSS software; bivariate correlations were obtained between the observed behavioral measures from the videotapes and the measures of empathy and emotions from the student interviews.

Table 8.1 shows that speaking initiative, openness, and inquiry were correlated more consistently and positively with emotions and empathy than either advancing a perspective or debate were. All three behaviors were positively related to the number of emotions students expressed in their interviews. Inquiry was also associated with a different measure—the student's awareness of the emotions of other students in the dialogue class—that con-

Table 8.1   Correlations of Videotape Measures of Student Behaviors with Interview Measures

	Initiative	Openness	Inquiry	Advancing a Perspective	Debate
Number of emotions	0.174**	0.167**	0.186*	ns	−0.325**
Awareness of other's emotions	ns	ns	0.218**	ns	ns
Emotional empathy	0.156*	0.156*	ns	ns	ns
Cognitive empathy	0.131**	ns	ns	ns	−0.254**
Relational empathy	0.184**	0.184**	ns	ns	−0.173*
Critical empathy	0.163**	0.163**	0.204**	ns	ns

Source: Authors' calculations.
$*p < .05; **p < .01; ***p < .001$

firms the interactional nature of the inquiry measure. In addition, speaking initiative, openness, and inquiry were positively related to most of the other measures of emotions and empathy. The pattern of correlations seen in table 8.1 involving the videotaping measures of speaking initiative, openness, and inquiry affirms that they are linked to desirable student outcomes, namely emotional and empathic involvement. Three points are worth noting:

Inquiry captures the students' orientation toward others as shown in its distinctive correlation of student behaviors with being aware of the emotions of others.

All three dialogic behaviors appear geared toward an empathic orientation at once emotional and cognizant of difference and power, as shown in their correlations with critical empathy.

Both speaking initiative and storytelling (the measure of openness) reflected what the student contributed, but also involved connection to others in the dialogue, as shown in their correlations with relational empathy.

Turning to the two nondialogic student behaviors, table 8.1 shows that they were either unrelated to most of these emotion and empathy measures, as is the case of advancing a perspective, or negatively related to them, as is the case of debating. Debating behaviors were negatively related to emotions, cognitive empathy, and relational empathy, confirming the nondialogic nature of debate. Although debate is useful in some communication situations, it is not supposed to occur in IGD.

In brief, the correlations between the observed behavior measures and the interview measures of emotions and empathy support the dialogic nature of speaking initiative, openness, and inquiry, and also validate the nondialogic nature of debating.

Impact of Topic, Session, and Activity Type on Behaviors

We have seen that listening and speaking initiative were widespread, that the dialogic behaviors of openness and inquiry were displayed frequently, but so too were the nondialogic behaviors of advancing a perspective and debating. An important question, therefore, is what was happening in the curriculum when these student behaviors were observed on the videotapes.

Table 8.2   Influences on Student Behaviors

	Topic[a]	Session[b]	Activity Type[c]
Speaking initiative	ns	$F = 10.36***$	$F = 9.49***$
Openness	ns	ns	$F = 5.21**$
Inquiry	$F = 3.95*$	$F = 4.40*$	$F = 4.07*$
Advancing a perspective	ns	$F = 12.88***$	$F = 12.10***$
Debate	$F = 5.47**$	ns	ns

Source: Authors' calculations.

[a]Inquiry and debate were both significantly greater in race than in gender dialogues.

[b]Verbal initiative and inquiry were both significantly greater in the fishbowl session than in the social identity and hot topics sessions. Advancing a perspective was significantly greater in the hot topics session than in both of the other two sessions.

[c]Verbal initiative, advancing a perspective, and openness were significantly greater during the activity. Inquiry was significantly greater in both reflection periods (reflection on the activity and reflection on the entire dialogue) than during the activity.

$*p < .05; **p < .01; ***p < .001$

We examined whether students behaved differently in three conditions: dialogue topic (race-ethnicity and gender dialogues), session (identity, fishbowls, and hot topics), and activity type (activity itself, collective reflection on learning from the activity, and collective reflection on the entire dialogue session). The results of these linear mixed model analyses are presented in table 8.2.

Several conclusions can be drawn about the impact of these design features of IGD pedagogy. Dialogue topic was influential. Debating and inquiry were both significantly more frequent in race-ethnicity than in gender dialogues, showing that both dialogic and nondialogic behaviors more frequently characterized the race dialogues. Both seem to relate to the fact that students often lacked knowledge about race, which led them to ask questions and sometimes to argue based on their beliefs, however accurate or inaccurate.

Session was also important. Session was related to speaking initiative, inquiry, and advancing a perspective. The fishbowl session stood out. Both speaking initiative and inquiry were significantly greater during the fishbowl session (session 2) than in either of the other two topics (social identity and hot topics). Not surprisingly in light of the controversial nature of the hot topics session, advancing one's own perspective occurred more frequently in that session than in either the identity or fishbowl sessions. However, because debating was not significantly more frequent during the hot topics session, and because advancing a perspective did not rise to the level of debate, it appears that the students were able to discuss controversial issues without reverting to debate mode even though they did not display as much listening and learning in the hot topics session as intergroup dialogue attempts to achieve.

Activity type was especially influential. It was related to all student behaviors except debating. Speaking initiative, openness, and advancing a perspective were greater during the activity than during the reflection activities, whereas inquiry was greater during both reflection activities (collective reflection on the activity and on the entire dialogue).

A CLOSER LOOK AT DIALOGIC BEHAVIORS: SPEAKING INITIATIVE, OPENNESS, AND INQUIRY

We turn next to one gender and one race-ethnicity transcript to examine what speaking initiative, openness, and inquiry looked like in actual IGD. The gender transcript is the first videotaped session (social identity); the race-ethnicity the third videotaped session (hot topics). Both were taken from dialogues at the same university. They illustrate how participants behaved when openness, inquiry, and speaking initiative were coded.

Gender Dialogue

The interactions described in the gender dialogue transcript of the social identity session occurred when the facilitators were guiding the participants in collective reflection on the entire dialogue session. The students were reflecting on what they had learned about their identities and those of the other students. The students in this example did not restrict themselves to gender identities but instead pondered other identities as well.

A man of color, using his hands to gesture, responded to something a white woman had just said.

I think what she just said goes with the "Who Am I?" reading. A person usually doesn't identify or think of themselves as dominant. For a rich person to think about themselves as rich, that doesn't happen, but for someone who doesn't have wealth, you sort of have to think about money because you are always striving to get more. That's one thing I liked about "Who Am I?" I mean as a man, I don't think about my gender or about being a woman. I don't have to deal with stereotypes or any predisposed notions, like "women can't do this, women can't do that." But I think about what I'm limited to as someone in a social class situation. I think that is what is important in making these connections about identities. It is what you cannot take for granted in a specific situation that makes you think about identity. (Man of color, gender dialogue)

This student was coded as displaying openness because he revealed something about himself and reflected on its meaning in relationship to other people and to how identities are expressed. He critically examined biases and assumptions, explaining his ignorance, as a man, of what women may go through. Inquiry was also suggested because he seemed to be trying to find common ground with the previous speaker and between gender and social class, even though he was not asking questions of other participants.

The two students sitting next to him, a woman of color and a man of color, demonstrated attentiveness. They turned toward him and paid attention as he was speaking. They nodded in agreement several times.

The facilitator, a man of color, then asked, "So, who decides which identities are more salient for us at different times? Who makes these decisions about our identities? What messages have you received and who did you receive them from?"

A white man sat forward, demonstrating openness through his reflection on his experience.

It's not something we have a lot of control over. It really depends on the environment you find yourself in. For example, when you find yourself a minority person in a group, then you think about that identity a lot. I often find myself the only male in my psychology classes and in that situation I think about my gender identity a lot. (White man, gender dialogue)

The importance of social context in making identity salient continued to be developed. An Asian American woman talked about what she had learned in a sociology class about the role of social context in making identity salient.

Identity changes when a person changes situations because almost everything is socially constructed. The labels we attach to each other probably come from our various cultural experiences and the environments we live in, but we usually aren't even aware of those influences. (Woman of color, gender dialogue)

A white woman, who had been listening attentively and looking directly at her, displayed inquiry in following up on the woman of color's perspective. She asked, "When do we think about ethnicity when we are here at college? Do we ever think about that?" Another white woman commented in a way that extended the dialogue and demonstrated both openness and inquiry:

> When we are immersed in mainstream American culture, we are sometimes surprised because we see that we don't quite fit in. For instance, when I watch the Super Bowl, I am aware of my French nationality. But when I am at home, I never think of myself as French. At work I think about my race because I am one of the few white people. Is that how it is for the rest of you? (White woman, gender dialogue)

Openness and inquiry were evident in these communicative exchanges because the students spoke personally about the meaning of identity, and they raised critical questions about the role of social context. They addressed power and privilege through references to stereotypes and environmental and contextual influences. They built on the comments made by the others. They perceived common ground in how identities across nationality, gender, and race-ethnicity were all contextualized. Two addressed explicit questions to the group. Several participants also displayed attentiveness through nonverbal gestures of listening and looking at other participants. We also note that the facilitator demonstrated two desirable facilitation qualities we discuss in a following section, namely, inquiry and reflection or redirection. He asked a thoughtful question on the origin of assumptions about the identities of both dominant and minority group members. He used the original speaker's openness and inquiry as a springboard for further analysis of identity salience.

Race-Ethnicity Dialogue

The transcript of the race-ethnicity dialogue, which covered a hot topics dialogue focused on affirmative action, occurred as a facilitator guided a transition to the collective reflection period when students dialogued about what they had learned during the entire session. The facilitator used reflection and redirection by referring to a comment a white woman had made earlier about "the tendency for the white men to dominate the dialogue." In doing this, the facilitator guided the dialogue to the final phase of collective reflection.

The facilitator then asked, "How do the rest of you see the racial and gender dynamics in our group?"

A white man immediately responded to the group, demonstrating speaking initiative, sharing, and reflection:

> I find this concern about white men's domination upsetting because it has been brought up in every class. I have been attacked in every class for the amount of time I talk, and this has created a frustrating, chilling effect on my openness and participation. In fact I made only one comment so far today. I *get* my white male privilege and I don't mean to invalidate the concern that [the white woman who had made the comment about white male domination] is expressing but I do think it is exaggerated. There are four white men in this class and that can create an illusion of them dominating discussion. (White man, race-ethnicity dialogue)

An African American man sitting next to the white man nodded and then displayed openness and inquiry in his response.

> I see what you mean, maybe it is exaggerated. But I also feel annoyed that you seem angry about being silenced since feeling silenced and attacked is something I—as a black male—have to deal with in so many of my classes. It is just commonplace for most of us students of color at this university. Do the rest of you experience that? (Man of color, race-ethnicity dialogue)

A Latina sitting across the room from both of these students started to speak, using one of her hands to point to herself and to others. She looked around the room but her eye contact rested on the African American man as she exhibited inquiry and openness.

> I just want to say, honestly, does it really make it right to put white students in the same position that we feel? Does it make it better? And I think this goes along with what we've been talking about today. Does affirmative action make it better when people who have been privileged in the past feel guilty? Does it make it better for white students to feel guilty about talking? I personally love it when white men in this class talk because I grow from hearing their experiences. Their experiences help me grow from my experiences. And this kind of silencing isn't what we should do in this class, even though silencing students of color instead of white students happens in a lot of other classes. If someone

feels silenced in this class, that's not okay. (Woman of color, race-ethnicity dialogue)

The white man and the African American man were coded for openness because they shared experiences of personal import and they attempted to explain why those experiences affected them. The African American man was also coded for inquiry. The Latina was also coded for inquiry because she asked questions of the entire dialogue, and in doing so she tried to find common ground. She also tied the controversy to the broader hot topic the dialogue had dealt with that day. She spoke personally about the impact of the controversy on her without directly countering the African American man. She used inquiry to build common ground and to encourage openness, trust, and mutual understanding between people of color and white men in the dialogue. She was also coded for attentiveness because of nonverbal gestures that she used to include everyone in the dialogue class and also to focus specifically on the African American man.

The dialogue about racial dynamics in the dialogue continued. An African American woman, speaking while looking at both the white and African American men as well as the Latina, said,

Um, I'm actually kind of torn, because I feel like it's a learning experience for white students to be in our shoes. It shouldn't be the only way to deal with the problem, but maybe now you [the white man] can see how we might feel when we don't feel comfortable enough to speak. I don't mean that feeling silenced is okay. And we are not solving the problem of racial silencing by silencing each other in this class. But still, how can you really understand our point of view until you've experienced it firsthand? Maybe having such an experience is a necessary thing. Maybe in a different situation white students will take into consideration the privileges they have. Also [looking directly at and addressing the white man] it isn't possible just from this one example to really understand—to "get it" so to speak, because I feel like that's like a lifelong process. (Woman of color, race-ethnicity dialogue)

The white man responded, displaying openness in reflecting on himself and what he was learning.

I understand that I do talk a lot and that can have an effect on other people. I wasn't saying that I experience the gambit of that. What I hear [the African

American female speaker] saying is that being silenced is a reality for students of color in other classes. Maybe it's a good experience for me to have. You know, I've walked a day in your shoes or something like that. But I did see that problem before. I did understand it even before today. And now I've felt it too, and I guess that does broaden, deepen my knowledge. (White man, race-ethnicity dialogue)

The African American woman continued,

It's okay. I was just going to say that I actually really enjoy the interaction you [pointing to all the white men] have. But sometimes I feel like all of you are only talking to each other. I see that a lot. And that actually does sort of bother me. Like one person will say one thing and you guys will automatically feel the need to answer to each other. And so that is what makes me uncomfortable. I definitely appreciate the things that you all say when you integrate the rest of us in what you contribute to the dialogue. What do the rest of you feel about how inclusive we have become in this class? Are we getting to where we want to go in dialogue? (Woman of color, race-ethnicity dialogue)

The white man was coded as open in this interaction because he was self-reflective about what the interaction had revealed about him, and because he responded to feedback acknowledging that he had learned from the interaction. The African American woman was coded for both openness and inquiry because she tried to build understanding of the different experiences of white students and students of color, and at the same time she challenged the white men to be more inclusive in their communications in the class. It was also important that she broadened the dialogue beyond just the one white man by challenging the whole class about how well everyone was achieving the goals of IGD.

In summary, these examples portray in real time what is supposed to happen in intergroup dialogue when dialogic interactions involve attentiveness, verbal initiative, openness, and inquiry.

FACILITATOR BEHAVIORS

Facilitation refers to the guidance provided in IGD to maximize the potential of content-based learning and structured interactions. Despite its importance in the practice of IGD, research examination of IGD facilitation has been scant. A recent book, *Facilitating Intergroup Dialogues: Building Bridges, Catalyzing Change*, is one of the first dedicated entirely to IGD facilitation (Maxwell, Nagda, and Thompson 2011). Yet, even that book shows little evidence of systematic efforts to observe how facilitators actually behave or to examine how their behaviors influence the behaviors of dialogue participants.

The main principles of facilitation in IGD, delineated by Biren (Ratnesh) Nagda and Kelly Maxwell (2011) and discussed in chapter 2, are worth noting again. First, facilitation is guiding, not didactic teaching. Facilitators are trained to guide learning by helping participants be open to the perspectives of others, share their perspectives, and inquire about the experiences and perspectives of their peers. "Whereas in debates or discussions the facilitator referees or directs the instruction and interactions, IGD facilitators pay keen attention to the conjoint learner-educator roles that every participant plays" (Nagda and Maxwell 2011, 7). To achieve this first goal, facilitators must be able to create an inclusive space for differences to emerge and they need to work effectively as a team of co-facilitators.

The second goal is that facilitators themselves learn through the practice of IGD. They do not come to their task as fully formed educators but rather as learners who recognize that learning is a "cyclical process of action and reflection" (Nagda and Maxwell 2011, 10). To realize this, facilitators use themselves and their experiences purposefully as ways to guide and deepen the dialogue. At the same time, facilitators are not supposed to make the dialogue about themselves. Using the self to promote openness, inquiry, and engagement in students is a skill that has to be learned and continually relearned because it differs significantly from traditional teaching, in which instructors in their course lectures may avoid saying anything about themselves or conversely may say too much about their experiences and points of view. In IGD, a productive use of self by facilitators involves sharing experiences and knowledge to deepen the dialogue and to model and activate engagement by the students.

This leads to the third goal of attending to process, not just procedures. Nagda and Maxwell (2011) stress that "as much as procedures are important in getting participants involved in structured activities, the subsequent debriefing process deepens and expands the learning through reflection, dialogue, and probing inquiry." This debriefing process is what we refer to as collective reflection (and dialogue about the dialogue) that follows the structured learning activity. When facilitators are effective, they sense when to reflect and redirect what is happening in the dialogue, when to listen and support what is happening, when to inquire and ask questions that encourage student reflection, and when to share their perspectives but not by being an advocate. They also need to be attentive to their triggered reactions and to monitor their emotions that can get in the way of staying mindful of group processes.

In this study, we approached facilitation in two ways. In the quantitative survey methods, students rated their facilitators (or instructors if they were part of the social science comparison groups) at the end of their courses on a number of behaviors. In the videotapes of the race-ethnicity and gender dialogues forming the intensive qualitative substudy, it was possible to examine facilitation behaviors through observations. Just as it was important to observe whether students behaved in ways supportive of the distinctive communication processes expected to characterize IGD, it was also important to observe whether facilitators behaved in ways supportive of the main principles of facilitation. In the videos, it was also possible to see whether particular facilitation behaviors were more effective than others because they related to dialogic behaviors among the students. That was not possible using the survey methods because student evaluations of facilitator behaviors were so highly interrelated. Additionally, the survey items measured dialogue-promoting behaviors whereas the video observations included nondialogic behaviors as well.

Facilitator Behavior Styles

Four facilitation styles were coded: reflection and redirection, inquiry, listening and support, and advocacy.

REFLECTION AND REDIRECTION *Reflection and redirection* were coded when the facilitator repeated or rephrased what someone had said, asked a question to clarify what a participant meant, or redirected the flow of conversation to transition to another topic. For example, a facilitator in the race-ethnicity dialogue previously discussed said, "It sounds like you are saying that affirmative action is a form of reverse racism. Am I hearing you correctly?" The participant responded, "Yeah, it's kind of racism against everyone who doesn't happen to be a minority." In another example, the facilitator redirected the dialogue from a debate that was taking place between two students. The facilitator said, "So, we've been talking about layers of identity, which relates to what the author of that paper was talking about, and to our next activity." The facilitator then described the next activity. In this instance, the facilitator effectively dealt with student debate by redirecting the students to focus on layers of identity and move them toward the next activity rather than simply letting the debate continue. In the race-ethnicity dialogue example discussed earlier, the facilitator made a transition to the collective reflection about the entire dialogue by bringing back a comment a white woman had made about what she considered conversational dominance by white men. The facilitator used that comment to encourage the whole group to consider what they had learned about power dynamics in that session.

INQUIRY   *Inquiry* was coded when the facilitator asked questions or probed the ideas of individuals in attempting to guide the dialogue in discerning commonalities and differences in the perspectives put forward and thus to establish common ground and build mutual understanding. For example, a facilitator in the gender dialogue asked, "So, who decides which identities are more salient for use at different times? Who makes those decisions about our identities? What messages did you receive and who did you receive them from?" A facilitator in a race-ethnicity dialogue probed the many reactions that students had about having been separated during the caucus-affinity group activity: "There are many different reactions to this experience. What was hard or easy about being split into the caucus groups? What did you learn that you haven't learned previously in the whole dialogue group?" Another facilitator in a gender group asked why women in the group sometimes insisted that gender discrimination is a thing of the past. The facilitator named the phenomenon and said, "You have agreed that women sometimes do this. Why is that? What is it in the gender experiences of women and men on college campuses that leads them to that conclusion?" Another facilitator named emotions, and described how everyone seemed sad and that everyone had become silent in response to a story told by a woman who had been raped: "We are all very sad not only for [the woman who told the story] but also because rape still happens, including here at [our university]. What is our sadness all about? Does it lead us to do something about rape?"

LISTENING AND SUPPORT   *Listening and support* were coded when the facilitator listened to or provided nonverbal support to the speaker. The facilitator demonstrated that he or she was listening by sitting quietly, looking directly at the speaker, turning to the speaker, or leaning forward toward the speaker. Facilitators showed nonverbal support by smiling, nodding, or gesturing. We see in the results that listening and support proved to be a fairly passive facilitation style, one that was associated with student debating rather than dialoguing.

ADVOCACY *Advocacy* was coded when the facilitator interrupted or talked over participants in support of the facilitator's position, or when the facilitator polarized an issue by presenting just one perspective, or when she or he disagreed with a participant in an adamant, emotional manner, often by presenting a counter argument. Facilitators are not to become advocates of a particular position because advocacy can easily shut down dialogue and silence individuals. An example from the videos showed a facilitator doing exactly that after a woman had explained how her religious values affected her political beliefs. The facilitator interjected, "I think that the conservative perspective is highly hypocritical when it comes to issues of church and state." The woman turned away, seemed hurt, and did not respond. The facilitator could have deepened the dialogue by asking how others thought about the connection between religious and political beliefs instead of offering this polarizing opinion. In another dialogue, after a gay participant said that cross-dressers undermine the gay rights movement's efforts to legalize gay marriage because cross-dressing is so flamboyant, a facilitator interrupted and said, "It is oppressive to dismiss or exclude a minority group like cross-dressers from a larger movement such as gay rights. Sometimes members of a minority group, like cross-dressers, behave stereotypically and nonnormatively. But they shouldn't be dismissed. That's just like not letting lesbians join the women's rights movement." The whole dialogue group went silent. Again, instead of admonishing the perspective shared by the participant, the facilitator could have deepened the dialogue by turning to the group and asking what they thought about balancing the need for individual expression with the need to establish a sense of commonality.

FREQUENCIES OF FACILITATOR BEHAVIORS

Figure 8.2 shows the distribution of the four facilitator behaviors across all codable minutes. The distribution of these four styles generally affirms what facilitators are expected to do in intergroup dialogue in that slightly over half of all facilitation minutes involved reflection and redirection; nearly a quarter

Figure 8.2   Observed Facilitation Styles

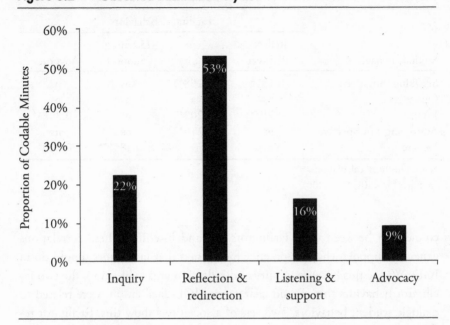

Source: Authors' calculations.

involved inquiry; advocacy was fairly rare, represented in less than a tenth of all facilitation minutes. We will see, however, that advocacy, though rare, was a negative facilitation behavior.

RELATIONSHIPS BETWEEN FACILITATOR AND STUDENT BEHAVIORS

We also examined how the observed facilitator behaviors related to the student behaviors. We did this two ways, although in neither is there a definitive causal connection because the analyses do not account for which student behaviors followed a facilitator behavior versus which facilitator behaviors followed a student behavior. What these analyses provide is evidence of which facilitator-student behavior relationships support what is expected to happen in IGD and which ones do not.

In one analysis, measures of the four facilitator behaviors were correlated with the measures of the five student speaking behaviors (see table 8.3). Listening attentively was so widespread that there was no possibility of finding a

Table 8.3   Correlations Between Facilitator and Student Behaviors

| Student Behaviors | Facilitator Behaviors | | | |
	Reflect-Redirect	Inquiry	Listening-Support	Advocacy
Speaking initiative	0.135*	0.258**	ns	ns
Openness	ns	ns	ns	ns
Inquiry	0.217**	0.202**	ns	−0.208**
Advancing a perspective	ns	−0.216**	ns	ns
Debate	ns	ns	0.485***	0.220*

Source: Authors' calculations.
*$p < .05$; **$p < .01$; ***$p < .001$

connection between what facilitators did and listening. These correlations generally support what the practice model says that facilitators should do in IGD. We see this because inquiry and reflection and redirection, the two facilitator behaviors that should characterize IGD facilitation, were related to dialogic student behaviors. Two sets of associations show this. Facilitator reflection and redirection and inquiry were associated with student speaking initiative and inquiry; facilitator inquiry was also associated with less student defense of their own perspectives. We also see support for the practice model in how facilitator advocacy related to student behaviors. Facilitator advocacy of his or her perspective was related to student debating and to less use of student inquiry. Thus, although facilitator advocacy was the least frequently observed behavior (as shown in figure 8.2), it had negative implications when it occurred.

These correlations further suggest that facilitator listening and support was a passive facilitation style in that it was not correlated with any student behaviors except student debating, which facilitators may let emerge and persist by just listening and supporting whatever is happening in the dialogue. Student debating, a nondialogic mode of communication, was associated with both facilitator advocacy and facilitator listening and support, suggesting that either too strong a stance or too passive a stance from facilitators resulted in (or went along with) student debating.

The second approach we took to examining the connections between facilitator and student behaviors was to use the linear mixed effects approach to compare the effects on student behaviors of facilitator advocacy, which is not consonant with IGD expectations, with those of the more desirable facilitation behaviors of reflection and redirection and inquiry. The results of this analysis show that facilitator advocacy, relative to the dialogic facilitator behaviors, was always negative. Student debating was more frequent when facilitators used advocacy more than reflection and redirection and advocacy more than inquiry. Student speaking initiative was lower when facilitators used advocacy more than reflection and redirection. Students exhibited less openness and less frequently used inquiry to learn from other students when facilitators used advocacy more than reflection and redirection. Thus, as a whole, facilitator advocacy was negatively related to dialogic behaviors among the students.

SUPPORT FOR THE PRACTICE MODEL IN THE OBSERVATIONS OF STUDENT AND FACILITATOR BEHAVIORS

In summary, our analysis of the video measures of student and facilitator behaviors supports the IGD practice model in several ways. Student openness and inquiry, the most dialogic of the student behaviors, made up more than half of all codable minutes of student behaviors. These two behaviors, along with speaking initiative, also proved important because they were associated with emotional and empathic processes intergroup dialogue is expected to foster. These dialogic behaviors were observed more frequently during certain features of the curriculum, in particular during the fishbowl session and actual fishbowl activity, which provided a powerful opportunity for students to listen to each other and probe the experiences described by members of the two identity groups. The importance of structured learning activities was also evident in that both speaking initiative and openness were more frequent when students were involved in the activity phase of each dialogue session. Collective reflection activities were especially and specifically influential when student inquiry was observed. Because inquiry even more than other behaviors distinguishes dialogue from other discursive learning methods, these two activities that occur at the end of a dialogue session are critical to ensuring that inquiry takes place. Dialogic facilitator behaviors were also influential. Facilitator reflection and redirection and inquiry were related to speaking initiative and also to student inquiry.

We have seen in the video observations that students did not always behave in dialogic ways. Student inquiry was less frequent than the practice model would expect. Some student behaviors were also more characteristic of debate and discussion than of dialogue. Student debating most dramatically counters what is supposed to take place in intergroup dialogue. Students observed to be debating also revealed in their interviews less emotionality and less cognitive and relational empathy. Students debated more when facilitators were advocating their perspectives on an issue, and when facilitators took a passive role, simply listening and supporting whatever was happening in the dialogue, thus doing little to intervene when debate emerged. Debate was also observed more frequently in race-ethnicity than in gender dialogues. Although not as clearly antithetical to dialogue principles and procedures as debate is, advancing personal perspectives is less dialogic than sharing with reflection and inquiring into the experiences and ideas of other students. The curriculum and facilitator behaviors were important here, too. Advancing personal perspectives occurred most frequently during hot topics, a session when it was hoped that students would be able to explore contentious issues dialogically rather than defensively. It was also more frequently observed during the fishbowl activity, which proved to be influential for both dialogic and nondialogic behaviors. Facilitators mattered as well in that students were not as likely to advance their perspectives when facilitators themselves used inquiry in guiding the dialogue.

In conclusion, the analysis of the videotaped material lends impressive support for the practice model by confirming the importance of certain features of the curriculum and of facilitator behaviors.

RELEVANCE TO THE PRACTICE MODEL OF FINDINGS FROM THE ANALYSES OF QUALITATIVE MATERIALS IN CHAPTERS 6, 7, AND 8

We turn now to what we have learned from the qualitative materials that complements what we learned from the survey analyses about the processes within IGDs. Depictions of processes are necessarily limited by what can be measured in surveys about what goes on when students interact with each other. Interviewing them about their experiences in a setting where they felt comfortable and observing them interacting with each other on the videotapes provide a much-needed depth in studying communication and interaction. Chapter 5 demonstrated that the communication processes, as measured in the surveys, proved especially influential in accounting for the impact of IGD on increases in students' intergroup understanding, intergroup empathy, and collaborative action. What we achieved from the qualitative parts of the study was a more nuanced picture of these communication processes. Let us look first at what we learned about the listening, speaking, and critical analysis that define the communication processes: engaging self, appreciating difference, critical reflection, and alliance building.

Listening, which is central to appreciating difference and in many ways distinguishes intergroup dialogue from other discursive educational approaches, was widespread. Nearly all students described listening at least once to the interviewer, and virtually all were observed to be listening attentively on the videotapes. Analyses of data from both the interviews and videos showed that listening was nearly equal for participants in the race and gender dialogues. Listening was especially evident when students displayed intergroup empathy in their interviews. Empathy was expressed when students were affected by stories they had listened to in their dialogue classes. Sometimes they were affected by the story of a given individual and sometimes they saw that individual as emblematic of a wider societal phenomenon, but in both cases they learned by listening to the experiences of their dialogue classmates. Appreciating difference also involves asking questions of other students or probing their stories to learn more about each other. Students did not exhibit inquiry as frequently as the practice model would indicate. Moreover, although students mentioned questioning as one of their motives for speaking in the interviews analyzed in the chapter on engagement, questioning was mentioned less often than speaking to share, challenge, educate, and defend.

One of the most important findings in the video analysis is that students asked questions more frequently when their facilitators also used inquiry in guiding the dialogue. Clearly, it is also possible that facilitators used inquiry because students were asking questions. Student listening, as revealed to the interviewers and observed as inquiry, was also connected to specific aspects of the curriculum. Listening in general and listening that led to intergroup empathy were both associated with testimonials and storytelling. Inquiry was observed more frequently during the fishbowl session and fishbowl activity. The testimonial and fishbowl activities both structure opportunities for students to listen. In testimonials, students listen while the other participants present their stories. In fishbowls, students sitting on the perimeter are instructed to listen while those sitting in the middle of the fishbowl conduct their own dialogue. In both activities students listen without interrupting or commenting as other students present what they want to say. Students are asked to listen attentively and try to understand what is being said and why it is important to the speaker. Thus, across chapters 6, 7, and 8, we see that specific features of the curriculum and facilitation behaviors are associated with this dialogic form of communication. What is encouraging is that students actually listened. Almost none of the behaviors showed students disengaged.

Speaking from life experience represents what is meant by the communication process of engaging self. Engaging self involves sharing, taking risks, voicing disagreements, reflecting on one's own learning, and opening up to others. That was what students were doing when they told the interviewer about speaking in the dialogue, something that three-quarters of the students did. Complementary evidence about speaking is seen in the videos, where three-quarters of observed speaking involved moderate to high initiative, indicated by speaking to the whole class or commenting on what was happening that generated additional dialogue. Speaking, like listening, was nearly equal in both race and gender dialogues, and with one exception nearly equal for all four racial-gender groups of students. The one exception was that men of color spoke more than other students in both race-ethnicity and gender dialogues. We learned that students had many motives for speaking, the most important of which was to share something from their lives with others in the dialogue. The videotapes confirmed that sharing was an important form of communication in that a large proportion of speaking engagement involved what we called openness—telling stories about themselves or others and making reflective comments about the meaning of the stories. Other features of the curriculum also seemed to have fostered speaking, taking initiative in speaking, and speaking dialogically. For example, the engagement chapter shows that speaking was greater not only during testimonials but also during the fishbowls and hot topics activities. Analysis of speaking on the videotapes complements and complicates what students revealed about the activities that stimulated speaking student behaviors. On the one hand, students spoke dialogically with openness and initiative during the fishbowl activity. On the other hand, they spoke nondialogically by advancing their personal perspectives without either asking about other perspectives or trying to find mutual understanding during the hot topics session. Facilitator behaviors were also important during dialogic speaking. When facilitators used reflection, redirection, and inquiry—something shown in both the transcripts of a gender dialogue and a race-ethnicity dialogue in this chapter and in many of the excerpts of intergroup empathy in chapter 6—students displayed engaging self in sharing their stories, taking risks, and reflecting on the meaning of their dialogue experiences with others. They were behaving with openness with others, which proved to be the most frequent of the speaking behaviors coded from the videotapes.

Critical reflection and alliance building were also displayed in these qualitative materials. We saw in chapter 6 that critical empathy was expressed when students described feeling for another student or taking his or her perspective with awareness that the student's situation or story represented something about his or her position in the social structure. That kind of intergroup empathy, which relates to critical reflection as a communication process, involves students reflecting about how power and privilege operate in society and in their own lives. Critical empathy was considerably more evident in the race than in the gender dialogues. Chapter 6 explored possible explanations for that difference. These are taken up again in chapter 9, where we discuss practice implications from the results based on the surveys, interviews, videos, and final papers. Critical reflection was also evident in the chapter on engagement. It was a form of active thinking that was coded when students used social justice language (power, privilege, discrimination, inequalities, and the like) in describing to the interviewer what they had learned in intergroup dialogue. Nearly all students displayed this kind of active thinking at least once in the interview. The interviews also made an important contribution by distinguishing two processes involved in active thinking, one in which students appeared to have been trying to figure out information or meaning, and the other when students gained insights in which they had learned something new or understood something on a deeper level. Insights they described involved critical reflection—insights into their biases and assumptions, how power and privilege operate and affected them personally, how the structural dynamics involving power and privilege within their dialogues often represent such dynamics in the wider society. These were not the only kind of insights the students gained, but they lend considerable support to critical reflection as a central communication process in intergroup dialogue.

Alliance building also was evident in these analyses of the qualitative materials, especially in the videotapes when students displayed inquiry. It was a specific kind of inquiry in which asking questions or probing the ideas of others was expressed as students were attempting to find or create mutual understanding. The excerpts revealing empathy, especially critical empathy, also frequently involved alliance building as students discovered commonalities within differences and motivation to collaborate across differences. The interview data showed students' motivation to speak, but the data were not coded specifically for alliance building behaviors, such as speaking to identify mutual understanding, or to identify ways in which students took initiative to work through some differences or conflicts. However, two reasons for speaking are noteworthy: speaking to make comments on the group process and speaking to facilitate. Both have the potential for alliance building and can be understood as promoting dialogue as a collective process. In speaking about group dynamics, the speakers are interested in having the group reflect on its dynamics to improve the common experience. Similarly, when speaking to facilitate, we may assume that the speakers are interested in moving the dialogue deeper or forward. One other reason for speaking discussed in chapter 6 has the quality of alliance building—speaking to educate. In the example shared in chapter 6, the African American woman, recognizing that some members of the dialogue knew very little about affirmative action, chose to educate them: "I was just generally trying to inform people. . . . I just wanted to let everybody know it affects everybody." The same concern for the overall group dialogue and searching for mutual understanding emblematic of alliance building is present in the students' interactions. What these reasons reveal is that alliance-oriented speaking must focus on the group rather than on individuals.

Speaking was not always dialogic, however. The videotapes in particular demonstrated that students sometimes spoke defending their points of view rather than attempting to understand other perspectives or why others might have different viewpoints. Advancing their perspectives, which constituted about two-fifths of all speaking, occurred most frequently during the hot topics session, when the practice model of IGD anticipates students to be able to talk about controversial issues dialogically. Facilitators also played a role when students advanced their perspectives. Students did so less often when facilitators used inquiry methods, thus modeling dialogic behavior for the students, or perhaps the facilitators were following the students and countering by asking questions.

Debating, which was rarer than advancing a perspective, was definitely nondialogic in that it went along with fewer emotions and less empathy. Students debated more when facilitators advocated for their positions, something facilitators are trained not to do. Although facilitators did not frequently advocate, their doing so was always a negative style relative to inquiry, reflection, and redirection. Students also debated more when facilitators simply listened and supported what was happening in the dialogue, letting nondialogic behaviors continue rather than more actively redirecting the students into more dialogic forms of communication.

Three features of the IGD pedagogy that emerged in these mixed-method analyses of the qualitative materials deserve special note. The fishbowl activity proved to be a compelling experience in both the interview and videotape data. That may be driven by the few opportunities students have in their ordinary lives to hear how students from other social groups (or even their own social groups) experience college and life in general as framed through their social identities, and to share their identity experiences knowing that they will be heard. Fishbowls provide a structured way for them to do this in the context of suspending judgment in a space designed for everyone to feel safe. Students who spoke in the center of the fishbowl describe feeling that their experiences were validated simply because others listened to them without interrupting, discounting, or critiquing what they said. Listeners are explicitly instructed to ask clarifying questions or questions that will advance understanding and not to argue or discount what the speakers share. This structure decreases the anxiety and vulnerability sometimes present when students attempt to share aspects of their lives with those from different backgrounds. Listeners learn a great deal from this communicative structure, and thus both speakers and listeners are able to discern commonalities and differences that can lead to building alliances across differences.

The second curricular feature the qualitative materials highlight as critical for dialogic exchange is collective reflection. We learned from the videotape analysis that the two activities, collective reflection on the focal activity of a given session and collective reflection on what students learned from the entire dialogue session, related specifically to student inquiry. We also saw in chapter 7 that active thinking, especially active insights students had reached, seemed to occur when facilitators invited students to reflect, sometimes privately in five-minute reflection papers and most importantly during the collective periods of reflection. In those periods, the students process what they had learned, what dynamics had been evident during the dialogue, and what they would need to do in the next dialogue to maximize learning for everyone. These two periods provide the time and space for reflective, relational, and integrative learning that provide the theoretical basis for learning in the practice model of IGD.

The third important feature of dialogue pedagogy to emerge is storytelling. Storytelling was introduced and encouraged early in the academic term when the curriculum called for students to present testimonials about how their racial or gender identities developed. Testimonials were one of the most frequently mentioned activities that engaged the students; storytelling defined when students behaved with openness. Telling stories about themselves, as well as listening to the stories of other students, was especially influential in expressions of empathy revealed in the interviews. In stressing the power of stories to enhance learning in IGD, we do not suggest that students discounted or minimized the importance of the readings. What we do stress is that, in IGD courses, readings are integrated with in-class interactive activities, reflection papers, whole group collective reflection, and facilitator role-modeling. They are intentionally assigned to strengthen, complicate, and deepen learning in particular modules of the curriculum. In dialogues, readings are intrinsic aspects of active learning. It is especially clear from the analysis of the final papers, even more than from the analysis of the interviews, that students integrated these sources, learning to produce a new kind of knowledge in which empathy and emotions were crucial. Overall, our qualitative analysis revealed that students learned from many sources—readings, exercises, stories, and collective reflection (what we call dialogue about the dialogue) among them. It also showed that the stories and emotional experiences of other students were especially powerful bases of learning.

The importance of storytelling and listening to stories has been stressed in many disciplines. Critical race theorists (Crenshaw 1995) and critical race feminists (Collins 2000; Hurtado and Sinha 2008) stress the telling of stories as a way to reclaim the voice and emotional experiences of historically marginalized groups. They also emphasize the power of stories to create empathy in people who practice law with marginalized populations (Barnes 2006; Delgado and Stefancic 2001). Through storytelling, people experience knowledge as emotional and relational, which critical race feminists and education scholars emphasize as an important means to acquire knowledge and understanding (Collins 2000; Delgado and Stefancic 2001; Freire 1993; Narayan 2004).

Storytelling also plays a role in many educational settings, among them medical education. For instance, Rita Charon (2001) examined the role of narrative competence in the practice of medicine. She states that the ability to elicit, hear, and connect with patient stories creates opportunities for respectful, empathic, and supportive medical care that bridges the gap between physicians and patients. Empathy training programs for physicians and clinical therapists increasingly incorporate narrative and storytelling competency training (DasGupta et al. 2006). Narration and storytelling in the training of medical professionals, as in intergroup dialogues, are viewed as important components in developing empathic relations, especially among medical professionals who need to connect with patients whose cultural backgrounds differ from their own.

The testimonial, fishbowl, and hot topics activities discussed in these chapters were among the most frequently mentioned learning activities in the students' final papers, along with the web of oppression activity. The web of oppression did not emerge in our analyses of either engagement or empathy and was not the focal activity during the videotaped sessions. Yet it was an influential learning experience as evidenced by being among the most frequently mentioned in the students' final papers and by its connection to writing about inequality, power, and privilege. NVivo provides a way to probe narrative materials for adjacent words and phrases, and a way to measure which of them are interconnected. The web of oppression was connected, as the curriculum expects, to words and phrases (social location, power, privilege, social structure, social position, inequality, institution, discrimination, injustice) that represent IGD's content emphasis on inequality and the role of social structure in producing or maintaining it. As discussed in chapter 2, the web of oppression activity, in conjunction with readings, is used to make explicit how privilege and inequality operate through institutions that create or reinforce racial, ethnic, gender, class, or sexuality inequalities. In this activity, students stand in a circle and hold a section of a web with labels of the different institutions. To show inequality within the respective institutions, statements on the labels specify aspects of institutional inequality. As students read the statements, they grasp the interconnections among the institutions and the historical and structural maintenance of inequalities. The physical web makes visible how the different institutions contribute to creating a pipeline of inequalities or multiplying inequalities. It is usually hard for people to understand what social structure is, how it is represented in everyday life, and how it influences people's life chances. It is easy, by contrast, to see individuals acting in a given situation and to attribute what happens in their lives primarily to their own actions, a phenomenon known as the fundamental attribution bias (Nisbett and Ross 1980; Ross 1977). Teaching how institutions are structured by laws, social policies, and cultural practices can be difficult because these phenomena are abstract and not immediately or visibly recognizable. The web of oppression makes them more concrete. Although not discussed by the students when they displayed empathy or talked about engagement, the web of oppression was critical in understanding individual and group bases of inequality.

CONCLUSION

The videotape data and analysis of student and facilitator behaviors provide a unique view of what happens inside a dialogue group, for both students and facilitators. The videotape data are different from any other data source in this study in its focus on facilitators and how they influence student behaviors. Our findings in this chapter confirm the practice model of intergroup dialogue by tying particular structured activities and facilitator behaviors to student listening and speaking. The findings also confirm the importance of communication processes proposed in both our theoretical and our practice models. We saw that students' communications involved openness, represented by sharing stories with each other. They also involved inquiry, represented by asking each other questions and probing each other's ideas to establish mutual understanding. These are dialogic behaviors that, according to the practice model, should occur in intergroup dialogue. However, the videotapes also revealed that the students sometimes displayed two nondialogic behaviors. They debated with each other and they advanced and defended their perspectives, much as students do in traditional discussion classes.

The findings discussed in this chapter coupled with those in chapters 6 and 7 provide a more complex view of both the classroom dialogue space, the interactions among the students, and the internal processes that occurred within them. The focus in chapter 6 on empathy showed the internal cognitive and affective processes that took place for students as they listened to other students share stories and experiences that fostered empathy among the listeners. Empathy, especially across dissimilarities, opened up newer connections and understandings for the students. Sometimes, as shown in chapter 7, these exchanges motivated students to speak and to think more actively. This chapter adds to findings of empathy and engagement by analyzing verbal and nonverbal behaviors of participants and facilitators that occur in the public space of IGD. Rich as the survey material was, it could not offer the in-depth and dynamic depiction of dialogue processes that these qualitative materials provided. These results from the qualitative and mixed methods analyses of empathy, engagement, and student and facilitator behaviors inform recommendations in the next chapter on how to improve IGD and what to attend to in using dialogue methods in other kinds of classrooms and settings.

Authored by Patricia Gurin, Elizabeth Meier, Biren (Ratnesh) A. Nagda, and Chloé Gurin-Sands.

PART III

Implications: Looking Forward

CHAPTER 9

Evidence, Criticisms, and Conclusions for Practice, Theory, and Research

The preceding chapters in this book have articulated the rationale for intergroup dialogue (IGD) in higher education and in our society, the overall methodology of the study, and the practice and theoretical foundations of a critical-dialogic model of intergroup dialogue. Chapters reporting on the quantitative and qualitative investigation undertaken in the Multi-University Intergroup Dialogue Research (MIGR) Project addressed both the impact of intergroup dialogue and the mechanisms of change in intergroup dialogue. In respect to impact, we have shown that intergroup dialogue increases students' intergroup understanding, strengthens positive intergroup relationships, and enhances commitment to intergroup action and collaboration. In respect to the mechanisms of change, we have shown how the pedagogy of intergroup dialogue works directly and indirectly through the communication processes and psychological processes to affect the outcomes of interest. The quantitative results on outcomes and processes support our theoretical model. The qualitative investigation of engagement and empathy provides a nuanced understanding of the ways in which students experience and understand the important processes and outcomes in intergroup dialogue. The intensive qualitative videotaping study provides confirmatory behavioral evidence for the IGD practice model. In this chapter and the next, we look back to move forward. In this chapter specifically, we return to the practice and theoretical foundations of intergroup dialogue (chapters 2 and 3) from the perspective of the empirical evidence of this study.

SUPPORT FOR THE PRACTICE AND THEORETICAL MODEL

The terms *dialogue* and *dialogue across differences* have become common parlance in a broad range of educational and community-based or organizational and policy projects that attempt to open discussion of different perspectives. Dialogue by itself evokes images of openness and engagement. Dialogue across differences evokes images of divergent perspectives held by people of diverse backgrounds brought into interactions with one another. In our conceptualization of intergroup dialogue, we referred to a specific model of dialoguing across and about differences—a critical-dialogic model of intergroup dialogue. We have applied that conceptualization in this study of engaging race and gender. The dialogic component emphasizes the centrality of building relationships across differences. These relationships are interpersonal in that they are built on sharing thoughts, experiences, and feelings with others. More important, however, these relationships are also intergroup because IGD intentionally brings different social identity groups together for students to have group-based interactions. This is not to say that students are confined to their identity groups but that their identity is engaged as an important lens for self- and other-understanding. The critical component addresses dialogue about differences, especially understanding the differences of identity that are contextualized in systems of power and privilege as well as in mutual responsibilities for individual and social change. The critical component not only involves race-ethnicity and gender, but also and in particular examines how they involve systemic racial-ethnic and gender inequalities and how interracial-interethnic and cross-gender collaborations for social justice can be achieved. Together, the critical-dialogic nature of intergroup dialogue allows for personalized and contextualized conversations about identities and inequalities while building relationships across these very kinds of difference. The critical-dialogic nature of intergroup dialogue guides those social relationships to be considered in the context of power and privilege. A white man in a race-ethnicity dialogue underscores this intentionality in structuring the intergroup collaborative projects (ICPs): "This strategy served as a catalyst to take us out of our comfort zones. It showed us how working across differences could lead to common ground." Even when students collaborate on projects, a critical analysis is brought to bear in understanding the dynamics of power and privilege that emerge in collaboration and working toward equality both inside and outside the dialogue setting. Critical-dialogic IGD is fundamentally about social change; it does not rest simply in opposition to what is, but has to be coupled with visions and experiments in collaboration for what is possible.

The quantitative and qualitative investigation in this study provides strong support for the practice model and theoretical framework of critical-dialogic intergroup dialogue as a distinctive approach to intergroup contact and multicultural education. As discussed in chapter 2, IGD integrates the core elements of diversity education on human relationships and the core elements of social justice education on critical consciousness. Furthermore, the study supports the importance of personal, intimate, positive intergroup relations, much as the emphasis on friendship does in intergroup relations scholarship. But the work on relationships within the social psychology of intergroup relationships is primarily interpersonal—relationships across difference but not about difference. Intergroup dialogue thus integrates across scholarship in diversity education, social justice education, and intergroup relations. The IGD practice model and theoretical framework show how dialogue about difference across difference is fostered over time and through collective communication and individual psychological processes.

Importance of Pedagogy

The theoretical model posits that intergroup dialogue pedagogy—content, structured interactions, and facilitation—provides the foundation from which the communication processes, psychological processes, and outcomes in intergroup dialogue emerge. In the structural equation model (SEM in chapter 5), the three pedagogical components formed a latent factor, meaning that they were interrelated and represent an underlying concept we call pedagogy. Content gives students knowledge for learning about identities, inequalities, and social change. In contrast to formalized lectures, the content in intergroup dialogue is delivered through discussion of readings and through in-class examination of conceptual frameworks and definitions. Structured interactions provide an active learning format through which students examine what a concept means, and dialogue with each other about their hands-on experiences. Facilitators, working in teams of two, provide guided learning rather than formalized instruction. They involve students in structured learning activities and guide the reflection and dialogue in which students individually and collectively make sense of what they learned from the activities. Facilitators help students integrate content with group dynamics. Both the quantitative and qualitative findings support the efficacy of the pedagogical features of intergroup dialogue.

The quantitative results showed that pedagogical features were related to the critical-dialogic communication processes, as we predicted they would be. In addition, pedagogy also had significant direct effects on the psychological processes of affective positivity and cognitive involvement. Thus, IGD pedagogy helped set up both the social-relational learning embedded in the communication processes and the individual learning represented by the psychological processes.

The qualitative analyses revealed several refined understandings of the pedagogical features. The interviews pointed to specific content that stimulated the communication processes of speaking (engaging self) and listening (appreciating difference). In the race-ethnicity dialogues, the most frequently mentioned content was about racism, especially individual experiences of racism, systemic racism, and race-related privilege. The next most common stimulus was social construction of race—what race means and how it is enacted in social relationships through assumptions, beliefs, and stereotypes. In the gender dialogues, students mentioned social construction of gender—through gender roles and gender socialization—as the most common stimulus for speaking. The next most common content was sexism—individual experiences of systemic gender oppression, instances of sexist behaviors, and gender-based privilege. Thus, although it might seem that the content in race-ethnicity and gender dialogues differed, the specific content that stimulated engagement was much the same in both.

The interviews also showed that specific structured activities cultivated student speaking and listening in intergroup dialogues. The learning activities of testimonials, caucus group and fishbowl, and hot topics seem to have engaged students the most in mutual speaking and listening. The testimonials encouraged individual storytelling and active listening to each story. The fishbowl activity following the separate identity-based caucus groups extended speaking and active listening to the group level. The video analyses also showed that the fishbowl especially fostered structured behaviors coded as engagement, specifically listening and responding to others. Hot topics were mentioned as important sources for students' engagement in intergroup dialogues, and particularly for speaking out on controversial issues. The hot topics sessions involved students in full-group dialogues. All of these structured interactions deepened students' speaking engagement by enabling them to move out of their comfort zones and taking risks to share their thoughts and experiences publicly. Students also refined their listening engagement in these structured interactions. They listened to diverse viewpoints in the dialogue among their peers, realized their opinions as one of many, and shared, hoping to be understood and expecting to be open to rethinking their own perspectives.

The role of the facilitator was most clearly investigated in the videotaping study that used recordings of three dialogue sessions and focused on facilitator behaviors of reflecting and redirecting, inquiring, listening and supporting, and advocating. Reflection and redirection accounted for half of all behaviors coded. Inquiry (asking questions) represented a quarter, followed by listening and support. Advocacy was evident in just less than a tenth. When facilitator behaviors were correlated with student behaviors in the video study, three clear trends emerged. One, listening-supporting and advocacy by facilitators were related to nondialogic student engagement (debating). Two, facilitator reflection and redirection and facilitator inquiry were related to student dialogic behaviors displaying more attentiveness and verbal initiative, openness, and inquiry in the dialogue. Three, the more the facilitators used inquiry in the dialogues, the less the students simply advanced their perspectives apart from other students' contributions, as they may do in discussion. As expected, facilitator reflection-redirection and inquiry appear to model for students positive dialogic engagement. Facilitator advocacy (discussed in chapter 8), although present in the least amount of facilitator behaviors, had consistently negative relationships to student dialogic engagement.

These findings are consistent with the facilitation principles discussed in chapter 2 (see Nagda and Maxwell 2011). Facilitator reflection and redirection is a good example of facilitators as guides, not teachers. By acknowledging participants' contributions and opening the dialogue to others, facilitators are maximizing participation and presumably creating a more inclusive environment. Facilitator inquiry expresses the third facilitation principle of attending to process, not just procedure. The inquiry process encourages students to think and share more reflectively and relationally—be it about the meaning of their experiences in structured activities, sharing their perspectives in relation to other students, or connecting their perspectives and experiences in relation to readings and larger social issues.

Centrality of Communication Processes

In the critical-dialogic theoretical framework, the four communication processes of engaging self, appreciating difference, critical reflection, and alliance building are posited as core processes that explain the way in which intergroup dialogue has an impact on learning. Prior work in social psychology of intergroup contact had emphasized the importance of psychological processes in helping explain the mechanism by which bias is reduced (Dovidio et al. 2004). As is evident from the structural equation modeling (chapter 5), the psychological processes were important processes in the study; cognitive involvement is directly related to all three outcomes; and affective positivity was directly related to intergroup empathy and intergroup collaboration and action immediately at the end of the dialogues. However, the psychological processes do not capture what happens sociorelationally among participants in contact situations. The communication processes do that, keeping group identity and group differences salient while they enable relationship building across differences for in-depth learning and empowerment for social change.

The quantitative and qualitative research conducted in this study provided support for the importance of communication processes in intergroup dialogues. The structural equation modeling (chapter 5) showed their importance in five ways. One, they were related to the psychological processes of affective positivity and cognitive openness, which directly affect outcomes. Two, they directly influenced both the immediate outcomes of intergroup understanding and intergroup collaboration and action at the end of the dialogues and indirectly influenced the outcome of intergroup empathy (through the affective and cognitive psychological processes). Three, they directly affected outcomes of intergroup understanding, intergroup empathy, and intergroup collaboration and action a year later. Four, they mediated the effect of pedagogical processes on psychological processes and outcomes at the end of the dialogues. Five, their mediation effect was still evident one year later.

The communication processes—engaging self, appreciating difference, critical reflection, and alliance building—were highly intercorrelated in the quantitative data and thus it was not possible to examine their separate effects in intergroup dialogue. The qualitative data, however, provided a more nuanced understanding of the role of each process. With respect to engaging self, the qualitative data showed many ways that students shared their perspectives and experiences and reflected on what they were learning as they engaged in the dialogue. In the video analysis, behaviorally observed openness was coded when students made self-reflective comments, often when they were telling stories about their lives. Openness was the most frequently observed student behavior, a finding that supports the importance of engaging self. Openness was related to measures of emotions and of empathy coded from the students' final papers. It often appeared together with student inquiry, as it did in the two examples of a race-ethnicity dialogue and a gender dialogue described in chapter 8. Facilitator behaviors were not especially correlated with times when students behaved with openness. Other qualitative data demonstrated the importance of structured activities. Analysis of engagement through speaking and listening, for example, showed that students engaged when they stepped out of their comfort zones and took risks to share their experiences. Student narratives in the interviews underscored the social nature of engaging self. Speaking, as an indicator of engaging self, was related to listening to others and to responding to questions from others. Importantly, students also spoke to share their perspectives, sometimes inspired by others' sharing. Finally, in a separately published article that also used final paper data, engaging self was related to the writing about action that the students did in the final papers, indicating that they were actually involved in taking some kind of action (see Gurin-Sands et al. 2012).

Appreciating difference involved listening, asking questions, and learning from others. It affirms that participants are not expected to know everything and need not pretend that they do. But they do have responsibilities to actively learn from and with each other by asking questions. Student inquiry, coded in the video tapes, in which students asked questions and tried to foster mutual understanding was coded most frequently during two collective reflection activities: dialogue about the activity that had occurred in that session and dialogue about the entire dialogue. Student inquiry was also related to awareness of the emotions of others in the dialogue and to empathic connections to others, as coded from the interviews. Thus, when students inquired of others, they were more oriented to their peers in these other ways as well. They also expressed more emotions overall in writing their papers. Inquiry's relationship to empathy was evident with respect to emotional empathy and to critical empathy involving the situation of a group, not merely an individual. Thus, behaviorally observed inquiry was both cognitive and emotional, and was related to student writing about intention to act and educating others in their final papers (Gurin-Sands et al. 2012). Facilitator behaviors were influential, especially when they were observed to reflect and redirect what was happening in the dialogue; when they used inquiry, student inquiry behaviors were also more evident. In contrast, when facilitators advocated their positions, students also displayed inquiry less often. The interviews also revealed the significance of appreciating difference through student listening and inquiry as foundations for intergroup empathy. Students listening intently to other students and asking them questions about their feelings and perspectives were especially evident in both relational and critical empathy. Listeners were affected by the content of the story, which was usually dissimilar to their experiences, and sometimes by how the students telling the stories were affected and expressed those emotions. Listeners tried to understand the experiences of others by perspective taking and asking questions. Because these interactions were in face-to-face encounters, students did not easily discount the experiences of others. Instead, they listened and asked questions to understand more fully what these experiences meant to their peers, and how those experiences had affected the feelings and thoughts of their peers. In critical empathy, listening led to seeing the broader group-based implications of a specific peer's story.

The communication process of critical reflection encouraged an analysis of identity and power. Be it in internal thoughts and assumptions about self and others or in external behaviors, students showed that learning with others made them more aware of social structural influences on both their and other students' lives. One kind of active thinking (from the analyses of engagement in the interviews) focused on power and privilege. In this critical reflection, students actively processed and arrived at insights about how power and privilege shaped their own and others' identities. They also thought about the impact of group dynamics on the quality of the dialogue. Critical reflection was also evident in the analyses of empathy from the interview data. Critical empathy, which was expressed more in the race-ethnicity dialogues than in the gender dialogues, showed that students recognized that another student's story was emblematic of something broader in society, and thus they empathized with that student both individually and on the basis of his or her position in a system of power and privilege. It was this critical analysis that distinguished critical empathy from relational empathy. Finally, critical reflection, coded from the students' final papers, was influential in the students' intention to act and to educate others (also see Gurin-Sands et al. 2012). Critical reflection influenced these two kinds of action indirectly through the psychological processes of emotions and politicized identity. Thus it is possible that critical reflection enabled participants to understand their identities in systems of privilege and inequality as well as acknowledge and understand their and others' emotions related to those systems.

Alliance building involves communication about commonalties and differences, about conflicts or tensions that underlie collaborations, and about ways to take actions. In this process, students search for commonalities while they maintain awareness of differences and inequalities. Chloé Gurin-Sands and her colleagues (2012) showed that alliance building was a predictor of levels of action (intention to act and actual action) as well as types of action (educating others and collaborative action). The interviews and papers also showed that alliance building was influential in relational empathy and critical empathy. Alliance building emerged in moments when other students took responsibility for their privileges or shared ways in which they had interrupted discriminatory actions. From listening to and probing these kinds of experiences, participants learned that people can collaborate across differences and inequalities. They could see possibilities for alliance building. These recollections were accompanied by words or phrases such as "I just felt I could relate to her" or "I could work with her," or "admiration."

As noted, psychological processes, which were fostered by the communication processes, were also important. In both the quantitative and qualitative results, affective and cognitive psychological processes proved influential for action, evident in the SEM analysis of survey measures and in the regression analyses of the final paper measures, as well as for intergroup empathy, evident in the SEM analysis of survey measures and mixed methods analyses of the interview measures. Cognitive processes were also related to critical analysis of inequality, evident in mixed-methods analysis of the interview measures, and to increased understanding of the structural causes of inequalities, evident in the SEM analysis of survey measures.

In summary, the comprehensive evidence accumulated from the mixed-methods study of intergroup dialogue shows two broad results. One, the evidence shows the overall effectiveness of the critical-dialogic model of intergroup dialogue as seen in the positive outcomes for intergroup understanding, intergroup relationships, and intergroup action and collaboration. Two, the evidence also shows the important role of communication and psychological processes in explaining how intergroup dialogue has the effects it does. This attention to both the communication and psychological processes is both of theoretical and practical significance. In the next section, we discuss the criticisms and concerns about intergroup dialogue and related fields in light of the evidence from the study.

CRITICISMS OF INTERGROUP DIALOGUE

Scholars and educators have articulated a number of criticisms of intergroup dialogue. These are sometimes directly about IGD, and at other times about related fields, such as intercultural education, multicultural education, antiracist education, and peace education. These criticisms fall in four main areas: too dialogic, focusing on interpersonal relations and lacking sociopolitical analyses; too critical, focusing on structural analysis that undermines relating across differences; too little action, focusing on the disconnection between dialogue and action; and, a concern about who benefits from intergroup dialogue. We map the critiques here to show how the critical-dialogic model of intergroup dialogue addresses them.

Too Dialogic

One set of critiques centers on an overly human relations focus of some intergroup dialogue efforts that results in too little or no attention to power, inequalities, and social change. Critics assert that focusing on building bridges across differences, fostering empathy, and increasing understanding of group perspectives can result in tokenizing and colonizing members of some groups (McPhail 2004; Miller and Donner 2000), leaving members of other groups to "enjoy personal growth and fulfillment from these intercultural practices" (Gorski 2008, 521). *Tokenizing* means education that simply involves learning about the other, and especially reducing social identities to learning about cultural artifacts—food, clothes, and holidays. These others are generally people of low-power groups who are assumed to have culture, whereas the dominant group members are seen as not having culture. *Colonizing* means education that perpetuates culturally imperialistic ways of learning and engagement that focus on intercultural-intergroup awareness at the individual level without attention to sociopolitical contexts, relations of domination, and social action. Thus, unequal power relationships continue to be reinforced rather than challenged, and learning and interactions continue to benefit the privileged.

Overreliance on interpersonal relationships has at least two consequences. One, dialogue becomes decontextualized and thus inadvertently privileges the privileged. Participants are not challenged to examine the context of different groups' locations in societal power structures. Nicholas Burbules (2000) attributes this to a "fetishization" of dialogue, by which he means an adherence to dialogue as the (only) way to work with differences and resolve conflicts. Originally a proponent of dialogue in teaching, Burbules eventually concluded that many dialogue practitioners reject any criticism of dialogue as being invalid and react to criticisms by suggesting that dialogue participants are just not willing or perhaps not able to engage fully in dialogue. Then, when dialogues prove ineffective, some dialogue educators simply persist in dialogue procedures they have used instead of examining barriers that might be hindering participant engagement. Dialogue becomes a procedural technique that some may call civility, masking important group differences and inequalities. The dialogue space then empowers the privileged and silences those who participate outside the boundaries of what is defined as civility. Jennifer Simpson quoted a participant in a study of racial dialogues that "civility functions not to level the playing field or to ensure just or equitable treatment for all but rather to silence even further the already marginalized" (2008, 153). Jodi Kaufmann, in an ethnographic study of a classroom, gives an example of how procedural tactics of dialogue silenced and diverted discussions of the reactions of members of less privileged groups:

> Cultural factors also appeared to influence the depth of interrogation required. Many students of color mentioned a desire to interrogate issues at more in-depth levels. In his interview, Richard noted, "It seemed like we talked about racism and feminism, but the conversations never went anywhere." I think it was kind of frustrating—"What do you think about racism? What do you think about feminism?" This frustration, however, was not noted by either of the white female students interviewed. . . . Not only did race, class, and gender influence who spoke, what was spoken, how it was spoken, and in what contexts, it appeared the fewer privileged positions one held the more aware one was of the politics of speech. (2010, 466)

Thus dialogue can become both prescriptive and decontextualized from the realities of the identities and experiences of participants. In its apparent neutral approach, a prescriptive and decontextualized dialogue reinforces dominant cultural ways of participation. This is a valid and important critique that educators should heed. Procedural techniques give little direction to how participants or facilitators deepen the dialogue organically.

Two, overreliance on interpersonal relationships may minimize the complexity and challenge of dialogue. In an often-quoted statement, Cornel West says, "Dialogue is a form of struggle; it's not chitchat" (Lerner and West 1995, 266). Dialogue needs to help participants struggle with complexities posed by bringing together people who are not only different in their social identities but also positioned unequally in the systems of privilege and inequality in which they live. Some dialogues may be primarily personal and apolitical (Abu-Nimer 1999; Bekerman 2007). A nonpolitically situated dialogue can perpetuate the myth that all identities are equally influential merely as cultural expressions, and that privileges accorded to particular cultural identities are both earned and deserved in a fair and color-blind society. Highly interpersonal or intercultural dialogues may therefore replicate unequal power dynamics in the wider society, constraining what can be learned (McPhail 2004). Simpson writes, "When discourses of color-blindness are invoked to discredit or dismiss the lived experiences of people of color as invalid, inaccurate, or irrelevant, the interaction can only be reproductive of color-blind beliefs. Because this stance also privileges the socially dominant position as correct and valid, it precludes a space where the status quo can be challenged, and, thus, is fundamentally antidialogic" (2008, 143).

Results in our study address the critique of intergroup dialogues as being too dialogic. The quantitative data showed that intergroup dialogue students increased significantly more than the control group students in endorsing structural attributions for both racial-ethnic and gender inequalities. A white woman in a race-ethnicity dialogue, quoted in chapter 3, captured her learning connecting individual experiences to structural realities through dialogue: "I am proud and confident of the fact that I am identifying my privileges. I could not have done it alone; it was the impact of everyone talking about privileges and disadvantages in their lives that I began to understand." It is also important that their understanding about structural causes of inequalities specific to their IGD topic generalized to increasingly seeing structural causes of inequalities not covered directly in their specific dialogues. These effects of intergroup dialogue are especially important in light of national studies showing that racial-ethnic groups differ greatly in their explanations for inequalities. African Americans and Latinos more often than whites attribute racial inequities, such as in occupation, income, and housing, to discrimination (Bobo 2011; Hunt 2007). Twice as many African American and Latino youth as white youth endorse that racism continues to be a problem in the United States, even after the 2008 election of President Obama (Cohen 2011), thus challenging the notion of a postracial society.

The quantitative findings were complemented by qualitative findings from interviews showing that dialogic participation through speaking and listening was accompanied by higher-order active thinking and critical reflection. Students conveyed a growing understanding that they are located in larger and often unequal social contexts. A woman of color in a gender intergroup dialogue, quoted in chapter 3, wrote about how the dialogic engagement fostered shared critical understanding: "By sharing our testimonials as a group, . . . I learned [that] our personal struggles are a result of our backgrounds and how we are raised. With that distinction, we connected and were able to build trust among us." A white woman in a race-ethnicity dialogue, also quoted in chapter 3, also wrote about the joint influence of dialogic and critical processes. "Sitting in class and hearing how we as a group represented so many different relationships to privilege, I looked at my life and how no one ever sat me down and told me about my privilege."

An appreciation for differences and understanding them in dynamics of power and privilege, as shown in the study of empathy, enabled students to develop critical empathy with each other. Even though their empathic connection to individuals who told stories about their experiences was relational, some students, especially in race-ethnicity dialogues, expressed critical empathy also. They related to the stories as emblematic of structures that produced inequalities. Furthermore, analyses of students' final paper data showed that a critical political perspective on their identities was an important influence on how much they wrote about action (Gurin-Sands et al. 2012). A politicized identity involves understanding one's location in systems of privilege and power as opposed to seeing oneself merely as an individual unmarked by social group memberships and status positions.

Taken together, findings of this study show that intergroup dialogue produced both relational outcomes—more positive emotions in intergroup situations, more positive intergroup relationships and increased empathy—and critical outcomes—increased structural understanding of inequality, more critical empathy and not only interpersonal empathy, and more understanding that identities have political implications.

Too Critical

Other educators and scholars have critiqued what may appear to be the exact opposite problem, that intergroup dialogues are too critical in having too heavy an emphasis on critical analysis (Brooks 2011; Conklin 2008; hooks 2003). Julia Brooks (2011), in discussing social justice education, specifically suggests that critically oriented efforts too frequently prevent attention to emotions, which are crucial in intergroup interactions. She explains that critical analysis "may *cover over* the rich and textured potential for non-violent and compassionate relations in the classroom" (Brooks 2011, 45, emphasis in the original). Building on Megan Boler's (1999) pedagogy of discomfort, Brooks further states that learning about social justice inevitably goes into the "unknown, uncomfortable and potentially violent territory" (Brooks 2001, 45). The discomfort, dissonance, and disequilibrium from examining personal and social realities can be jarring for students and inevitably require attention to emotions (Conklin 2008; hooks 2003). Overly relying on critical, cognitive understanding of social relations and institutional practices may divert students from dealing with emotions, some of which are violent. Not only are efforts toward change stifled, but relations of respect, care, and joint sense-making are diminished as well. Focusing on emotions as much as critical analysis makes it possible, Brooks (2011) says, to question what kinds of relations support nonviolence toward others. Jodi Kaufmann (2010) recounts two particular teaching experiences in her classes in which students' critical consciousness of differences produced different emotional reactions and behaviors from students with less privilege and those with more privilege. In response to Kaufmann's sharing of her white identity development and coming to consciousness about whiteness and racism, a white student denied having any racism herself and listed her accomplishments as a teacher of African American children. In another incident between two students, an African American man, who was constantly bothered by a white male student's twitching foot touching him, finally exploded one day and challenged him "to take it outside." Both of these students, the white woman and the African American man, were dealing with underlying emotions and reacted defensively and offensively. Their reactions conveyed strong emotions that likely built up over the academic term. Instead of constructively engaging emotional reactions to learning about inequalities both outside and inside the classroom, the tensions led to shout-outs or fight-outs. Reflecting on these troubling but instructive issues, Julia Brooks says,

> We can choose to participate alongside our students' grappling, modeling respect and care, and mitigating some of the violence they might experience by recognizing, naming and attending to the various elements of their struggle in the classroom. . . . our efforts might afford us opportunities to co-construct and promote, again alongside our students, a less violent and relational dialogic process . . . amidst the struggle and pain that might lead to individual and social transformation. (2011, 46)

In critical cognitive analysis, terms such as *agent* and *target*, or *privileged* and *oppressed*, indicating the social locations of individuals in larger systems of power and privilege, may be useful in highlighting the consequences of power and inequalities. However, they may also produce almost stereotypical characteristics such that they are the only way individuals are seen in intergroup interactions. Identity can be perceived as too fixed and static, conflated with status, rather than as dynamic, evolving, and affected by the intergroup interactions and critical awareness of inequality. For members of groups with less privilege in the encounter, such labeling usually puts them as victims and underplays their resiliency (hooks 2003). For members of groups with more privilege, such labeling puts them as perpetrators and discounts their attempts at self-directed change, alliance building, or social justice advocacy. How one is seen, or sees oneself, as a member of a particular identity group can override complex life experiences. Chimamanda Ngozi Adichie (2009) refers to this as the "danger of a single story," whereby we see each other in limited, unidimensional, and constricting ways. Critical analysis should not produce simplistic and dichotomous ways of thinking about identities and groups. Instead, members of both groups in intergroup dialogue have multiple and intersecting identities that must enter the analyses of power and privilege. Even when dialogues may be primarily focused on singular identities, a consideration of multiple identities can be a resource in deepening collective reflection and shared understanding of singular identities. Elizabeth Cole (2008) urges exploring multiple identities and intersectionality as an avenue to build bridges across differences. Grappling with intersectionalities of one's multiple identities and how they interface with others opens the possibility of finding commonalities in experiences, emotions, and life stories. Dealing with intersectionality allows for one to recognize both similarities in the context of differences and differences in the context of similarities (Alperin 1990; Anzaldúa 2002; Cole 2008). Rather than seeing ourselves as separate from each other, we can see ourselves as social beings influenced by social practices and in interrelation with each other (Asher 2003).

The quantitative results of our study demonstrate that these race-ethnic and gender dialogue courses did not produce an overemphasis on critical analysis to the exclusion of intergroup relationships. Intergroup dialogue students increased more than control group students in intergroup empathy and motivation to bridge differences. They became more attuned to the emotional impact of power and privilege on each other. These emotions were not simply stereotypical feelings of despair and shame for members of less privileged and more privileged groups, but also feelings of admiration and hope related to the resiliency of both less and more advantaged people as they interact with each other. Furthermore, increased understanding of structural inequality did not create divisions between the groups in dialogue. Rather, students became simultaneously more structural in their orientations, more motivated to bridge differences, more empathic, and more involved in educating and collaborating with others. A woman of color in a race-ethnicity intergroup dialogue (quoted in chapter 3) contrasted her relational experience in intergroup dialogue to other courses: "Often in [other] classes I feel that no one is interested in what I say. I learned to trust people in my dialogue that they would actually listen and care what I said."

The qualitative data from student interviews showed positive engagement across differences. Speaking enabled students to share their perspectives— both unique and common—with their peers. Listening enabled students to appreciate differences among them, to learn from each other, and to develop further understanding of one another through inquiry. The more nuanced understanding of empathy, from analyzing students' interviews and papers, also showed that students developed both relational empathy and critical empathy. Both types come from face-to-face interactions, and both involve emotions. A heterosexual, white man in a gender dialogue, quoted in chapter 6, shared his strong emotions in empathizing both relationally and critically with a gay man of color. "I just couldn't even grasp that I would have to, if I were gay, think . . . how people are going to look at me, how they're going to treat me . . . I felt a lot of anger . . . [and] sadness."

Taken together, the quantitative and qualitative results showed that both critical analysis and relationships fostered through speaking, listening, and inquiry produced both more positive intergroup relationships and greater understanding of inequalities. Even when analysis of inequality within the dialogue group or in the wider society highlights the disadvantages and advantages across groups in dialogue, these relational connections allowed them to bridge differences and learn to collaborate. A man of color in a gender dialogue, quoted in chapter 3, recalled his shift from defensiveness to greater dialogic engagement: "When [another student] kept asking me questions about why I think the way I do, I was pretty defensive at first. . . . When I actually dug into my feelings on the matter, I realized it helped me to have to listen to how other students thought I was behaving in the class." Most important, grappling with the reality of inequalities did not reinforce divisions; the intentional attention to dialogic relationship building in the context of power differences enhanced motivations for continued learning and engagement with each other.

Too Little Action

Some critics, concerned about an overemphasis on dialogic relationships, have claimed that intergroup dialogue does not pay enough attention to action, that dialogue is simply all talk, and that it is too oriented to intergroup harmony instead of leading to social and structural change (Gorski 2008). Similarly, an overemphasis on critical analysis could hinder capacity for action because problems that are revealed in critical consciousness-raising may seem intractable and, for some, evoke a sense of helplessness (Sue et al. 2010). Mark Chesler states that for intergroup dialogues to fulfill their potential, they must help participants translate the new cognitive and affective understandings of themselves and others into new actions. Barring that, "when new individual behaviors are not translated into action with others, in forms of collective action, fundamental social structures maintaining privilege and oppression go unchecked" (Chesler 2001, 29). Thus, linking dialogic relationships and critical analysis to action is a crucial part of intergroup dialogue.

A second critique about action sometimes levied against intergroup dialogue concerns when and how practitioners frame action. Simpson (2008) warns against focusing too early or too exclusively on finding common ground as a basis for action. Before forming alliances, differences need to be fully explored regarding the groups' perspectives about problems and about appropriate action to undertake. Even in exploring collaborative social action, an imbalanced focus on commonalties can emerge to the exclusion of exploring differences. Furthermore, critics are concerned that a heavy emphasis on dialogic relationships in intergroup dialogue means that change will be conceived of as individual change to the exclusion of social change (Gorski 2008; Maoz 2011). Simply changing interpersonal relationships and promoting individual knowledge alone will not alter the status quo, and can favor privileged groups. As documented in many studies, members of more privileged groups hope for closer interpersonal relationships, not social change, whereas members of less privileged groups hope that intergroup encounters will mobilize social change efforts (Dixon et al. 2010; Wright and Lubensky 2009). Another particular problem in how action is addressed in dialogue is by not differentiating between intention and action. Mere intention to act may reinforce alienation and distrust that can emerge in interracial encounters (McPhail 2004). Successful intergroup encounters must involve actual actions both inside and outside the dialogue, and a collective reflection on those actions in order to build efficacy and understanding of the shared and unique responsibilities across groups.

A third issue, perhaps not a critique, is who acts, with whom, and on behalf of whom. As discussed in chapter 3, collective action is defined mostly as action aimed at improving the status, power, and influence of a group, and in most cases a disadvantaged group. Little is known about what collective action means for advantaged groups except as they become allies to disadvantaged groups. There is also the tension between solidarity, intragroup-based action, and collaborative action in intergroup alliances (Pheterson 1990). Zvi Bekerman (2007), in reviewing twenty years of Palestinian-Israeli intergroup encounters, argues that collaborative action by its nature does not allow for strengthening group identity and group solidarity. Yet solidarity-based action by separate identity groups is a vital form of creating social change, especially for disadvantaged groups. Others note that solidarity-based action is important for advantaged groups also, so that they can develop a politicized identity and understanding of their privilege without being overwhelmed by feelings of guilt and shame (Pheterson 1990). The question is whether both solidarity and collective action can result from intergroup dialogue. Mohammed Abu-Nimer answers affirmatively. Intergroup dialogue, he explains, can lead all groups to be able to "critique their empowerment while emphasizing at the same time that encounters in and of themselves are not a substitute for structural change" (1999, 24).

Regarding action, our quantitative results showed that intergroup dialogue increased frequency and efficacy of action in both race-ethnicity and gender dialogues and for students from both advantaged and disadvantaged groups. Relative to students in the control group, students participating in intergroup dialogue became more confident in self-directed, other-directed, and collaborative actions, and participated in these different kinds of action more frequently as well. One man (not previously quoted) stressed the importance of the intergroup collaborative project in showing him that he could work with others to make a difference on his campus.

> What I found remarkable about the project was that it taught us how to promote awareness of different cultures and cultural issues. . . . At [his university] and in general, it is difficult to get people to listen and pay attention to a problem. . . . The ICP project showed us that it is possible to effect some kind of change. That is a life-long lesson for me—that collaborating with others will make a difference. (White man, race-ethnicity dialogue)

The positive impact of intergroup dialogue was also evident in students' commitments to postcollege community action. The structural equation modeling further shows how dialogue pedagogy and both communication and psychological processes are connected to intergroup collaboration and action. IGD pedagogy had an impact on both processes, each of which was then related to increased action at the end of the academic term. The effect of pedagogy on action was thus indirect. The effect of communication processes, by contrast, was both direct and indirect through fostering the psychological processes. The students who reported that engaging self, appreciating difference, critical reflection, and alliance building happened frequently in their dialogues and were important to their learning gained more than their counterparts in both efficacy and frequency of action. Moreover, that direct effect of communication processes was significant both immediately at the end of the intergroup dialogue course and a year later.

The mixed-methods study of action conducted by Gurin-Sands and her colleagues (2012) provides further support for the theoretical model of how intergroup dialogue fosters action. Pedagogy, communication processes, and psychological processes were influential, sometimes indirectly, sometimes directly in accounting for both levels of action and types of action. Gurin-Sands and her colleagues show that the more the students mentioned structured activities and readings in their papers, the more they mentioned each of the communication processes. The more references to communication processes, the more to psychological processes (active thinking and politicized identity) and to action. The more references to politicized identity and emotions, the more references to action. Alliance building was particularly influential for both levels of action—intention to act and actual acting—and targets of action—educating others and collaborating with others.

Who Benefits from Intergroup Dialogue?

The question of who benefits from IGD cuts across all the criticisms discussed thus far. At the heart of the other criticisms is an overriding concern that intergroup dialogue falls into the same trap as some other diversity and social justice education efforts, namely that it supports rather than challenges the dynamics of inequalities that exist in the wider society. Some critics claim that IGD benefits students from more privileged backgrounds at the expense of their less privileged counterparts. Relating to our earlier discussion about an overemphasis on dialogic relationships, several critics claim that this happens by not challenging more privileged students to examine structural and institutional causes of inequality that advantage them and disadvantage others (Gorski 2008), and by not supporting the desires of less privileged students to confront inequalities and talk about social change (Chesler 2001; McPhail 2004; Miller and Donner 2000; Saguy, Dovidio, and Pratto 2008). Paradoxically, an overemphasis on critical analyses may also favor the privileged because it too frequently focuses on "what the privileged don't know." By contrast, less privileged groups, by their life experiences "already know" how privilege and power operate (Narayan 1988). Thus, whether IGD favors the learning of one group, and especially the privileged group, over another is an important concern.

Two areas of research and practice are informative in addressing the question of who benefits. The first is an emerging scholarship on divergences in motivations and expectations of low-power and high-power groups in intergroup interactions. Developed mostly by social psychologists and extending intergroup contact theory, these divergences are commonly referred to as intergroup misunderstandings. Especially important for the question of who benefits from intergroup dialogue is the possibility that the expectations and motivations of high-power groups take precedence over those of low-power groups. If and when that happens, intergroup dialogues would privilege the privileged. The second area is the emerging scholarship on microaggressions in dialogues. Developed mostly by educational and clinical psychologists, and critical theorists, this body of knowledge looks at the negative effects, especially on but not limited to low-power groups, that sometimes occur in interactional exchanges between low-power and high-power groups. Especially important for the question of who benefits in intergroup dialogue are the negative affective, cognitive, and behavioral effects that undermine the learning in intergroup dialogue and further marginalize the marginalized. It is noteworthy that the scholarship on intergroup misunderstandings and the scholarship on microaggressions have not yet been brought together. Doing so enables us to underscore the relational nature of privilege and marginalization. In other words, privileging the privileged (by focusing on high-power group needs and goals in intergroup contact) occurs with direct consequences in marginalizing the marginalized (low-power groups). We turn now to how IGD has dealt with these two lines of scholarship.

MOTIVATIONS OF LOW- AND HIGH-POWER GROUPS IN INTERGROUP CONTACT   As discussed in chapter 3, the recent shift in intergroup contact research to explicitly attend to issues of power has revealed several possibilities of misunderstandings and disagreements when members of low-power and high-power groups interact. These asymmetries in understanding parallel our discussion of the first three criticisms of intergroup dialogue—too dialogic, too critical, and too little action. In relation to social identities, low-power groups often enter intergroup encounters with their particular identities being salient, whereas high-power group members often come identified just as persons or with some superordinate identity (for example, all college students). Low-power groups tend to prefer exploration of differences, and high-power groups tend to prefer exploration of similarities in perspectives and experiences (Eggins, Haslam, and Reynolds 2002; Maoz 2011; Saguy et al. 2009; Trawalter and Richeson 2008). It is important that the low-power groups are not interested in talking only about differences; they also want to explore both differences and similarities. In relation to understanding inequality, low-power groups reject the legitimacy of hierarchical power relationships, whereas high-power groups may endorse them (Pratto et al. 1994; Saguy, Dovidio, and Pratto 2008). In relation to change, low-power groups want collective action, but high-power groups usually focus on the goals of individual prejudice reduction (Wright and Lubensky 2009). These differing motivations, cognitions, and goals in intergroup encounters also mean that low-power and high-power groups expect different processes to foster their desired outcomes. With the goal of collective action and social change, low-power groups expect to build alliances through exploring both similarities and differences in group-based experiences and through being respected in those explorations (Bergsieker, Shelton, and Richeson 2010; Dixon et al. 2010; Wright and Lubensky 2009). With the goal of individual prejudice reduction, high-power groups expect to build friendships based on similarities, interpersonal affective ties, and being liked. Low-power groups prefer that the content of the conversations include political issues and conflicts, whereas high-power groups tend to prefer more personal and cultural topics (Abu-Nimer 1999).

These divergent motivations and expectations pose challenges in intergroup interactions. In interracial interactions, and nearly all these studies have focused on race, researchers have found that a variety of negative affective and behavioral reactions are evoked for both whites and people of color. People of color often fear being targets of prejudice, experience negative emotions, feel inauthentic, and use compensatory strategies to buffer the stress of such interactions. White people fear being perceived as prejudiced, exhibit nervous behaviors, and have high intergroup anxiety, increased cardiovascular reactivity, and depleted executive functioning (Richeson and Shelton 2007; Trawalter and Richeson 2008). Given the elucidation of the differences in preferences involved in intergroup contact, we can assert that favoring the preferences of the privileged group—a focus on personal talk, intergroup similarities, superordinate identity, and individual change only with a goal of building friendships—will advantage high-power groups. Almost all of the studies looking at these intergroup divergences in motivations and expectations are laboratory-based and have helped delineate elements that can contribute to intergroup misunderstandings in controlled laboratory situations. What happens in everyday, real-time interactions, which are undoubtedly more complex? We turn to the second body of knowledge that focuses specifically on the verbal and nonverbal face-to-face intergroup exchanges.

MICROAGGRESSIONS   A number of scholars and practitioners have pointed out the difficulties in talking across differences for people with more and less privilege. Conversation stoppers (discussed in chapter 1) and intergroup mis-understanding (discussed also in chapter 4), when unaddressed, replicate un-equal power relations; they marginalize and silence members of both groups, although for different reasons and thus affect the learning in intergroup dia-logues. Derald Wing Sue and his colleagues (2007, 2009, 2010) acknowledge that racial and gender dialogues can be difficult because of what is known as microaggressions—brief, everyday exchanges that send denigrating messages from well-intentioned privileged people to the less privileged (Sue et al. 2007). These microaggressions may be experienced by low-power groups in the defensive behaviors of the more privileged, in acts of conversational dom-inance, and in disjunctures in interactions.

Sherry Watt (2007) identifies defensive behaviors that privileged people sometimes exhibit that can be experienced as microaggressions by those with less privilege. One, a principium defense, is driven by personal or political belief systems that judge others' cultures, lifestyles, and life circumstances and does not permit self-criticism of culture or situation. For example, con-sider the statement "Although I feel really badly for the homeless having to suffer in the cold, I do believe that anyone who tries hard enough can get a job and have a roof over their heads." It carries sympathy, but primarily ad-herence to the value of meritocracy. Two, a false envy defense, is characterized by a display of personal affection or admiration of a person while denying the complexity of how power and privilege affect that person. False envy is often conveyed in statements of what is termed exoticization and token recogni-tion. It marks the other as having culture and at the same time keeps one's privileges invisible and cultureless. An example may be, "Oh, I wish I had a distinctive culture with special traditions and special holidays. I am just an ordinary American." Three, a benevolence defense, is based on an attitude of charity in which the more privileged are givers displaying generosity, and the less privileged are the receivers expected to display gratitude. Examples in-clude compensatory behaviors, like "coming down to their level" or personal feelings of goodness because of giving to others. A charity attitude is ex-pressed in a statement like "I sent some money and I got a thank you note with a picture of a child. It made me feel so good that I am making a differ-ence. I can't imagine how difficult it must be for those children in the refugee camps." Each of these defenses is likely well-intentioned, but each also has a quality of focusing paternalistically on others while distancing oneself with little critical reflection, either on one's identities and positions in a system of power and privilege or on the impact of one's statements on others in the learning situation.

Uma Narayan (1988) focuses on emotional costs of working across differences, especially when microaggressions are experienced in acts of invalidation or dominance in interactions. She uses the term *epistemic privilege* to indicate a disjuncture in who knows what and who does not know what. Using examples from relationship interactions between women and men, and women of color and white women, she asserts that low-power groups have epistemic privilege about oppression because of their lived experience. The lack of such epistemic privilege can lead even well-meaning members of high-power groups to negatively affect members of low-power groups in interactions. Even if more privileged group members are critical of inequalities and sympathetic to the experiences of the less privileged group members, they may not understand the deeper impact and emotions involved in assaults to self-identity and self-respect. Thus, people with more privilege may overtly and, sometimes inadvertently, invalidate how members of low-power groups think, feel, and deal with oppression. They may react insensitively to low-power group members' emotional responses by discounting, dismissing, or diverting their emotions. They may even accuse low-power group members of paranoia and of exaggerating emotions. In these ways, members of more privileged groups may exercise their dominance by prescribing what the less privileged ought to think, do, or feel about certain situations.

As subtle or overt as these defenses, disjunctures, and conversation stoppers may be, they convey an impact and struggle in dealing with the realities of inequalities on the part of both the less privileged and the more privileged. Looking specifically at difficult racial dialogues, Derald Wing Sue and his colleagues (2009) found that students of color experienced microaggressions as insulting, derogating, and denigrating. They reported students of color feeling a variety of emotions—angry that their integrity was being challenged, anxious because of their concern of personal consequences, and exhausted from having to continuously deal with microaggressions, and continuing defensiveness on the part of white people in the dialogue. Behaviorally, students of color questioned whether to participate in the dialogues, usually fearing retribution, lack of emotional support, and evaluations by peers and instructors or facilitators. Interestingly, and powerfully so, difficult race-ethnicity dialogues have a parallel impact on white participants. That is, they too experienced—though differently—affective, cognitive, and behavioral impact. Affectively, difficult racial dialogues often evoked anxiety for white students because they were out of their comfort zones; they felt helpless because they did not know how to engage in racial dialogue; they were fearful of appearing racist; they also felt guilty (Spanierman et al. 2006; Sue et al. 2010). Cognitively, white students struggled, often denying their whiteness and white privilege and adhering to a colorblind ideology (Spanierman et al 2008; Sue et al. 2010). Behaviorally, some white students retreated and participated in more passive and appeasing ways or moved on to other topics. When fear and anxiety were especially salient, participants stammered and expressed their perspectives in vague and diffuse ways, thus leading to more misunderstandings. Sometimes, as an expression of their color-blindness, some white students said things like "we are all the same under the skin" or "we are all human beings" in concluding the dialogues.

For all these reasons, it is not surprising that critics would be concerned about both the potential beneficial learning for only one group in dialogue and the potential detriment to the other group. If the dynamics were occurring and had not been addressed constructively in the intergroup dialogues studied in the project, the effects would have differed for the students from the more and less privileged backgrounds. We did not find such evidence. Intergroup dialogue neither privileged the privileged nor marginalized the marginalized. In the quantitative results, similar effects of dialogue were found for students from groups that differed in societal privilege on all but six of the twenty-four measures presented in chapter 5. In four of these exceptions, dialogue was effective for both groups but had larger effects for groups with more societal privilege, that is, white people in the race-ethnicity dialogues and men in the gender dialogues. In other words, larger effects for students from more privileged groups were not associated with negative effects for students from less privileged groups. It was only on two measures that dialogue had an impact only on the more privileged students. Moreover, on twenty-two measures covering intergroup understanding, intergroup relationships, intergroup action, and cognitive involvement and emotions, both groups showed positive significant effects.

In the qualitative results, we also found similar subjective accounts of the dialogue experience by members of more and less privileged backgrounds. The qualitative findings on student engagement in chapter 7 showed no differences among the four demographic groups in how frequently they were coded in the interview material as being engaged by listening, speaking, and actively thinking—with one exception. That exception was that the men of color were coded as more engaged in speaking compared with the other three groups. The findings on empathy in chapter 6 also showed similar amounts of writing about empathy in the final papers. That was true of cognitive empathy, emotional empathy, relational empathy, and critical empathy. A man of color in a race-ethnicity intergroup dialogue, quoted in chapter 3, underscores the importance of empathy (listening, understanding, and relating to his experiences) as a path to realizing how everyone, including himself, can benefit in intergroup dialogue: "Coming into the course, I had a hard time listening to white people's complaints and concerns about whether or not they actually hold privilege in society. This class taught me to be . . . there for people along their journeys . . . just as I was helped as well . . . I have begun to understand that learning is a two-way street and we both benefit from listening to each other." A woman of color, also in a race-ethnicity intergroup dialogue and quoted at the beginning of chapter 1, stressed the importance of honest talk about race, something she rarely had experienced on her campus but did experience in her dialogue class. "I came to this class hoping . . . to be able to talk honest about race. . . . What I hoped for was a small community where I could speak about racial issues without feeling people would point to me as the 'angry, black woman.' In fact, I did get a place to speak comfortably about issues of race."

It was not only students of color in race-ethnicity intergroup dialogues or women in gender intergroup dialogues who talked and wrote about what they learned in their dialogue classes. A white woman in a race dialogue (not previously quoted) talked to the interviewer at the end of her class about learning to communicate across differences.

> Beyond the lessons I have learned about myself, the most important skill I have obtained is the ability to successfully communicate cross-culturally. . . . This could not have happened if I had not built relationships with all the unique members of the group and I did that by bridging the differences between us. . . . I am confident in saying that by the end of the class, I was able to abandon any confusion, resentment, and anger that sometimes gets in the way and do whatever I could to communicate and relate with everyone. That is a huge learning for me. (White woman, race dialogue)

A white man in a gender dialogue (not quoted before) wrote in his final paper about "the single most important valuable lesson" that he learned, what he called his epiphany. "The whole experience has taught me countless lessons about gender roles and stereotypes, as well as important skills that have to be there for dialogue to take place. I have learned to listen and try to understand when women talk about feeling put down. I have dropped my defensiveness, and I can be an ally in improving gender relationships."

In both the quantitative and qualitative analyses, we also found no differences in the responses about the communication processes by the four groups of students. They did not differ in how frequently they reported on the surveys that engaging self, appreciating difference, critical reflection, and alliance building occurred in their dialogues or how important those four processes were for their learning. In the qualitative analyses, they did not differ in how much they wrote about these processes in their final papers. Furthermore, the impact of the processes on the students' commitments to action in their final papers did not differ for the more and less privileged students (Gurin-Sands et al. 2012).

HOW INTERGROUP DIALOGUE ADDRESSES POWER ASYMMETRIES AND MICROAGGRESSIONS

The evidence is clear that the project did not support critiques of power asymmetries and microagressions that have been levied against intergroup dialogue. Why might that be? The primary answer is that the critical-dialogic communication processes address the potential cognitive, affective, and behavioral challenges and misunderstandings that may arise in intergroup relationships across differences in power and privilege. Our findings show three ways that the communication processes address such misunderstandings. One, the dialogic communication processes of engaging self and appreciating difference set the stage for both preventing these problems or addressing them constructively as they developed. Prevention occurred because the practice model (chapter 2) addresses students' fears and hopes immediately in the beginning of the intergroup dialogue course. Realizing that fears are not theirs alone but common for others helps allay initial anxiety and promotes the process of engaging self. A white woman in a gender dialogue, quoted in chapter 3, stressed the impact on her of respect that she saw directed to her peers in the dialogue.

When students shared their testimonials, I was blown away with how everyone really listened and how each person who shared was treated with such respect and without judgment. . . . When I saw how the facilitators and students asked thoughtful and respectful questions, I was a whole lot more comfortable sharing my own story and beginning to be a fully participating member of this dialogue.

Moreover, building dialogue skills of active listening and setting guidelines for engagement early in the dialogue help students have productive interactions. The qualitative analysis of interviews shows that the processes of engaging self (speaking) and appreciating difference (listening) were mutually influential. Having others listen to one's perspectives helps one share more, and sharing by others inspires one to share as well. As demonstrated in the qualitative data from videotaping, interviews, and final papers, dialogic processes of listening and responding to others through openness and behavioral engagement influenced relational empathy engagement (from interview data). The dialogic process of appreciating difference through asking questions and conveying interest in others influenced awareness of others' emotions (interview data), critical empathy (interview data), and intention to act and educating others (final paper data as shown in Gurin-Sands et al. 2012). In contrast, nondialogic behaviors of debating were consistently negatively related to empathy and action. The dialogic skills (speaking openly, listening and responding to others, and inquiring), contrasted with debating (forceful and defensive sharing of one's thinking) seem to set the stage for more critical skills—critical reflection and alliance building. Building these foundation processes and skills helps students acknowledge anxieties and helps them inquire into commonalities and differences. Complementing student narratives, the structural equation model (using quantitative data) presented in chapter 5 also showed that communication processes fostered affective positivity in intergroup dialogues.

Two, the critical process of analysis and reflection was important in addressing the misunderstandings that may arise in intergroup dialogue. Analyses of the video data showed that misunderstandings were not submerged but instead actively surfaced and processed within the dialogue groups. In the video example from the race-ethnicity dialogue, students' openness and inquiry, which involved active critical reflection on the interactions in the dialogue group, allowed many points of connection to be formed. The social nature of learning was evident as the students renegotiated how the white men and students of color could contribute in more equal ways. The dialogue process encouraged the students to share a variety of perspectives, even disagreements, and to critically examine what the impact of privileged participation had been on the diverse group members. The white man's lack of awareness of how his behaviors had been visible to others was brought to his attention. His willingness to listen to his peers' perspectives, many of them students of color, heightened his awareness and allowed him to understand dialogue dynamics in a new way. The collective critical reflections in the dialogue helped him critically appraise himself. What could have been under-the-surface, unexplored misunderstandings were dealt with productively through critical reflection, inquiry, and openness. The structural equation model (using quantitative data), presented in chapter 5, also showed that communication processes foster such cognitive involvement. The specific focus in intergroup dialogue on identity and inequality helps all students critically analyze their similar and different social locations and the possible impact their identities may have in the dialogue group. Critical analysis and reflection can be learned, as it was in these race-ethnicity and gender dialogues, through sustained contact with people different from oneself and through facilitative guidance as those sustained interactions take place. A woman of color in a race-ethnicity dialogue (quoted in chapter 3) stressed the importance of her facilitator pressing "us to see who was talking and who was silent [sending] us all into reflection and thinking together. We realized that our dynamics were silencing people from minority groups that weren't black, and that there were many different points of view in our dialogue." As our discussion of roommate studies in chapter 3 shows, sustained contact by itself produces mixed outcomes. Without facilitation, roommates may not talk about their racial-ethnic differences, may not reflect on how their socialization experiences influence the ways they see each other, and may not explore how power and privilege affect ways in which they negotiate the shared living quarters.

Three, the communication process of alliance building specifically addresses the challenges posed by the divergent goals of high-power and low-power groups in relation to action, namely, preferences for prejudice reduction and individual change versus collective action for social change. By seeking collaboration between low-power and high-power groups in action, alliance building specifies a process by which these different goals can be engaged. The goal of collaboration does not submerge differences and con-flicts, but engages these very divergences to build greater trust and strengthen alliances.

A woman of color in a gender intergroup dialogue stressed that alliances depend on differences. "Alliances were formed in our ICP experience. The ICP was designed to challenge our previous beliefs, views, and opinions and to step outside of our comfort zones to work with people we would not nor-mally interact with. It taught me, as in the poem on alliances that we read, that alliances arise out of the fact that we are different. With these differences we were able to find a common goal and carry out a successful action proj-ect." A man of color in a race-ethnicity intergroup dialogue, quoted in chap-ter 3, emphasized the importance of conflict. "From these moments of con-flict, I also felt a sense of hope when I realized that it was possible for diverse people to use their differences in pursuit of a common goal, which in the case of dialogue is shared meaning."

In the quantitative data, distinctions were drawn between types of action. Educating self is closely related to personal change and reducing prejudice. Educating others and collaborating with others are more related to collective action. The quantitative data showed that intergroup dialogue increased all three types of action, both their frequency and the confidence that students felt in enacting them. A mixed-methods analysis of the interviews and final papers confirmed the importance of both educating others and collaborating with others (see Gurin-Sands et al. 2012; Nagda 2006; Nagda, Kim, and Truelove 2004). Additional analyses showed the importance of both engag-ing self and alliance building in explaining how students conceive of their intention to act and actually act in the service of social justice (Gurin-Sands et al. 2012).

In summary, the quantitative and qualitative analyses support the conclu-sion that joint critical and dialogic communication processes result in inter-group interactions that are not plagued by misunderstandings but instead deal with divergent motivations and expectations. The communication pro-cesses help students understand these asymmetries as part of the challenges posed in interacting across and about difference, engage students in critical collective dialogue about them, and offer newer ways of thinking, relating, and acting that help bridge the differences. Together, the dialogic and critical processes played important roles in students' understanding of inequalities, building relationships, and building collaborations for action.

PRACTICE, THEORY, AND RESEARCH REVISITED

Throughout this chapter, we have presented practice and theoretical implications based on our findings as well as implications for scholarship on intergroup relations. In this section, we summarize the important conclusions in two broad areas. In the area of practice and theory, we discuss implications for improving IGD practice based on the research evidence. In the area of research and evaluation, we note conclusions for how small-group educational interventions may be evaluated.

From Theory and Evidence to Improving Practice

The research evidence accumulated in this study and its validation of the theoretical framework of intergroup dialogue provide a basis for thinking about improving IGD practice. We focus on implications specifically for intergroup dialogue but what we suggest here applies generally to other courses in which student interaction is important and to other guided intergroup interactions. We use the critical-dialogic theoretical framework presented in chapter 3 to organize practice implications to strengthen IGD pedagogy, communication processes, and psychological processes.

INTERGROUP DIALOGUE PEDAGOGY   Both the quantitative and qualitative evidence shows the importance of IGD pedagogy—content, structured interactions, and facilitation—for student learning. All three are important for improving intergroup dialogue practice.

Understanding how the different learning processes of reflective, relational, and integrative learning work illuminates some of the weaknesses in IGD and ways learning can be enhanced. Learning in intergroup dialogue can be biased toward reflective and relational learning without thoroughly integrating content. Students need to learn more about inequality and its multiple causes, the controversies that exist in many disciplinary literatures about the positives and negatives of in-group identifications, and the factors that explain when conflict can be constructive or destructive. Readings provide such materials but the compelling nature of relational learning in the dialogues sometimes deters sufficient engagement with content and readings. Some collaborators in the MIGR project are experimenting with colleagues across disciplines, and with attaching dialogue courses to lecture courses (sociology courses on inequality, comparative religion courses, international politics courses, social work courses on diversity and justice, and others) that connect in-depth information with the relational aspects of intergroup dialogue.

A second content-related issue is how IGD meets or fails to meet the challenge of dispersion noted in chapter 1. IGD courses need to challenge participants to deal with their identities as world citizens and actors with responsibilities at both local and global levels. IGD course content, as implemented in this study, is far too bounded by material about the United States and identities defined within the United States. Although several collaborators have extended the dialogue method to international settings, most IGD programs that currently exist on college campuses focus almost exclusively on issues within the United States. Course content needs to draw connections between the intersectional identities across race, ethnicity, religion, gender, sexuality, and class as experienced within the United States with similar intersectional identities of people in other countries. It also needs to help students understand that local and national identities fit with and are enhanced by identities as world citizens.

The qualitative data provided evidence of the importance of structured activities for student learning. Students, in interviews about their learning, cited testimonials, caucus and fishbowl activity, and hot topics as the three most important activities that helped engage them in speaking and listening in intergroup dialogue. These three activities, together with the web of oppression and intergroup collaborative project (ICP), were cited in students' papers as the five structured activities most important for their learning. Two of these five, hot topics and ICP, are designed for students to integrate and apply their learning. However, the videotape data analyses revealed that student speaking in the hot topics session was often nondialogic. Although hot topics was influential in their speaking engagement in intergroup dialogue, the observed behaviors show that student debating was more evident during that activity. These findings suggest that facilitators need to help students apply and deepen their dialogue skills when contentious issues arise, as they do during hot topics. Facilitators need to remind students of the ground rules for engaging in dialogue, and of what students have learned during the first two IGD stages, which should have prepared them to have a dialogue rather than a debate during hot topics in the third stage. Facilitators must help students suspend judgments of each other's perspectives through active listening and identify each other's assumptions by asking questions.

It also appears that IGD courses do not always maximize the integrative learning potential of the ICPs. Those projects are intended to foster reflection on the dynamics of intergroup collaboration and provide practice in collaborating across differences. The student presentations of their ICP experience too often emphasize the product of collaboration rather than the process of collaborating (Gurin-Sands et al. 2012). ICP thus sometimes fails to meet its full potential for integrative learning. Although we do not wish to diminish students' possible excitement about their action projects, we do wish to increase the amount of time that students reflect on what made their collaboration successful or not. This may require a two-phase dialogue. The first phase would allow students to present their action projects, and the second would ask them to step back and reflect on their collaborative process as an example of alliance building. In both phases, collective reflection that encourages students to discern the lessons across the presentations of actions and the processes of collaboration can contribute to integrative learning.

In addition to strengthening the learning from specific activities, the role of collective reflection in every dialogue needs attention. Collective reflection, as the last part of each dialogue session, can deepen what the students have learned and guide them to imagine how that learning can be used in the future. The collective reflection phase of a session is sometimes incomplete because of shortness of time or lack of direction on how to build collective learning from structured interaction. We offer two suggestions for improvement to incorporate into the intergroup curriculum design. First, curriculum designers should not include too many structured activities per session lest the focus of intergroup dialogue become procedural—merely participating in structured activities—rather than process oriented—deriving learning from structured activities (Nagda and Maxwell 2011). In chapter 2, we described a template for a typical IGD session. Beyond the brief check-in and check-out parts of a session, we recommend one main activity per session. Observing this as a general rule will increase time for collective reflection about the structured activities and for integrating learning from readings and group processes. Second, we suggest using a general developmental guide for the collective reflection and dialogue to deepen the learning. Barbara Steinwachs (1992) offers a helpful rubric for thinking about different levels of learning: description, analogy-analysis, and application. The description phase encourages students to begin collective reflection on the activity through questions such as "What happened during this activity?" "How did we feel participating in this activity?" "How did our thinking and feeling change during the course of the activity?" The analogy-analysis phase encourages students to connect learning in the activity to real-world situations and content. Reflection questions may include "How do our experiences in this activity represent concepts discussed in the readings and real-life situations?" "How were our experiences in the activity different from real-life situations?" "What may be some reasons for that?" Finally, the applications phase encourages participants to consider how they can apply what they have learned to their lives. They may reflect and dialogue about "How can we apply our learning to situations outside the dialogue group?" "How might we continue to learn more about what we have experienced and discussed?" "What are some next steps in learning more about the issues raised?"

Facilitators are crucial in structuring these different phases of collective reflection and in framing relevant questions. We turn to the facilitation component of IGD pedagogy next.

Many intergroup contact and social justice education efforts stress the importance of structured interactions and sustained contact as opposed to one-time interventions. The evidence, especially from the videotape study and as part of pedagogy in the structural equation modeling, shows how critical facilitators are. Although IGD facilitators do not take on traditional instructional roles, they are active in engaging participants in the structured activities, help frame the learning significance of relevant content, foster collective dialogic interactions among participants, support individual participant learning, and intervene as necessary to address intergroup dynamics that impede dialogue. The videotape data showed that dialogic facilitation behaviors were related to student dialogic behaviors; facilitator reflection-redirection and inquiry were positively related to students' initiative to speak and inquire. The video data further showed that either extreme of facilitation—too passive or too active—does not promote dialogic participation among students. Facilitators need to be active guides without letting go of the dialogue or taking over.

Facilitator training, therefore, needs to deepen facilitation skills in guiding dialogue and to avoid becoming advocates for their positions. Facilitators may resort to advocacy when they are triggered by something participants say or by particular participants in the dialogue. Or, some facilitators may freeze and just listen and support whatever is happening rather than guiding the dialogue in a productive manner. Merely listening and supporting students may actually represent facilitator distance and disengagement when they do not know what to say or how to reflect, redirect, and use inquiry to promote student dialogue. Consequently, students may perceive the dialogue as being rudderless.

Many IGD programs use the concepts and language of triggers and hot buttons in training facilitators (Hardiman, Jackson, and Griffin 2007; Rodriguez et al. 2011). Facilitators are asked to identify thoughts, feelings, and behaviors that can be emotionally triggering for them and become obstacles in facilitating effectively. What is important is training them to move this awareness to action, that is, how to use their awareness of their triggers to become more effective facilitators. For example, to move from passive listening and support, facilitators need to actively validate the different perspectives emerging in the dialogue. They need to understand that validation does not mean agreement but simply that every participant's perspective is acknowledged. To move from advancing their positions to cultivating diverse perspectives, facilitators can use inquiry, model examination of the underlying assumptions of their and others' perspectives, and contextualize these perspectives in the dynamics of identity, power, and privilege.

Critically reflective practice is one approach used to encourage facilitators to "examine their personal motives, reactions, skills, or experiences in the moment (reflection-in-action) and after a dialogue session took place (reflection-on-action)" (Zúñiga et al. 2011, 74). Such practice enables facilitators to step back to examine both the internal and situational factors at play when they may have acted on their triggers or fears. With feedback from co-facilitators and trainers, facilitators can learn to recognize when they are advocating particular perspectives or letting student debate or perspective-advancement persist when they instead should intervene. Trainers may engage facilitators in role-playing or other theater techniques to act out scenarios with different possible interventions to increase facilitator self-confidence in responding to unproductive dynamics in IGD and continue to develop their skills in effective IGD facilitation.

The elucidation of communication and psychological processes as the mediating processes in our theoretical model between IGD pedagogy and outcomes also has implications for strengthening facilitation training. Facilitators can both directly influence ways in which participants interact with each other through communication and constantly attend to the affective and cognitive processes for participants. Facilitators must also attend to the impact of power asymmetries that can manifest as misunderstandings or experienced as microaggressions. Students may not always be able to verbalize the impact of power asymmetries and they may disengage or resist the dialogue. Facilitators, informed by the knowledge of intergroup misunderstandings and microaggressions, need to surface such dynamics and engage the students in exploring the dynamics through collective reflection and dialogue. We turn now to how facilitators can link IGD pedagogy to these processes.

COMMUNICATION PROCESSES   In our view, the importance of communication processes in intergroup dialogue cannot be overstated. The quantitative and qualitative findings of the study converge on the immediate and long-term benefits of communication processes in fostering cognitive and affective psychological processes as well as outcomes of intergroup understanding, intergroup relationships, and intergroup collaboration. We have noted both the theoretical and practical importance of communication processes throughout the volume, and especially in this chapter, in addressing the cross-group interactional challenges that arise from power asymmetries and microaggressions. The dialogic and critical communication processes together denote a social-relational process that moves away from simply learning about others or being critical of society to conceiving oneself in relation to others, understanding oneself and one's relationships in a larger societal context. Additionally, and perhaps most important, these communication processes engage students in participating in and experimenting with new ways of relating and thinking together that foster individual and collaborative action. The communication processes play a vital role through which students come to understand how relationships across differences and power statuses can become the nexus of social change. Through facilitator guidance, modeling, and skill-building among participants, the communication processes engage all participants in speaking, listening, and critical thinking. Given the emphasis on building self-other relationships and equalizing relationships in the context of inequalities, the communication processes offer a way of speaking and listening different than the norm. Speaking becomes relational because it involves careful listening and critical reflection rather than merely speaking one's mind. Listening is also relational because each participant learns how to attend to both the content and feeling that others convey. Listening may be conveyed both in responsive speaking (through validation, clarification, sharing, and inquiry), and connective nonverbal communication. In both speaking and listening, the communication processes involve responsibility to participate in the interactions, rather than removal from them. The communication processes enable students to build connection through understanding how all participants are both differently and similarly affected by systems of power and inequalities. Students can use these connections to strengthen their capacities for collective action. Alliance building is a process, not merely an outcome; it involves grappling with roles, relationships, and actions so that unequal power dynamics are challenged as students experience agency-in-community rather than self-separate-from-community (Miller 1982; Nagda et al. 2011).

These findings have important implications for facilitator training and how facilitators can mobilize communication processes. Facilitators need to understand the theoretical, empirical, and practical significance of communication processes in IGD. We see two important ways in which facilitator knowledge can improve IGD practice: facilitators can, one, promote critical-dialogic communication processes among students to deepen the dialogue through inquiry, and, two, learn how to intervene when nondialogic behaviors and dynamics occur and then redirect the dialogue toward more dialogic engagement.

DEEPENING THE DIALOGUE THROUGH INQUIRY   With knowledge of critical-dialogic communication processes, facilitators can work to balance engaging self and appreciating difference as students tell and listen to each others' stories. The analysis of empathy (chapter 6) revealed that when students saw others take risks in telling stories, they were inspired and encouraged to tell their own. When students tell stories, sometimes with considerable courage, facilitators need to validate the risks the students may have taken. Facilitators can encourage students to appreciate their peers' courage and risk-taking by requesting them to verbally connect their stories to what their peers have shared. Facilitators can also encourage students to ask each other clarifying questions, share more of their stories sparked by what they have heard from others, or even revise the meaning of their stories based on feedback.

For the dialogue to go beyond just simple sharing of experience in the structured activity, facilitator inquiry and fostering student-student inquiry are crucial in deepening the learning. The videotape data (chapter 8) showed that students moved beyond attentiveness and verbal initiative to more inquiry in the collective reflection parts of a dialogue session. Inquiry was more present in dialogue about learning from the activity and about learning from the entire session than during the activity. Moreover, the videotape analysis showed that student inquiry involved being attuned to the emotions of others. Thus, facilitators must ensure that collective reflection occurs rather than let dialogue activities predominate over processing their collective meaning. During that period, facilitators should use their knowledge of and practice with communication processes to encourage both private, individual learning and public, collective learning. Individual-directed inquiry invites participants to share their learning through open-ended questions, such as "Can you please say more about that?" or "How did that experience affect you?" Individual-in-collective-directed inquiry invites participants to consider what they have learned in relation to each other through questions such as "What do others think about what has been shared?" or "She has shared something very powerful—how do others connect with her sharing?" or "How are all of us affected by what has been shared in the group?" Collective-directed inquiry includes open-ended questions to the group that help people connect their learning and the dialogue dynamics to larger social arrangements and issues. For example, facilitators may ask, "I wonder how the different issues we have been talking about are connected to the definitions of individual and institutional discrimination we went over at the beginning of the session?" or "How do the different experiences that have been shared connect to our social identities and how we feel on this campus?"

Facilitators can further deepen the dialogue by explicitly connecting the dialogic and critical communication processes. To build on the exchanges, facilitators can use inquiry to guide students to analyze how issues of power and privilege may be reflected in their individual stories as well as in the similarities and differences among those of their peers. Conversely, when students participate in the web of oppression activity, which elucidates the structural nature of power and privilege, facilitators can encourage students to personalize the information so that it does not stand apart as abstract knowledge. In both cases, inquiry and dialogue may also parallel the alliance-building communication process and the ways in which students can collectively build on their dialogic relations and critical analysis for the next steps in their learning and joint actions.

Of course, the responsibility for deepening the dialogue through inquiry does not rest solely with the facilitators. Biren (Ratnesh) Nagda and Kelly Maxwell (2011) emphasize the empowering impact of facilitation in supporting skill development for students. Two particular suggestions are helpful here. One, Stephen Brookfield and Stephen Preskill (1999) suggest giving each student an index card with a particular dialogic conversational move to practice in a dialogue session. Moves that convey listening, responding, or inquiring can include connective behaviors (body leaning in) and statements (such as commenting on someone's idea to show interest, asking questions, encouraging others to elaborate on ideas introduced in the dialogue). They may also include ways to deepen the dialogue, such as asking cause-and-effect questions, slowing the group's pace by asking for silence to reflect on the conversation, expressing appreciation for how what she or he may have gained from the conversation, and offering a different perspective or disagreeing respectfully. In the collective reflection part of the dialogue, facilitators can share the entire list of conversational moves and engage students in a dialogue about what moves they noticed among their peers and how they practiced their own. Two, Steinwachs's (1992) conceptual map of description, analogy, and application discussed earlier may also serve as a guide for designing small and large group dialogues that involve student-led inquiry following the structured activities. Then facilitators can foster metadialogues that focus on the importance of inquiry, the level of confidence students felt when they inquired of their peers, the depth of their responses, and ways to continue to apply those skills in the open dialogues. In both these suggestions, facilitators become coaches, walking alongside students in developing dialogue-promoting behaviors through practice and collective reflection.

INTERVENING IN NONDIALOGIC DYNAMICS AND BEHAVIORS The prevalence of students' nondialogic behaviors, such as advancing their perspectives and debating, requires active intervention on the part of facilitators and trainers. To do so, facilitators need to understand that nondialogic behaviors signify an area for facilitator intervention. For example, when students are advancing their perspectives, facilitators may ask questions about how those perspectives are related to others shared in the dialogue or how they are related to a particular reading. Facilitators may also reflect, redirect, and invite different perspectives by asking other students to contribute, or by using content in readings that sheds a different light on the perspectives. When students engage in debate rather than dialogue, facilitators can note what has happened. They can remind and reaffirm the group's guidelines for engagement, or ask how the group can collectively continue the conversation in a more dialogic manner. Sometimes nondialogic communication may be experienced by students who are in less privileged groups as microaggressions. As discussed earlier in chapters 2 and 8, Nagda and Maxwell (2011) offer the importance of framing and naming whereby facilitators name group dynamics and frame them in a broader context of societal inequalities. Thus, even nondialogic behaviors offer in vivo opportunities to examine intergroup dynamics, to reflect on how they may represent societal dynamics, and to collectively problem solve.

Nondialogic dynamics, when facilitated effectively, can produce teachable moments for students to learn about inequalities and how they can be addressed rather than avoided so that alliances will prove effective. Anna Yeakley (2011) urges using conflicts that emerge in intergroup dialogue as teachable moments because unresolved conflicts often lead to negative outcomes, such as increased separation, stereotyping, resentment, and disconnection. Facilitators must be able to detect signs of conflict that may lie beneath the surface of dialogue interactions, bring them into the open, and create a space where all participants can share what they have learned from the conflict and connect the dynamics to larger societal conflicts.

COGNITIVE AND AFFECTIVE PSYCHOLOGICAL PROCESSES   Like the communication processes, the critical-dialogic intergroup dialogue model underscores the importance of two sets of psychological processes—cognitive involvement and affective positivity. The links of pedagogy and communication processes to cognitive-affective engagement predicted in the theoretical model was supported in both the quantitative and qualitative findings. Thomas Pettigrew and Linda Tropp (2011), in their meta-analysis of intergroup contact to reduce prejudice, found very few research studies that looked at both cognitive and affective processes in the same study. In intergroup dialogue, the joint impact of the two types of psychological processes is evident in critical relational empathy, which has both cognitive elements, which help students understand particular experiences and perspectives as part of larger social patterns, and affective elements, which arise in connecting with these experiences and perspectives. Our qualitative findings on engagement showed the significance of internal active thinking and active processing in response to what occurs in dialogue. Two specific processes, one cognitive and one affective, deserve elaboration in thinking about implications for practice.

IDENTITY SALIENCE   In contrast to the previous emphasis on similarity at the exclusion of difference, intergroup dialogue addresses more recent scholarship that emphasizes an understanding of power and differences in intergroup interactions. Intergroup dialogue provides one way—a demonstrably effective one—that divergences in motivations, expectations, and goals resulting from differences in power and status can be addressed in the contact situation. Identity salience also means that students see themselves as part of social groups, not just as individuals, and that they develop critical thinking skills to question societal and institutional influences on individual and group behavior. Both of these processes—seeing oneself as social and knowing the ways in which society and institutions "do race"—are among six antidotes Paula Moya and Hazel Markus (2010) recommend to "undo" common, negative practices of "doing race." As our evidence shows, making group identity salient, positioning identity within power and privilege, and having dialogues about misunderstandings and power asymmetries as they emerge in the interactions contribute to positive learning in intergroup dialogue.

Students came to active insights especially when they were able to interrogate the differences in their experiences and those of the other identity group. When that happened, students were able to understand that social identities influence everyone in the dialogue; they can grasp that identities are inevitably political in the sense that they are located in social structure and are not merely characteristics of individuals (Cole 2008; Gurin-Sands et al. 2012). Identity engagement in our practice and research in this study focused on particular identities (race-ethnicity and gender). Students, however, extended their thinking about structural inequality to topics that were not the focus of their particular dialogue, demonstrating that intersectionality of their multiple identities can become a resource for coalition building (Cole 2008) and for connecting their identities to their roles as local and global citizens.

EMOTIONS   Emotions are also an important part of the learning process in connecting personal and group experiences to social and structural arrangements. The strategies for "undoing race" that Moya and Markus (2010) suggest are entirely cognitive and informational, such as becoming more knowledgeable about concepts of race and of the history of racism and practices that lead to racial disparities. In line with suggestions by Sherry Watt (2007), Sue and his colleagues (2009, 2010), and Uma Narayan (1988), our evidence points to the complementary importance of emotions and the need to address them in intergroup encounters. In the structural equation modeling, affective positivity, which is fostered by pedagogy and communication processes, then influences intergroup empathy and intergroup collaboration and action. In addition, emotional processing evident in our qualitative findings on empathy shows how students were individually affected by listening to their peers' stories.

The recognition and expression of emotions in intergroup dialogue need to be normalized. To do so facilitators may ask any one of several questions: "You have shared something very important about how you felt about this situation; can you share more about how that affected you?" "We are hearing many different perspectives and experiences in our dialogue. How are we feeling hearing all these different experiences?" "What is emotionally challenging for you in acknowledging privilege? What makes it hard to acknowledge disadvantages?" Alternately, when participants explicitly share their feelings, facilitators should validate those feelings, check back for accuracy, and then open the dialogue to others who may feel similarly or differently. They may follow with inquiry such as "If we take all the feelings as valid, can we think about how our identities and locations of privilege and disadvantages may be connected to these feelings?"

Another way for surfacing emotions to increase dialogue is to use in-class reflection papers, which IGD pedagogy calls for so that students check in with themselves in the moment. Reflection questions are generally directed at individual learning: "How would you describe what happened during the —— activity? Feel free to describe a particular moment or interchange." "Describe the reactions (such as thoughts, feelings) that came up for you at the time?" "Why do you think you had these reactions?" and "How do you think these reactions relate to what you are learning in the dialogue?" Because both active cognitive processing (as in engagement) and emotional processing (as in empathy) are important and occur in the context of collective reflection and learning, additional reflection questions should focus on collective learning: "What are all of us thinking about the perspective that your peers have shared?" "Describe your feelings in relation to what you are hearing from your peers" "How do we see our social identities influencing our perspectives and feelings in relation to our peers?" After the private reflection and writing, facilitators may ask students to share their thoughts and feelings publicly to generate collective reflection.

In describing ways to improve IGD practice, we have built directly on the research evidence that identified the pedagogical features and the communication and psychological processes that influence the outcomes in our study. We turn now to implications of our research for studying the effectiveness of intergroup interventions, both intergroup dialogue and other guided interactions.

Research and Evaluation Conclusions: Intervention Effectiveness

The experimental design comparing students randomly assigned to experimental and to control groups allowed us to attribute participation as the cause of the observed change. The evidence accrued in this study further shows that small group educational interventions can be effective. This effectiveness is shown through the impact of IGD on multiple measures of intergroup understanding, relationships, and collaboration and action. Not only do participants build substantive relationships in the group and learn together about social inequalities, they also learn to work together to take action aimed at fostering greater equality and justice. However, the study design could not control for another kind of selectivity, namely, that both the experimental and the control groups were motivated to be in the intergroup dialogues. Thus, the findings from this study cannot be generalized to undergraduate students who have not expressed interest in intergroup dialogues.

As discussed in chapter 4, the study was also designed to address limitations of previous intergroup dialogue research studies that lacked longitudinal follow-up. Our research was designed specifically to assess the long-term impact of intergroup dialogue. Almost all of the effects found immediately at the end of the intergroup dialogue course endured and were evident a year later.

The study was based on an interdisciplinary theoretical model that integrated insights from psychology, sociology, social work, education, communication, and women's studies. The theoretical model specified the immediate and long-term outcomes of IGDs and the communication and psychological processes that mediate the impact of intergroup dialogue pedagogy on the outcomes. Including communication processes among individuals in IGD in addition to the psychological processes within individuals is a unique theoretical and practical contribution of the study. Based on the theoretical model, we found evidence for the effectiveness of communication processes (group) and psychological processes (individual) as mechanisms of change in helping explain the impact of intergroup dialogue. Thus our findings can be applied to other settings that use intergroup contact and diversity–social justice education. Communication processes and psychological processes can be fostered within those settings to enhance intervention effectiveness.

The conclusions of this study have been demonstrated both quantitatively and qualitatively. The mixed-methods approach provided stronger conclusions than would have been possible by depending on any one method. Take intergroup empathy as an example. The survey data results, based on a large sample size, gave us confidence that pedagogy and communication processes both fostered the affective and cognitive psychological processes, which in turn related to increased intergroup empathy. We also are confident that these processes operate similarly in both race and gender dialogues. The qualitative interview results support these results in that intergroup empathy has both affective and cognitive elements in both race and gender dialogues. However, we also learn something new from the interview analyses, namely, a distinction between two kinds of intergroup empathy that were not measured by the survey items. One, relational intergroup empathy, was more evident in gender dialogues where 80 percent of the empathy coded in the interviews was relational, whereas in the race-ethnicity dialogues 50 percent was. The other, critical intergroup empathy, was more evident in the race dialogues, where 50 percent of the empathy coded was critical, whereas in the gender dialogues only 20 percent was. We would have missed this important distinction and missed a difference between the two types of dialogues had we not used mixed methods.

We also learn more about how the communication processes relate to students' action through using mixed methods. We know from the survey results that increases in action (a combined measure of frequency and efficacy) resulted from communication processes both directly and indirectly through the psychological processes. We also know that the level of action students showed a year later was also directly affected by the communication processes during the dialogue course. We know that the role of communication processes was similar in both race and gender dialogues. In the analyses of the students' final papers, we were able to distinguish among the communication processes and learned that the communication process of alliance building was especially related to students' writing about two kinds of action: educating others and collaborating with others (see Gurin-Sands et al. 2012). Moreover, we learned that this connection between alliance building in intergroup dialogue was connected directly to action outside it.

CONCLUSION

In this chapter, we focused on what we have learned from the overall quantitative and qualitative results of the MIGR project. We have done so in three ways. We first examined the overall results in light of the practice and theoretical models of intergroup dialogue. We then mapped the criticisms of intergroup dialogues and related social justice education efforts and showed how the results address the criticisms. Finally, we concluded with the practice and research implications of our study, highlighting important aspects that can be useful for current and future practice, research and theory of intergroup relations interventions and social justice education efforts. In the next and final chapter, we expand the focus of implications to the challenges facing the world and the role of higher education in an increasingly global world.

Authored by Biren (Ratnesh) A. Nagda and Patricia Gurin.

CHAPTER 10

Intergroup Dialogue: A Response to the Challenges of Demography, Democracy, and Dispersion

In chapter 1, we argued that intergroup dialogue (IGD) is an increasingly important form of communication because the United States as a whole and higher education institutions in particular must deal with three major challenges:

a demographic challenge arising from demographic shifts producing a much more ethnically and racially diverse United States that will be majority nonwhite by 2050 and earlier among youth,

a democracy challenge arising from increasing inequality that raises questions for the vitality of a democracy, and

a dispersion challenge arising from shifts in the global position of the United States as other countries assume critical roles on the world stage.

In this chapter, we take up each of these challenges as they specifically involve higher education. We argue that demographic trends among young people will mean that higher education institutions will have much larger proportions of nonwhite students. Rather than assuming that interaction and mutual learning across demographic groups will automatically increase, we contend that intergroup dialogue will continue to be needed, perhaps even more than now, because students will find it easier to insulate themselves in the larger communities of students from their same backgrounds. We also argue that intergroup dialogue addresses the democratic challenge of assuring that members of all groups have a stake in sustaining and invigorating democratic processes. Intergroup dialogue does this by educating students about inequalities and about the need for and capacity of groups differing in power and privilege to collaborate with each other. Finally, we argue that the importance of dialogue, consultation, and cooperation has grown as many more countries have increased economic and political influence in the world. The challenge of dispersion demands a more cosmopolitan education for young people in the United States (Appiah 2006b; Nussbaum 1996, 2007). Intergroup dialogue fosters competencies that future leaders will need in interacting across nationalities in diplomacy, multinational corporations, and both governmental and nongovernmental organizations. In discussing the relevance of intergroup dialogue for how higher education addresses these challenges, we also describe examples that have been developed since the conclusion of this study at some of the nine participating institutions and at other institutions where the Multi-University Intergroup Dialogue Research (MIGR) collaborators have consulted. We offer them as illustrative of possible programs institutions might implement in the future, not necessarily recommended ones because none of them have yet been evaluated as rigorously as the dialogues presented in this book.

THE DEMOGRAPHIC CHALLENGE: INCREASING DIVERSITY IN HIGHER EDUCATION INSTITUTIONS

The capacity and importance of people of different racial-ethnic backgrounds to dialogue with each other will increase in importance as the nation's colleges and universities themselves become more racially and ethnically diverse.

Several demographic trends foretell more diverse higher education institutions in the United States. For one, the recent overall increase in student enrollment in higher education institutions, which, according to the Pew Research Center (Fry 2010), was 6 percent just between the fall of 2007 and 2008, was driven primarily by an increase in racial and ethnic minority enrollment. Almost three-quarters of that year's increase came from racial-ethnic minority students: Hispanic[1] students leading the growth at 15 percent, black students at 8 percent, Asian background students at 6 percent, and white students at 3 percent. For another, a report from the Pew Hispanic Center shows a second single-year surge of Hispanic enrollment in higher education institutions between 2009 and 2010 (Fry 2011). In that year, Hispanic enrollment increased by 349,000, African American by 88,000, and Asian Americans by 43,000, but white enrollment dropped by 320,000. These increases reflect overall changes in proportions of high school graduates from various ethnic-racial backgrounds. The Western Interstate Commission for Higher Education (2008) estimates that the nation's public schools are expected to produce 54 percent more Hispanic high school graduates, 32 percent more Asian/Pacific Islander graduates, 3 percent more African American graduates, 7 percent more American Indian and Alaska Native graduates but 11 percent fewer non-Hispanic white graduates between 2004 and 2014. The increasingly nonwhite pipeline from high school graduation to higher education means that higher education will rapidly become more diversified racially and ethnically.

The dramatic increases expected in ethnic-racial minority enrollment in higher education are apt to continue for three reasons. In the first place, racial and ethnic minorities are becoming a larger proportion of the youth cohort in the United States and thus will be a larger portion of the pipeline to higher education. By 2050, the pipeline to higher education is estimated to include 5 million more African American students, 17 million more Hispanic, and 5 million more from other groups (largely Asian background), along with 6 million fewer white students in K-12 schools (Lopez 2006).

Second, the increases in ethnic or minority enrollment are fueled by immigration from South and East Asia and from Latin America, which is expected to continue. Projections of the Census Bureau suggest that more than half of the likely U.S. population growth rate of 0.77 per year between 2000 and 2050 will be due to immigration (Murdock and Hoque 1999). Immigration has resulted from many factors, including globalization of markets, migrations of populations across the world, and change in 1965 in the U.S. immigration law that increased the annual number of immigrants allowed to come to the United States and permitted immigration from non-European countries (Passel and Cohn 2008). These factors will likely continue to stimulate immigration, short of a change in the 1965 immigration law. Thus, immigrants and children of immigrants will continue to be a significant presence on the campuses of U.S. colleges and universities. Third, because fertility rates are higher among Hispanic immigrants than among all other groups in the United States, including other immigrant groups, Hispanic students in particular will have a much larger presence on college campuses.

Impact of Demographic Changes in Higher Education Institutions

The impact of these demographic changes will likely affect higher education differently in community colleges, public universities, and private universities. It is projected that community colleges will have 57 percent Hispanics, 25 percent whites, 10 percent Asian Americans, and 8 percent African Americans in 2050. Public universities are expected to have 44 percent Hispanics, 33 percent whites, 15 percent Asian Americans, and 8 percent African Americans (Lopez 2006, 11). Only in private institutions will non-Hispanic white students be a majority. The primary reason to expect continuing racial-ethnic diversification of most higher education institutions in the United States is that immigration and higher fertility rates among Hispanics than among other groups will continue to produce a significantly increased presence of students of color in the K-12 pipeline to higher education.

Two other demographic influences should be considered in the likely increase in student diversity in higher education institutions in the United States. First, a greater complexity should be expected in what racial-ethnic diversity means. That complexity will result from an increasing number of students from mixed racial-ethnic backgrounds who identify with more than one race. Between 1990 and 2008, the proportion of students who identify with more than one racial-ethnic group has risen unevenly but unmistakably, a phenomenon likely to increase because about half of the 7 million people who marked more than one race in the American Community Survey of 2009 were under the age of eighteen (Hochschild, Weaver, and Burch 2011).

Second, complexity within the increasing diversification in higher education will also come from the presence of international students at U.S. colleges and universities. Projections of the likely numbers of international students for 2050 are difficult to draw because many factors affect how many students are likely to study abroad and where they are likely to study. The global economic downturn in 2008 produced a decrease in the number of international students enrolled in U.S. higher education institutions (Institute of International Education 2010). But in the 2009–2010 school year, the number of students from other countries entering U.S. schools and colleges rose by 3 percent. The increase was driven primarily by a 30 percent increase in Chinese student enrollment, making China the leading country sending students to the United States. India is next. The top countries sending students to the United States, which together make up 44 percent of the total international enrollments in U.S. higher education, are now China, India, and South Korea, followed by Canada, Taiwan, Japan, and Saudi Arabia (Institute of International Education 2010). Although the numbers of students choosing to study in countries other than the United States are expected to rise, the United States will continue to be among the top receiving countries because of the prestige and attractiveness of its institutions of higher education. Fourteen of the top twenty most highly rated institutions in the world are in the United States.[2]

In summary, demographic shifts will produce higher education institutions in which non-Hispanic white students will make up a smaller proportion of all students, and students of color will make up a larger proportion and a majority of the enrollments in public universities. Hispanic students will greatly outnumber other U.S. resident student groups of color in universities, and the number of students who identify with multiple races or ethnicities will increase. International students will have a significant presence, as will students whose families have migrated from other countries, often maintaining close ties with those countries. What colleges and universities do to educate these much more diverse students and to tap the increasing student diversity for educational benefit will largely determine how successful the United States will be in the increasingly competitive global world and how effective its future leaders will be in multilateral relationships.

A further demographic challenge is that the more diverse students entering U.S. colleges and universities may not have had more experience in multiracial-multicultural relationships by the time they reach college. If patterns of racial-ethnic segregation that exist today were to define the home environments of the 2050 college students, many still will come from K-12 schools where their racial-ethnic group is a majority of the school. Currently, white students are the most isolated group in K-12 schools. Gary Orfield and Chungmei Lee (2006) contrast the racial-ethnic composition of what they call the average student from each of the racial-ethnic groups. The average white student attends a school where slightly more than three-quarters of his or her peers are also white. The average African American student attends a school where slightly more than half of his or her peers are also African American. That is also true of the average Latino student. It is only the average student of Asian background and the average American Indian student who attends a school where less than half of their peers are also from their racial-ethnic backgrounds. Of course, with the hugely increasing share of the K-12 population being racial and ethnic minorities in the upcoming years, the relative isolation of white, African American, and Latino students may change. That depends on what happens to patterns of residential segregation and whether pupil assignment continues to be as residentially based as it is now.

The Opportunity and Challenge of Demographic Shifts for Higher Education

The expected increase in racial-ethnic diversity in colleges and universities offers both an opportunity and challenge. The opportunity is obvious. The possibility of interaction among students from different racial-ethnic backgrounds and from different countries of origin will increase dramatically. The challenge is just as great. The more diverse students will not necessarily have lived in multiracial neighborhoods or attended multiracial schools. They may or may not have had experiences of learning, collaborating, and relating across differences. The larger numbers of multiple groups on many college campuses may also lead to more separate racial-ethnic and nationality organizations and living spaces, what we think of as educational silos. It may be even easier for students to stay within the comfort zones of their own nationality, racial, ethnic group, replicating rather than challenging the experiences they brought to college from their precollege environments. Some of the most diverse institutions today with the greatest potential for interaction and learning across difference are in actuality highly siloed. Sometimes those silos are crucial safe havens for students on campuses where the campus climate is not supportive of racial and ethnic minority students (Powell 1998; McCabe 2009; Smith, Hung, and Franklin 2011). Important as within-group interaction is for fostering a sense of belonging among students of color (Harper and Hurtado 2007; Miller and Sujitparapitaya 2010), it is also important to encourage cross-group interaction if the benefits of diversity are to be realized. What institutions do now and in the future in response to the increasing racial-ethnic diversity will greatly affect whether the increase in diversity will positively influence student learning. A critical question, therefore, is how higher education institutions will utilize this increasing diversity among students at both the undergraduate and graduate levels.

Intergroup dialogue courses use diversity explicitly and intentionally. Each course comprises an equal number of students from two demographically different identity groups. The pedagogy of intergroup dialogue intentionally uses diversity to promote student interactions and learning. The curriculum stimulates students through readings and in-class structured learning activities to learn about inequality, empathize across differences, and practice (in the intergroup collaboration project) how to work across differences. We have shown evidence that the interactions across differences that the pedagogy and communication processes produced were influential in dialogue's effects on intergroup understanding, intergroup empathy, and action.

Diversity Through Intergroup Dialogue

Many institutions of higher education are interested in learning how to implement IGD courses and dialogue-based co-curricular initiatives on their campuses to ensure greater interaction across students from different demographic backgrounds. In 2008, collaborators in the MIGR project conducted a four-day intergroup dialogue institute that was attended by faculty and staff from thirty-five colleges and universities. This MIGR institute presented the theory and practice of intergroup dialogue and offered opportunities for the participants to experience many of the in-class structured learning activities, and to practice how to use collective reflection for students to process what they learn from these activities. The institute also facilitated discussion of institutional factors that can foster or inhibit the introduction of intergroup dialogues on their campuses. The Program on Intergroup Relations at the University of Michigan has also conducted additional summer institutes now spanning five years and 110 institutions. The effectiveness of these institutes has been demonstrated both by outstanding participant evaluations at the close of each institute, and by follow-up efforts at thirty-seven colleges and universities.

We turn now to a few examples of dialogue initiatives that have been created, sometimes at the same institutions that participated in this research project and sometimes at other institutions where the MIGR collaborators have consulted with faculty, staff, and administrators involved in creating their versions of intergroup dialogue.

One of the co-authors of this book, Ximena Zúñiga, extended the University of Massachusetts Amherst dialogue program by developing a multi-institutional collaboration with the Five Colleges, Inc., called the Five College Intergroup Dialogue (IGD) Initiative, which has broadened its focus and has become the Diversity and Dialogue Initiative Group. The collaboration includes Hampshire College, Mount Holyoke College, Smith College, and the Social Justice Education Program of the University of Massachusetts Amherst. The partnership trains staff and faculty across these institutions to facilitate and host both short-term and longer-term intergroup dialogues on a range of topics. The goal is to create a sustainable process for dialoguing on these campuses, to incorporate dialogue methods and skills into many types of classrooms, to increase collaboration across the five colleges through development of a cadre of trained IGD facilitators, to build the capacity for institutional change to make these campuses genuinely welcoming and inclusive campus communities, and to promote increased understanding of how identities affect daily work experiences on these campuses. Since 2009, 120 participants, of whom approximately one-fifth were people of color, have attended one of the three-day IGD facilitation training institutes created by the Five-College partnership.

In 2009, the partnership initiated a new project, called the Five College Days of Dialogue, in which each campus conducts several introductory two and a half hour dialogues for staff and faculty on the same day each year. It has attracted between 300 and 350 participants across the five campuses. In these dialogues, facilitated by faculty and staff previously trained by the partnership, participants explore identities that include race-ethnicity, social class, academic rank status, gender, and religion. They also discuss the impact of these identities in creating inclusive campus work environments. The Days of Dialogue project has motivated participants to take part in longer six-week dialogues that the partnership has instituted on each campus later during each academic year. About eighty-five faculty and staff have engaged in these longer dialogues each year (Kennedy 2011).

The projects initiated by the Five College partnership are being evaluated. In surveys completed immediately after the Days of Dialogue, 70 percent of the participants indicated that they would apply dialogue skills in interactions with people who are different from them; another 64 percent expected to apply dialogue skills in meetings; 54 percent expected to talk with their co-workers about their dialogue experience (Zúñiga, Dimmitt, and Neely 2011). A participant in one of the introductory dialogues focusing on academic rank observed a year later, "I was reinvigorated to bring the conversations back to my workplace and make sure the conversations continued and were respectful." From a different perspective, an individual who participated in an introductory race-ethnicity dialogue said, "Getting to know people a bit across the spectrum of the college and talking with them about issues of inclusion has made me feel more comfortable in general discussing these issues."

Analysis of pre-post measures of reactions to the longer (six-week) dialogues show that participants significantly increased knowledge of "issues pertinent to race-racism dialogues" and "issues pertinent to class-classism and academic rank." One participant explained, "I have been more tuned into how social class and academic rank dynamics play out on campus [and] felt more empowered to take action." Participants also expressed greater ability to initiate conversations about diversity issues at work and create a more open and inclusive work environment. Another participant said, "I have had a few conversations with co-workers and also asked leadership if diversity is something our department can incorporate into our ongoing conversations" (Zúñiga, Dimmitt, and Neely 2011).

Two additional examples of institutions using intergroup dialogue to tap student diversity have taken place on campuses that are among the most diverse in the United States. Both institutions have sent representatives to the summer institutes at the University of Michigan and subsequently developed new initiatives on their campuses.

The University of Illinois at Chicago (UIC), the thirteenth most diverse national university in the United States, provides an excellent example of the Michigan summer institute experience.[3] In 2008, two senior administrators from UIC, one from academic affairs and one from student affairs, attended the institute and saw the relevance of intergroup dialogue for using that institution's considerable student diversity to foster intergroup interactions and student learning. A plan was developed under the guidance of a small working group from the two units to pilot an intergroup dialogue course in the UIC Honors College and to develop co-curricular intergroup dialogue workshops. In the winter of 2009, a pilot was developed to introduce basic dialogic methods in an existing Honors College diversity course. This pilot was soon followed by a full semester honors course offered in the fall of 2010 cofacilitated by two faculty members. Based on evidence of its impact, additional courses and co-curricular activities have been developed. Under the leadership of Charu Thakral, diversity planning specialist in the Office of Diversity, and Valerie Holmes, associate director of Student Development Services (and most recently Philip Vasquez in the same position), a campuswide UIC dialogue initiative has been implemented into curricular and co-curricular dialogue offerings that provide students with opportunities to benefit educationally from UIC's student diversity. UIC is now developing a plan to provide some type of intergroup dialogue experience during first-year orientation to initiate new students into a campus culture that values student interactions across the many racial-ethnic and religious groups that make up the UIC student body.

These curricular and co-curricular developments are guided by an executive committee that establishes, maintains, and coordinates intergroup dialogue programming efforts on campus. An ongoing task force of representatives from key campus units involved in the dialogue initiative—the Honors College, Department of Communication, College of Pharmacy, College of Education, Urban and Public Affairs Undergraduate Program, the Centers for Diversity, Center for Research on Women and Gender, the Counseling Center, Student Development Services, Campus Housing, and Campus Programs—guides the implementation of intergroup dialogue across the campus.

The University of California at Riverside, the seventh most diverse institution in the United States,[4] has sent representatives to the University of Michigan summer institutes to explore how intergroup dialogue might be used to encourage cross-group interactions on the Riverside campus. With the leadership of Marcela Ramirez, Diversity Initiatives coordinator, and Joseph Virata, interim director of Diversity Initiatives, the university has created programs that both support and challenge separate homogeneous racial-ethnic groupings by helping members of these groups to sustain relationships across identity groups. As at many universities, the safe spaces that students of color have developed at Riverside can turn into silos that discourage intergroup interaction. Separate safe spaces are important because they create group solidarity and support, but they can also reduce interactions across difference. Lack of intergroup connections can produce awkward encounters and conflicts, particularly when groups find themselves on opposite sides of campus issues. This dynamic occurs because, as at many other universities, the Ethnic and Gender Program Offices—comprising African American Student Programs, Asian Pacific Student Programs, Chicano Student Programs, LGBT Resource Center, Native American Student Programs, and the Women's Resource Center—offer separate services to separate historically targeted groups. These group-specific offices provide important services but at the same time may insulate these groups from one another.

The IGD program initiated by the Diversity Initiatives Office aims to promote community building across these groups and to foster civic engagement among students in all groups. Without sacrificing the ability to provide targeted support for specific student communities, the program brings different identity groups together to dialogue across difference. These dialogues give the students a language and skills they can use in intergroup interactions on the campus and help them discover connections and commonalities within differences. Another way in which this dialogue program tries to foster intergroup interaction is by training staff from across the university in dialogue methods they can use to help design and develop dialogue-based programs for academic tutors, peer mentors, resident advisors, fraternities and sororities, tour guides, student organization leaders and many others. This tiered approach builds connections at all levels, across many units of the university, and across a wide range of aspects of student life and campus culture. To institutionalize and strengthen the influence of the dialogue program, the Diversity Initiatives Office will become a core member of the Ethnic and Gender Programs Office.

One example of intergroup dialogue on the Riverside campus is a three-day Common Ground Retreat, which brings together leaders from all groups served by the Ethnic and Gender Program Offices. Another is a first-year student orientation program called Building Our Common Ground Workshop, which aims to create positive peer-to-peer interactions among diverse entering students, to facilitate understanding of the complexities of identity, and to build interest in establishing community across differences. For most incoming first-year students, it is the first time they have addressed the meaning of diversity and what diversity involves at the University of California, Riverside.

In these three institutions, IGD training has allowed faculty and staff to develop new programs that attempt to use the student diversity that has resulted from demographic shifts to promote educational benefits for students. They differ in their emphases, one focusing especially on how IGD helps faculty and staff in their daily work environments and fosters interuniversity collaboration, another focusing on integrating IGD in both co-curricular and especially curricular settings across the entire campus, and the third focusing on ways that the staff in student affairs can use dialogue to foster intergroup interaction across student groups. Evaluations are under way at all three campuses, but of course these initiatives have not been subjected to the rigorous, experimental methods that the MIGR used in the research reported in this volume. They demonstrate how intergroup dialogue can be used to leverage the increasing student diversity resulting from demographic shifts in the United States.

THE DEMOCRATIC CHALLENGE: DEMOCRATIC ENGAGEMENT

Since the founding of public higher education institutions in the last quarter of the eighteenth century, higher education has played an important role in creating an educated citizenry to assure the vitality of the U.S. democracy. Thomas Jefferson, whose vision of democracy included only individuals who were already defined as citizens, that is, white men with property, argued that citizens are made, not born (Barber 1998). His great vision for education—to provide the knowledge citizens would need to invent, reinvent, and sustain democracy—was fulfilled in the founding of the University of Virginia in 1819. Jefferson spent the last years of his life guiding how that institution would provide the kind of education that would make students into citizens. His impact on education in the service of democracy is reflected in the in-scription on his tombstone, which he composed:

Here was buried
Thomas Jefferson
Author of the Declaration of American Independence
of the Statute of Virginia for religious freedom
and Father of the University of Virginia[5]

Jefferson included in his directive for his tombstone not a word about being governor of Virginia, U.S. minister to France, secretary of state, vice president in the administration of John Adams, and president of the United States from 1801 to 1809. However Thomas Jefferson is judged with respect to slavery, he was an important figure in the evolution of higher education's mission of educating and preparing citizens for democratic participation. The University of Virginia, along with a few other public institutions, including the University of Michigan, founded in 1817, created an alternative to the classical education then normative in private colleges, offering instead a vision related to the needs of a democratic society.

Even now agreement is not universal about the appropriate role of higher education in ensuring a vital democracy of people from widely differing life circumstances. Critics of affirmative action argued at the time of the University of Michigan lawsuits that preparation for citizenship is not the business of higher education. The National Association of Scholars, which submitted an amicus brief in support of the plaintiffs who sued the University of Michigan, argued that the democracy outcomes included in the Gurin expert report (1999) on the educational value of diversity were not legitimate educational goals. The outcomes they disparaged included cross-racial understanding, perspective taking, preparation for an increasingly diverse workforce and society, and participatory citizenship. The National Association of Scholars contended that these outcomes simply reflected the liberal, politically correct framing that the University of Michigan mounted to defend affirmative action (Wood and Sherman 2001).[6] The university countered that higher education does have the responsibility to prepare citizens capable of understanding different cultural and life experiences and of collaborating across differences in a diverse democracy. It is up to higher education to provide learning opportunities that help students understand and work with difference and connection (Guarasci, Cornwell et al. 1997), something that the MIGR does throughout its curriculum.

The relationship between diversity and democracy has long been debated. In *Fear of Diversity*, the political scientist Arlene Saxonhouse (1992) details the debates of the ancient Greeks about the impact of diversity on capacity for democracy. According to Saxonhouse, Plato envisioned a city-state in which unity and harmony would be based on the shared characteristics of a homogeneous citizenry. Aristotle, by contrast, envisioned a democracy that incorporated difference within unity, which he contended would more likely thrive than would one based on homogeneity. What makes democracy work, Aristotle argued, is equality among citizens who are peers (at the time, only free men, not women or slaves), who hold diverse perspectives and whose relationships in the polis are governed by freedom and the rules of civil discourse (Pitkin and Shumer 1982). Discourse involving differing views, not unanimity, is what helps democracy thrive.

The United States, with its increasingly diverse population, needs a vision of democracy compatible with diversity—a vision in which people from a range of economic circumstances and cultural experiences are integrated into the democratic project. Higher education has a critical role in modeling how that integration can be accomplished. In educating students from diverse backgrounds, higher education should prepare all of them to become civic as well as scientific, business, intellectual, and professional leaders. All of the students, whatever their disciplinary commitments, should learn about the growing inequality in the United States as an important public concern. They need to grasp the necessity of considering different perspectives on public issues, including what to do about inequality. They should be knowledgeable about the struggles for democracy in other countries (Aung San Suu Kyi 2011), and hone their capacities to understand and collaborate with people from multiple cultures and political persuasions.

Practicing democratic engagement and interacting with diverse peers while they are in college advances the development of civic sentiments that are important for a vital democracy. Nancy Cantor, chancellor of Syracuse University, in speaking of the value of diversity in higher education, calls for engaging students, staff, and faculty from diverse backgrounds in connecting universities with communities where they are situated. She urges that members of university communities use their "prodigious intellectual capital, . . . energetic human capital, and . . . social capital . . . to address the 'sticky issues' of our day—reclaiming public education, our environment, our economy or our ability to make peace" (2011a, 11). For Cantor, work with communities that are themselves racially, ethnically, or economically diverse requires diverse members of the university community that can bring to bear multiple and differing perspectives on joint community-university endeavors.

As we have seen in this book, IGD courses provide practice in collaboration across differences (the ICP projects described in chapter 2), an experience that teaches the importance of personal and social responsibility (Association of American Colleges and Universities 2007) in a democratic society. As students carry out these projects with peers whose backgrounds, experiences, and perspectives differ because of growing up in different racial-ethnic, religious, and economic situations, they are asked to be mindful of power dynamics that can validate some voices and silence others. Our results show that participants learned to listen, ask questions, and probe the ideas of others, preparing them to work productively in cross-racial and cross-gender collaborative projects. Group identities remained salient and were examined so that students would discern both commonalities and differences. Intergroup dialogue is explicitly group-conscious rather than color-blind or gender-blind, but it is also inclusive. Participants learned about inequality and its structural and institutional influences. They became critical thinkers about society. They learned to consider different perspectives on public issues. They learned that relationships can bind diverse participants to a common democratic enterprise. They became more empathic and motivated to bridge differences rather than to erase them. They simultaneously increased both their involvement in their own group identities and their commitments to intergroup collaborations. In all these ways, intergroup dialogue is a democratic project.

Projects to Foster Democratic Capacity through Intergroup Dialogue

Intergroup dialogue programs at the nine collaborating institutions have gone beyond the academic courses evaluated in the Multi-University Intergroup Dialogue Research Project to apply what we have learned in this democratic project to other educational settings. Two in particular demonstrate applications to high school youth in racially segregated cities, Detroit, Michigan, and Syracuse, New York.

The importance of young people in Detroit dialoguing across race and ethnicity could not be greater because of Detroit's residential racial-ethnic segregation and lack of public transportation that could connect different neighborhoods. Detroit is one of the most racially and ethnically segregated cities in the United States. The Detroit Plan, which called for city-suburban desegregation of schools in metropolitan Detroit, was overturned by the Supreme Court in 1974. The city then moved through rapid residential segregation, producing schools attended by black students that Gary Orfield and Chungmei Lee (2006) describe as close to complete apartheid. They also point out that in recent decades Detroit consistently has rated among the most hypersegregated housing markets in the United States. These patterns mean that few students in the schools in metropolitan Detroit have opportunities to interact across race and ethnicity.

Summer Youth Dialogues, created in 2003 by Barry Checkoway, professor of Social Work, and Roger Fisher, associate director of the Program on Intergroup Relations at the University of Michigan, directly addresses the isolation of Detroit students from various racial-ethnic backgrounds. The program brings high school youth from both the city of Detroit and Detroit suburbs together to dialogue with each other over a nine-week period during the summer. The program, which involves a collaboration between the University of Michigan, community-based organizations (CBOs), and the Skillman Foundation, has three aims: to promote young people's understanding of their own racial and ethnic identity, as well understanding of the identities of their dialogue peers; to familiarize them with historical and contemporary patterns of segregation, racial-ethnic inequalities, and social-economic justice issues in the metropolitan Detroit area; and to strengthen their capacities for democratic engagement and social change (Fisher and Checkoway 2011).

The youth dialogues follow a curriculum closely aligned with the one described in chapter 2. The college student facilitators are recruited and trained by the University of Michigan's Program on Intergroup Relations. Thus, the Summer Youth Dialogues are a direct extension of intergroup dialogues at the college level. There are differences as well. Roger Fisher and Barry Checkoway (2011) point out that the Summer Youth Dialogues take place in communities, not in high schools or on college campuses; they rely heavily on experiential learning; and they lead explicitly to action projects at the community level, empowering the youth to create social change and providing them with practice in democratic engagement. Over its eight-year history, Summer Youth Dialogues has involved approximately 600 students in dialogic education promoting social responsibility. Students who would normally not interact across racial and ethnic residential boundaries get to know each other and collaborate with each other in intensive weekly dialogues over a sustained period. They see that it is possible for democracy and diversity to be compatible when opportunities are structured for intergroup interaction. They learn about economic, social, and political inequalities that can produce fissures in the fabric of democracy. They learn that they can do something about those divides. In the year following their summer experiences, the students develop some kind of learning experience for their peers living in their segregated neighborhoods and in so doing, practice social responsibility, which is needed in a diverse democracy.

An important feature of Summer Youth Dialogues is participatory research in which a team of high school students, usually drawn from participants from a previous summer, serves as research assistants gathering information they deem important for understanding the impact of the Summer Youth Dialogues. Such information includes weekly journals, interviews, and focus groups with participants. The research involvement of youth supports critical thinking about society, inequalities, and potentials for neighborhood collaborations (for an overview of the history, activities, and impact of Summer Youth Dialogues, see Fisher and Checkoway 2011).

Young people in Syracuse, New York, also have few opportunities to interact across race and ethnicity because Syracuse, like most other large and smaller cities in the United States, is divided economically and racially between the city and its suburbs. Gretchen Lopez, social psychologist on the faculty of the School of Education and also Syracuse University's collaborator in the Multi-University Intergroup Dialogue Research Project, has developed a high school initiative, an extension of the university's intergroup dialogue program, that is geared to bringing together students from a largely minority city high school and from a largely white suburban high school in a series of one-day dialogue experiences (Lopez and Nastasi 2012). The most recent High School Institute drew eighty high school students. The students explored their identities and shared personal narratives of their school and community lives in two racially and ethnically different communities. They participated in poetry workshops and collaborated across their school affiliations in writing letters to public officials to advocate for specific actions to reduce racial-ethnic inequalities. This was democracy in action whereby students gained a voice spoken at the institute and written in their action projects.

In contrast to Summer Youth Dialogues, this youth dialogue program was connected directly to the two high schools, led by one teacher from each high school in collaboration with Lopez and the staff from the Syracuse University's Intergroup Dialogue Program. Like Summer Youth Dialogues, this project used participatory research in which the students themselves served as evaluators to understand what participants learned in the day-long dialogue experience. Gretchen Lopez and Wendy Nastasi (2012) report new awareness by the participants of the racial-ethnic contexts in which they lived. The participants also gained a sense of agency in being able to express their concerns through poetry and the action letters. They especially valued the time they spent with peers from different schools—one might say from different worlds—with whom they had never before interacted. The teachers who accompanied the students reported that the students were deeply involved in the dialogue experience and many said that they did not want the day to end. Lopez and Nastasi describe a connected community of young people who became actors in a multiracial democratic project. They conclude that

democracy itself is the leitmotif that unites the research and students' stories we have explored. Youth action and intergroup dialogue are not mere dress rehearsals for the civic responsibilities of adult life. They are genuine interactions with the democratic process that education must take up, not only to prepare our students for their futures, but also to empower our youth to impact the institutions and communities in their present. (2012, 155)

Connecting Syracuse University's Program on Intergroup Relations with city and suburban high schools to promote intergroup understanding, relationships, and action—the same three goals of the IGD project evaluated in this book—is part of a broad democratic project launched by Syracuse's chancellor, Nancy Cantor. Named the Academic Plan and Scholarship in Action, this project, supported broadly by faculty across many disciplines as well as by staff and students, connects resources of Syracuse University with the Syracuse schools and with economic development in upstate New York. The Academic Plan and Scholarship in Action is the center of Cantor's vision of higher education as an incubator of innovation and a catalyst for university-community collaborations for the public good. It is a vision

that prepares students *for the world, in the world,* with a sense of social responsibility for its failures and solutions for its future. Scholarship in Action opens up the university to learning and scholarship through deep academic engagement with outside partners to address the grand problems, the critical social issues of our day in which the big and the little, the blatant and the hidden, and the local and the global are inevitably intertwined. (Cantor 2011b, 2)

These Detroit and Syracuse projects demonstrate that intergroup dialogue is a relevant educational approach for helping young people develop understanding of what is needed to make democracy work at a local level, become motivated to take personal and social responsibility for finding solutions to racial-ethnic separation of the city's youth, and gain skills for implementing projects to apply intergroup dialogue in their own schools. They are examples of democracy in action.

THE DISPERSION CHALLENGE: THE IMPORTANCE OF DIALOGUE AND COLLABORATION

The third challenge that the country faces in which higher education has an important role is what Fareed Zakaria terms "the rise of the rest" (2008, 2011). Countries other than the United States—China, India, Brazil, Russia, and South Africa (the BRICS), and increasingly others as well—have greater economic and international political influence than they once had. Other countries too are rising in a "hybrid international system—more democratic, more dynamic, more open, more connected." Zakaria says that "in the long run this secular trend—the rise of the rest—will only gather strength, whatever the temporary ups and downs. At a military-political level, America still dominates the world, but the larger structure of unipolarity—economic, financial, cultural—is weakening" (2011, 53, 242). The United States' role in the world will be different but not diminished. The new role will require consultation, cooperation, and dialogue. This is obvious in public diplomacy, which, according to Geoffrey Cowan and Amelia Arsenault (2008), already has moved in the past decade from a monologue, top-down, unilateral approach to one of dialogue, consultation, and multilateral relationships. They point to the 2002 Council on Foreign Relations report on public diplomacy, which called for increased, customized two-way dialogue, as contrasted with conventional one-way, push-down mass communication. In their view, dialogue in public diplomacy involves exchange of ideas and information in which communication is reciprocal and multidirectional. The importance of dialogue has grown not only as more countries have risen in influence but also as people in many countries across broad reaches of the affluent and the poor have called for a voice in their destinations.

Having a larger and stronger voice in their countries' governance and direction is what the Arab Spring of 2011 was all about. Other protests elsewhere during 2010 and 2011 also reflected opposition to government decisions that affected people's lives without what they considered sufficient governmental consideration of their perspectives. In England, approximately 52,000 students marched through London on November 24, 2010, to protest the government's plans to increase tuition fees while cutting state funding for university teaching, something the government deemed necessary in light of its commitment to reduce the public debt (Coughlan 2010). In Israel on October 24, 2011, more than 100,000 people protested rising costs of living with marches and rallies in eleven cities across the country, including protests involving both Jews and Arabs in Nazareth.[7] In the United States, the Occupy Wall Street movement, protesting corporate power and government cut-backs affecting education and the poor, grew through September and October 2011 in cities across the country and in cities in other parts of the world.[8] The particulars of each of these examples differ, but they all represent aspirations for a voice and often represent opposition to growing inequality worldwide. People want to be heard, have a voice, and be in dialogue with government officials, corporations, and groups that historically have made decisions affecting the lives of ordinary people. Cowan and Arsenault provide evidence of widespread desire to be heard from a landmark World Bank survey of 60,000 people living below the poverty line around the world, and conclude that this desire for a voice extends beyond the people's local communities and specific societies, noting that dialogue is needed across boundaries of all kinds:

> It seems fair to assume that people around the world would like to be heard by leaders in neighboring countries as well as by America and other industrialized nations. By providing opportunities for people to express themselves and to be heard, and to engage in a dialogue, those concerned with public diplomacy can begin to address that need. (2008, 19)

In a world in which many more countries are increasingly influential economically and politically, students being educated in higher education institutions in the United States will need knowledge of other countries and dialogue skills in interactions with people across nationalities if they are to become effective leaders in public diplomacy and in global and local profit and nonprofit organizations. There are also many other arenas, nongovernmental initiatives in particular, where dialogue experience and skills are already valuable assets that will only grow in importance. Zakaria (2011) points to situations where nonstate actors have become influential because groups and individuals have been empowered, and because hierarchy, centralization, and control have been undermined. Nongovernmental organizations are mushrooming every day on many issues in many countries. Leaders of these organizations need the kinds of skills that students learn in intergroup dialogue courses.

Kwame Anthony Appiah, professor of philosophy at Princeton University, and Martha Nussbaum, professor of philosophy at the University of Chicago, have written extensively about the importance of an outward orientation as a goal of education, what they call cosmopolitanism. Although cosmopolitanism sometimes evokes elitist images of well-traveled people, Appiah and Nussbaum argue that cosmopolitanism does not require travel and can occur in many settings. More than anything, cosmopolitanism is a way of thinking about oneself and the world. Their discussions of cosmopolitanism include four related ideas. One is a pluralistic perspective. Cosmopolitans understand "there are many values worth living by" and therefore "expect that different people and different societies will embody different ideas and values" within an overall common humanity (Appiah 2006a, 36). To embrace pluralism, Nussbaum (2007) urges students to see themselves as members of a heterogeneous nation and world. Understanding difference is perfectly consistent with common humanity—that all people everywhere are social beings, connected with each other, and share a capacity to care for one another. It is our social nature that enables people with different perspectives to be bound to each other, even as they disagree. Desmond Tutu, quoted in chapter 3, speaks similarly of common humanity: "Our humanity is caught up in that of all others. We are humans because we belong. We are made for community, for togetherness, for family, to exist in a delicate network of interdependence" (1999, 196).

The second feature of cosmopolitanism is critical thinking. According to Nussbaum, a cosmopolitan education that prepares students to become citizens of the world demands that "They step away from the comfort of assured truths, from the nestling feeling of being surrounded by people who share one's convictions and passions. . . . Through cross-cultural inquiry, students may realize that what they have taken to be natural and normal—and therefore what they are most comfortable with—is merely parochial and habitual" (2007, 39). Nussbaum emphasizes "the capacity for Socratic self-criticism and critical thought about one's own traditions" as crucial elements in cosmopolitanism (38).

A third feature is empathy. A key aim of cosmopolitanism is what Nussbaum calls narrative imagination, being able to imagine the lives of people different from oneself and what it might be like to be in their shoes. Appiah (2006b) uses the same language, saying that we need to learn about other people's situations and then use our imagination to walk in their shoes.

Finally, a fourth defining feature of cosmopolitanism is the importance of integrating specific group-based identities with a broad global identification that transcends them. Both of these scholars are critical of specific group-based identities if they restrict either individuality or common humanity. Such identities too often insist on a correct way to "be" a woman or to "be" a member of the royal Oyoko clan, as Appiah is. Everyone has multiple identities, and cosmopolitans accept multiplicity. They reject pressures to conform to the expectations of any one identity group. They appreciate solidarity with others who share that identity but they also recognize the contingent nature of when any one identity becomes salient in their lives (Appiah and Gutmann 1996, 104).

In a similar vein, Nussbaum stresses that the spirit of multiculturalism and the goal of producing world citizens are profoundly opposed to identity politics, which "sometimes has led to a new anti-humanist view that celebrates difference in an uncritical way and that denies the very possibility of common interests and understandings that take one outside one's own group" (2007, 40). Cosmopolitanism does not minimize the importance of specific-group identities, be they religious, nationality, racial, ethnic, gender, or sexual orientation, but it does recognize that people hold multiple identities and see themselves in complex ways. Specific identities and an identity as a world citizen can exist alongside each other.

> We need not give up our special affections and identifications, whether ethnic or gender-based or religious. We need not think of them as superficial, and we may think of our identity as constituted partly by them. We may and should devote special attention to them in education. But we should also work to make all human beings part of our community of dialogue and concern, base our political deliberations on that interlocking commonality, and give the circle that defines our humanity special attention and respect.
>
> In educational terms, this means that students . . . may continue to regard themselves as defined partly by their particular loves—their families, their religious, ethnic, or racial communities, or even their country. But they must also, and centrally, learn to recognize humanity wherever they encounter it, undeterred by traits that are strange to them, and be eager to understand humanity in all its strange guises. (Nussbaum 1996, 9)

The arguments that Appiah and Nussbaum make for cosmopolitanism fit with a vision for higher education that has been proposed by the Association of American Colleges and Universities and by the Partnership for 21st Century Skills, an organization that has brought together the business community, education leaders, and policymakers. The language that each organization uses differs somewhat but their rationales are similar. The Association of American Colleges and Universities frames its rationale this way:

In recent years, the ground has shifted for Americans in virtually every important sphere of life—economic, global, cross-cultural, environmental, civic. The world is being dramatically reshaped by scientific and technological innovations, global interdependence, cross-cultural encounters, and changes in the balance of economic and political power. . . . The context in which today's students will make choices and compose lives is one of disruption rather than certainty, and of interdependence rather than insularity. . . . Taking stock of these developments, educators and employers have begun to reach similar conclusions—an emerging consensus—about the kinds of learning Americans need from college. (2007, 1–2)

The Partnership for 21st Century Skills frames its rationale similarly:

In an economy driven by innovation and knowledge . . . in marketplaces engaged in intense competition and constant renewal . . . in a world of tremendous opportunities and risks . . . in a society facing complex business, political, scientific, technological, health and environmental challenges . . . and in diverse workplaces and communities that hinge on collaborative relationships and social networking . . . the ingenuity, agility and skills of the American people are crucial to U.S. competitiveness. (2008, 1)

Three sets of outcomes, cast mostly as desired skills, characterize the emerging consensus that these two organizations reflect and that intergroup dialogue produces. For one, both organizations stress the need for broad knowledge, especially based in science and technology but also in the arts, languages, and social sciences. Second, they also both stress communication, collaboration, and problem solving with teams of people across cultural, geographic, and language boundaries both within the United States and internationally. Third, they both stress critical, creative, adaptive, and flexible thinking that is built on quantitative, informational, financial, organizational, and civic literacy.

Not everyone would agree with these three classes of outcomes, including some who accept them as important but want them to be accepted because of their intrinsic value and not because they would increase the competitiveness of the United States. Some worry that an excessive focus on international competitiveness and economic growth can be reflected sometimes in too exclusive an emphasis on science learning and technological skills. The social sciences, humanities, and the arts may be undervalued in the current discourse about "the rise of the rest" and what higher education needs to be doing to ensure the future of the United States as a leader in the world (Walker 2009). Michael Crow, president of Arizona State University, responding to the call by Florida Governor Rick Scott to reduce support for academic disciplines other than science, technology, engineering, and math, asserted the importance of other disciplines in the liberal arts that teach skills of critical thinking, analytic reasoning, creativity, and leadership. "It is essential that we develop in our students the ability to understand the complexity and interrelatedness of our cultural, economic, natural, political, social, and technological systems. The point here is that we need all of the skill sets from anthropology to zoology" (Crow 2011). Neither the American Association of Colleges and Universities nor the Partnership for 21st Century Skills can be accused of stressing only science, technology, engineering, and math or of stressing only immediate workplace skills. They both advance a broad vision for higher education that is consistent with the aims of intergroup dialogue.

The critical-dialogic model of intergroup dialogue we have discussed in this book provides a cosmopolitan education that reflects the goals these organizations stress. The dialogic aspect of our model directly addresses the emphasis Appiah and Nussbaum place on developing pluralistic and empathic orientations in which difference is embraced to be understood and accepted, as well as the emphasis given by the American Association of Colleges and Universities and the Partnership for 21st Century Skills to the development of skills of communication, collaboration, and problem-solving across difference. The critical aspect of our model directly addresses the emphasis by all of these writers on critical thinking. Our model also considers identities in ways that encourage students to recognize multiplicity and complexity, as well as the compatibility of specific group-based identities and intergroup collaborations. We challenge students to understand why many kinds of group-based differences exist. We ask them to think critically in general and in particular about inequality. We encourage them to communicate and collaborate with others whose life experiences—either their own or those of others in their groups—have been affected by inequalities embedded in various types of power and privilege. Our model also offers a process—a relational, reflective, integrative model of learning—by which these desired outcomes of education can be achieved. The outcomes are relational, in Zakaria's terms the skills of collaboration, cooperation, and dialogue, but so too are the processes by which students learn.

Fostering Cosmopolitanism through Intergroup Dialogue and Leadership Development

One of the co-authors of this book, Biren (Ratnesh) Nagda, a social worker and psychologist, collaborated with colleagues at the Desmond Tutu Peace Center (DTPC) in South Africa to develop cosmopolitanism through a youth leadership program with intergroup dialogue at its heart. This project needs to be cast in the historical context of transition from apartheid to democracy in South Africa in the early 1990s. Deliberations among politicians, clergy, academics, and community leaders made clear that a new vision for democracy in South Africa was imperative to avert a civil war or a fate similar to other postindependence African nations (Tutu 2004). The political revolution was only one part of a larger transformation; a social revolution was also necessary. The Truth and Reconciliation Commission (TRC), headed by Nobel Peace Laureate Archbishop Desmond Tutu, was one such national effort to heal the past, bridge estranged groups, and build a new future. Guided by the foundational principle of restorative justice in contrast to retributive justice, the TRC sought to document testimonies of violent atrocities of apartheid, to move toward forgiveness and reconciliation among the victimized and perpetrators, and grant amnesty to perpetrators when appropriate.

The DTPC was founded in 1998 to honor and continue the legacy of Archbishop Tutu in building restorative justice and peace worldwide. One aim was to recognize and cultivate leadership among historically marginalized groups, especially young people. The Emerging Leadership Program was established in 2003 to promote values-based leadership among youth, a collaborative, community-based effort toward sustainable peace, hope, and nation building. Nagda collaborated with colleagues at DTPC to formalize the effort, to establish pedagogical principles and practices, and to build international collaborations. Intergroup dialogue became the foundational methodology for leadership development and peace-building initiatives (Van Wyk, Nagda, and Robertson 2005).

The leadership curriculum has three components. The first, peace within, involves youth in developing knowledge and values related to leadership, dialogue, and self-identity. They examine their conceptions and experiences of leadership, and think critically about prominent national and international leaders (comparing and contrasting leaders such as Nelson Mandela, Adolf Hitler, Wangari Matthai, Aung San Suu Kyi, and the Dalai Lama, among others) as well as everyday leaders (parents, teachers, and peers). They also examine their conceptions of peace and conflict, again reflecting on both domestic and international examples. They develop interpersonal dialogue communication skills, especially related to publicly narrating difficult experiences and listening to others. They examine their and their peers' social identities and how those play out in their daily lives. The second, peace between, is a week-long wilderness hiking experience. The youth learn not only about physical wellness but also about social wellness in diverse teams and environmental wellness in taking care of the natural environment. They also spend time reading and in personal reflection and in group dialogues to deepen their learning by bridging the peace between and peace within components of the curriculum. The third, peace among, engages the youth in examining critical global and local issues (such as education, xenophobia, and HIV/AIDS). An important feature of this component is future scenario planning, modeled after deliberations leading to and following the dismantling of apartheid, in which the youth imagine "high road—win/win," "middle road—win-lose/win-lose," and "low road—lose/lose" scenarios for problems facing their communities. They imagine the scenarios, think critically about the trade-offs, and think creatively about collaborations and partnerships necessary for best possible outcomes that promote human development. The youth are officially recognized during this time as Emerging Leadership Awardees at a "Tea with Tutu," at which they dialogue with Archbishop Tutu or other renowned peace-builders about pressing world issues.

Hundreds of youth in South Africa, Kenya, Uganda, Thailand, Philippines, Indonesia, Myanmar (formerly Burma), and Norway have now participated in leadership programs based on the model. The leadership development principles and curriculum conform to the four dimensions of cosmopolitanism delineated by Appiah and Nussbaum: a pluralist perspective, empathy, critical thinking, and integration of group-specific and global identifications. The Emerging Leadership Program directly addresses what new leaders will need in a world characterized by "the rise of the rest."

CONCLUSION

We began and ended this volume claiming that intergroup dialogue provides the kind of education that addresses the demographic, democratic, and dispersion challenges facing the United States and other countries in the twenty-first century. Our Multi-University Intergroup Dialogue Research Project's evidence for the impact of intergroup dialogue spanned an eighteen-month period from pretest to the longitudinal post-posttest. We would have liked to have been able to assess impact over an even longer period, and particularly to know how students who participated in intergroup dialogue during college might be using their dialogue experience in their postcollege work and personal lives. That was not possible in a systematic longer-term follow-up, but we did ask a few graduates to describe what they are currently doing professionally and how their experiences in intergroup dialogue may have played a role in their professional and personal directions. We also specifically probed the ways they are professionally and personally addressing the demographic, democratic, and dispersion challenges. We turn to their responses in the epilogue.

Authored by Patricia Gurin, Biren (Ratnesh) A. Nagda, Walter G. Stephan, Cookie White Stephan, Gary Anderson, Delia Saenz, and Gloria Bouis.

EPILOGUE

Intergroup Dialogue Alumni in a Changing World

As we were finishing this book, it seemed only right that we end with words and lives of students who were actively involved in intergroup dialogue (IGD) as undergraduates and who have now graduated. We invited twelve graduates to share their experiences in intergroup dialogue, and all of them responded with reflection essays. These essays convey purposefulness as engaged graduates who are trying to advance social justice across a range of professional fields—medicine, nursing, social work, law, public health, business and finance, the arts, education, and public policy. They write of the continuing impact of their intergroup dialogue experiences in what they are doing professionally and personally. By no means are we claiming that they are representative of the participants in the broader study. They are simply graduates from the universities of two of the authors. We knew them to have been actively involved with intergroup dialogue during their college years and as graduates who could reflect on how their postcollege years address the demographic, democratic, and dispersion challenges that frame this book. When we asked them to respond to us about their current lives, we knew little about their lives after graduation. We chose them because they were leaders during their college years. They participated in intergroup dialogue and facilitated dialogues, and in some cases played other leadership roles in IGD programs. They are still leaders trying to foster the major aims of

IGD—greater intergroup understanding, positive intergroup relationships, and collaborative social action.

We specifically asked them to describe what they are currently doing and to reflect on how their work and lives deal with the three challenges that frame this book. To elucidate those challenges, we sent them a draft of chapter 10 of the book and asked them to write essay responses to the following four questions:

What are you currently doing professionally and how did your experiences in intergroup dialogue play a role in your professional direction?

In what ways is your work addressing inequalities and is aimed at creating greater social justice? (the democratic challenge)

In what ways are you professionally and personally engaged with people from various identity groups and how are you bridging differences by bringing people together? (the demographic challenge)

In what ways are you involved with people in or from other countries? In what ways do you consider yourself a global citizen? (the dispersion challenge)

In the remainder of this epilogue, we share the uniqueness of each of the graduates and the themes we discerned across their essays in relation to the three challenges.

THE DEMOCRATIC CHALLENGE: ADDRESSING INEQUALITIES

We begin by introducing these twelve graduates, identifying them—with their agreement—by name, and showing how their current work, preparation for future work, and personal lives address inequalities. The democratic challenge drew the lion's share of their writing. We believe that reflects that the primary continuing impact of intergroup dialogue is pressing them to do something about inequalities and to conceive of themselves as responsible social change agents. They write of rural-urban inequalities, health disparities, educational inequalities, and economic inequalities.

Adam Falkner, a white man, is in his sixth year teaching eleventh-grade English and Creative Writing at the Academy for Young Writers in Brooklyn,

New York. He is also a poet, performer, educational consultant, and the founder and executive director of the Dialogue Arts Project, a nonprofit organization dedicated to using creative writing and performing arts in what we call a democratic project—promoting the exploration of identity and critical dialogue between students, artists, and educators to make society more just. Its primary aim is to help young people, especially less privileged young people whose opportunities are constrained by inequalities that they face, to become healthy, contributing members of society. Adam writes,

> To say that my experience in intergroup dialogue influenced my professional direction would be a wild understatement. . . . [As a teacher] I knew that I wanted to be responsible for facilitating dialogue and balancing voices in an intergroup setting, and I was given an early look at a highly effective classroom. I was also moved by IGR's [The Program on Intergroup Relations at the University of Michigan] belief in the universal human need for communication across lines of identity, and the extent to which the dialogue environments IGR created gave permission for that unspoken want to surface in the form of empathic, courageous conversation. . . . In my current high school classroom, I am constantly attempting to create settings that "uncork" something similar and grant my students permission to connect with that same universal human desire for communication.

He sees the same connection with identity and communication in his work as a poet, artist, and consultant. "I think of writing as an opportunity to explore the silent spaces—the dialogue that is often overlooked or purposefully brushed under the carpet. . . . As an artist as well as an educator, I recognized the ability of performance art and self-created participant art to allow for broader and yet more personalized dialogue." In the Dialogue Arts Project, Adam uses "creative writing and the arts to promote the exploration of identity and thus to improve self-understanding, self-expression and cultural awareness. . . . The Dialogue Arts Project is inspired largely by my participation in intergroup dialogue and my subsequent development as an artist and teacher of self-authored curricula to facilitate similar dialogue through the use of art."

Annabel Cholico is a Latina and a first-year student at the University of San Francisco School of Law, an achievement she describes as having taken several years of hardships as a Latina and being the first in her family to go to college. Some of the hardships arose from self-doubts that first-generation college students often harbor; others arose from financial difficulties and identity issues. She writes, "As a Latina, it has always been hard to feel comfortable in a professional field, because you tend to feel like you are the only one. I've learned over time to embrace this feeling because it is an honor to my family, my culture, and my roots to be a Latina pursuing a professional career." Through it all, she credits her involvement with intergroup dialogue at the University of Washington as supporting her goals because it was there that she was able to speak openly about how class, gender, race, and socioeconomic status affected her educationally and professionally. "That class taught me to have a voice and use it. . . . I now know that my voice matters because everyone learns from each other, you learn from other people's stories and they learn from yours." She realizes that her struggle to eventually become a lawyer is not over but the goal that guides her is to help make the law available to low-income people, especially those who are not English speakers. As a law student, she has volunteered to interpret for a non-Spanish-speaking attorney who has Spanish-speaking clients. She writes that she is confident she will accomplish her goal of helping the law become an instrument available to all. She is aware that when she speaks now that others listen to her. It is not only about speaking up but also about speaking how—using the communication processes she learned in intergroup dialogue to speak, listen, and critically analyze with others so that her voice counts.

Denny Chan, a Chinese American man, is also a law student. Now in his third year of law school at the University of California, Irvine, he has strengthened the resolve that originally took him into law, that is, to use the law "as a vehicle toward progressive social change." During his college years at the University of Michigan, he became a facilitator of intergroup dialogue courses and also applied what he learned as a dialogue facilitator in his role as a minority peer advisor in Michigan's residence halls. As a senior, he was selected to be a facilitator in the training course required of undergraduates who were to be residence hall staff the following year. His facilitation skills, honed in intergroup dialogue, were highly valued in the training course, where professional staff frequently asked Denny for pedagogical suggestions deriving directly from intergroup dialogue. It was Denny who taught others how to use five-minute reflection papers immediately following conflict in the classroom, or for that matter immediately following a period of passive engagement, to stimulate students to think about what they were learning from the group dynamics that would be relevant to their work as future undergraduate resident advisors. Although he knew that he would not become a teacher either in K-12 or higher education, he—like Adam—saw in intergroup dialogue what an effective classroom would look like. On graduating, he was selected as a Fulbright grant recipient to teach English for a year in Macau, China. It proved to be another opportunity for applying dialogic pedagogy and communication skills that he had learned in intergroup dialogue. Denny is not certain what follows law school graduation, although he is sure that he will find a way to become a public interest lawyer. During the first two summers of law school, Denny spent time addressing inequalities through the power of the law. At the American Civil Liberties Union, he helped litigate cases involving federal voting rights laws. At a law firm specializing in plaintiffs' class-action lawsuits, he worked on a sexual discrimination case against a large corporate retailer and on a financial mortgage case involving one of the nation's largest banks. Although Denny came to the law from a more affluent background than Annabel did, both are motivated to make the law an effective instrument to be used by people from all backgrounds.

Clare Wrobel, a white woman who earned both an undergraduate degree and master's in health services administration from the University of Michigan, is now working in the U.S. Department of Health and Human Services. As an undergraduate, Clare facilitated intergroup dialogues, created a video that portrayed how dialogues operate, and worked on the research project this book has presented. As a graduate student, she was an instructor for a Women's Studies health course and participated with a team from the Program on Intergroup Relations that consulted with colleges and universities in Wisconsin interested in initiating IGD programs. Clare credits her involvement with intergroup dialogue with nurturing her interest in "reducing the inequities in delivery of health care in the United States that are rooted in social identity differences between provider and patient, and particularly, the earned distrust of the medical community by communities of color." She describes stories she heard from fellow intergroup dialogue participants about mistreatment in the medical system: "An Asian American man expressed disappointment when his trusted family pediatrician referred to him as 'Oriental;' a transgender man expressed many barriers to receiving competent care. . . . My experience with intergroup dialogue led me to be very conscious of my identities and the identities of people I engage with." She writes that effective professional and meaningful personal relationships across difference require being aware of assumptions that people often make, as, for example, when a young woman related her experience with a gynecologist, who, demanding that she reveal what birth control she was using, just assumed she was sexually active with a male partner. Changing assumptions and the often unbalanced power relationship between doctor and patient are two major professional goals that Clare attributes directly to her involvement in intergroup dialogue. They figure prominently in her current work with a federal program that provides grants to providers and assistance to states to support providers in implementing health information technology to improve the delivery of care and population health outcomes. She writes that "the priority providers in this program care for a high proportion of Medicaid-eligible patients. They are incentivized to give patients open access to their personal health data, supporting a shift to seeing patients as equal and active partners in their own health care."

Nathaniel Swartz is a white, male social worker, who, after his undergraduate years, enrolled in a nursing school in Chicago to obtain another degree in nursing. He is now a nurse in an acute care surgical unit in a regional pediatric hospital providing direct services to children and families. He is also involved organizationally to improve cultural competency training for new hospital employees. Participating in intergroup dialogue at the University of Washington led directly to his search for a career in which he could be in alliance with others to make society more just. Intergroup dialogue gave him a way of understanding himself as a "white, middle-class, straight, twenty-something male brought up to feel deserving of my privilege." He writes, "The easiest way for me to sum up my experience in intergroup dialogue is that it has helped me to see the air—something I was raised not to see but that surrounds me and benefits me every day. . . . There is no final destination for the intergroup dialogue process . . . [because] the power of intergroup dialogue lies in conveying truths that are all but impossible to walk away from." He has chosen a profession in which, as a male, he is in the minority numbers-wise. It is a profession that he describes as requiring reciprocity and alliances in order to be effective, one in which he "directly applies what he learned in intergroup dialogue." His goal as a nurse, like Clare's in public health, is to address "the power imbalance between patients and practitioners, especially as they pertain to people belonging to less privileged populations." He continues, "I chose nursing because I wanted to find a place with great power discrepancy where I could use my skills as a social worker and social justice worker to help balance the power. . . . Events that transpire in a hospital have far-reaching consequences affecting people's finances, employment, transportation, and overall ability to live healthy, fulfilling, and productive lives. The nurse is the primary contact and gatekeeper for hospital resources, so my goal is to use advocacy, education, and alliance to hand as much power as possible to the patients and families for whom I care."

Chloé Gurin-Sands is a multiracial/multi-ethnic (Latina African American) recent graduate whose professional goal is to do health-related research, especially research on health disparities. Fluent in Spanish, Chloé expects to work and do research in and with Latino and African American communities after obtaining a master's degree in public health and possibly a Ph.D. Her involvement in intergroup dialogue at the University of Michigan was multifaceted in that she participated in dialogues, facilitated them, and worked for four years as an undergraduate research assistant on the project this book has presented. With no awareness that she would enjoy research when she entered college, she relished her experiences learning both quantitative and qualitative skills and later teaching those skills to other undergraduate students. She has also worked as a research assistant at Michigan's School of Public Health on a project evaluating an intervention connecting nonresident African American fathers with their sons. She writes, "My experience in intergroup dialogue helped confirm that not only do I want to be involved in research, but also I want to be involved in interpersonal face-to-face work with people." During her college years, Chloé combined her strong commitment to research with applied community work, just as she hopes to do in her eventual career. She has provided leadership in an organization that works with Latino youth and adults—anything from help with schoolwork for the youth to increasing English-speaking skills for the adults. Beyond solidifying both the importance and possibility of integrating research and practice, intergroup dialogue helped her "build knowledge about and ability to discuss identity-based oppression, and frame health issues in a social justice way. . . . In my classes I have tried to bring up alternate viewpoints and concerns of people whose identities may not be present in the class. [Intergroup dialogue] has educated me about how the personal is political (and vice versa), meaning how people's positions in society really affect how we interact together. It has given me confidence in speaking up about injustice or 'single-perspective' thinking, and it has given me the ability to analyze nearly everything through the lens of multipartiality, that is, taking several identities into account at once."

Aaron James, a white man, graduated with an undergraduate degree, an MS, and an MBA from the University of Michigan. Aaron participated in and facilitated intergroup dialogues as an undergraduate, took a professional position for three years in the Program on Intergroup Relations before pursuing the MS and MBA, and also supervised a variety of peer-education programs at the university. Thus, he came to our request to write about his dialogue experience with both the broadest and longest involvement with intergroup dialogue, and has applied his experience in perhaps the most unlikely direction. He is now working in finance and notes that his interest in finance arose, at least in part, from realizing from his IGD experience that people do not like to talk about money. Even in college, he described his interest in dialogue as "giving voice to human experience often silenced by taboos on talking about money." Then, as an MBA student when the financial crisis hit in 2008, he became more rather than less committed to understanding finance. He writes, "While my peers fled finance to safer havens for their next jobs, I became fascinated. My experience with intergroup dialogue had raised my awareness of the human consequences of our financial system, both good and bad. For me, the crisis appeared as an opportunity for change on a grand scale. So I dove into the study and practice of finance." Aaron is currently working in impact investing, a type of finance committed to positive social and environmental outcomes as well as to financial returns. His most recent project aims to connect rural communities to urban capital, both philanthropic and for-profit investment. His work often involves detailed analysis of financial data and accountability metrics. What is striking about Aaron's path, however, is the extent to which he stresses the importance of the interpersonal, communication skills he acquired in intergroup dialogue. "Finance evaluates the present and future value of investments in the context of uncertainty. It involves deal-making between individuals and organizations, and relies on trust built up over time. My work certainly requires analytic skills, but it is distinguished by the kind of interpersonal skills nurtured through the crucible of intergroup dialogue in conflict and community." And what are those skills? He delineates several: attuned communication, emotional balance, response flexibility, intuition, fear modulation, insight, empathy, and more awareness, all of which Aaron writes were "honed in me by intergroup dialogue at a formative time in my education."

Tara Hackel, a white woman, is a recent graduate of the University of Michigan's School of Engineering, where she majored in nuclear engineering and bioengineering. She is a researcher in a cancer research project where her engineering skills and her experience in intergroup dialogue are used directly. She writes of her current work and how she has used her knowledge of group dynamics and conflict resolution from intergroup dialogue "to engage with people across differences in order to develop solutions to complex problems. I have a language to effectively challenge my co-workers' statements rather than remain silent. Being able to productively engage in dialogue related to social identity with my co-workers on a daily basis has been highly reward-ing." She attributes her participation in intergroup dialogue and her subse-quent facilitation experiences as raising her consciousness of the role of social identity in engineering education and engineering practice as well as increas-ing her commitment to make engineering more accessible and successful for a broad range of people. She writes, "Participating in intergroup dialogues helped me to better recognize inequalities that I faced as a woman in the en-gineering program. . . . Then becoming more in touch with problems within the STEM [science, technology, engineering, and mathematics] fields helped me recognize inequalities affecting others, not merely women." Tara's ulti-mate goal is to become a faculty member in a school of engineering. To achieve that goal, she writes that she will need a Ph.D. as well as several more years of practical experience within diverse engineering fields. She aims for "a leadership position in a top engineering program so that I can bring about changes to make engineering a place where students and faculty from many backgrounds communicate and collaborate in ways that are needed in the global economy." After graduating, Tara took the first step toward this goal by becoming a dialogue course facilitator in a summer engineering academy for students admitted to the University of Michigan School of Engineering from less affluent communities and from high schools with few advanced placement classes. She was influential in the teaching team by using her knowledge of the motivations of incoming engineering students and the spe-cific ways that dialogue communication processes could address their fears and goals.

Jaimée Marsh is a multiracial/multi-ethnic (African American and indige-nous) woman, and a recent graduate of the University of Washington whose professional goals are to become a university faculty member in a school of social work, where she will use social science and social work training in both teaching and developing intergroup dialogue experiences for students. Cur-rently she is an administrator in a student affairs division of a large university, where she manages programs that empower students to explore their social identities and collaborate in social justice activities. The unit in which she works focuses on enrollment and retention of underrepresented students of color. Retention is enhanced, she contends, by implementing co-curricular programs that empower underrepresented students to explore their multiple and intersecting identities and that build and strengthen their leadership skills and competencies. It is sometimes considered exclusively intragroup identity work, in that she relates primarily to leaders within specific cultural communities on the campus. However, she stresses that it is also intergroup identity work because she fosters cross-cultural partnerships among these cultural groups. This work derives in obvious ways from her IGD experience at the University of Washington, where she learned to "navigate social spaces and institutions while negotiating my identities as a multiracial, queer, spiritual woman from a working-class background in a conservative, predominantly white region of the Pacific Northwest." She writes that intergroup dialogue was "a space in which my peers and I exchanged our deepest experiences of trauma and triumph. . . . Professionally speaking, I find that I am successful at connecting with students in part because of my ability to leverage my own identities, experiences, and intercultural competency, but also because of my ability to incorporate dialogic methods in my work with them." Jaimée writes that her goal of empowerment of students is richly met in her current work, but she is applying to graduate programs to earn a doctorate because she believes that she will be most effective in creating greater educational equality by having an academic position where she can press for policy and programmatic changes.

Joshua Johnson, an African American man, is a community organizer in the greater Seattle area, focusing currently on income inequality. He works with a coalition of labor unions, community organizations, and faith-based groups working for a fair economy within Washington State. Reflecting on his professional path, Josh says that "intergroup dialogue was the spark that awakened my destiny in community organizing, for inspiring me to use my skills to build bridges across race and class, for gaining a sense of urgency to do this work, and most important, for inspiring others to take up this duty as well." Joshua facilitated intergroup dialogue as an undergraduate and credits the skills he learned as crucial in his community organizing: He writes that "As a community organizer, the awareness of how we relate on the bases of our multiple identities is essential in canvassing across diverse neighborhoods and personalities, building power with hundreds of diverse people ... and empowering people to make change in the narrative of change in our country. . . . We've gathered students, community members and faith leaders to march for corporate accountability and tax reform, and to demand good jobs in our community." Joshua is also involved in promoting spaces in the larger community, where dialogue can take place, locating his activism as a legacy of many who have come before him and many with whom he walks alongside today. He writes about a recent experience of facilitating an intergenerational dialogue among community activists: "I facilitated a workshop in Seattle's MLK Celebration titled *Healing Through Our Struggle*. Each participant shared his/her background and then we began to realize that although we varied in both age and experience, a significant spark for social justice had been ignited for each of us along our journeys. Some were activists who had very real and punishing experiences dealing with racism in the South, one had felt a religious calling through missionary work, and so on. Yet each perspective connected through dialogue about social change. It was an inspiring moment." Be it in his community organizing work, his community activism service, or in his world travels, it is this sense of connection through dialogue that Joshua sees as the path to "recognizing our humanness in others and growing in relationships. The only way to unmask this keen awareness, I've found, is through dialogue."

Colleen Campbell is a white woman who graduated from the University of Michigan and is currently working in the office of financial aid at a small, private college in New York City. Her current position is an outgrowth of her involvement in intergroup dialogue and also in undergraduate positions that she held in Michigan's Office of Admissions and Office of New Student Programs. It was a broad Michigan investment that she describes as "opening me up to a completely different worldview from the one of my small mostly white, working class hometown." In her leadership positions during college, she found people who were "intellectually curious, challenging, and confident," and those were qualities that led her to intergroup dialogue. She writes, "The semester of training [to be a facilitator of intergroup dialogue] was transformative for me. At the end of the semester, I felt like a different person and I found myself seeking out those with whom I could candidly discuss race, gender, sexuality, socioeconomic status, and religion. These were people that I trusted more deeply because we challenged each other." In her current work in financial aid, she uses her reflective and communication skills gained in intergroup dialogue to discuss sensitive topics with students and parents. She has also had an impact on inequalities within the financial aid office by recording how frequently the scholarship committee "clandestinely noted that a student should appeal for additional aid because they were being offered too little, how often it happened, and how that correlated to income." With evidence in hand, Colleen's suggestions that the office alert all students about the appeal process on the college website and make awarding guidelines more transparent were adopted by the office. Learning that financial aid has enormous effects on the capacities of many young people to enroll in college and complete a degree, Colleen is now applying to master of public policy programs so that she "can better understand how higher education policy is made and how colleges can recruit and retain high-achieving, truly diverse populations, and how such populations can interact in meaningful ways." She doesn't know how she will accomplish the goal of making higher education accessible for all people but does know that goal is what motivates her professional path. She writes that she has come to see that she can and must be an advocate for change at a systemic level, something she attributes to both her postcollege work experience and her IGD participation and facilitation.

Kartik Sidhar is a South Asian man who graduated from the University of Michigan. He combined pre-medical and sociology studies leading him to medical school, also at the University of Michigan, and likely to a joint master's degree in public health. He has both participated in and facilitated intergroup dialogues and provided leadership in developing a new dialogue course focused on ability-disability status. He entered the university expecting to become a doctor but credits his experience in intergroup dialogue, along with internships and volunteer work in New Orleans and in Detroit hospitals, with shifting his focus in medicine from an exclusively academic, research-based role to one that combines research and practice, especially practice in medically underserved communities. His course work in sociology and his multiple responsibilities in the Program on Intergroup Relations have sharpened his understanding of health disparities and deepened his commitment to create change in that arena. It was especially in developing the new course on ability-disability that he was able to connect medicine and intergroup dialogue practice. It helped him see, like Nathaniel now practicing in nursing, that doctor-patient (and other provider-patient) conversations involve power imbalances that have important life consequences for patients and their families. Learning a language of power and communication and discerning how social identities affect communication are what Kartik credits intergroup dialogue doing for him as he begins his professional path as a doctor. More than any other responder to our questions, Kartik emphasizes the experience of learning to communicate at many levels with his co-facilitator. He writes, "Co-facilitating a dialogue was one of the most challenging and rewarding experiences I faced as an undergraduate. It enhanced my listening skills and allowed me to understand individuals beyond their surface levels. The depth of communication and transparency required between my co-facilitator and me was immense." He stresses their joint planning for each class session and, most important, their joint reflections on the group dynamics in their classroom that propelled them to think critically and creatively about how to deal with dominance and assertions of privilege that inevitably arise in intergroup dialogue courses. He recounts that when he was interviewed for medical school admission and was asked what changes he would make if he were the dean of the medical school, he didn't hesitate. "I didn't have to think for a second because I knew my first project would be to implement intergroup dialogues. Medical students would definitely benefit from intergroup dialogues—between students with each other, between students and faculty, and especially between doctors and patients. In an ever-diversifying society, social awareness and understanding are crucial for physicians if they are to offer unbiased care." Although Kartik is just beginning his medical school journey, he envisions working in a free health clinic and doing policy work to reduce the disparities in health care in the United States.

THE DEMOGRAPHIC CHALLENGE: CROSSING BOUNDARIES AND BRIDGING DIFFERENCES

Demographic diversity and bridging identity differences pervade the public roles and personal lives of these graduates. They are all working in situations or preparing for careers that involve a range of potential demographic divides. They all reveal a strong commitment to bridging those divides. However, most of these graduates did not enter college with either frequent or meaningful interactions with diverse peers. Even when they grew up in diverse communities, as Kartik did, pre-college social life was separated by race-ethnicity and religion—what he called the Black Table, the Asian Table, the Jewish Table, and the Chaldean Table. He and others write that intergroup dialogue provided the kind of experience that led to bridging differences.

Kartik explains that it offered him a new lens with which to view his experiences—to find a new normal in heterogeneity. That social diversity, among students, faculty, and patients, was a core criterion in Kartik's choice of medical schools. Colleen also attributes the growing diversity within her college friendship circles to her involvement with intergroup dialogue. As she reveals in her case, exploration of her identities fostered rather than prevented bridging differences.

Others also write about bridging differences. Annabel attributes her abilities to listen and appreciate each person's uniqueness to intergroup dialogue, and at the same time discusses the struggle to do exactly that. "Differences are always bridged through conversations when you get to learn about another person's upbringing, privilege, or struggle to get to the same place. There are times when I struggle hearing conversations of privilege because I was raised otherwise." This struggle, and a subsequent examination of one's life, often accompanies bridging differences. Aaron writes that the cultural, political, and economic separation between urban and rural communities has captured his attention because poverty rates and unemployment are generally higher in rural communities. He also notes that local elections in his state generally reveal Democratic majorities in cities and Republican majorities in rural areas, and that his life has been too circumscribed by living in liberal urban enclaves. His work focuses on economic development in rural areas. In his personal life, Aaron is trying to cross rural-urban cultural boundaries and to bond with rural residents at a level not often attempted by urban residents.

Joshua joins the theme of active listening to a sense of curiosity. Like Annabel, he bridges his understanding of the complexity of identities to connecting with others: "I have become more aware of the many lenses through which we perceive understanding. It becomes an almost immediate responsibility for me to dig deeper with others with whom I speak, both professionally and personally. I try to relate with their background through dialogue and especially active listening." Like Aaron, Joshua focuses on economic issues and finds that the habits of relating—active listening, engaging identity, and bridging differences—are crucial in mobilizing residents across race and class to dialogue about the economy.

Many of them, like Clare and Adam, have made choices to live in multiracial-ethnic communities, Clare in Washington, D.C., and Adam in Brooklyn, New York. Clare writes that, having grown up in the Detroit metropolitan area, one of the most segregated urban areas in the United States, she was no stranger to urban borders and boundaries. Yet, she was surprised that the "District of Columbia, half the size of Detroit, manages to maintain borders as distinct as 8 Mile." When she was searching for housing, she heard warnings such as "Don't live east of 14th Street," and was told that the apartment where she now lives and has many important, personal engagements is a bad neighborhood.

The importance of exploring identity and of examining oneself to connect with others is stressed by all of these graduates. Both Nathaniel and Adam write about coming to understand whiteness, albeit in very different ways, and yet they express similar views of using their professional roles and understanding of whiteness to advance social justice. Adam describes a process in which he, as a white male, tried for many years to live through the music and art of others. He says, "My understanding of whiteness was determined not by an actual understanding of white racial identity but rather an absence of it in other cultures that were not mine." But eventually he had to examine his whiteness so that his poetry and performance art would reveal his complexity and connections to others. Nathaniel describes his process of going from denial and color-blindness to then struggling to understand and take ownership of racism and now reaching a place of acceptance and questioning how to build genuine relationships: "How can I have genuine interactions with people in a target population if all I see is racism, oppression, and privilege staring me in the face?" Adam resonates with the centrality of relationships. He learned through intergroup dialogue that connection, rather than preemption, was a way forward. In his educational and performance work, Adam aims "to cultivate a culture of empathy wherein participants develop the capacity to recognize and to some extent share feelings experienced by others. . . . And the only way to develop empathy for others is first by examining oneself. . . . My experience as a participant in and facilitator of intergroup dialogue helped me to ask—or, at least start to ask—difficult questions of myself . . . so that I might eventually be able to pursue social justice work not from a place of guilt or sympathy but rather one of empowerment rooted in ownership and pedagogy."

Nathaniel too contrasts relationship and agency coming originally from sympathy to becoming grounded in social justice. "The greatest struggle is to deny that which benefits me, and to help other [privileged people] understand how they are privileged in the same vein. I will do it through social justice work and through friendship. I will not do it through sympathy, as sympathy is a passive emotion. I have never solved anything through sympathy. I will continue to do it through the active process of building alliances. So if asked what I do at work every day, I would say that I continue to strive for alliance with those around me."

Nathaniel describes getting involved in a hospital diversity committee, the ethics committee, and in efforts to broaden cultural orientation training as ways he is building alliances across differences and influencing change.

What we found most interesting in their responses to our demographic question is the extent to which they write about diversity and bridging differences in both their professional and personal lives. Chloé in particular exhibits this intentionality. She writes, "My personal and professional lives are completely intertwined. My circle of friends includes people from all identity groups. . . . Most of my closest friends during college were involved in intergroup dialogue, the tutoring group in which I worked, my jobs, or lived in the same community service-focused residence hall that I did during my first two years in college. I feel that I was bridging differences and bringing people together all the time by being part of these different groups."

Denny shares a sense of internalizing his lesson about the importance of diversity in professional and personal lives. Noting the barriers of entry into law school for students of color and the poor, Denny writes about how he has acted on this internalized commitment to diversity. "When I had concerns about the diversity of the faculty and the student body at my law school, I took to the student newspaper, and my article began a series of conversations within the community about the institutional commitment to diversity. At both of my summer internship placements, I spoke at length with my supervisors and others about the need for attorneys of color who are well trained and competent professionals." Denny also writes about collaborating with other law students to serve as mentors for aspiring lawyers as a way of supporting the educational pipeline to diversify law schools. Similarly, Tara extends her personal learning about identity to changing the professional culture in engineering. "I am now personally committed to interrupting the cycle of silence surrounding identity, oppression, and privilege, especially within the engineering community. I believe it is important for engineers to recognize how identity influences the functioning of groups and to understand the role group dynamics plays in the overall experience of being an engineer within a global economy."

Like Chloé, Tara, and Denny, Jaimée stresses the intertwining of the personal and professional. "Navigating social spaces and institutions, while negotiating my social identities, is both my work and my life." Paralleling her journey of self-empowerment through identity exploration, understanding inequalities and activism through intergroup dialogue, she elaborates on her current work in student affairs. "Our framework and approach focus on intragroup development, multicultural development, and intercultural development simultaneously so that students feel empowered by their own identities while learning to engage with students whose cultural identities are different from their own."

These reflections about the demographic challenge convey that the graduates see themselves not only as individually valuing diversity and bridging differences, but also as being actively and demonstrably committed to realizing these values and effecting change in the context of their own spheres of influence—whether personal, academic, or professional. For many, these values both provide guidance for how they aspire to live and permeate all aspects of their lives.

THE DISPERSION CHALLENGE: BEING GLOBAL CITIZENS

Of the three challenges framing this book, the dispersion challenge as reflected in being global citizens was the one that could be deemed as still a work in progress. The graduates varied in how much they claimed being global citizens and how they exercised global citizenship. None is currently working internationally, but some have studied and worked abroad, and several continue to work in diverse settings that include people originally from countries outside the United States.

Several graduates began their responses stating that they do not really know what a global citizen means, suggesting that the term denotes the kind of elitism that comes with privileged economic resources that makes it possible to travel and study abroad. Colleen represents this concern: "Right now, I can't claim being a global citizen as I don't really know what that means. . . . I imagine a global citizen to be one who is able to travel or live abroad, to put themselves out of a country where they are the majority and become foreign in another place. This requires money and time, things that are available only to some."

For others who had found opportunities (many of which did not require personal financial resources) to travel and work abroad, being a global citizen meant acknowledging this privilege and using their international experiences to fundamentally change their life directions. Jaimée writes, "As I continue to connect my intellectual and spiritual growth with my profession, I will never cease to think of myself as a global citizen even though I no longer physically live in a foreign country."

Colleen's and Jaimée's perspectives represent the two ends of a continuum on which the graduates thought of themselves as global citizens. Other graduates, in writing about their sense of global citizenship, convey the idea that the global is local. They credit their work in the United States with broadening their outlooks and their sense of themselves as global citizens. Chloé writes of her work tutoring Spanish-speaking adults with being in touch with the concerns of people in and from other countries, cementing for her the impact that studying in Argentina, Mexico, and Spain had on her earlier in her high school and college years. For Adam, living and working in New York City propelled him to see his work as an artist in a global sense. "Being a global citizen means to consider one's own role as a contributing member of a society not in isolation from, but rather in the context of, the most pressing and urgent of global concerns." For Annabel, the global is not just local as in place and people; it is also home and embodied in her. "I consider myself a global citizen because although I was born in the United States, both of my parents are from Mexico and raised me in Mexican traditional ways. . . . Before attending law school, I was employed as a paralegal–legal assistant at an immigration law firm where I constantly worked with individuals from many countries. Working with people from other countries intrigues me because I see my parents, my community and myself in them."

Turning to influences on their sense of being global citizens, the essays highlight the significance of college friendships, studying and working in other countries, and, equally as important, working in the United States. Nearly all of these graduates attribute their sense of being global citizens to having become friends when they were in college with students from many countries.

Aaron writes of staying in touch with students he originally met at an intercultural leadership seminar and staying in touch through Facebook and other social media. He says that "events across the globe are personal to me now in ways that they were not before I had an international community." A few who have worked and studied abroad stress its enormous impact on their worldly views. Jaimée writes of having been blessed with opportunities to "explore research, work with community-based and nongovernmental organizations, and sustain relationships with mentors in Egypt, Italy, Guatemala, South Africa, Ethiopia, and Brazil." She lived for some time in Johannesburg, South Africa, working in youth engagement and public health projects. She continues to unpack the meaning of these experiences, especially recognizing her privilege and at the same time that "these journeys solidified a sense of global interconnectivity and interdependency in my mind to a depth that I would not have grasped if I had only learned such concepts in class." Joshua resonates with the sense of global interconnectedness developed through traveling, working, and being amid a diversity of cultures. In the final year of his undergraduate education, Joshua was awarded a year-long global travel fellowship so that he could understand himself as a global citizen by finding commonalities in places of different races, cultures and religions. He traveled to Iceland, the United Kingdom, Turkey, Syria, Jordan, Egypt, the Sudan, Ethiopia, and India. He also interned at nonprofit agencies in South Africa and India. Through all these experiences, he found that the quality of relationships across national borders have to be "built on respect and allyship, a result of culturally competent dialogue." Working with young people in South Africa, exchanging life stories, and witnessing their emergence into youth leadership remains a cornerstone life experience for Joshua. He acknowledges the powerful reciprocal impact on his and their lives: "Our presence represented the greater global thread of leadership as well as the interconnectedness of social justice work." Denny, too, also stresses the import of working in another country on his sense of being a global citizen. He credits the experience of being a Fulbright scholar in Macau with his sense of global citizenship. He affirms the crucial role that social media now play in solidifying the impact of studying or working abroad because it is now possible to maintain relationships created during those experiences in mutual lifelong interactions. Nearly all of them also stress that intergroup dialogue inculcated a sense of responsibility for learning by reading and in other ways gaining information about other countries and about U.S.-international relationships. Clare writes that she gained a commitment in intergroup dialogue to "keep up-to-date about international political movements. It should not be up to my Egyptian American friend to explain to me what is going on in Egypt. It is my responsibility to continue to educate myself to have meaningful conversations with people from other countries." Knowledge and commitment to learn—those are critical elements of being global citizens.

Finally, we found their essays displaying a remarkable sense of humility and a corollary sense of responsibility in making the claim of being global citizens. Jaimée expresses humility about the opportunities she has had to study and work in other countries. She vows that as she makes sense of the impact of those opportunities, she has responsibility to be "a voice and a witness to interrupting ignorance and xenophobia" wherever she finds it. Joshua resonates with this sense of humility in witnessing social change that is possible in the lives of young people in South Africa and how that ignited in him an "urgency for international social justice work." Chloé writes that being a global citizen means that she must continue to try to "understand things on a global level and think more critically about how things that happen in the United States will affect things elsewhere." Colleen, reflecting her humility and responsibility, reverses this connection between the United States and the rest of the world; she writes about learning from other countries. "With a growing interest in policy, I have started to read about models of education in other countries and thinking about how an internationally focused education will affect students in this country. I believe my generation will be stewards of the movement toward a less-Americanized society." Denny echoes a similar commitment in connecting responsibility with curiosity about looking outward to other countries to improve what is within the United States. "My Fulbright experience also sparked curiosity toward international law, and I constantly look for opportunities to improve our legal system by seeing what has worked in other countries." Tara writes of reading publications from authors all over the world in connection with the research she is doing on cancer. Adam emphasizes his responsibility as a global citizen, aside from teaching and living in a neighborhood comprised mostly of Puerto Rican and Dominican families. "I would like to think that my work, at its very core, recognizes the urgency with which we as citizens of our respective communities, our nation, and our globe must begin to examine ourselves and our identities as a way of more fully understanding the social and cultural disparities that exist in our world, and that art—language even more so—can be the most fundamental key in unlocking that process of empowerment."

FINAL WORDS

Although we asked each graduate to write specifically about each of the challenges—democratic, demographic, and dispersion—it was remarkable how intertwined the three challenges are for them, and for us. As many of the graduates have shared, to be effective collaborators, both globally and locally, they need to be aware of their identities, including what it means to be an American in an increasingly diverse United States and the larger world. They need to be aware of others' identities and of the complexity and multiplicity of inequalities domestically and internationally that may or may not parallel their own experiences. They need to develop intercultural competencies to work with people and communities at home and abroad, and at the same time stay tuned to the commonalities and heterogeneities within any community in which they engage. Most important, be it global or local, the graduates share a clear sense of responsibility to advance social justice in ways that embody consciousness of privilege, respect for unique and shared humanity, and global interconnectivity. Thinking globally, this means to check their privileges as Americans in order to learn from systems and practices in other countries so that they can be effective collaborators. Thinking locally, this means a responsibility to use the privilege of education in general, and opportunities such as intergroup dialogue specifically, to build and follow through on their commitments to social change.

The graduates' reflections show the important ways in which they think about the enduring impact of intergroup dialogue. More than the content of their intergroup dialogues, they write richly about the reflective, dialogic, analytical, and collaborative learning and communication processes that form the foundation of intergroup dialogue. They have internalized these learning and interaction processes and translated them into concrete skills to advance concerns of social diversity and social justice in a variety of settings. Beyond their individual benefit of self-reflection, relationship building, and critical analysis, the graduates are effecting change in their arenas for the public good. Their responses convey a sense of empowerment in engaging difference and identity, recognizing their agency and voice not only in surfacing inequalities but also in taking responsibility to bring about change, and, most important, intentionally practicing their commitments to power sharing and alliance building. They are all leaders in their own right, perhaps not in the traditional sense of having power over decision making and advancing their agendas, but in the sense of generative, collaborative power to build capacity for diversity and equality in their professional and personal lives. Many of the graduates are finding their niche within traditionally hierarchical settings, attempting to build what critical race theorists call counterspaces, that is, spaces that challenge unequal power relations and provide more egalitarian environments. Perhaps most impressive in their reflections is the dedicated and creative ways they traverse the boundaries of the theoretical and the practical, the personal and the professional, the individual and the collective, and the global and the local to apply their learning in intergroup dialogue to concrete practices and programs in the real world. A glimpse into the lives of these graduates gives a sense of the possible futures for the intergroup dialogue students whose learning has been the main subject of this book.

Authored by Patricia Gurin and Biren (Ratnesh) A. Nagda.

APPENDIX A

Survey Measures

Table A.1   Affective Positivity

	Reverse Coded	Pretest α	Posttest α
Positive interactions across difference (Matlock, Wade-Golden, and Gurin 2007)		.776	.784
In interactions with people from racial-ethnic (genders) groups different from your own, how frequently have you done or experienced the following since you have been at the university? (Mark one for each item) (1 = Not at all; 7 = Very much) • had meaningful and honest discussions outside of class about race and ethnic (gender) relations • shared our personal feelings and problems • had close friendships			
Positive emotions in interactions across difference (adapted from Stephan and Stephan 1985)		.698	.718
How do you generally feel when interacting with people from racial-ethnic (gender) groups different from your own? Look at the pairs of emotions below and place yourself somewhere on that continuum. (Mark one for each pair). (Scale: 1–10) • trusting (1 = Not trusting at all; 10 = Extremely trusting)			

Table A.1   (continued)

	Reverse Coded	Pretest α	Postest α

- excited (1 = Not at all excited; 10 = Extremely excited)
- open (1 = Not at all open; 10 = Extremely open)
- engaged (1 = Not at all engaged; 10 = Extremely engaged)

Comfort in communicating with people of other groups (Nagda and Zúñiga 2003; Zúñiga et al. 1995)		.696	.732

For each item below, indicate how well you think it describes your motivation and skills in learning about people of racial-ethnic (gender) groups different from your own and interacting with them. (Mark one for each item) (1 = Not at all like me; 7 = Very much like me)

- I find it hard to challenge opinions of people in other racial-ethnic (gender) groups.   *
- I have difficulty expressing myself when discussing sensitive issues with people in other racial-ethnic (gender) groups.   *
- I feel comfortable asking people of other racial-ethnic (gender) groups about their perspectives on issues involving their groups.
- I avoid conversations with people of other racial-ethnic (gender) groups who hold really different perspectives from my own.   *
- I worry about offending people from a different gender/race when I disagree with their points of view.   *

Source: Authors' compilation.
*Indicates reverse coding.

Table A.2   Cognitive Openness

	Reverse Coded	Pretest α	Posttest α
The following statements concern your thinking about people, society, and the world. For each statement, indicate how well each statement describes you. (1 = Not at all like me; 7 = Very much like me)			
Complexity of thinking (adapted from Cacioppo and Petty 1982; Fletcher, Danilovics, Fernandez, Peterson, and Reeder 1986)		.793	.818
• I like tasks that require little thought once I've learned them.	*		
• I prefer simple rather than complex explanations for people's behavior.	*		
• I would rather do something that requires little thought than something that is sure to challenge my thinking abilities.			
• The world is too complicated for me to spend time trying to figure out how it operates.	*		
• I don't like to have the responsibility of handling a situation that requires a lot of thinking.	*		
Thinking about society (adapted from Lopez, Abboushi, and Reifmann 1992)		.729	.735
• I think a lot about the influence that society has on my behaviors.			
• I am fascinated by the complexity of the social institutions that affect people's lives.			
• I think a lot about the influence that society has on other people.			
• I really enjoy analyzing the reasons or causes for people's behavior.			
Openness to multiple perspectives (adapted from Davis 1983)		.737	.760
• I strive to see issues from many points of view.			
• If I am sure about something, I don't waste too much time listening to other people's arguments.	*		
• I believe there are many sides to every issue and try to look at most of them.			

Table A.2   (continued)

	Reverse Coded	Pretest α	Posttest α
• I am willing to listen to the variety of views that can emerge in talking about social issues and problems.			
• I sometimes find it difficult to see things from the "other person's" point of view.	*		
Identity involvement (Gurin and Markus 1989; Luhtanen and Crocker 1992)		.833	.853

Thinking about the racial-ethnic (gender) identity group that you mentioned as your primary racial-ethnic (gender) identification, please indicate how much you agree or disagree with the following statements. (1 = Disagree strongly; 7 = Agree strongly)
- I have spent time trying to find out more about my racial-ethnic (gender) identity group.
- To learn more about my racial-ethnic (gender) group, I have often talked to other people about it.
- I participate in activities that express my racial-ethnic (gender) group.
- I think a lot about how my life will be affected by my race/ethnicity (gender).
- I think a lot about how the group history and traditions of my racial-ethnic (gender) group have influenced me.

Source: Authors' compilation.
*Indicates reverse coding.

Table A.3   Intergroup Understanding

	Reverse Coded	Pretest α	Posttest α
Attributions for race and gender inequality Please indicate how much you agree or disagree with the following statements about gender, racial-ethnic issues. (1 = Disagree strongly; 7 = Agree strongly)			
Structural attribution for racial-ethnic inequality (Gurin, Miller, and Gurin 1980) • What one can achieve in life is still limited by one's race or ethnicity. • Prejudice and discrimination in the educational system limit the success of people of color. • Unfair hiring and promotion practices help keep many people of color from gaining positions of power. • Most people of color are no longer discriminated against in this country.	 *	.771	.796
Structural attribution for gender inequality (Gurin, Miller, and Gurin 1980) • In the United States there is still great gender inequality. • Discrimination in the workplace still limits the success of many women. • It is harder for women candidates to raise campaign funds than it is men candidates. • Most women are no longer discriminated against in the country.	 *	.728	.756
Individual attributions for racial-ethnic inequality (Gurin, Miller, and Gurin 1980) • People of color are responsible for their lack of accomplishments in society. • People of color aren't as successful in the workplace as whites because they don't have the same work ethic.		.669	.729
Individual attributions for gender inequality (Gurin, Miller, and Gurin 1980) • Women are responsible for their lack of accomplishments in society.		.618	.674

Table A.3   (continued)

	Reverse Coded	Pretest α	Posttest α
• Women are less willing to make the personal sacrifices needed to make it in American society.			
Critique of inequality[a]		.645	.694
• Racial-ethnic profiling is a serious problem in our society.			
• There should be stronger legislation against perpetrators of hate crimes.			
• The biases built into the legal and justice systems contribute to the inequality in our country.			
Attitudes toward diversity (Matlock, Wade-Golden, and Gurin 2007)		.693	.731
Below are statements about the value of diversity in higher education. How much do you agree or disagree with each of them? (1 = Disagree strongly; 7 = Agree strongly)			
• The focus on diversity in colleges and universities puts too much emphasis on differences between racial-ethnic groups.	*		
• A diverse student body is essential to teaching students the skills they need to succeed and lead in the work environments of the twenty-first century.			
• The emphasis on diversity means I can't talk honestly about ethnic, racial, and gender issues.	*		
• Leaders in science and engineering should reflect the racial-ethnic diversity of the United States.			
• The current focus on diversity undermines the common ties that bind us as a nation.	*		
• Exposure to diverse peers makes college graduates better-informed participants in public life.			

Source: Authors' compilation.
*Indicates reverse coding.
[a]Measure developed for this study.

Table A.4   Intergroup Relationships

	Reverse Coded	Pretest α	Posttest α
Intergroup empathy[a]		.863	.882

Here is another way of describing your feelings in conversations with people from racial-ethnic (gender) groups different from your own. (1 = Not at all like me; 7 = Very much like me)

- When people feel frustrated about racial-ethnic (gender) stereotypes applied to their group, I feel some of their frustration too.
- When people feel proud of the accomplishments of someone of their racial-ethnic (gender) group, I feel some of their pride as well.
- When people express regret about the racial-ethnic (gender) biases they were taught, I can empathize with their feelings.
- When I learn about the injustices that people of different races/ethnicities (genders) have experienced, I tend to feel some of the anger that they do.
- When I hear others use their positions of privilege to promote greater racial-gender equality, I feel hopeful.
- I feel despair when I hear about the impact of racial-gender inequalities on others in our society.
- I feel hopeful hearing how others have overcome disadvantages because of their race or gender.
- I feel angry when people don't acknowledge the privileges they have in society because of their race or gender.

	Reverse Coded	Pretest α	Posttest α
Motivation to bridge differences (adapted from Nagda and Zúñiga 2003; Nagda, Kim, and Truelove 2004)		.766	.788

For each item below, indicate how well you think it describes your motivation and skills in learning about people of racial-ethnic (gender) groups different from your own and interacting with them. (Mark one for each item) (1 = Not at all like me; 7 = Very much like me)

- It is important for me to educate others about my racial-ethnic (gender) group.

Table A.4   (continued)

	Reverse Coded	Pretest α	Posttest α
• I like to learn about racial-ethnic (gender) groups different from my own.			
• Sharing stories and experiences of my racial-ethnic (gender) groups with others matters a lot to me.			
• I want to bridge differences between different racial-ethnic groups (women and men).			
• As I learn more about other racial-ethnic (gender) groups, I find myself wanting to learn more about people of my own racial-ethnic (gender) group.			
• I don't feel the need to help people from different racial-ethnic (women and men) groups learn from each other.	*		
• I don't care if other people understand my racial-ethnic/gender group.	*		
• I don't enjoy getting into unfamiliar situations involving members of other racial-ethnic (gender) groups.	*		

Source: Authors' compilation.

*Indicates reverse coding.

[a]Measure developed for this study.

Table A.5   Intergroup Collaboration and Action

	Reverse Coded	Pretest α	Posttest α
Confidence and frequency of action			

People can take a variety of actions to address issues of prejudice, discrimination, and injustices. Listed below are different actions. First, indicate how confident you feel about your abilities in each of the actions listed. (1 = Not at all confident; 7 = Extremely confident). Second, indicate how often you have engaged in each of the actions during the last few months. (1 = Never; 7 = Very often)

	Reverse Coded	Pretest α	Posttest α
Self-directed action (Nagda, Kim, and Truelove 2004)			
confidence		.713	.755
frequency		.704	.755

- Recognize and challenge the biases that affect my own thinking
- Avoid using language that reinforces negative stereotypes
- Make efforts to educate myself about other groups
- Make efforts to get to know people from diverse backgrounds

	Reverse Coded	Pretest α	Posttest α
Other-directed action (Nagda, Kim, and Truelove 2004)			
confidence		.692	.707
frequency		.681	.700

- Challenge others on derogatory comments
- Reinforce others for behaviors that support cultural diversity

	Reverse Coded	Pretest α	Posttest α
Intergroup collaboration[a]			
confidence		.880	.890
frequency		.861	.887

- Join a community group/organization that promotes diversity
- Get together with others to challenge discrimination
- Participate in a coalition of different groups to address some social issues

Table A.5   (continued)

	Reverse Coded	Pretest α	Posttest α
Composite of action items			
confidence		.870	.885
frequency		.849	.862
Postcollege involvement (Gurin, Dey, Hurtado, and Gurin 2002)		.883	.893

How important do you think the following activities will be to you personally after college? (Mark one for each item). (1 = Not at all important; 7 = Extremely important)
- Influencing the political structure (for example, voting, education campaigns, and get-out-the-vote)
- Influencing social policy
- Working to correct social and economic inequalities
- Helping promote inter-racial-inter-ethnic understanding
- Working to achieve greater gender equality

Involvement in social justice activities[a]		.717	.739

To what extent have you been involved in the following campus activities and organizations while at college?
- Groups and activities reflecting my own cultural-ethnic background (such as Black Student Union, La Raza, and Asian American Association)
- Groups and activities reflecting other cultural-ethnic backgrounds
- Groups promoting gender awareness and equality (such as antisexual harassment and violence)
- Lesbian, gay, bisexual, transgendered people, and allies (LGBTA)

Table A.5   (continued)

	Reverse Coded	Pretest α	Posttest α
Skills in dealing with conflict[a]		.739	.758

Please indicate how much you agree or disagree with these statements about how you deal with conflict. By conflict, we mean situations or interactions in which there are important and emotionally charged disagreements and differences in points of view (1 = Disagree strongly; 7 = Agree strongly)

- I generally try to avoid conflict.   *
- I can help people from different groups use conflict constructively.
- I clam up (freeze) when conflict involves strong emotions.   *
- I can work effectively with conflicts that involve me.
- I am usually uncertain how to help people learn from conflicts.   *
- I learn a lot about myself in conflict situations.
- I'd like for groups to just get along rather than deal openly with their conflicts.   *
- I can help people from different groups deal with conflicts that break out between groups.

Source: Authors' compilation.

*Indicates reverse coding.

[a]Measure developed for this study.

Table A.6   Negative Processes

	Reverse Coded	Pretest α	Posttest α
Negative emotions (adapted from Stephan and Stephan 1985)		.843	.872

How do you generally feel when interacting with people from racial-ethnic (gender) groups different from your own? Look at the pairs of emotions below and place yourself somewhere on that continuum. (Scale: 1–10)
- Worried (1 = Not at all worried; 10 = Extremely worried)
- Anxious (1 = Not at all anxious; 10 = Extremely anxious)
- Tense (1 = Not at all tense; 10 = Extremely tense)
- Fearful (1 = Not at all fearful; 10 = Extremely fearful)

	Reverse Coded	Pretest α	Posttest α
Negative interactions (Matlock, Wade-Golden, and Gurin 2007)		.792	.774

In interactions with people from racial-ethnic (gender) groups different from your own, how frequently have you done or experienced the following since you have been at the university? (1 = Not at all; 7 = Very much)
- Been put down, made to feel uncomfortable
- Had tense, somewhat hostile interactions
- Had guarded, cautious interactions
- Felt excluded, ignored

Source: Authors' compilation.

Table A.7   Pedagogy

	Reverse Coded	Pretest α	Posttest α
Listed here are different educational features that characterize courses or programs. How much did each component contribute to your learning? (Mark one for each item) (1 = Not at all; 7 = Very much; 9 = Does not apply)			
Content (Lopez, Gurin, and Nagda 1998; Nagda, Kim, and Truelove 2004) • Assigned readings • Journals or reflection papers • Other written assignments			.776
Structured interactions (Nagda, Kim, and Truelove 2004; Nagda and Zúñiga 2003) • Structured activities and exercises • Ground rules for discussion • A small group of students • A diverse group of students • Collaborative projects with other students			.786
IGD facilitator effectiveness (Nagda 1999)			.955
How effective were your facilitators/instructors in the following areas: (1 = Not at all effective; 7 = Extremely effective) • Facilitators/instructors • Creating an inclusive climate • Modeling good communication skills • Actively involving me in learning experiences • Intervening when some group or class members dominated discussion • Encouraging group or class members to talk to each other, not just to the facilitators/instructors • Intervening when some group or class members were quiet • Handling conflict situations • Helping to clarify misunderstandings • Offering their perspectives in a helpful way • Bringing in a different perspective when everyone seemed to be agreeing • Encouraging us to continue discussion when it became uncomfortable			

Source: Authors' compilation.

Table A.8 Communication Processes

	Reverse Coded	Pretest α	Posttest α
A variety of learning and communication processes are found in courses and programs involving group discussions. Listed below are a number of such processes. Indicate the extent to which each of the communication processes occurred during your course/program. (1 = Not at all; 7 = Very much).			
Engaging self (Nagda 2006) • Being able to disagree • Sharing my views and experiences • Asking questions that I felt I wasn't able to ask before • Addressing difficult issues • Speaking openly without feeling judged			.836
Appreciating difference (Nagda 2006) • Hearing different points of view • Learning from each other • Hearing other students' personal stories • Appreciating experiences different from my own			.837
Critical reflection (Nagda 2006) • Examining the sources of my biases and assumptions • Making mistakes and reconsidering my opinions • Thinking about issues that I may not have before • Understanding how privilege and oppression affect our lives			.807
Alliance building (Nagda 2006) • Working through disagreements and conflicts • Other students' willingness to understand their own biases and assumptions • Listening to other students' commitment to work against injustices • Understanding other students' passion about social issues • Talking about ways to take action on social issues • Sharing ways to collaborate with other groups to take action • Feeling a sense of hope about being able to challenge injustices			.915

Source: Authors' compilation.

APPENDIX B

Analytic Procedures, Effects Tables

Appendix B details the estimation methods used to account for missing data, test for baseline equivalence, examine the impact of intergroup dialogue on the hypothesized outcomes, and test the theoretical model for intergroup dialogue.

MISSING DATA

As detailed in chapter 2, the project successfully tracked students who were randomly assigned to dialogue, control, and the social science comparison groups. Nearly all (95 percent) of participants completed the posttest administered at the end the term in which dialogue and comparison courses were offered and the study team successfully followed up with 82 percent of the original sample one year after the posttest. While these retention rates are high for longitudinal studies, analyses conducted with missing data can introduce bias into the results. Specifically, if those students who did not take the posttest or the survey one year later were systematically different than their counterparts who did, the analyses can lead to erroneous conclusions if applied to the sample as a whole.

To adjust for the potential bias introduced by missing data, we used multiple imputation. Multiple imputation was used to create ten imputed datasets for subsequent analysis, which reduces the potential bias introduced when estimating the effect of intergroup dialogue using only observed data. Multiple imputation procedures (Rubin 1987) replace each missing value with a set of plausible values (across ten datasets) that represent the uncertainty about the right value to impute. Analyses are then conducted separately on each dataset using standard procedures and results are combined across datasets in ways that appropriately account for between and within imputation variance.

Multiple imputation, as a strategy to reduce bias associated with missing data, assumes that the data were missing at random (MAR) such that missing data depend on observed data but not on unobserved data. Multiple imputation corrects for this kind of bias using the available observed data to predict and impute missing values. After these relationships are accounted for, MAR assumes that the patterns of missingness are completely random. In contrast, including only observed data in analyses assumes that missing data are missing completely at random (MCAR) before adjustment, a less tenable assumption.

Initial analyses of missing data patterns suggest that a number of measured variables were associated with missingness in a predictable pattern such that multiple measures collected on the pretest (including demographic information) predicted patterns of missingness on the posttest and at one year follow-up. In choosing the number of variables to enter in the imputation model, we erred on the side of inclusion. The general recommendation for imputation models is to use every available variable in the imputation model (Little and Raghunathan 2004), including the dependent variables (Little and Rubin 2002; Allison 2009).

IMPACT ANALYSES

To create a multiply-imputed dataset for analyses examining the impact of intergroup dialogue, we included all of the outcome measures at each time point (pretest, posttest, one-year follow-up) in the imputation model, as well as a range of demographic variables (institution, gender, race, topic of dialogue, privileged group status, major, immigration status, religion, year in school, parental education, pre-college exposure to diversity—racial-ethnic composition of neighborhood, high school, and place of worship, religiosity, liberalism, and students' prior participation in courses or programs that focused on issues related to race, ethnicity or gender). Multiple imputation was conducted using SAS PROC MI; the procedure was performed separately for the dialogue, wait-list control, and social science comparison groups to create ten imputed datasets and the data files were subsequently combined for analysis.

SEM ANALYSES

To create a variance-covariance matrix based on a multiply-imputed dataset for the SEM analyses testing theoretical framework, we included all individual indicator variables included in the SEM model (pedagogical features, communication processes, psychological processes, outcomes) as well as demographic variables (gender, race, topic of dialogue, status, year in school, pre-college exposure to and students' prior participation in courses or programs that focused on issues related to race-ethnicity or gender). Because the SEM analyses focused on the processes that took place within intergroup dialogue, only students who participated in dialogue were included. Multiple imputation was conducted using SAS PROC MI; however, to maximize reliability and the stability of the variance and covariance of the variables used in the estimated model, missing data were multiply imputed 100 times and a combined dataset was used to calculate a variance-covariance matrix, corrected for the original sample size of students in the dialogue condition (n = 720 rather than 72,000 = 720 × 100).

BASELINE EQUIVALENCE ANALYSES

This project utilized an experimental design to test the impact of intergroup dialogue, such that students were randomly assigned to participate in an intergroup dialogue or in a wait-list control group. Although random assignment procedures are used to produce equivalent groups of students in each condition before implementing and evaluating an intervention (in this case, the intergroup dialogue course), these procedures can, in some cases, produce random differences. To examine whether our random assignment procedure was successful in producing two equivalent groups of students, we tested for statistical differences between dialogue group and control group students on the twenty-six pretest measures used to assess the impact of intergroup dialogue (twenty-four positive outcomes and two additional measures assessing negative interactions).

The equivalent distribution of students across the four demographic groups—women of color, men of color, white women, white men—in each condition was explicitly controlled by randomly assigning students to condition within each of these four demographic blocks. However, we also examined whether dialogue and control group students differed significantly at baseline on nine additional variables that might importantly shape students' experience in intergroup dialogue. These variables included their year in school, exposure to pre-college diversity in their neighborhoods, high schools and places of worship, liberal-conservatism, and prior courses that they had taken in college that involved race-ethnicity (two measures) or gender content (two measures). In total, we examined baseline differences across thirty-five measures (twenty-six pretest outcome measures and nine auxiliary measures of baseline characteristics).

To test for statistical differences at baseline on each outcome, we estimated the following two-level model:

$$PRETESTMEASURE_{ij} = \beta_{0j} + \beta_{1j}\,(Condition) + \varepsilon_{ij} \qquad \text{(B.1a)}$$

$$\beta_{0j} = \gamma_{00} + u_{0j} \qquad \text{(B.1b)}$$

$$\beta_{1j} = \gamma_{10} \qquad \text{(B.1c)}$$

where $PRETESTMEASURE_{ij}$ is the pretest score of student i in dialogue/control group j. Condition (0 = control; 1 = IGD) was uncentered and γ_{10} represents an unstandardized estimate of the difference on the pretest measure between students randomly assigned to take an intergroup dialogue course or to a wait-list control group. A statistically significant effect γ_{10} where $p < .05$ would indicate non-equivalence at baseline.

Across the twenty-six outcome measures, we observed statistically significant differences on only two—comfort in communicating across differences and frequency of self-directed action. For comfort in communicating across differences, students in intergroup dialogue were significantly lower at baseline than their counterparts in the control group (see table B.1 for means and standard deviations); for frequency of self-directed action, students in dialogue were significantly higher than controls (see table B.5 for means and standard deviations). Across the additional nine auxiliary measures of baseline characteristics, we observed a statistically significant difference on only one—the number of courses that students had previously taken in a race-ethnicity studies department or program. Specifically, control group students had previously taken more courses in a race-ethnic studies department or program ($M = .78$, $SD = .94$) than students randomly assigned to take intergroup dialogue ($M = .65$, $SD = .90$). Thus, we did not observe statistical differences between students randomized to take intergroup dialogue or to a wait-list control group across thirty-three of thirty-six baseline measures tested. These findings show that randomization was successful.

PRE-POST EXPERIMENTAL IMPACT ANALYSES

To estimate the effect of intergroup dialogue on each outcome, we conducted a series of multilevel models to examine change over time and account for the nested data structure (observations over time within person, persons within dialogue or control groups). In this study, the units of data at each level are not statistically independent of one another and ignoring this interdependency yields misleadingly small standard errors when estimating the effect of intergroup dialogue on the outcomes of interest (see Seltzer 2004; Raudenbush and Bryk 2002; Snijders and Bosker 1999). MLM properly estimates the effect of intergroup dialogue by accounting for the nesting of multiple time points of data within each student and the multiple students within each dialogue or control group. Specifically, the following three-level growth model was specified:

Level 1 Model

$$OUTCOME_{ijk} = \pi_{0jk} + \pi_{1jk}(PREvsPOST_{ijk}) + \pi_{2jk}{}^*(Quadratic_{ijk}) + e_{ijk} \quad \text{(B.2a)}$$

Level 2 Model

$$\pi_{0jk} = \beta_{00k} + \beta_{01k}(Condition_{jk}) + \beta_{02k}(YEAR_{jk}) + \beta_{03k}(NEIGHDIV_{jk})$$
$$+ \beta_{04k}(HSDIV_{jk}) + \beta_{05k}(RELIGDIV_{jk}) + \beta_{06k}(CONSERVATISM_{jk})$$
$$+ \beta_{07k}(RACECOURSE1_{jk}) + \beta_{08k}(RACECOURSE2_{jk})$$
$$+ \beta_{09k}(GENDERCOURSE1_{jk})$$
$$+ \beta_{010k}(GENDERCOURSE2_{jk}) + r_{0jk} \quad \text{(B.2b)}$$

$$\pi_{1jk} = \beta_{10k} + \beta_{11k}(Condition_{jk}) + \beta_{12k}(YEAR_{jk}) + \beta_{13k}(NEIGHDIV_{jk})$$
$$+ \beta_{14k}(HSDIV_{jk}) + \beta_{15k}(RELIGDIV_{jk}) + \beta_{16k}(CONSERVATISM_{jk})$$
$$+ \beta_{17k}(RACECOURSE1_{jk}) + \beta_{18k}(RACECOURSE2_{jk})$$
$$+ \beta_{19k}(GENDERCOURSE1_{jk}) + \beta_{110k}(GENDERCOURSE2_{jk})$$
$$+ r_{1jk} \quad \text{(B.2c)}$$

$$\pi_{2jk} = \beta_{20k} + \beta_{21k}(Condition_{jk}) + \beta_{22k}(YEAR_{jk}) + \beta_{23k}(INEIGHDIV_{jk})$$
$$+ \beta_{24k}(HSDIV_{jk}) + \beta_{25k}(RELIGDIV_{jk}) + \beta_{26k}(CONSERVATISM_{jk})$$
$$+ \beta_{27k}(I\,RACECOURSE1_{jk}) + \beta_{28k}(RACECOURSE2_{jk})$$

$$+ \beta_{29k}(GENDERCOURSE1_{jk})$$
$$+ \beta_{210k}(GENDERCOURSE2_{jk}) \tag{B.2d}$$

Level 3 Model

$$\beta_{00k} = \gamma_{000} + u_{00k} \tag{B.2e}$$
$$\beta_{01k} = \gamma_{010} \tag{B.2f}$$
$$\beta_{02k} = \gamma_{020} \tag{B.2g}$$
$$\beta_{03k} = \gamma_{030} \tag{B.2h}$$
$$\beta_{04k} = \gamma_{040} \tag{B.2i}$$
$$\beta_{05k} = \gamma_{050} \tag{B.2j}$$
$$\beta_{06k} = \gamma_{060} \tag{B.2k}$$
$$\beta_{07k} = \gamma_{070} \tag{B.2l}$$
$$\beta_{08k} = \gamma_{080} \tag{B.2m}$$
$$\beta_{09k} = \gamma_{090} \tag{B.2n}$$
$$\beta_{010k} = \gamma_{0100} \tag{B.2o}$$
$$\beta_{10k} = \gamma_{100} \tag{B.2p}$$
$$\beta_{11k} = \gamma_{110} + u_{11k} \tag{B.2q}$$
$$\beta_{12k} = \gamma_{120} \tag{B.2r}$$
$$\beta_{13k} = \gamma_{130} \tag{B.2s}$$
$$\beta_{14k} = \gamma_{140} \tag{B.2t}$$
$$\beta_{15k} = \gamma_{150} \tag{B.2u}$$
$$\beta_{16k} = \gamma_{160} \tag{B.2v}$$
$$\beta_{17k} = \gamma_{170} \tag{B.2w}$$
$$\beta_{18k} = \gamma_{180} \tag{B.2x}$$
$$\beta_{19k} = \gamma_{190} \tag{B.2y}$$
$$\beta_{110k} = \gamma_{1100} \tag{B.2z}$$
$$\beta_{20k} = \gamma_{200} \tag{B.2aa}$$
$$\beta_{21k} = \gamma_{210} \tag{B.2ab}$$
$$\beta_{22k} = \gamma_{220} \tag{B.2ac}$$
$$\beta_{23k} = \gamma_{230} \tag{B.2ad}$$
$$\beta_{24k} = \gamma_{240} \tag{B.2ae}$$
$$\beta_{25k} = \gamma_{250} \tag{B.2af}$$
$$\beta_{26k} = \gamma_{260} \tag{B.2ag}$$
$$\beta_{27k} = \gamma_{270} \tag{B.2ah}$$
$$\beta_{28k} = \gamma_{280} \tag{B.2ai}$$
$$\beta_{29k} = \gamma_{290} \tag{B.2aj}$$
$$\beta_{210k} = \gamma_{2100} \tag{B.2ak}$$

Alternatively, this three-level growth model can be represented concisely in mixed form as follows:

$$
\begin{aligned}
OUTCOME_{ijk} = {} & \gamma_{000} + \gamma_{010}(Condition_{jk}) + \gamma_{020}(YEAR_{jk}) \\
& + \gamma_{030}(NEIGHDIV_{jk}) + \gamma_{040}(HSDIV_{jk}) + \gamma_{050}(RELIGDIV_{jk}) \\
& + \gamma_{060}(CONSERVATISM_{jk}) + \gamma_{070}(RACECOURSE1_{jk}) \\
& + \gamma_{080}(RACECOURSE2_{jk}) + \gamma_{090}(GENDERCOURSE1_{jk}) \\
& + \gamma_{0100}(GENDERCOURSE2_{jk}) + \gamma_{100}(PREvsPOST_{ijk}) \\
& + \gamma_{110}(PREvsPOST_{ijk}*Condition_{jk}) \\
& + \gamma_{120}(PREvsPOST_{ijk}*YEAR_{jk}) \\
& + \gamma_{130}(PREvsPOST_{ijk}*NEIGHDIV_{jk}) \\
& + \gamma_{140}(PREvsPOST_{ijk}*HSDIV_{jk}) \\
& + \gamma_{150}(PREvsPOST_{ijk}*RELIGDIV_{jk}) \\
& + \gamma_{160}(PREvsPOST_{ijk}*CONSERVATISM_{jk}) \\
& + \gamma_{170}(PREvsPOST_{ijk}*RACECOURSE1_{jk}) \\
& + \gamma_{180}(PREvsPOST_{ijk}*RACECOURSE2_{jk}) \\
& + \gamma_{190}(PREvsPOST_{ijk}*GENDERCOURSE1_{jk}) \\
& + \gamma_{1100}(PREvsPOST_{ijk}*GENDERCOURSE2_{jk}) \\
& + \gamma_{200}(Quadratic_{ijk}) + \gamma_{210}(Quadratic_{ijk}*Condition_{jk}) \\
& + \gamma_{220}(Quadratic_{ijk}*YEAR_{jk}) \\
& + \gamma_{230}(Quadratic_{ijk}*NEIGHDIV_{jk}) \\
& + \gamma_{240}(Quadratic_{ijk}*HSDIV_{jk}) \\
& + \gamma_{250}(Quadratic_{ijk}*RELIGDIV_{jk}) \\
& + \gamma_{260}(Quadratic_{ijk}*CONSERVATISM_{jk}) \\
& + \gamma_{270}(Quadratic_{ijk}*RACECOURSE1_{jk}) \\
& + \gamma_{280}(Quadratic_{ijk}*RACECOURSE2_{jk}) \\
& + \gamma_{290}(Quadratic_{ijk}*GENDERCOURSE1_{jk}) \\
& + \gamma_{2100}(Quadratic_{ijk}*GENDERCOURSE2_{jk}) + r_{0jk} \\
& + r_{1jk}(PREvsPOST_{ijk}) + u_{00k} \\
& + u_{11k}(PREvsPOST_{ijk}*Condition_{jk}) + e_{ijk} \qquad\qquad (B.3)
\end{aligned}
$$

where $OUTCOME_{ijk}$ represents the outcome score at time point i (pretest, posttest, one-year follow-up) for student j in dialogue/control group k. While an interpretation of each coefficient in this multilevel growth model is beyond the scope of this text, conceptually, this model accounts for the following:

Estimates a time by condition interaction. To estimate the impact of intergroup dialogue at posttest, we tested for a time (pre- versus post-) by condition (dialogue versus control) interaction. To estimate changes pre-post, model B.3 estimates a linear "main effect" pre-post contrast for time (pre = –1, post = 1, one-year follow-up = 0) represented by γ_{100}. The time by condition interaction is represented by γ_{110}. Additionally, these estimates of pre-post change and its interaction with condition control for a potential quadratic effect of time γ_{200} (by including an orthogonal quadratic contrast) and a quadratic time by condition interaction γ_{210} across the three observed time points. Thus, reported linear impacts at posttest account for the differential growth patterns between dialogue and control students where in many cases, dialogue students increase pre-post and diminish over time, while controls do not change either between pre-post or pre- to post-post (see tables B.1 through B.5). A statistically significant positive coefficient for γ_{110} would demonstrate a positive impact of dialogue, with students in intergroup dialogue showing greater change over the course of the academic term than their counterparts in the wait-list control group.

Includes student-level covariates. Because this project employed experimental methodology to randomly assign students to take intergroup dialogue course or to a wait-list control, it was not necessary to control student-level differences at baseline. Theoretically, random assignment ought to ensure equivalent groups and the analyses of baseline equivalence demonstrate that with only a few exceptions, students in intergroup dialogue did not differ from their counterparts in the control on the pretest measures. However, including covariates, particularly those that may be theoretically important (in that they might predict the outcome of interest), increases the precision of the impact estimates (see Bloom, Richburg-Hayes, and Black 2005). For this reason, we included student-level covariates including students' year in school, their prior exposure to diversity in their neighborhood (*NEIGHDIV*), their high school (*HSDIV*), and their place of worship (*RELIGDIV*), political orientation (*CONSERVATISM*), the number of courses students have taken in a race-ethnic studies department or program (*RACE-COURSE1*), the number of courses taken in other departments that primarily cover race-ethnicity content (*RACECOURSE2*), the number of courses taken in women's studies department or program (*GEN-DERCOURSE1*), and the number of courses taken in other departments that primarily cover gender content. The student-level covariates including *YEAR, NEIGHDIV, HSDIV, RELIGDIV, CONSERVATIVISM, RACECOURSE1, RACECOURSE2, GENDERCOURSE1*, and *GENDERCOURSE2* were centered around the grand mean.

Estimates random effects of pre-post impact. The model estimates a random effect for the intercept and pre-post linear contrast for students (allowing estimates to vary across students at level 2) and for dialogue and control groups (allowing estimates to vary across groups at level 3).

Given that we used multiple imputation (see Missing Data section) to impute missing data, all analyses were conducted separately on each of ten imputed datasets and averaged using MLM.

We report effect sizes d for differential change in empathy over time following Raudenbush and Liu (2001; see also Feingold 2009). Effect sizes were calculated by multiplying the coefficient for a time by condition interaction by time and dividing the product by the pooled standard deviation of the raw empathy pretest scores.

ONE-YEAR FOLLOW-UP EXPERIMENTAL IMPACT ANALYSES

To estimate the effect of intergroup dialogue on each outcome at one year follow-up, we used the same analytic strategy as for the estimates of pre-post impact with one exception. We used model B.3 but replaced the *PREvsPOST* linear contrast with a contrast γ_{100} that tested linear change between baseline and the one-year follow-up (where pre = –1, post = 0, one-year follow-up = 1). Accordingly the impact of intergroup dialogue was tested using a time (pre versus one-year follow-up) by condition (dialogue versus control) interaction γ_{110} and this model controlled for a potential quadratic effect of time γ_{200} (by including an orthogonal quadratic contrast) and a quadratic time by condition interaction γ_{210} across the three observed time points. As was the case for the estimates of pre-post impact, a statistically significant positive coefficient for γ_{110} would demonstrate a positive impact of dialogue, with students in intergroup dialogue showing greater change over the course of the academic term than their counterparts in the wait-list control group.

SOCIAL SCIENCE COMPARISON ANALYSES

To estimate the effect of intergroup dialogue relative to the non-randomized social science comparison groups, we employed the same analytic strategy presented for the pre-post experimental impact analyses using model B.3. A statistically significant positive coefficient for γ_{110} would demonstrate a positive impact of dialogue, with students in intergroup dialogue showing greater change over the course of the academic term than their counterparts in the nonrandomized social science group. Analyses were conducted using ten multiply-imputed datasets and effect sizes were calculated using the approach outlined above. A summary of the social science comparison analyses is presented in tables B.7 and B.8.

MODERATION ANALYSES

In addition to testing the impact of intergroup dialogue, we also examined whether the impact estimates differed: for students in race and gender dialogues and by whether students had more or less societal privilege within the context of the topic of the dialogue. To do so, we tested whether the impact estimates were moderated by the topic (race versus gender) of the dialogue or students' privileged status. Students were defined as having more privilege if they were white within a race dialogue or men within a gender dialogue; they were defined as having less privilege if they were a person of color within a race dialogue or a woman within a gender dialogue.

TOPIC MODERATION ANALYSES

To examine whether the effect of intergroup dialogue relative to a randomized wait-list control differed for race and gender dialogue, we tested a three-way cross-level interaction, time (pre versus post, level 1), by condition (dialogue versus control, level 2), by topic (race versus gender, level 3). The model used to estimate this interaction for each outcome was similar to model B.3 but additionally included a main effect of topic (race versus gender) at level 3 as well as the three-way cross-level interaction. Specifically, the following three-level growth model can be specified in mixed form as

$$
\begin{aligned}
OUTCOME_{ijk} = \ & \gamma_{000} + \gamma_{010}(Condition_{jk}) + \gamma_{020}(YEAR_{jk}) \\
& + \gamma_{030}(NEIGHDIV_{jk}) + \gamma_{040}(HSDIV_{jk}) + \gamma_{050}(RELIGDIV_{jk}) \\
& + \gamma_{060}(CONSERVATISM_{jk}) + \gamma_{070}(RACECOURSE1_{jk})
\end{aligned}
$$

$$+ \gamma_{080}(RACECOURSE2_{jk}) + \gamma_{090}(GENDERCOURSE1_{jk})$$
$$+ \gamma_{0100}(GENDERCOURSE2_{jk}) + \gamma_{0110}(Topic_k)$$
$$+ \gamma_{0120}(Condition_{jk}{}^* Topic_k) + \gamma_{100}(PREvsPOST_{ijk})$$
$$+ \gamma_{110}(PREvsPOST_{ijk}{}^*Condition_{jk})$$
$$+ \gamma_{120}(PREvsPOST_{ijk}{}^*YEAR_{jk})$$
$$+ \gamma_{130}(PREvsPOST_{ijk}{}^*NEIGHDIV_{jk})$$
$$+ \gamma_{140}(PREvsPOST_{ijk}{}^*HSDIV_{jk})$$
$$+ \gamma_{150}(PREvsPOST_{ijk}{}^*RELIGDIV_{jk})$$
$$+ \gamma_{160}(PREvsPOST_{ijk}{}^*CONSERVATISM_{jk})$$
$$+ \gamma_{170}(PREvsPOST_{ijk}{}^*RACECOURSE1_{jk})$$
$$+ \gamma_{180}(PREvsPOST_{ijk}{}^*RACECOURSE2_{jk})$$
$$+ \gamma_{190}(PREvsPOST_{ijk}{}^*GENDERCOURSE1_{jk})$$
$$+ \gamma_{1100}(PREvsPOST_{ijk}{}^*GENDERCOURSE2_{jk})$$
$$+ \gamma_{1110}(PREvsPOST_{ijk}{}^*Topic_k)$$
$$+ \gamma_{1120}(PREvsPOST_{ijk}{}^*Condition_{jk}{}^*Topic_k)$$
$$+ \gamma_{200}(Quadratic_{ijk}) + \gamma_{210}(Quadratic_{ijk}{}^*Condition_{jk})$$
$$+ \gamma_{220}(Quadratic_{ijk}{}^*YEAR_{jk}) + \gamma_{230}(Quadratic_{ijk}{}^*NEIGHDIV_{jk})$$
$$+ \gamma_{240}(Quadratic_{ijk}{}^*HSDIV_{jk}) + \gamma_{250}(Quadratic_{ijk}{}^*RELIGDIV_{jk})$$
$$+ \gamma_{260}(Quadratic_{ijk}{}^*CONSERVATISM_{jk})$$
$$+ \gamma_{270}(Quadratic_{ijk}{}^*RACECOURSE1_{jk})$$
$$+ \gamma_{280}(Quadratic_{ijk}{}^*RACECOURSE2_{jk})$$
$$+ \gamma_{290}(Quadratic_{ijk}{}^*GENDERCOURSE1_{jk})$$
$$+ \gamma_{2100}(Quadratic_{ijk}{}^*GENDERCOURSE2_{jk})$$
$$+ \gamma_{2110}(Quadratic_{ijk}{}^*Topic_k)$$
$$+ \gamma_{2120}(Quadratric_{ijk}{}^*Condition_{jk}{}^*Topic_k) + r_{0jk}$$
$$+ r_{1jk}(PREvsPOST_{ijk}) + u_{00k}$$
$$+ u_{11k}(PREvsPOST_{ijk}{}^*Condition_{jk}) + e_{ijk} \qquad \text{(B.4)}$$

A statistically significant ($p < .05$) coefficient for γ_{1120} would demonstrate a differential impact of intergroup dialogue relative to control between pretest and posttest for students in race and gender dialogues.

STATUS MODERATION ANALYSES

To examine whether the effect of intergroup dialogue relative to a randomized wait-list control differed for students with more or less societal privilege (within the context of the topic of their dialogue) we tested a three-way cross-level interaction, time (pre versus post, level 1), by condition (dialogue versus control, level 2), by status (more versus less privilege, level 2). The model used to estimate this interaction for each outcome was similar to model B.3 but additionally included a main effect of status (more versus less privilege) at level 2 as well as the three-way cross-level interaction. Specifically, the following three-level growth model can be specified in mixed form as follows:

$$
\begin{aligned}
OUTCOME_{ijk} = \ & \gamma_{000} + \gamma_{010}(Condition_{jk}) + \gamma_{020}(YEAR_{jk}) + \gamma_{030}(NEIGHDIV_{jk}) \\
& + \gamma_{040}(HSDIV_{jk}) + \gamma_{050}(RELIGDIV_{jk}) \\
& + \gamma_{060}(CONSERVATISM_{jk}) + \gamma_{070}(RACECOURSE1_{jk}) \\
& + \gamma_{080}(RACECOURSE2_{jk}) + \gamma_{090}(GENDERCOURSE1_{jk}) \\
& + \gamma_{0100}(GENDERCOURSE2_{jk}) + \gamma_{0110}(Status_{jk}) \\
& + \gamma_{0120}(Condition*Status_{jk}) + \gamma_{100}(PREvsPOST_{ijk}) \\
& + \gamma_{110}(PREvsPOST_{ijk}*Condition_{jk}) \\
& + \gamma_{120}(PREvsPOST_{ijk}*YEAR_{jk}) \\
& + \gamma_{130}(PREvsPOST_{ijk}*NEIGHDIV_{jk}) \\
& + \gamma_{140}(PREvsPOST_{ijk}*HSDIV_{jk}) \\
& + \gamma_{150}(PREvsPOST_{ijk}*RELIGDIV_{jk}) \\
& + \gamma_{160}(PREvsPOST_{ijk}*CONSERVATISM_{jk}) \\
& + \gamma_{170}(PREvsPOST_{ijk}*RACECOURSE1_{jk}) \\
& + \gamma_{180}(PREvsPOST_{ijk}*RACECOURSE2_{jk}) \\
& + \gamma_{190}(PREvsPOST_{ijk}*GENDERCOURSE1_{jk}) \\
& + \gamma_{1100}(PREvsPOST_{ijk}*GENDERCOURSE2_{jk}) \\
& + \gamma_{1110}(PREvsPOST_{ijk}*Status_{jk}) \\
& + \gamma_{1120}(PREvsPOST_{ijk}*Condition*Status_{jk}) \\
& + \gamma_{200}(Quadratic_{ijk}) + \gamma_{210}(Quadratic_{ijk}*Condition_{jk}) \\
& + \gamma_{220}(Quadratic_{ijk}*YEAR_{jk}) \\
& + \gamma_{230}(Quadratic_{ijk}*NEIGHDIV_{jk}) \\
& + \gamma_{240}(Quadratic_{ijk}*HSDIV_{jk}) \\
& + \gamma_{250}(Quadratic_{ijk}*RELIGDIV_{jk}) \\
& + \gamma_{260}(Quadratic_{ijk}*CONSERVATISM_{jk}) \\
& + \gamma_{270}(Quadratic_{ijk}*RACECOURSE1_{jk}) \\
& + \gamma_{280}(Quadratic_{ijk}*RACECOURSE2_{jk}) \\
& + \gamma_{290}(Quadratic_{ijk}*GENDERCOURSE1_{jk}) \\
& + \gamma_{2100}(Quadratic_{ijk}*GENDERCOURSE2_{jk}) \\
& + \gamma_{2110}(Quadratic_{ijk}*Status_{jk}) \\
& + \gamma_{2120}(Quadratric_{ijk}*Condition*Status_{jk}) + r_{0jk}
\end{aligned}
$$

$$+ r_{1jk} \, (PREvsPOST_{ijk}) + u_{00k}$$
$$+ u_{11k} \, (PREvsPOST_{ijk}*Condition_{jk}) + e_{ijk} \qquad \text{(B.5)}$$

A statistically significant (p < .05) coefficient for γ_{1120} would demonstrate a differential impact of intergroup dialogue relative to control between pretest and posttest for students with more or less societal privilege within the context of their race or gender dialogue.

A summary of the moderation analyses is presented in table B.6.

STRUCTURAL EQUATION MODELING ANALYSES

Structural equation modeling (SEM) with latent constructs was used to test the theoretical process model for how intergroup dialogue fosters pre-post increases in intergroup understanding, intergroup relationships, and intergroup collaboration and action as well as where students end up one year later. Analyses were conducted using AMOS 17.0 software (Arbuckle 2008) with students who participated in dialogue (n = 720).

Measurement

As detailed in chapter 5, the structural equation model includes six latent constructs: dialogue pedagogy, communication processes, two psychological process constructs (affective positivity, cognitive involvement) and three outcomes (structural understanding of inequality, intergroup empathy, and intergroup action (for a thorough description of the measures that contributed to each latent construct, see chapter 5). The indicators that we used to measure the dialogue pedagogy and communication processes were measured at posttest only (students were asked to reflect on the processes that transpired within the dialogue). Therefore, indicators for these two measures are raw means for each subscale. The indicators for the two psychological processes and the three outcomes measuring pre-post change are residual scores, that is, using pretest scores to predict posttest scores. However, indicators for outcomes at one-year follow-up are raw means of each subscale or individual item scores (for empathy) one year after the dialogue ended.

Latent constructs were each verified with reliability, factor, and confirmatory factor analyses. To increase the replicability of the structural parameters (that is, minimize over fitting) while also providing a more conservative test of the hypothesized model, they do not include correlated error terms between indicators within a latent construct.

Structural Parameters

To test the proposed theoretical model, we tested an "all ends" model where all latent constructs earlier (to the left) in the model are allowed to have direct pathways to every latent construct later in the model (to the right) up to the prediction of pre-post change in the outcomes. To examine whether pre-post change in each outcome predicts where students ended up on each outcome one year later, only three direct pathways were included for each outcome at one-year follow-up:

the measure of pre-post change for that outcome;

the latent construct of intergroup pedagogy; and

the latent construct of communication processes.

Given the prominent role of pedagogy and communication processes in intergroup dialogue, we were interested in testing if pedagogy and communication processes that took place during the dialogue courses had lasting direct effects on the outcomes one year later.

Only significant pathways are reported. Indirect pathways were tested using 2000 bootstrap samples; bootstrapped standard errors and bias-corrected 95 percent confidence intervals are reported (see Shrout and Bolger 2002). A summary of the direct pathways is presented in table 5.1, and a summary of the indirect pathways is presented in table 5.2.

Estimation Procedure, Nesting, and Model Fits

We used a maximum likelihood (ML) estimation procedure to estimate the specified model based on a variance-covariance matrix. The variance-covariance matrix was calculated from a dataset where missing data at posttest and at one-year follow-up were multiply imputed. Given that participants were nested within dialogue groups, the findings presented below were also tested controlling for dialogue group means. No changes in the direction or significant of parameters were found, suggesting that the individual processes that are presented cannot be attributed to "dialogue group" effects. Acceptable model fit was indicated by a root mean squared error (RMSEA) less than .06, χ^2/df ratio less than 3.00 and .85 or higher for the goodness of fit (GFI), Tucker Lewis (TLI), and comparative fit (CFI) indexes.

Table B.1 Scores on Affective Positivity

	Pretest		Posttest		One Year Later		Effect of Dialogue at Posttest				Effect of Dialogue One Year Later			
	M	SD	M	SD	M	SD	γ	SE	t	d	γ	SE	t	d
Frequency of positive interactions														
dialogue	4.80	1.47	5.28	1.30	5.07	1.44	0.18	0.04	4.46****	0.07	0.11	0.05	2.27**	0.05
control	4.87	1.47	5.00	1.41	4.94	1.50								
Positive emotions														
dialogue	6.35	1.55	6.66	1.49	6.55	1.61	0.12	0.05	2.61**	0.16	0.07	0.06	1.26	0.09
control	6.46	1.47	6.53	1.48	6.52	1.53								
Comfort in communicating across difference														
dialogue	5.11	0.98	5.06	0.92	5.24	0.96	0.04	0.03	1.35	0.08	0.12	0.03	3.93****	0.24
control	5.23	0.99	5.11	0.98	5.11	1.02								

Source: Authors' calculations.

*p < .10; **p < .05; ***p < .01; ****p < .001

Table B.2   Scores on Cognitive Involvement

	Pretest		Posttest		One Year later		Effect of Dialogue at Posttest				Effect of Dialogue One Year Later			
	M	SD	M	SD	M	SD	γ	SE	t	d	γ	SE	t	d
Complexity of thinking														
dialogue	5.06	1.07	5.09	1.16	5.24	1.13	0.04	0.03	1.51	0.07	0.08	0.03	2.51**	0.15
control	5.06	1.10	4.99	1.12	5.08	1.20								
Thinking about society														
dialogue	5.50	1.15	5.65	1.13	5.58	1.19	0.11	0.03	4.16****	0.19	0.05	0.03	1.73*	0.09
control	5.55	1.15	5.48	1.17	5.52	1.21								
Consideration of multiple perspectives														
dialogue	5.40	0.93	5.45	0.93	5.48	0.97	0.03	0.02	1.30	0.06	0.01	0.03	0.54	0.02
control	5.39	0.95	5.37	0.97	5.43	1.03								
Identity involvement														
dialogue	4.36	1.50	5.07	1.31	4.79	1.46	0.32	0.04	8.47****	0.42	0.16	0.04	4.12****	0.21
control	4.35	1.55	4.42	1.47	4.48	1.53								

Source: Authors' calculations.
*$p < .10$; **$p < .05$; ***$p < .01$; ****$p < .001$

Table B.3 Scores on Intergroup Understanding

	Pretest		Posttest		One Year Later		Effect of Dialogue at Posttest				Effect of Dialogue One Year Later			
	M	SD	M	SD	M	SD	γ	SE	t	d	γ	SE	t	d
Structural race														
dialogue	5.20	1.28	5.58	1.21	5.48	1.23	0.16	0.03	4.82****	0.25	0.13	0.03	3.85****	0.20
control	5.16	1.30	5.23	1.27	5.20	1.37								
Structural gender														
dialogue	5.31	1.15	5.67	1.06	5.53	1.12	0.16	0.03	5.61****	0.28	0.15	0.03	4.53****	0.26
control	5.26	1.13	5.30	1.17	5.20	1.29								
Individual race														
dialogue	2.08	1.19	1.97	1.19	1.93	1.22	−0.08	0.03	−2.39**	−0.13	−0.1	0.04	−2.62***	−0.16
control	2.18	1.33	2.24	1.37	2.24	1.38								
Individual gender														
dialogue	2.26	1.26	2.16	1.24	2.14	1.25	−0.09	0.04	−2.28**	−0.14	−0.09	0.04	−2.34**	−0.14
control	2.26	1.24	2.33	1.28	2.33	1.39								
Critique of inequality														
dialogue	5.46	1.18	5.69	1.16	5.62	1.14	0.14	0.03	4.51****	0.24	0.07	0.03	2.15**	0.12
control	5.44	1.15	5.39	1.20	5.46	1.27								
Attitudes toward diversity														
dialogue	5.08	0.98	5.25	1.05	5.28	1.08	0.05	0.03	2.03**	0.10	0.06	0.03	2.06**	0.12
control	5.01	0.99	5.07	1.03	5.10	1.10								

Source: Authors' calculations.

*p < .10; **p < .05; ***p < .01; ****p < .001

Table B.4 Scores on Intergroup Relationships

	Pretest		Posttest		One Year Later		Effect of Dialogue at Posttest				Effect of Dialogue One Year Later			
	M	SD	M	SD	M	SD	γ	SE	t	d	γ	SE	t	d
Intergroup empathy														
dialogue	4.97	1.16	5.35	1.05	5.17	1.20	0.21	0.03	7.78****	0.36	0.10	0.03	3.31***	0.17
control	4.99	1.15	4.96	1.16	4.98	1.19								
Motivation to bridge differences														
dialogue	4.73	1.20	5.28	1.08	5.02	1.19	0.27	0.03	9.69****	0.45	0.15	0.03	4.44****	0.25
control	4.70	1.18	4.70	1.20	4.69	1.26								

Source: Authors' calculations.

*p < .10; **p < .05; ***p < .01; ****p < .001

Table B.5 Scores on Intergroup Collaboration and Action

	Pretest		Posttest		One Year Later		Effect of Dialogue at Posttest				Effect of Dialogue One Year Later			
	M	SD	M	SD	M	SD	γ	SE	t	d	γ	SE	t	d
Frequency of self-directed action														
dialogue	4.88	1.17	5.39	1.14	5.27	1.16	0.28	0.03	9.28****	0.47	0.17	0.03	4.99****	0.29
control	5.05	1.19	4.99	1.20	5.11	1.23								
Frequency of other-directed action														
dialogue	4.32	1.45	4.76	1.45	4.80	1.47	0.25	0.04	5.67****	0.34	0.12	0.05	2.59**	0.16
control	4.37	1.48	4.32	1.45	4.62	1.46								
Frequency of intergroup collaboration														
dialogue	3.16	1.68	3.75	1.77	3.63	1.78	0.32	0.05	6.52****	0.38	0.13	0.05	2.67**	0.15
control	3.22	1.73	3.19	1.70	3.42	1.83								
Confidence in self-directed action														
dialogue	5.42	0.94	5.65	0.97	5.64	0.99	0.10	0.03	3.57****	0.21	0.07	0.03	2.54**	0.15
control	5.47	0.98	5.49	0.97	5.54	1.02								

Table B.5 (continued)

	Pretest		Posttest		One Year Later		Effect of Dialogue at Posttest				Effect of Dialogue One Year Later			
	M	SD	M	SD	M	SD	γ	SE	t	d	γ	SE	t	d
Confidence in other-directed action														
dialogue	5.13	1.25	5.38	1.22	5.41	1.20	0.10	0.04	2.67***	0.16	0.10	0.04	2.65***	0.16
control	5.13	1.32	5.19	1.24	5.22	1.31								
Confidence in intergroup collaboration														
dialogue	4.79	1.56	5.04	1.51	5.03	1.49	0.09	0.04	2.15**	0.12	0.07	0.05	1.45	0.09
control	4.73	1.56	4.81	1.54	4.85	1.60								
Postcollege involvement														
dialogue	4.91	1.44	5.13	1.39	5.24	1.29	0.15	0.03	4.27****	0.21	0.11	0.04	2.81***	0.15
control	4.89	1.44	4.80	1.47	4.99	1.39								
Involvement in social justice activities														
dialogue	2.37	1.28	2.58	1.38	2.55	1.39	0.13	0.03	4.25****	0.20	0.10	0.04	2.71***	0.16
control	2.45	1.29	2.41	1.30	2.44	1.39								
Skills in dealing with conflict														
dialogue	4.78	0.89	4.92	0.93	4.97	0.92	0.04	0.02	1.64	0.09	0.07	0.02	3.11***	0.15
control	4.76	0.94	4.79	0.94	4.79	0.97								

Source: Authors' calculations.

*$p < .10$; **$p < .05$; ***$p < .01$; ****$p < .001$

Table B.6   Summary of Treatment Effects Moderated by Dialogue Topic or Status

Outcomes	Time × Condition Effect Moderated by	
	Race-Gender Topic	More Prv or Less Prv Status
Affective positivity		
Frequency of positive interactions	ns	**
Positive emotions	ns	ns
Comfort	ns	*
Cognitive involvement		
Complexity of thinking	ns	ns
Thinking about society	ns	ns
Openness to multiple perspectives	ns	ns
Identity involvement	ns	***
Intergroup understanding		
Structural race	ns	ns
Structural gender	ns	ns
Individual race	ns	ns
Individual gender	ns	ns
Critique of inequality	*	ns
Attitudes toward diversity	ns	ns
Intergroup relationships		
Intergroup empathy	ns	ns
Motivation to bridge differences	ns	**
Intergroup action		
Frequency of self-directed action	**	ns
Frequency of other-directed action	**	ns
Frequency of intergroup collaboration	ns	ns
Confidence in self-directed action	ns	ns
Confidence in other-directed action	ns	ns
Confidence in intergroup collaboration	ns	ns
Postcollege involvement	ns	**
Involvement in social justice activities	ns	ns
Skills in dealing with conflict	ns	*
Negative interactions		
Frequency of negative interactions	ns	**
Negative emotions	ns	*

Source: Authors' calculations.

Note: Moderation was tested using three-way interactions with topic (time by condition by topic) or status (time by condition by status).

*$p < .10$; **$p < .05$; ***$p < .01$; ****$p < .001$

Table B.7   Comparison of Intergroup Dialogues to Social Science Courses

	Pretest		Posttest		Effect of Dialogue at Posttest			
	M	SD	M	SD	γ	SE	t	d
Affective positivity								
Frequency of positive interactions								
Dialogue	4.89	1.44	5.33	1.30	0.03	0.05	0.51	0.04
SS comparison	4.52	1.48	4.92	1.42				
Positive emotions								
Dialogue	6.50	1.52	6.76	1.47	0.07	0.05	1.35	0.10
SS comparison	6.49	1.39	6.59	1.44				
Comfort								
Dialogue	5.10	0.94	5.09	0.90	0.01	0.03	0.20	0.02
SS comparison	5.01	1.00	5.00	0.99				
Cognitive involvement								
Complex thinking								
Dialogue	5.15	1.07	5.18	1.14	0.01	0.03	0.46	0.02
SS comparison	4.92	1.08	4.93	1.15				
Analytical thinking about society								
Dialogue	5.64	1.11	5.78	1.09	0.05	0.03	1.45	0.09
SS comparison	5.44	1.11	5.47	1.18				
Consideration of multiple perspectives								
Dialogue	5.47	0.90	5.54	0.91	0.06	0.03	1.91*	0.13
SS comparison	5.35	0.90	5.31	0.91				
Identity involvement								
Dialogue	4.44	1.53	5.14	1.29	0.27	0.04	6.15****	0.36
SS comparison	4.13	1.49	4.29	1.46				
Intergroup understanding								
Structural race								
Dialogue	5.24	1.28	5.70	1.19	0.18	0.04	4.38****	0.31
SS comparison	5.35	1.14	5.49	1.15				
Structural gender								
Dialogue	5.40	1.08	5.75	1.01	0.12	0.04	3.40***	0.23
SS comparison	5.39	1.05	5.50	1.04				
Individual race								
Dialogue	1.99	1.13	1.78	1.06	−0.07	0.04	−1.65	−0.12
SS comparison	2.08	1.22	2.02	1.18				
Individual gender								
Dialogue	2.22	1.29	1.95	1.10	−0.12	0.04	−2.65***	−0.20
SS comparison	2.24	1.20	2.20	1.17				

Table B.7   (Continued)

	Pretest		Posttest		Effect of Dialogue at Posttest			
	M	SD	M	SD	γ	SE	t	d
Critique of inequality								
Dialogue	5.51	1.17	5.83	1.09	0.16	0.04	4.46****	0.30
SS comparison	5.52	1.04	5.52	1.07				
Attitudes toward diversity								
Dialogue	5.13	0.97	5.35	1.02	0.10	0.03	2.99***	0.21
SS comparison	5.02	0.95	5.02	1.01				
Intergroup relationships								
Intergroup empathy								
Dialogue	5.15	1.14	5.50	1.00	0.12	0.04	3.16***	0.21
SS comparison	4.95	1.11	5.07	1.09				
Motivation to bridge differences								
Dialogue	4.87	1.20	5.37	1.10	0.17	0.03	5.24****	0.30
SS comparison	4.55	1.13	4.69	1.10				
Intergroup collaboration and action								
Frequency of self-directed actions								
Dialogue	4.96	1.12	5.54	1.06	0.33	0.04	8.23***	0.60
SS comparison	4.99	1.09	4.89	1.12				
Frequency of other-directed actions								
Dialogue	4.34	1.42	4.73	1.42	0.20	0.05	3.73****	0.27
SS comparison	4.16	1.49	4.17	1.40				
Frequency of intergroup collaboration								
Dialogue	3.29	1.70	3.84	1.81	0.26	0.06	4.38****	0.32
SS comparison	2.88	1.58	2.92	1.61				
Confidence in self-directed actions								
Dialogue	5.38	0.95	5.69	0.95	0.11	0.03	3.41***	0.23
SS comparison	5.34	0.95	5.41	0.94				
Confidence in other-directed actions								
Dialogue	5.09	1.24	5.35	1.20	0.09	0.05	1.79*	0.13
SS comparison	4.92	1.39	5.00	1.26				
Confidence in intergroup collaboration								
Dialogue	4.86	1.49	5.11	1.52	0.08	0.06	1.46	0.10
SS comparison	4.44	1.59	4.52	1.54				

Table B.7   (Continued)

	Pretest		Posttest		Effect of Dialogue at Posttest			
	M	*SD*	*M*	*SD*	γ	*SE*	*t*	*d*
Postcollege involvement								
Dialogue	4.96	1.42	5.20	1.41	0.13	0.04	2.96***	0.19
SS comparison	4.77	1.36	4.76	1.39				
Involvement in social justice activities								
Dialogue	2.52	1.35	2.71	1.42	0.15	0.04	3.84***	0.25
SS comparison	2.24	1.14	2.18	1.12				
Skills in dealing with conflict								
Dialogue	4.83	0.91	4.97	0.98	0.02	0.03	0.69	0.04
SS comparison	4.54	0.90	4.62	0.89				
Negative interactions								
Frequency of negative interactions								
Dialogue	2.94	1.31	3.35	1.28	0.15	0.04	3.31***	0.25
SS comparison	2.63	1.17	2.75	1.18				
Negative emotions								
Dialogue	3.27	1.59	3.36	1.63	0.11	0.06	1.87*	0.14
SS comparison	3.25	1.61	3.15	1.56				

Source: Authors' calculations.

*p < .10; **p < .05; ***p < .01; ****p < .001

Table B.8   Scores on Negative Interactions

	Pretest		Posttest		One Year Later		Effect of Dialogue at Posttest				Effect of Dialogue One Year Later			
	M	SD	M	SD	M	SD	γ	SE	t	d	γ	SE	t	d
Frequency of negative interactions														
dialogue	3.01	1.32	3.37	1.29	2.91	1.32	0.16	0.04	4.50****	0.24	−0.03	0.04	−0.63	−0.05
control	2.97	1.30	3.03	1.30	2.95	1.36								
Negative emotions														
dialogue	3.24	1.58	3.39	1.64	3.12	1.68	0.04	0.04	1.02	0.05	−0.04	0.05	−0.81	−0.05
control	3.12	1.59	3.20	1.71	3.09	1.71								

Source: Authors' calculations.

*$p < .10$; **$p < .05$; ***$p < .01$; ****$p < .001$

Authored by Nicholas Sorensen.

NOTES

CHAPTER 1

1. Brown v. Board of Education, 347 US 483 (1954).
2. Grutter v. Bollinger, 539 US 306 (2003).
3. Ibid, 3–4.
4. Actual practices and experiences with diversity—not merely attending a diverse campus—were held to be the way in which diversity produces educational impact in amicus briefs submitted by the American Psychological Association and the American Educational Research Association (citing Chang 1999; Hurtado 2001; Gurin et al. 2002; Orfield and Kurlaender 2001).
5. Scott Page, private communication.

CHAPTER 2

1. A curriculum design team developed a standard curriculum that was implemented at the nine collaborating institutions (Multi-University Intergroup Dialogue Research Project 2005). The team members included Craig Alimo, Gary Anderson, Margarita M. Arellano, Gloria J. Bouis, Teresa Brett, Dominic Cobb, Eva Fatigoni, Patricia Gurin, Joycelyn Landrum-Brown, Gretchen Lopez, Kelly Maxwell, Biren (Ratnesh) Nagda, Jaclyn Rodriguez, Thomas Walker, Kathleen Wong (Lau), Anna Yeakley, and Ximena Zúñiga. The team drew heavily from intergroup dialogue curricula developed at Arizona State University (Treviño and Maxwell 1999), University of Massachusetts (Zúñiga and Cytron-Walker 2003), University of Michigan (Program on Intergroup Relations 2003) and University of Washington (Nagda 2001). For a more detailed description of se-

lect activities, see the *ASHE Higher Education Report* by Ximena Zúñiga and her colleagues (2007).

CHAPTER 3

1. This work shows that the same affective brain circuits are activated both when people feel their own pain and the pain or distress of others. In one of the first studies, Vittorio Gallese and his colleagues (1996) demonstrated through single-cell recordings in macaque monkeys that brain cells, called mirror neurons, located in area F5 of the premotor cortex fired not only when a monkey acted but also when the monkey observed another one making the same action. "Later on, by mapping regions of the human brain using Functional Magnetic Resonance Imaging (fMRI), it was discovered that human areas that presumably had mirror neurons also communicated with the brain's emotional or limbic system, facilitating connection with another's feelings, probably by mirroring those feelings. This neural circuitry is presumed to be the basis of empathic behavior, in which actions in response to the distress of others are virtually instantaneous" (Olson 2008, 2). A related area of research has investigated the network of brain regions thought to support mental inference and the processes by which we understand stories (Mar 2011). Raymond Mar concludes that although a quantitative meta-analysis reveals an overlap in the brain regions associated with mental inference and story comprehension, the exact relationship between these two processes is not yet clear. Both of these processes are involved in empathy.

2. Wil Haygood, "One Family's Plunge from the Middle Class into Poverty," *Washington Post*, November 19, 2010. Available at: http://www.washingtonpost.com/wp-dyn/content/story/2010/11/19/ST2010111900317.html (accessed January 23, 2013).

CHAPTER 4

1. Detailed presentation of all these methods and consent forms is available in a project guidebook on the Russell Sage Foundation website.

2. In this study, the units of data at each level are not statistically independent of one another and ignoring this interdependency yields misleadingly small standard errors when estimating the effect of intergroup dialogue on the outcomes of interest. MLM properly estimates the effect of IGD by accounting for the nesting of multiple time points of data within each student and the multiple students within each dialogue, control, or social science comparison groups.

3. Although our structural equation model (SEM) does not account for the hierar-

chical structure of the data for this study, we conducted sensitivity analyses that partial out students' dialogue group means from their individual scores to bolster confidence in the estimation of the reported pathways to the outcomes of intergroup dialogue.

4. Multiple imputations were done with ten datasets, which reduces the potential bias introduced when estimating the effect of intergroup dialogue using only observed data. Analyses of missing data patterns suggest that a number of measured variables were associated with missingness in a predictable pattern. Thus, we assume that the data were missing at random (MAR) such that missing data depend on observed data but not on unobserved data. Multiple imputation corrects for this kind of bias using the available observed data to predict and impute missing values. After these relationships are accounted for, MAR assumes that the patterns of missingness are completely random. In contrast, including only observed data in analyses assumes that missing data are missing completely at random (MCAR) before adjustment, a less tenable assumption.

CHAPTER 5

1. In this study, the units of data at each level are not statistically independent of one another and ignoring this interdependency yields misleadingly small standard errors when estimating the effect of intergroup dialogue on the outcomes of interest. MLM properly estimates the effect of intergroup dialogue by accounting for the nesting of multiple time points of data within each student and the multiple students within each dialogue, control, or social science comparison groups. See appendix B for greater detail for the procedures used to determine effects.

2. As detailed in appendix B, the models used to estimate the effect of intergroup dialogue test for a time by condition interaction. For estimates of immediate effects at post-test, an effect of intergroup dialogue is observed by a significant linear time (pre- versus post-) by condition interaction. Similarly, an effect of intergroup dialogue one year later (discussed later in this chapter) is observed by a significant linear time (pre- versus one-year follow-up) by condition interaction. All estimates of immediate and long-term effects control potential quadratic effects of time and quadratic time by condition interactions across the three observed time points. Thus, reported linear effects at one-year follow-up account for the differential growth patterns between dialogue and control students where in many cases dialogue students increase pre-post and diminish over time, whereas controls do not change either between pre-post or pre- to post-post. Additionally, these models allow the estimated treatment effect to vary

across individuals and across dialogue groups by estimating random effects for each (see appendix B). Given that we used multiple imputation to impute missing data, all analyses were conducted separately on each of ten imputed datasets and averaged using MLM.

3. Tests for differences between dialogue and control students at baseline were conducted with multilevel models that accounted for the clustering of students within dialogue and control groups.

4. Effect sizes were calculated by multiplying the coefficient for a time × condition interaction by time and dividing the product by the pooled standard deviation of the pretest scores.

5. Measures for this study were drawn from previous studies of intergroup relations and of the impact of diversity in higher education. Where certain of the proposed outcomes and processes of dialogue had not been measured in previous studies, we adapted closely aligned measures and created some measures specifically for this study. Before constructing the final surveys to be used in the study, we pilot tested possible measures with 200 students. Because all the measures involved multiple survey items, we factor analyzed the pilot data to select items that clustered together and that together had high internal consistency. The average internal consistency (alphas) across all multi-item scales used in the final surveys was 0.762, range 0.618 to 0.877. These measures also showed enough variance to be useful for quantitative analyses. In the study there were two versions of the pre-test, post-test, and post-post-test surveys, one for gender dialogues and one for race dialogues. The questions and items were identical except for the phrases racial identity or gender identity. The post-test and post-post test surveys repeated items from the pretest survey so that change over time could be measured. These two later surveys also asked questions of students in the dialogue and social science classes about their experiences in those classes. These questions on classroom experience were not included in the surveys given to the control group students.

6. A third measure, sense of comfort in interactions across race or gender, appears in appendix A but is not included in the affective positivity summary score presented in figure 5.2. We discuss possible reasons that dialogue did not significantly affect comfort at post-test in the discussion at the end of this chapter, as well as why there was a significant effect of dialogue a year later. One reason may be that comfort was one of the two measures when randomization did not produce pretest equivalence between dialogue and control group students. Di-

alogue students were already more comfortable than control group students at pre-test in interacting across difference.

7. This measure of self-assessed skills was the second of two, of a total of twenty-four, where randomization did not produce equivalence between dialogue and control group students at pretest. Dialogue group students had higher pre-test scores than control group students.

8. In three instances—analytic thinking about society, frequency of positive interactions, and positive emotions—a significant effect of dialogue was found in the experiments but not found comparing the dialogue courses that were paired with the social science courses. Because of randomization, results from the experiments give a more valid picture of the effects of dialogue on these three psychological processes.

9. Indirect pathways were tested using 2,000 bootstrap samples; bootstrapped standard errors and bias-corrected; 95 percent confidence intervals are reported (Shrout and Bolger 2002).

10. To maximize reliability and the stability of the variance and covariance of the variables used in the estimated model, missing data were multiply imputed 100 times and a combined dataset was used to calculate a variance-covariance matrix, corrected for the original sample size ($n = 720$ rather than $72,000 = 720 \times 100$).

CHAPTER 7

1. Once codes were developed, trained coders worked in teams of two to code each interview and then to confirm that their coding work was consistent (discussing any areas of discrepancy). As time went on and the codes became clear, coders proceeded individually. Importantly, though, the dyads checked for consistency every tenth interview, working for a 75 percent intercoder agreement rate. When this rate was not achieved, dyads met to discuss primary discrepancies and developed better consistency together. The interviews that were coded in common had a reliability rate of more than 80 percent.

CHAPTER 8

1. Linear mixed effects make full use of all the minute-by-minute observational data available for each individual. Second, a lot of variability observed over time in the data is lost when data are aggregated but is not lost when linear mixed effects analyses are used. Third, aggregating to a single mean per individual pre-

vents modeling linear and nonlinear changes that occurred over time in one variable, as they predict changes that occur over time in another variable.

Linear mixed effects models procedure in SPSS was selected as an additional method of analysis of the data because it allows for correlations (for example, between coding scales) to be accounted for in observations by including random effects. The linear mixed effects procedure also allows one to model the relationships between covariates and dependent variables, such as student engagement, as they change in the presence of different predictive factors, such as video session (Verbeke and Molenberghs 2000). This allows one to flexibly estimate average trends over time in specific subgroups, such as students in race dialogues and in gender dialogues, and estimate how much individual variation exists around a subgroup-level trend (Gueorguieva and Krystal 2004). Linear mixed-effect models were fit including random effects, which allow for effects of time-varying variables such as student engagement to vary by student.

CHAPTER 10

1. Although we use the term *Latino* throughout the book, nearly all of the demographic studies use the term *Hispanic* and so we use that term in referring to research on demographic changes.

2. "The World University Rankings 2011–2012," *Times Higher Education*. Available at: http://www.timeshighereducation.co.uk/world-university-rankings/2011-12/world-ranking (accessed January 23, 2013).

3. "U.S. News College Compass," *U.S. News and World Report Education* 2012. Available at: http://www.usnews.com/usnews/store/college_compass.htm (accessed January 23, 2013).

4. Ibid.

5. "Jefferson's Gravestone," 2011.

6. The National Association of Scholars has more recently specifically critiqued intergroup dialogue, along with eight other critiques of what they call "the progressivist near-monopoly of American higher education" (Wood 2008). Thomas Wood criticizes the role of undergraduate peer facilitators (which some institutions but not all institutions use) and the problem, as he sees it, of the Michigan intergroup dialogue courses being only under the sponsorship of the College of Literature, Sciences, and the Arts and the Division of Student Affairs rather than under the faculty senate. He also charges that there is an imbalance and bias in political perspectives, too much emphasis on action and change, and an inappropriate pedagogy emphasizing personal experience. His view that reading and

dialoguing about inequality and listening to students' own experiences with inequality promote a deep distrust of American society underestimates the capacities of undergraduates to balance societal problems with appreciation for historical change and progress.

7. By Ilan Lior, Gili Cohen, Jack Khoury, Nir Hasson, Yanir Yagna, and Eli Ashkenazi, "More than 150,000 Take to Streets Across Israel in Largest Housing Protest Yet," *Haaretz*, July 30, 2011. Available at: http://www.haaretz.com/news/national/more-than-150-000-take-to-streets-across-israel-in-largest-housing-protest-yet-1.376102 (accessed January 23, 2013).

8. Josie Ensor, "Occupy Wall Street Protests Stepped Up Around the World," *The Telegraph*, October 16, 2011. Available at: http://www.telegraph.co.uk/finance/financialcrisis/8829838/Occupy-Wall-Street-protests-stepped-up-around-the-world.html (accessed January 23, 2013).

REFERENCES

Abu-Nimer, Mohammed. 1999. *Dialogue, Conflict Resolution, and Change: Arab-Jewish Encounters in Israel.* Blue Mountain Lake: State University of New York Press.

Adams, Glenn, Laurie T. O'Brien, and Jessica C. Nelson. 2006. "Perceptions of Racism in Hurricane Katrina: A Liberation Psychology Analysis." *Analyses of Social Issues and Public Policy* 6(1): 215–35. doi:10.1111/j.1530-2415.2006.00112.x.

Adams, Maurianne. 2007. "Pedagogical Frameworks for Social Justice Education." In *Teaching for Diversity and Social Justice*, 2nd ed., edited by Maurianne Adams, Lee Anne Bell, and Pat Griffin. New York: Routledge.

Adams, Maurianne, Lee Anne Bell, and Pat Griffin, eds. 2007. *Teaching for Diversity and Social Justice*, 2nd ed. New York: Routledge.

Adichie, Chimamanda. 2009. "The Danger of a Single Story." *TED Talks*, July 2009. Available at: http://www.ted.com/talks/lang/en/chimamanda_adichie_the_danger _of_a_single_story.html (accessed January 21, 2013).

Allen, Jodie T., and Andrew Kohut. 2008. "Pinched Pocketbooks: Do Average Americans Spot Something That Most Economists Miss?" Pew Research Center Publications. Available at: http://pewresearch.org/pubs/13/pinched-pocketbooks (accessed January 23, 2013).

Allison, Paul D. 2009. "Missing Data." In *The SAGE Handbook of Quantitative Methods in Psychology*, edited by Roger E. Millsap and Alberto Maydeu-Olivares. Thousand Oaks, Calif.: Sage Publications.

Allport, Gordon W. 1954. *The Nature of Prejudice.* Cambridge, Mass.: Addison-Wesley.

Alperin, Davida J. 1990. "Social Diversity and the Necessity of Alliances: A Developing Feminist Perspective." In *Bridges of Power: Women's Multicultural Alliances*, edited by Lisa Albrecht and Rose M. Brewer. Philadelphia, Pa.: New Society.

American Association of University Women. 2012. *The Simple Truth about the Gender Pay Gap*. Available at: http://www.aauw.org/learn/research/simpletruth.cfm (accessed January 23, 2013).

Antonio, Anthony Lising. 2001. "The Role of Interracial Interaction in the Development of Leadership Skills and Cultural Knowledge and Understanding." *Research in Higher Education* 42(5): 593–617. doi:10.1023/a:1011054427581.

———. 2004. "The Influence of Friendship Groups on Intellectual Self-Confidence and Educational Aspirations in College." *Journal of Higher Education* 75(4): 446–71. doi:10.1353/jhe.2004.0019.

Antonio, Anthony Lising, Mitchell J. Chang, Kenji Hakuta, David A. Kenny, Shana Levin, and Jeffrey F. Milem. 2004. "Effects of Racial Diversity on Complex Thinking in College Students." *Psychological Science* 15(8): 507–10. doi:10.1111/j.0956-7976.2004.00710.x.

Anzaldúa, Gloria E. 2002. "(Un)Natural Bridges, (Un)Safe Spaces." In *This Bridge We Call Home: Radical Visions for Transformation*, edited by Gloria E. Anzaldúa and AnaLouise Keating. New York: Routledge.

Anzaldúa, Gloria E., and AnaLouise Keating, eds. 2002. *This Bridge We Call Home: Radical Visions for Transformation*. New York: Routledge.

Apfelbaum, Erika. 1979. "Relations of Domination and Movements for Liberation: An Analysis of Power Between Groups," trans. Ian Lubek. In *The Social Psychology of Intergroup Relations*, edited by William G. Austin and Stephen Worchel. Monterey, Calif.: Brooks/Cole.

Appiah, Kwame Anthony. 2006a. "The Case for Contamination: No to Purity. No to Tribalism. No to Cultural Protectionism. Toward a New Cosmopolitanism." *New York Times Magazine*, January 1, pp. 30–37, 52. Available at: http://www.nytimes.com/2006/01/01/magazine/01cosmopolitan.html (accessed January 21, 2013).

———. 2006b. *Cosmopolitanism: Ethics in a World of Strangers*. New York: W. W. Norton.

Appiah, Kwame Anthony, and Amy Gutmann. 1996. *Color Conscious: The Political Morality of Race*. Princeton, N.J.: Princeton University Press.

Arbuckle, James L. 2008. *Amos 17.0 User's Guide*. Crawfordville, Fla.: Amos Development Corporation.

Aron, Arthur, and Tracy McLaughlin-Volpe. 2001. "Including Others in the Self: Extensions to Own and Partner's Group Memberships." In *Individual Self, Rela-*

tional Self, Collective Self, edited by Constantine Sedikides and Marilynn B. Brewer. Philadelphia, Pa.: Psychology Press.

Asher, Nina. 2003. "Engaging Difference: Towards a Pedagogy of Interbeing." *Teaching Education* 14(3): 235–47. doi:10.1080/1047621032000135159.

Association of American Colleges and Universities. 2002. *Greater Expectations: A New Vision for Learning as a Nation Goes to College.* Washington, D.C.: Association of American Colleges and Universities, Greater Expectations National Panel. Available at: http://www.greaterexpectations.org/ (accessed January 21, 2013).

———. 2007. *College Learning for the New Global Century.* Washington,. D.C.: Association of American Colleges and Universities, National Leadership Council for Liberal Education and America's Promise. Available at: http://www.aacu.org/advocacy/leap/documents/globalcentury_final.pdf (accessed January 21, 2013).

Astin, Alexander W. 1993. *What Matters in College? Four Critical Years Revisited.* San Francisco: Jossey-Bass.

Aung San Suu Kyi. 2011. "21st Annual Raoul Wallenberg Lecture." University of Michigan, Ann Arbor (October 25, 2011).

Ayvazian, Andrea. 2007. "Interrupting the Cycle of Oppression: The Role of Allies as Agents of Change." In *Race, Class, and Gender in the United States: An Integrated Study,* 7th ed., edited by Paula S. Rothenberg. New York: Worth.

Bäckström, Martin, and Fredrik Björklund. 2007. "Structural Modeling of Generalized Prejudice: The Role of Social Dominance, Authoritarianism, and Empathy." *Journal of Individual Differences* 28(1): 10–17. doi:10.1027/1614-0001.28.1.10.

Bailey, Alison. 1998. "Locating Traitorous Identities: Toward a View of Privilege-Cognizant White Character." *Hypatia* 13(3): 27–42. doi:10.1111/j.1527-2001.1998.tb01368.x.

Bakhtin, M. M. 1981. *The Dialogic Imagination: Four Essays,* edited by Michael Holquist, translated by Caryl Emerson and Michael Holquist. Austin: University of Texas Press.

Banks, James A. 2009. "Multicultural Education: Dimensions and Paradigms." In *The Routledge International Companion to Multicultural Education,* edited by James A. Banks. New York: Routledge.

Banse, Rainer, Bertram Gawronski, Christine Rebetez, Hélène Gutt, and J. Bruce Morton. 2010. "The Development of Spontaneous Gender Stereotyping in Childhood: Relations to Stereotype Knowledge and Stereotype Flexibility." *Developmental Science* 13(2): 298–306. doi:10.1111/j.1467-7687.2009.00880.x.

Barber, Benjamin R. 1998. *A Passion for Democracy: American Essays.* Princeton, N.J.: Princeton University Press.

Barge, J. Kevin, and Martin Little. 2002. "Dialogical Wisdom, Communicative Practice, and Organizational Life." *Communication Theory* 12(4): 375–97. doi:10.1111/j.1468-2885.2002.tb00275.x.

Barnes, Mario L. 2006. "Black Women's Stories and the Criminal Law: Restating the Power of Narrative." *U.C. Davis Law Review* 39(2006): 941–90.

Bartels, Larry M. 2008. *Unequal Democracy: The Political Economy of the New Gilded Age.* Princeton, N.J.: Princeton University Press.

Batson, C. Daniel, David A. Lishner, Amy Carpenter, Luis Dulin, Sanna Harjusola-Webb, E. L. Stocks, Shawna Gale, Omar Hassan, and Brenda Sampat. 2003. "'. . . As You Would Have Them Do Unto You': Does Imagining Yourself in the Other's Place Stimulate Moral Action?" *Personality and Social Psychology Bulletin* 29(9): 1190–201. doi:10.1177/0146167203254600.

Batson, C. Daniel, Marina P. Polycarpou, Eddie Harmon-Jones, Heidi J. Imhoff, Erin C. Mitchener, Lori L. Bednar, Tricia R. Klein, and Lori Highberger. 1997. "Empathy and Attitudes: Can Feeling for a Member of a Stigmatized Group Improve Feelings Toward That Group?" *Journal of Personality and Social Psychology* 72(1): 105–118. doi:10.1037/0022-3514.72.1.105.

Baumgardner, Jennifer, and Amy Richards. 2000. *Manifesta: Young Women, Feminism, and the Future.* New York: Farrar, Straus and Giroux.

Baxter, Leslie A. 2004. "Dialogues of Relating." In *Dialogue: Theorizing Difference in Communication Studies*, edited by Rob Anderson, Leslie A. Baxter, and Kenneth N. Cissna. Thousand Oaks, Calif.: Sage Publications.

———. 2011. *Voicing Relationships: A Dialogic Perspective.* Thousand Oaks, Calif.: Sage Publications.

Bekerman, Zvi. 2007. "Rethinking Intergroup Encounters: Rescuing Praxis from Theory, Activity from Education, and Peace/Co-Existence from Identity and Culture." *Journal of Peace Education* 4(1): 21–37. doi:10.1080/17400200601171198.

Bell, Derrick. 1980. *Shades of Brown: New Perspectives on School Desegregation.* New York: Teachers College Press.

Bell, Lee Anne. 2007. "Theoretical Foundations for Social Justice Education." In *Teaching for Diversity and Social Justice*, 2nd ed., edited by Maurianne Adams, Lee Anne Bell, and Pat Griffin. New York: Routledge.

Bell, Lee Anne, Barbara J. Love, and Rosemarie A. Roberts. 2007. "Racism and White Privilege Curriculum Design." In *Teaching for Diversity and Social Justice*, 2nd ed., edited by Maurianne Adams, Lee Anne Bell, and Pat Griffin. New York: Routledge.

Benhabib, Seyla. 2002. *The Claims of Culture: Equality and Diversity in the Global Era*. Princeton, N.J.: Princeton University Press.

Bergsieker, Hilary B., J. Nicole Shelton, and Jennifer A. Richeson. 2010. "To Be Liked Versus Respected: Divergent Goals in Interracial Interactions." *Journal of Personality and Social Psychology* 99(2): 248–64. doi:10.1037/a0018474.

Bjork, Elizabeth L., and Robert Bjork. 2011. "Making Things Hard on Yourself, But in a Good Way: Creating Desirable Difficulties to Enhance Learning." In *Psychology and the Real World: Essays Illustrating Fundamental Contributions to Society*, edited by Morton Ann Gernsbacher, Richard W. Pew, Leaetta M. Hough, and James R. Pomerantz. New York: Worth Publishers.

Blair, Irene V., Bernadette Park, and Jonathan Bachelor. 2003. "Understanding Intergroup Anxiety: Are Some People More Anxious Than Others?" *Group Processes and Intergroup Relations* 6(2): 151–69. doi:10.1177/1368430203006002002.

Blascovich, Jim, Wendy Berry Mendes, Sarah B. Hunter, Brian Lickel, and Neneh Kowai-Bell. 2001. "Perceiver Threat in Social Interactions with Stigmatized Others." *Journal of Personality and Social Psychology* 80(2): 253–67. doi:10.1037/0022-3514.80.2.253.

Bloom, Howard S., Carolyn J. Hill, Alison Rebeck Black, and Mark W. Lipsey. 2008. "Performance Trajectories and Performance Gaps as Achievement Effect-Size Benchmarks for Educational Interventions." *MDRC Working Papers on Research Methodology*. New York: MDRC. Available at: http://www.mdrc.org/sites/default/files/full_473.pdf (accessed January 21, 2013).

Bloom, Howard S., Lashawn Richburg-Hayes, and Alison Rebeck Black. 2005. "Using Covariates to Improve Precision: Empirical Guidance for Studies That Randomize Schools to Measure the Impacts of Educational Interventions." *MDRC Working Papers on Research Metholodology.* New York: MDRC. Available at: http://www.mdrc.org/sites/default/files/full_598.pdf (accessed January 21, 2013).

Bobo, Lawrence D. 2011. "Somewhere Between Jim Crow and Post-Racialism: Reflections on the Racial Divide in America Today." *Daedalus* 140(2): 11–36. doi:10.1162/DAED_a_00091.

Bobo, Lawrence D., and Cybelle Fox. 2003. "Race, Racism, and Discrimination: Bridging Problems, Methods, and Theory in Social Psychological Research." *Social Psychology Quarterly* 66(4): 319–32. doi:10.2307/1519832.

Bohm, David. 1996. *On Dialogue*, edited by Lee Nichol. New York: Routledge.

Boisjoly, Johanne, Greg J. Duncan, Michael Kremer, Dan M. Levy, and Jacque Eccles. 2006. "Empathy or Antipathy? The Impact of Diversity." *American Economic Review* 96(5): 1890–905. doi:10.1257/aer.96.5.1890.

Boler, Megan. 1999. *Feeling Power: Emotions and Education*. New York: Routledge.

Bonilla-Silva, Eduardo. 2003. *Racism Without Racists: Color-Blind Racism and the Persistence of Racial Inequality in the United States*. Lanham, Md.: Rowman and Littlefield.

Botkin, Steven, JoAnne Jones, and Tanya Kachwaha. 2007. "Sexism Curriculum Design." In *Teaching for Diversity and Social Justice*, 2nd ed., edited by Maurianne Adams, Lee Anne Bell, and Pat Griffin. New York: Routledge.

Bowman, Nicholas A. 2010. "College Diversity Experiences and Cognitive Development: A Meta-Analysis." *Review of Educational Research* 80(1): 4–33. doi:10.3102/0034654309352495.

Brewer, Marilynn B., and Norman Miller. 1984. "Beyond the Contact Hypothesis: Theoretical Perspectives on Desegregation." In *Groups in Contact: The Psychology of Desegregation*, edited by Norman Miller and Marilynn B. Brewer. Orlando, Fla.: Academic Press.

Broido, Ellen M. 2000. "The Development of Social Justice Allies During College: A Phenomenological Investigation." *Journal of College Student Development* 41(1): 3–18.

Brookfield, Stephen D., and Stephen Preskill. 1999. *Discussion as a Way of Teaching: Tools and Techniques for Democratic Classrooms*. San Francisco: Jossey-Bass.

Brooks, Julia G. 2011. "Bearing the Weight: Discomfort as Necessary Condition for 'Less Violent' and More Equitable Learning." *Educational Foundations* 25(1–2): 43–62.

Brown, Ryan P., Michael J. A. Wohl, and Julie Juola Exline. 2008. "Taking Up Offenses: Secondhand Forgiveness and Group Identification." *Personality and Social Psychology Bulletin* 34(10): 1406–419. doi:10.1177/0146167208321538.

Bryman, Alan. 2001. *Social Research Methods*. New York: Oxford University Press.

———. 2008. "Why Do Researchers Integrate/Combine/Mesh/Blend/Mix/Merge/Fuse Quantitative and Qualitative Research?" In *Advances in Mixed Methods Research: Theories and Applications*, edited by Manfred Max Bergman. Los Angeles, Calif.: Sage Publications.

Buber, Martin. 1970. *I and Thou*, trans. Walter Kaufmann. New York: Charles Scribner's Sons.

Bullock, Heather E. 1999. "Attributions for Poverty: A Comparison of Middle-Class and Welfare Recipient Attitudes." *Journal of Applied Social Psychology* 29(10): 2059–82. doi:10.1111/j.1559-1816.1999.tb02295.x.

———. 2006. "Justifying Inequality: A Social Psychological Analysis of Beliefs about Poverty and the Poor." *National Poverty Center Working Paper Series no.* 06–08. Ann Arbor: University of Michigan. Available at: http://www.npc.umich.edu/ publications/workingpaper06/paper08/working_paper06-08.pdf (accessed January 21, 2013).

Bullock, Heather E., Wendy R. Williams, and Wendy M. Limbert. 2003. "Predicting Support for Welfare Policies: The Impact of Attributions and Beliefs about Inequality." *Journal of Poverty* 7(3): 35–56. doi:10.1300/j134v07n03_03.

Burbules, Nicholas C. 2000. "The Limits of Dialogue as a Critical Pedagogy." In ·*Revolutionary Pedagogies: Cultural Politics, Instituting Education, and the Discourse of Theory*, edited by Peter Pericles Trifonas. New York: Routledge.

Cacioppo, John T., and Richard E. Petty. 1982. "The Need for Cognition." *Journal of Personality and Social Psychology* 42(1): 116–31. doi:10.1037/0022-3514.42.1 .116.

Cacioppo, John T., Richard E. Petty, Jeffrey A. Feinstein, and W. Blair G. Jarvis. 1996. "Dispositional Differences in Cognitive Motivation: The Life and Times of Individuals Varying in Need for Cognition." *Psychological Bulletin* 119(2): 197– 253. doi:10.1037/0033-2909.119.2.197.

Camargo, Braz, Ralph Stinebrickner, and Todd R. Stinebrickner. 2010. "Interracial Friendships in College." *NBER* working paper 15970. Cambridge, Mass.: National Bureau of Economic Research.

Cantor, Nancy. 2011a. "'One Nation, Indivisible': The Value of Diversity in Higher Education." Lecture, University of Michigan, Ann Arbor (March 6, 2011). Available at: http://surface.syr.edu/chancellor/45 (accessed January 21, 2013).

———. 2011b. "Scholarship in Action: Remapping Higher Education." Anna and Samuel Pinanski Lecture, Wellesley College (April 20, 2011). Available at: http:// surface.syr.edu/chancellor/44 (accessed January 21, 2013).

Caracelli, Valerie J., and Jennifer C. Greene. 1997. "Crafting Mixed-Method Evaluation Designs." In *New Directions for Evaluation*, no. 74. *Advances in Mixed-Method Evaluation: The Challenges and Benefits of Integrating Diverse Paradigms*, edited by Jennifer C. Greene and Valerie J. Caracelli. San Francisco: Jossey-Bass. doi:10.1002/ev.1069.

Cehajic, Sabina, Rupert Brown, and Emanuele Castano. 2008. "Forgive and Forget? Antecedents and Consequences of Intergroup Forgiveness in Bosnia and Herzegovina." *Political Psychology* 29(3): 351–67. doi:10.1111/j.1467-9221.2008 .00634.x.

Chang, Mitchell J. 1999. "Does Racial Diversity Matter? The Educational Impact of a Racially Diverse Undergraduate Population." *Journal of College Student Development* 40(4): 377–95.

———. 2003. "Racial Differences in Viewpoints about Contemporary Issues Among Entering College Students: Fact or Fiction?" *NASPA Journal* 40(4): 55–71. doi:10.2202/1949-6605.1280.

Chang, Mitchell J., Nida Denson, Victor Sáenz, and Kimberly Misa. 2006. "The Educational Benefits of Sustaining Cross-Racial Interaction Among Undergraduates." *Journal of Higher Education* 77(3): 430–55. doi:10.1353/jhe.2006.0018.

Chang, Mitchell J., Daria Witt, James Jones, and Kenji Hakuta. 2003. *Compelling Interest: Examining the Evidence on Racial Dynamics in Colleges and Universities.* Stanford, Calif.: Stanford Education.

Charmaz, Kathleen. 2006. *Constructing Grounded Theory: A Practical Guide Through Qualitative Analysis.* London: Sage Publications.

Chasin, Richard, Margaret Herzig, Sallyann Roth, Laura Chasin, Carol Becker, and Robert R. Stains, Jr. 1996. "From Diatribe to Dialogue on Divisive Public Issues: Approaches Drawn from Family Therapy." *Mediation Quarterly* 13(4): 323–44. doi:10.1002/crq.3900130408.

Chesler, Mark. 2001. "Extending Intergroup Dialogue: From Talk to Action." In *Intergroup Dialogue: Deliberative Democracy in School, College, Community, and Workplace,* edited by David Schoem and Sylvia Hurtado. Ann Arbor: University of Michigan Press.

Chesler, Mark, Amanda Lewis, and James Crowfoot. 2005. *Challenging Racism in Higher Education: Promoting Justice.* Lanham, Md.: Rowman and Littlefield.

Cohen, Cathy J. 2011. "Millennials and the Myth of the Post-Racial Society: Black Youth, Intra-Generational Divisions and the Continuing Racial Divide in American Politics." *Daedalus* 140(2): 197–205. doi:10.1162/DAED_a_00087.

Cole, Elizabeth R. 2008. "Coalitions as a Model for Intersectionality: From Practice to Theory." *Sex Roles* 59(5–6): 443–53. doi:10.1007/s11199-008-9419-1.

Collins, Patricia Hill. 2000. *Black Feminist Thought: Knowledge, Consciousness, and the Politics of Empowerment,* 2nd ed. New York: Routledge.

Congressional Budget Office. 2011. "Trends in the Distribution of Household Income between 1979 and 2007." *CBO* publication no. 4031. Washington, D.C.: Government Printing Office. Available at: http://cbo.gov/publication/42729 (accessed January 21, 2013).

Conklin, Hilary Gehlbach. 2008. "Modeling Compassion in Critical, Justice-Oriented Teacher Education." *Harvard Educational Review* 78(4): 652–74.

Coughlan, Sean. 2010. "Students Stage Day of Protests over Tuition Fee Rises." *BBC*

News, Education and Family, November 24. Available at: http://www.bbc.co.uk/news/education-11829102 (accessed January 21, 2013).

Cowan, Geoffrey, and Amelia Arsenault. 2008. "Moving from Monologue to Dialogue to Collaboration: The Three Layers of Public Diplomacy." *Annals of the American Academy of Political and Social Science* 616(1): 10–30. doi:10.1177/0002716207311863.

Crenshaw, Kimberlé W. 1995. "Mapping the Margins: Intersectionality, Identity Politics, and Violence against Women of Color." In *Critical Race Theory: The Key Writings That Formed the Movement*, edited by Kimberlé W. Crenshaw, Neil Gotanda, Gary Peller, and Kendall Thomas. New York: New Press.

Creswell, John W. 1998. *Qualitative Inquiry and Research Design: Choosing Among Five Traditions*. Thousand Oaks, Calif.: Sage Publications.

Crocker, Jennifer, and Riia Luhtanen. 1990. "Collective Self-Esteem and Ingroup Bias." *Journal of Personality and Social Psychology* 58(1): 60–67. doi:10.1037/0022-3514.58.1.60.

Crosby, Faye. 1984. "The Denial of Personal Discrimination." *American Behavioral Scientist* 27(3): 371–86. doi:10.1177/000276484027003008.

Crow, Michael M. 2011. "America Needs Broadly Educated Citizens, Even Anthropologists." *Slate*, October 21. Available at: http://www.slate.com/articles/news_and_politics/politics/2011/10/michael_m_crow_president_of_arizona_state_university_explains_wh.html (accessed January 20, 2013).

Damasio, Antonio R. 2000. *Descartes' Error: Emotion, Reason, and the Human Brain*. New York: Quill.

DasGupta, Sayantani, Dodi Meyer, Ayxa Calero-Breckheimer, Alex W. Costley, and Sobeira Guillen. 2006. "Teaching Cultural Competency Through Narrative Medicine: Intersections of Classroom and Community." *Teaching and Learning in Medicine* 18(1): 14–17. doi:10.1207/s15328015tlm1801_4.

Davis, Mark H. 1983. "Measuring Individual Differences in Empathy: Evidence for a Multidimensional Approach." *Journal of Personality and Social Psychology* 44(1): 113–26. doi:10.1037/0022-3514.44.1.113.

Daye, Charles E., A. T. Panter, Walter R. Allen, and Linda F. Wightman. Forthcoming. "Does Race Matter in Educational Diversity? A Legal and Empirical Analysis." *Rutgers Race and the Law Review* 13(2). Available at: http://ssrn.com/abstract-2101253 (accessed January 21, 2013).

de Waal, Frans. 2009. *The Age of Empathy: Nature's Lessons for a Kinder Society*. New York: Harmony Books.

Deffenbacher, David M., Bernadette Park, Charles M. Judd, and Joshua Correll. 2009. "Category Boundaries Can Be Accentuated Without Increasing Intergroup Bias." *Group Processes and Intergroup Relations* 12(2): 175–93. doi:10.1177/136 8430208101055.

Delgado, Richard, and Jean Stefancic. 2001. *Critical Race Theory: An Introduction.* New York: New York University Press.

Demoulin, Stéphanie, Jacques-Philippe Leyens, and John F. Dovidio. 2009. *Intergroup Misunderstandings: Impact of Divergent Social Realities.* New York: Psychology Press.

Denson, Nida. 2009. "Do Curricular and Co-Curricular Diversity Activities Influence Racial Bias? A Meta-Analysis." *Review of Educational Research* 79(2): 805–38. doi:10.3102/0034654309331551.

Denson, Nida, and Mitchell J. Chang. 2009. "Racial Diversity Matters: The Impact of Diversity-Related Student Engagement and Institutional Context." *American Educational Research Journal* 46(2): 322–53. doi:10.3102/0002831208323278.

Denvir, Daniel. 2011. "The 10 Most Segregated Urban Areas in America." *Salon*, March 10. Available at: http://www.salon.com/2011/03/29/most_segregated _cities/ (accessed January 21, 2013).

Deo, Meera E. 2011. "The Promise of *Grutter*: Diverse Interactions at the University of Michigan Law School." *Michigan Journal of Race and Law* 17(1): 63–118.

Dessel, Adrienne, Mary E. Rogge, and Sarah B. Garlington. 2006. "Using Intergroup Dialogue to Promote Social Justice and Change." *Social Work* 51(4): 303–15. doi:10.1093/sw/51.4.303.

DeStigter, Todd. 1999. "Public Displays of Affection: Political Community Through Critical Empathy." *Research in the Teaching of English* 33(3): 235–44. Available at: http://www.jstor.org/stable/40171438.

Devine, Patricia G. 1989. "Stereotypes and Prejudice: Their Automatic and Controlled Components." *Journal of Personality and Social Psychology* 56(1): 5–18. doi:10.1037/0022-3514.56.1.5.

Dietz, Mary G. 2003. "Current Controversies in Feminist Theory." *Annual Review of Political Science* 6: 399–431. doi:10.1146/annurev.polisci.6.121901.085635.

Dixon, John, Linda R. Tropp, Kevin Durrheim, and Colin Tredoux. 2010. "'Let Them Eat Harmony': Prejudice-Reduction Strategies and Attitudes of Historically Disadvantaged Groups." *Current Directions in Psychological Science* 19(2): 76–80. doi:10.1177/0963721410363366.

Doosje, Bertjan, Nyla R. Branscombe, Russell Spears, and Antony S. R. Manstead. 1998. "Guilty by Association: When One's Group Has a Negative History." *Jour-*

nal of Personality and Social Psychology 75(4): 872–86. doi:10.1037/00223514
.75.4.872.

Dovidio, John F., Samuel L. Gaertner, Tracie L. Stewart, Victoria M. Esses, Marleen
ten Vergert, and Gordon Hodson. 2004. "From Intervention to Outcome: Processes in the Reduction of Bias." In *Education Programs for Improving Intergroup Relations: Theory, Research, and Practice*, edited by Walter G. Stephan and W. Paul Vogt. New York: Teachers College Press.

Dovidio, John F., Tamar Saguy, and Nurit Shnabel. 2009. "Cooperation and Conflict Within Groups: Bridging Intragroup and Intergroup Processes." *Journal of Social Issues* 65(2): 429–49. doi:10.1111/j.1540-4560.2009.01607.x.

Duncan, Lauren E., and Abigail J. Stewart. 2007. "Personal Political Salience: The Role of Personality in Collective Identity and Action." *Political Psychology* 28(2): 143–64. doi:10.1111/j.1467-9221.2007.00560.x.

Eagly, Alice H., and Linda L. Carli. 2007. *Through the Labyrinth: The Truth About How Women Become Leaders*. Boston, Mass.: Harvard Business School Press.

Eggins, Rachael A., S. Alexander Haslam, and Katherine J. Reynolds. 2002. "Social Identity and Negotiation: Subgroup Representation and Superordinate Consensus." *Personality and Social Psychology Bulletin* 28(7): 887–99.

Ellemers, Naomi, and Manuela Barreto. 2009. "Collective Action in Modern Times: How Modern Expressions of Prejudice Prevent Collective Action." *Journal of Social Issues* 65(4): 749–68. doi:10.1111/j.1540-4560.2009.01621.x.

Ellinor, Linda, and Glenna Gerard. 1998. *Dialogue: Rediscover the Transforming Power of Conversation*. New York: John Wiley and Sons.

Engberg, Mark E., and Sylvia Hurtado. 2011. "Developing Pluralistic Skills and Dispositions in College: Examining Racial/Ethnic Group Differences." *Journal of Higher Education* 82(4): 416–43. doi:10.1353/jhe.2011.0025.

Ensari, Nurcan Karamolla, and Norman Miller. 2006. "The Application of the Personalization Model in Diversity Management." *Group Processes and Intergroup Relations* 9(4): 589–607. doi:10.1177/1368430206067679.

Evans, Nancy J., Deanna S. Forney, and Florence Guido-DiBrito. 1998. *Student Development in College: Theory, Research, and Practice*. San Francisco: Jossey-Bass.

Fazio, Russell H. 1990. "Multiple Processes by Which Attitudes Guide Behavior: The MODE Model as an Integrative Framework." *Advances in Experimental Social Psychology* 23: 75–109. doi:10.1016/S0065-2601(08)60318-4.

Feagin, Joe R. 1975. *Subordinating the Poor: Welfare and American Beliefs*. Englewood Cliffs, N.J.: Prentice-Hall.

———. 2006. *Systemic Racism: A Theory of Oppression*. New York: Routledge.

Feingold, Alan. 2009. "Effect Sizes for Growth-Modeling Analysis for Controlled Clinical Trials in the Same Metric as for Classical Analysis." *Psychological Methods* 14(1): 43–53. doi:10.1037/a0014699.

Finlay, Krystina A., and Walter G. Stephan. 2000. "Improving Intergroup Relations: The Effects of Empathy on Racial Attitudes." *Journal of Applied Social Psychology* 30(8): 1720–37. doi:10.1111/j.1559-1816.2000.tb02464.x.

Fischer, Mary J. 2008. "Does Campus Diversity Promote Friendship Diversity? A Look at Interracial Friendships in College." *Social Science Quarterly* 89(3): 631–55. doi:10.1111/j.1540-6237.2008.00552.x.

Fisher, Roger B., and Barry N. Checkoway. 2011. "Intergroup Dialogue Facilitation for Youth Empowerment and Community Change." In *Facilitating Intergroup Dialogues: Bridging Differences, Catalyzing Change*, edited by Kelly E. Maxwell, Biren (Ratnesh) A. Nagda, and Monita C. Thompson. Sterling, Va.: Stylus.

Fletcher, Garth J. O., Paula Danilovics, Guadalupe Fernandez, Dena Peterson, and Glenn D. Reeder. 1986. "Attributional Complexity: An Individual Differences Measure." *Journal of Personality and Social Psychology* 51(4): 875–84. doi:10.1037/0022-3514.51.4.875.

Fook, Jan, and Gurid Aga Askeland. 2007. "Challenges of Critical Reflection: 'Nothing Ventured, Nothing Gained.'" *Social Work Education* 26(5): 520–33. doi:10.1080/02615470601118662.

Freire, Paulo. 1970. *Pedagogy of the Oppressed*, trans. Myra Bergman Ramos. New York: Seabury Press.

———. 1993. *Pedagogy of the Oppressed*, 20th anniversary ed., trans. Myra Bergman Ramos. New York: Continuum.

Fry, Richard. 2010. "Minorities and the Recession-Era College Enrollment Boom." Washington, D.C.: Pew Research Center. Available at: http://www.pewsocial trends.org/2010/06/16/minorities-and-the-recession-era-college-enrollment-boom/ (accessed January 21, 2013).

———. 2011. "Hispanic College Enrollment Spikes, Narrowing Gaps with Other Groups." Washington, D.C.: Pew Research Center. Available at: http://www.pewhispanic.org/files/2011/08/146.pdf (accessed January 21, 2013).

Gaertner, Samuel L., and John F. Dovidio. 1986. "The Aversive Form of Racism." In *Prejudice, Discrimination, and Racism*, edited by John F. Dovidio and Samuel L. Gaertner, 61–89. Orlando, Fla.: Academic Press.

———. 2000. *Reducing Intergroup Bias: The Common Ingroup Identity Model.* Philadelphia, Pa.: Psychology Press.

Gaertner, Samuel L., John F. Dovidio, Jason A. Nier, Christine M. Ward, and Brenda S. Banker. 1999. "Across Cultural Divides: The Value of a Superordinate Identity." In *Cultural Divides: Understanding and Overcoming Group Conflict*, edited by Deborah A. Prentice and Dale T. Miller. New York: Russell Sage Foundation.

Galinsky, Adam D., and Gordon B. Moskowitz. 2000. "Perspective-Taking: Decreasing Stereotype Expression, Stereotype Accessibility, and In-Group Favoritism." *Journal of Personality and Social Psychology* 78(4): 708–24. doi:10.1037/0022 -3514.78.4.708.

Galinsky, Adam D., William W. Maddux, Debra Gilin, and Judith B. White. 2008. "Why It Pays to Get Inside the Head of Your Opponent: The Differential Effects of Perspective Taking and Empathy." *Psychological Science* 19(4): 378–84. doi:10.1111/j.1467-9280.2008.02096.x.

Gallese, Vittorio, Luciano Fadiga, Leonardo Fogassi, and Giacomo Rizzolatti. 1996. "Action Recognition in the Premotor Cortex." *Brain* 119(2): 593–609. doi:10 .1093/brain/119.2.593.

Glick, Peter, and Susan T. Fiske. 2001. "An Ambivalent Alliance: Hostile and Benevolent Sexism as Complementary Justifications for Gender Inequality." *American Psychologist* 56(2): 109–18. doi:10.1037/0003-066x.56.2.109.

Goodenough, Ward H. 1970. "Describing a Culture." In *Description and Comparison in Cultural Anthropology*, 104–119. Chicago: Aldine Publishing.

Goodman, Diane, and Steven Schapiro. 1997. "Sexism Curriculum Design." In *Teaching for Diversity and Social Justice: A Sourcebook*, edited by Maurianne Adams, Lee Anne Bell, and Pat Griffin. New York: Routledge.

Gorski, Paul C. 2008. "Good Intentions Are Not Enough: A Decolonizing Intercultural Education." *Intercultural Education* 19(6): 515–25. doi:10.1080/1467598 0802568319.

Gottfredson, Nisha C., A. T. Panter, Charles E. Daye, Walter A. Allen, Linda F. Wightman, and Meera E. Deo. 2008. "Does Diversity at Undergraduate Institutions Influence Student Outcomes?" *Journal of Diversity in Higher Education* 1(2): 80–94. doi:10.1037/1938-8926.1.2.80.

Guarasci, Richard, Grant H. Cornwell et al. 1997. *Democratic Education in an Age of Difference: Redefining Citizenship in Higher Education.* San Francisco: Jossey-Bass.

Gueorguieva, Ralitza, and John H. Krystal. 2004. "Move over ANOVA: Progress in Analyzing Repeated-Measures Data and Its Reflection in Papers Published in the *Archives of General Psychiatry*." *Archives of General Psychiatry* 61(3): 310–17. doi:10.1001/archpsyc.61.3.310.

Gurin, Patricia. 1999. *The Compelling Need for Diversity in Higher Education.* Ann Arbor: University of Michigan. Available at: http://www.vpcomm.umich.edu/admissions/research/expert/gurintoc.html (accessed January 21, 2013).

————. 2011. "Learning in a Diverse Environment." Keynote address at the Provost's Seminar on Teaching, Center for Research on Teaching and Learning. University of Michigan, Ann Arbor (March 15, 2011).

Gurin, Patricia, Eric L. Dey, Gerald Gurin, and Sylvia Hurtado. 2004. "The Educational Value of Diversity." In *Defending Diversity: Affirmative Action at the University of Michigan,* edited by Patricia Gurin, Jeffrey S. Lehman, and Earl Lewis. Ann Arbor: University of Michigan Press.

Gurin, Patricia, Eric L. Dey, Sylvia Hurtado, and Gerald Gurin. 2002. "Diversity and Higher Education: Theory and Impact on Educational Outcomes." *Harvard Educational Review* 72(3): 330–66.

Gurin, Patricia, Shirley Hatchett, and James S. Jackson. 1989. *Hope and Independence: Blacks' Response to Electoral and Party Politics.* New York: Russell Sage Foundation.

Gurin, Patricia, and Hazel Markus. 1989. "Cognitive Consequences of Gender Identity." In *The Social Identity of Women,* edited by Suzanne Skevington and Deborah Baker. London: Sage Publications.

Gurin, Patricia, Arthur H. Miller, and Gerald Gurin. 1980. "Stratum Identification and Consciousness." *Social Psychology Quarterly* 43(1): 30–47. doi:10.2307/3033746.

Gurin, Patricia, and Biren (Ratnesh) A. Nagda. 2006. "Getting to the *What, How,* and *Why* of Diversity on Campus." *Educational Researcher* 35(1): 20–24. doi:10.3102/0013189x035001020.

Gurin, Patricia, Biren (Ratnesh) A. Nagda, and Gretchen E. López. 2004. "The Benefits of Diversity in Education for Democratic Citizenship." *Journal of Social Issues* 60(1): 17–34. doi:10.1111/j.0022-4537.2004.00097.x.

Gurin, Patricia, Timothy Peng, Gretchen Lopez, and Biren (Ratnesh) A. Nagda. 1999. "Context, Identity, and Intergroup Relations." In *Cultural Divides: Understanding and Overcoming Group Conflict,* edited by Deborah A. Prentice and Dale T. Miller. New York: Russell Sage Foundation.

Gurin-Sands, Chloé, Patricia Gurin, Biren (Ratnesh) A. Nagda, and Shardae Osuna. 2012. "Fostering a Commitment to Social Action: How Talking, Thinking, and Feeling Make a Difference in Intergroup Dialogue." *Equity and Excellence in Education* 45(1): 60–79. doi:10.1080/10665684.2012.643699.

Gutiérrez, Lorraine M., and Edith A. Lewis. 1999. *Empowering Women of Color.* New York: Columbia University Press.

Habermas, Jürgen. 1984. *The Theory of Communicative Action*, trans. Thomas McCarthy. Boston, Mass.: Beacon Press.

Hardiman, Rita, Bailey Jackson, and Pat Griffin. 2007. "Conceptual Foundations for Social Justice Education." In *Teaching for Diversity and Social Justice*, 2nd ed., edited by Maurianne Adams, Lee Anne Bell, and Pat Griffin. New York: Routledge.

Harper, Shaun R., and Sylvia Hurtado. 2007. "Nine Themes in Campus Racial Climates and Implications for Institutional Transformation." *New Directions for Student Services: No. 120. Responding to the Realities of Race on Campus.* San Francisco: Jossey-Bass. doi:10.1002/ss.254.

Harro, Bobbie. 2000a. "The Cycle of Socialization." In *Readings for Diversity and Social Justice*, edited by Maurianne Adams, Warren J. Blumenfeld, Rosie Castañeda, Heather W. Hackman, Madeline L. Peters, and Ximena Zúñiga. New York: Routledge.

———. 2000b. "The Cycle of Liberation." In *Readings for Diversity and Social Justice*, edited by Maurianne Adams, Warren J. Blumenfeld, Rosie Castañeda, Heather W. Hackman, Madeline L. Peters, and Ximena Zúñiga. New York: Routledge.

Herring, Cedric. 2009. "Does Diversity Pay? Race, Gender, and the Business Case for Diversity." *American Sociological Review* 74(2): 208–24. doi:10.1177/000312240907400203.

Hewstone, Miles, and Rupert Brown. 1986. "Contact Is Not Enough: An Intergroup Perspective on the 'Contact Hypothesis.'" In *Contact and Conflict in Intergroup Encounters*, edited by Miles Hewstone and Rupert Brown. Oxford: Basil Blackwell.

Hewstone, Miles, Ed Cairns, Alberto Voci, Juergen Hamberger, and Ulrike Niens. 2006. "Intergroup Contact, Forgiveness, and Experience of 'The Troubles' in Northern Ireland." *Journal of Social Issues* 62(1): 99–120. doi:10.1111/j.1540-4560.2006.00441.x.

Hewstone, Miles, Mark Rubin, and Hazel Willis. 2002. "Intergroup Bias." *Annual Review of Psychology* 53: 575–604. doi:10.1146/annurev.psych.53.100901.135109.

Hill, Catherine, Christianne Corbett, and Andresse St. Rose. 2010. *Why So Few? Women in Science, Technology, Engineering, and Mathematics.* Washington, D.C.: American Association of University Women.

Hochschild, Jennifer L., Vesla M. Weaver, and Traci Burch. 2011. "Destabilizing the American Racial Order." *Daedalus* 140(2): 151–65. doi:10.1162/daed_a_00084.

Hoffman, Martin L. 2000. *Empathy and Moral Development: Implications for Caring and Justice.* Cambridge: Cambridge University Press.

hooks, bell. 2003. *Teaching Community: A Pedagogy of Hope.* New York: Routledge.

Huber, Mary Taylor, and Pat Hutchings. 2004. *Integrative Learning: Mapping the Terrain.* Washington, D.C.: Association of American Colleges and Universities.

Hughes, Michael, and Steven A. Tuch. 2000. "How Beliefs about Poverty Influence Racial Policy Attitudes: A Study of Whites, African Americans, Hispanics, and Asians in the United States." In *Racialized Politics: The Debate about Racism in America*, edited by David O. Sears, Jim Sidanius, and Lawrence Bobo. Chicago: University of Chicago Press.

Hunt, Matthew O. 2004. "Race/Ethnicity and Beliefs about Wealth and Poverty." *Social Science Quarterly* 85(3): 827–53. doi:10.1111/j.0038-4941.2004.00247.x.

———. 2007. "African American, Hispanic, and White Beliefs about Black/White Inequality, 1977–2004." *American Sociological Review* 72(3): 390–415. doi:10.1177/000312240707200304.

Hurtado, Aída. 1996. *The Color of Privilege: Three Blasphemies on Race and Feminism.* Ann Arbor: University of Michigan Press.

Hurtado, Aida, and Mrinal Sinha. 2008. "More than Men: Latino Feminist Masculinities and Intersectionality." *Sex Roles* 59(5–6): 337–49. doi:10.1007/s11199-008-9405-7.

Hurtado, Sylvia. 2001. "Linking Diversity and Educational Purpose: How Diversity Affects the Classroom Environment and Student Development." In *Diversity Challenged: Evidence on the Impact of Affirmative Action*, edited by Gary Orfield and Michal Kurlaender. Cambridge, Mass.: Harvard Educational Publishing Group.

———. 2005. "The Next Generation of Diversity and Intergroup Relations Research." *Journal of Social Issues* 61(3): 595–610. doi:10.1111/j.1540-4560.2005.00422.x.

Iacoboni, Marco. 2008. *Mirroring People: The New Science of How We Connect with Others.* New York: Farrar, Straus and Giroux.

Iceland, John. 2004. "Beyond Black and White: Metropolitan Residential Segregation in Multi-Ethnic America." *Social Science Research* 33(2): 248–71. doi:10.1016/s0049-089x(03)00056-5.

Institute of International Education. 2010. "International Student Enrollments Rose Modestly in 2009/10, Led by Strong Increase in Students from China." Press release. Washington, D.C.: IIE. Available at: http://www.iie.org/who-we-are/news

-and-events/press-center/press-releases/2010/2010-11-15-open-door-interna
tional-students-in-the-us (accessed January 21, 2013).

Isaacs, William. 1999. *Dialogue and the Art of Thinking Together: A Pioneering Approach to Communicating in Business and in Life*. New York: Currency.

Iyer, Aarti, and Michelle K. Ryan. 2009. "Why Do Men and Women Challenge Gender Discrimination in the Workplace? The Role of Group Status and In-Group Identification in Predicting Pathways to Collective Action." *Journal of Social Issues* 65(4): 791–814. doi:10.1111/j.1540-4560.2009.01625.x.

Iyer, Aarti, Toni Schmader, and Brian Lickel. 2007. "Why Individuals Protest the Perceived Transgressions of Their Country: The Role of Anger, Shame, and Guilt." *Personality and Social Psychology Bulletin* 33(4): 572–87. doi:10.1177/0146 167206297402.

Jackson, Susan E., Aparna Joshi, and Niclas L. Erhardt. 2003. "Recent Research on Team and Organizational Diversity: SWOT Analysis and Implications." *Journal of Management* 29(6): 801–30. doi:10.1016/s0149-2063_03_00080-1.

Jayakumar, Uma M. 2008. "Can Higher Education Meet the Needs of an Increasingly Diverse and Global Society? Campus Diversity and Cross-Cultural Workforce Competencies." *Harvard Educational Review* 78(4): 615–51.

"Jefferson's Gravestone." 2011. In *The Thomas Jefferson Encyclopedia*. Available at: http://www.monticello.org/site/research-and-collections/jeffersons-gravestone (accessed January 21, 2013).

Johnson, David W., and Roger T. Johnson. 1996. "Conflict Resolution and Peer Mediation Programs in Elementary and Secondary Schools: A Review of the Research." *Review of Educational Research* 66(4): 459–506. doi:10.3102/0034654 3066004459.

Jones, James M., Shelly Engelman, Carl E. Turner, Jr., and Santiba Campbell. 2009. "Worlds Apart: The Universality of Racism Leads to Divergent Social Realities." In *Intergroup Misunderstandings: Impact of Divergent Social Realities*, edited by Stéphanie Demoulin, Jacques-Philippe Leyens, and John F. Dovidio. New York: Psychology Press.

Judit. 1987. "Alliances." In Juanita Ramos, ed., *Compañeras: Latina Lesbians*. New York: Latina Lesbian History Project.

Kahn, Jack S., and Kathy Ferguson. 2009. "Men as Allies in Feminist Pedagogy in the Undergraduate Psychology Curriculum." *Women and Therapy* 33(1–2): 121–39. doi:10.1080/02703140903404853.

Kalev, Alexandra, Frank Dobbin, and Erin Kelly. 2006. "Best Practices or Best

Guesses? Assessing the Efficacy of Corporate Affirmative Action and Diversity Policies." *American Sociological Review* 71(4): 589–617. doi:10.1177/0003122 40607100404.

Kaufmann, Jodi Jan. 2010. "The Practice of Dialogue in Critical Pedagogy." *Adult Education Quarterly* 60(5): 456–76. doi:10.1177/0741713610363021.

Kelly, Caroline, and Sara Breinlinger. 1996. *The Social Psychology of Collective Action: Identity, Injustice and Gender*. London: Taylor and Francis.

Kennedy, Kevin. 2011. "People of Different Backgrounds, Races, Roles Gather for Days of Dialogue." *Five College Ink* 23(2010–2011): 9. Available at: https://www .fivecolleges.edu/consortium/publications/ink (accessed January 21, 2013).

Khuri, M. Lydia. 2004. "Working with Emotion in Educational Intergroup Dialogue." *International Journal of Intercultural Relations* 28(6): 595–612. doi:10 .1016/j.ijintrel.2005.01.012.

King, Patricia M., and Bettina C. Shuford. 1996. "A Multicultural View Is a More Cognitively Complex View: Cognitive Development and Multicultural Education." *American Behavioral Scientist* 40(2): 153–64. doi:10.1177/0002764296040 002006.

Kitayama, Shinobu, and Dov Cohen. 2007. *Handbook of Cultural Psychology*. New York: Guilford Press.

Kochhar, Rakesh, Richard Fry, and Paul Taylor. 2011. "Twenty-to-One: Wealth Gaps Rise to Record Highs Between Whites, Blacks, Hispanics." Pew Social and Demographic Trends. Washington, D.C.: Pew Research Center. Available at: http:// www.pewsocialtrends.org/2011/07/26/wealth-gaps-rise-to-record-highs -between-whites-blacks-hispanics/ (accessed January 21, 2013).

Konrad, Shelley Cohen. 2010. "Relational Learning in Social Work Education: Transformative Education for Teaching a Course on Loss, Grief and Death." *Journal of Teaching in Social Work* 30(1): 15–28. doi:10.1080/08841230903479458.

Krysan, Maria, and Nakesha Faison. 2008. "Racial Attitudes in America: An Update." Institute of Government and Public Affairs, University of Illinois. Available at: http://igpa.uillinois.edu/programs/racial-attitudes/detailed8 (accessed January 21, 2013).

Kumashiro, Kevin K. 2000. "Toward a Theory of Anti-Oppressive Education." *Review of Educational Research* 70(1): 25–53. doi:10.3102/00346543070001025.

Laird, Thomas F. Nelson. 2005. "College Students' Experiences with Diversity and Their Effects on Academic Self-Confidence, Social Agency, and Disposition Toward Critical Thinking." *Research in Higher Education* 46(4): 365–87. doi:10.1007/ s11162-005-2966-1.

Laird, Thomas F. Nelson, Mark E. Engberg, and Sylvia Hurtado. 2005. "Modeling Accentuation Effects: Enrolling in a Diversity Course and the Importance of Social Action Engagement." *Journal of Higher Education* 76(4): 448–76. doi:10.1353/jhe.2005.0028.

Lalljee, Mansur, Tania Tam, Miles Hewstone, Simon Laham, and Jessica Lee. 2009. "Unconditional Respect for Persons and the Prediction of Intergroup Action Tendencies." *European Journal of Social Psychology* 39(5): 666–83. doi:10.1002/ejsp.564.

Lawless, Jennifer L., and Richard L. Fox. 2010. *It Still Takes a Candidate: Why Women Don't Run for Office*, rev. ed. Cambridge: Cambridge University Press.

Lea, Susan J., David Stephenson, and Juliette Troy. 2003. "Higher Education Students' Attitudes to Student-Centred Learning: Beyond 'Educational Bulimia'?" *Studies in Higher Education* 28(3): 321–34. doi:10.1080/03075070309293.

Leach, Colin Wayne, Aarti Iyer, and Anne Pedersen. 2006. "Anger and Guilt about Ingroup Advantage Explain the Willingness for Political Action." *Personality and Social Psychology Bulletin* 32(9): 1232–45. doi:10.1177/0146167206289729.

Lerner, Michael, and Cornel West. 1995. *Jews and Blacks: Let the Healing Begin*. New York: G. P. Putnam's Sons.

Levy, Sheri R., Tara L. West, Luisa F. Ramirez, and John E. Pachankis. 2004. "Racial and Ethnic Prejudice Among Children." In *The Psychology of Prejudice and Discrimination*, vol. 1, *Racism in America*, edited by Jean Lau Chin. Westport, Conn.: Praeger Publishers / Greenwood Publishing Group.

Little, Roderick J. A., and Trivellore Raghunathan. 2004. "Statistical Analysis with Missing Data." Course materials presentation. Arlington, Va. (May 4–5, 2004).

Little, Roderick J. A., and Donald B. Rubin. 2002. *Statistical Analysis with Missing Data*, 2nd ed. Hoboken, N.J.: John Wiley and Sons.

Littlejohn, Stephen W. 2004. "The Transcendent Communication Project: Searching for a Praxis of Dialogue." *Conflict Resolution Quarterly* 21(3): 337–59. doi:10.1002/crq.66.

Logan, Amanda, and Christian E. Weller. 2009. "The State of Minorities: The Recession Issue." Washington, D.C.: Center for American Progress. Available at: http://www.americanprogress.org/issues/2009/01/state_of_minorities.html (accessed January 21, 2013).

Lopez, Gretchen, Mark Abboushi, and Alan Reifman. 1992. "Interest in Social and Political Thinking." Unpublished manuscript. University of Michigan, Ann Arbor.

Lopez, Gretchen E., Patricia Gurin, and Biren (Ratnesh) A. Nagda. 1998. "Education and Understanding Structural Causes for Group Inequalities." *Political Psychology* 19(2): 305–39. doi:10.1111/0162-895x.00106.

Lopez, Gretchen E., and A. Wendy Nastasi. 2012. "Writing the Divide: High School Students Crossing Urban-Suburban Contexts." *Equity and Excellence in Education* 45(1): 138–58. doi:10.1080/10665684.2012.643676.

Lopez, Janet. 2006. "The Impact of Demographic Changes on United States Higher Education, 2000–2050." State Higher Education Executive Offices, University of North Carolina at Chapel Hill. Available at: http://archive.sheeo.org/pubs/demographics-lopez.pdf (accessed January 21, 2013).

Louis, Winnifred R. 2009. "Collective Action—And Then What?" *Journal of Social Issues* 65(4): 727–48. doi:10.1111/j.1540-4560.2009.01623.x.

Love, Patrick G., and Victoria L. Guthrie. 1999. "King and Kitchener's Reflective Judgment Model." In *New Directions for Student Services*, No. 88: *Understanding and Applying Cognitive Development Theory.* San Francisco: Jossey-Bass. doi:10.1002/ss.8804.

Lowenstein, Roger. 2007. "The Inequality Conundrum." *New York Times Magazine*, June 10. Available at: http://www.nytimes.com/2007/06/10/magazine/10wwln-lede-t.html (accessed January 25, 2013).

Luhtanen, Riia, and Jennifer Crocker. 1992. "A Collective Self-Esteem Scale: Self-Evaluation of One's Social Identity." *Personality and Social Psychology Bulletin* 18(3): 302–18. doi:10.1177/0146167292183006.

Maoz, Ifat. 2011. "Does Contact Work in Protracted Asymmetrical Conflict? Appraising 20 Years of Reconciliation-Aimed Encounters Between Israeli Jews and Palestinians." *Journal of Peace Research* 48(1): 115–25. doi:10.1177/0022343310389506.

Mar, Raymond A. 2011. "The Neural Bases of Social Cognition and Story Comprehension." *Annual Review of Psychology* 62: 103–34. doi:10.1146/annurev-psych-120709-145406.

Matlock, John, Wade-Golden, Katrina, and Gerald Gurin. 2007. *Michigan Student Study Guidebook.* Ann Arbor: University of Michigan Office of Academic Multicultural Initiatives. Available at: http://www.oami.umich.edu/images/MSS%20FINAL%20GUIDEBOOK.pdf (accessed January 21, 2013).

Maxwell, Kelly E., Biren (Ratnesh) A. Nagda, and Monita C. Thompson, eds. 2011. *Facilitating Intergroup Dialogues: Bridging Differences, Catalyzing Change.* Sterling, Va.: Stylus.

May, Stephen. 2009. "Critical Multiculturalism and Education." In *The Routledge*

International Companion to Multicultural Education, edited by James A. Banks. New York: Routledge.

McCabe, Janice. 2009. "Racial and Gender Microaggressions on a Predominantly-White Campus: Experiences of Black, Latina/o and White Undergraduates." *Race, Gender and Class* 16(1–2): 133–51.

McCombs, Barbara L., and Jo Sue Whisler. 1997. *The Learner-Centered Classroom and School: Strategies for Increasing Student Motivation and Achievement.* San Francisco: Jossey-Bass.

McConahay, John B. 1986. "Modern Racism, Ambivalence, and the Modern Racism Scale." In *Prejudice, Discrimination, and Racism*, edited by John F. Dovidio and Samuel L. Gaertner. Orlando, Fla.: Academic Press.

McCoy, Martha L., and Patrick L. Scully. 2002. "Deliberative Dialogue to Expand Civic Engagement: What Kind of Talk Does Democracy Need?" *National Civic Review* 91(2): 117–35. doi:10.1002/ncr.91202.

McIntosh, Peggy. 1989. "White Privilege: Unpacking the Invisible Knapsack." *Peace and Freedom* (July/August): 10–12.

McNamee, Sheila, and Kenneth J. Gergen, eds. 1999. *Relational Responsibility: Resources for Sustainable Dialogue.* Thousand Oaks, Calif.: Sage Publications.

McPhail, M. L. 2004. "Race and the (Im)Possibility of Dialogue." In *Dialogue: Theorizing Difference in Communication Studies*, edited by Rob Anderson, Leslie A. Baxter, and Kenneth N. Cissna. Thousand Oaks, Calif.: Sage Publications.

Milem, Jeffrey F., Mitchell J. Chang, and Anthony Lising Antonio. 2005. *Making Diversity Work on Campus: A Research-Based Perspective.* Washington, D.C.: Association of American Colleges and Universities.

Miller, Berkeley, and Sutee Sujitparapitaya. 2010. "Campus Climate in the Twenty-First Century: Estimating Perceptions of Discrimination at a Racially Mixed Institution, 1994–2006." *New Directions for Institutional Research* 145(Spring): 29–52. doi:10.1002/ir.321.

Miller, Jean Baker. 1982. "Women and Power." *Work in Progress* no. 82–01. Wellesley, Mass.: Stone Center Working Paper Series.

Miller, Joshua, and Susan Donner. 2000. "More Than Just Talk: The Use of Racial Dialogues to Combat Racism." *Social Work with Groups* 23(1): 31–53. doi:10.1300/J009v23n01_03.

Moya, Paula M. L., and Hazel Rose Markus. 2010. "Doing Race: An Introduction." In *Doing Race: 21 Essays for the 21st Century*, edited by Hazel Rose Markus and Paula M. L. Moya. New York: W. W. Norton.

Multi-University Intergroup Dialogue Research Project. 2005. "Multi-University Intergroup Dialogue Curriculum." Ann Arbor: University of Michigan.

Murdock, Steve H., and Md. Nazrul Hoque. 1999. "Demographic Factors Affecting Higher Education in the United States in the Twenty-First Century." *New Directions for Higher Education* 108: 5–13. doi:10.1002/he.10801.

Nadler, Arie. 2012. "Intergroup Reconciliation: Definitions, Processes, and Future Directions." In *The Oxford Handbook of Intergroup Conflict*, edited by Linda R. Tropp. Oxford: Oxford University Press.

Nadler, Arie, and Ido Liviatan. 2006. "Intergroup Reconciliation: Effects of Adversary's Expressions of Empathy, Responsibility, and Recipients' Trust." *Personality and Social Psychology Bulletin* 32(4): 459–70. doi:10.1177/0146167205276431.

Nadler, Arie, and Nurit Shnabel. 2011. "Promoting Intergroup Reconciliation in Conflicts Involving Direct or Structural Violence: Implications of the Needs-Based Model." In *Moving Beyond Prejudice Reduction: Pathways to Positive Intergroup Relations*, edited by Linda R. Tropp and Robyn K. Mallett. Washington, D.C.: American Psychological Association.

Nagda, Biren (Ratnesh) A. 1999. "An End-of-Quarter Survey for Cultural Diversity and Justice Course." Unpublished manuscript. University of Washington School of Social Work, Seattle.

———. 2001. *Creating Spaces of Hope and Possibility: A Curriculum Guide for Intergroup Dialogues.* Seattle, Wash.: IDEA Center.

———. 2006. "Breaking Barriers, Crossing Borders, Building Bridges: Communication Processes in Intergroup Dialogues." *Journal of Social Issues* 62(3): 553–76. doi:10.1111/j.1540-4560.2006.00473.x.

Nagda, Biren (Ratnesh) A., and Patricia Gurin. 2007. "Intergroup Dialogue: A Critical-Dialogic Approach to Learning about Difference, Inequality, and Social Justice." *New Directions for Teaching and Learning* 111: 35–45. doi:10.1002/tl.284.

———. 2012. "Intergroup Contact and Social Justice." In *Encyclopedia of Diversity in Education*, vol. 2, edited by James A. Banks. Thousand Oaks, Calif.: Sage Publications.

Nagda, Biren (Ratnesh) A., Patricia Gurin, and Gretchen E. Lopez. 2003. "Transformative Pedagogy for Democracy and Social Justice." *Race Ethnicity and Education* 6(2): 165–91. doi:10.1080/13613320308199.

Nagda, Biren (Ratnesh) A., Patricia Gurin, Nicholas Sorensen, Chloé Gurin-Sands, and Shardae M. Osuna. 2009. "From Separate Corners to Dialogue and Action." *Race and Social Problems* 1(1): 45–55. doi:10.1007/s12552-009-9002-6.

Nagda, Biren (Ratnesh) A., Chan-woo Kim, and Yaffa Truelove. 2004. "Learning about Difference, Learning with Others, Learning to Transgress." *Journal of Social Issues* 60(1): 195–214. doi:10.1111/j.0022-4537.2004.00106.x.

Nagda, Biren (Ratnesh) A., and Kelly E. Maxwell. 2011. "Deepening the Layers of Understanding and Connection: A Critical-Dialogic Approach to Facilitating Intergroup Dialogues." In *Facilitating Intergroup Dialogues: Bridging Differences, Catalyzing Change*, edited by Kelly E. Maxwell, Biren (Ratnesh) A. Nagda, and Monita C. Thompson. Sterling, Va.: Stylus Publishing.

Nagda, Biren (Ratnesh) A., Norma Timbang, Nichola G. Fulmer, and Thai Hung V. Tran. 2011. "Not *for* Others, But *with* Others *for All of Us*: Weaving Relationships, Co-Creating Spaces of Justice." In *Facilitating Intergroup Dialogues: Bridging Differences, Catalyzing Change*, edited by Kelly E. Maxwell, Biren (Ratnesh) A. Nagda, and Monita C. Thompson. Sterling, Va.: Stylus.

Nagda, Biren (Ratnesh) A., Anna Yeakley, Patricia Gurin, and Nicholas Sorensen. 2012. "Intergroup Dialogue: A Critical-Dialogic Model for Conflict Engagement." In *Oxford Handbook of Intergroup Conflict*, edited by Linda R. Tropp. Oxford: Oxford University Press.

Nagda, Biren (Ratnesh) A., and Ximena Zúñiga. 2003. "Fostering Meaningful Racial Engagement through Intergroup Dialogues." *Group Processes and Intergroup Relations* 6(1): 111–28. doi:10.1177/1368430203006001015.

Nagda, Biren (Ratnesh) A., Ximena Zúñiga, and Todd Sevig. 1995. "Bridging Differences through Peer-Facilitated Intergroup Dialogues." In *Peer Programs on the College Campus: Theory, Training, and "Voice of the Peers,"* edited by Sherry L. Hatcher. San José, Calif.: Resources Publications.

Narayan, Uma. 1988. "Working Together Across Difference: Some Considerations on Emotions and Political Practice." *Hypatia* 3(2): 31–47. doi:10.1111/j.1527-2001.1988.tb00067.x.

———. 2004. "The Project of Feminist Epistemology: Perspectives from a Non-Western Feminist." In *The Feminist Standpoint Theory Reader: Intellectual and Political Controversies*, edited by Sandra G. Harding. New York: Routledge.

National Urban League. 2009. *The State of Black America 2009: Message to the President*. New York: National Urban League.

Nedeau, Jen. 2008. "Is Feminism Dead? An Overview of Post-Feminism." *Change.org News*, October 4. Available at: http://jjgp.pbworks.com/w/page/18951263/Relevant%20Article%20-%20Is%20Feminism%20Dead (original URL defunct; copy accessed January 22, 2013).

Nisbett, Richard E., and Lee Ross. 1980. *Human Inference: Strategies and Shortcomings of Social Judgment*. Englewood Cliffs, N.J.: Prentice-Hall.

Nussbaum, Martha C. 1996. "Patriotism and Cosmopolitanism." In *For Love of Country: Debating the Limits of Patriotism*, edited by Joshua Cohen. Boston, Mass.: Beacon Press.

———. 2001. *Upheavals of Thought: The Intelligence of Emotions*. Cambridge: Cambridge University Press.

———. 2007. "Cultivating Humanity and World Citizenship." In *Forum Futures 2007*. Cambridge, Mass.: Forum for the Future of Higher Education. Available at: http://net.educause.edu/ir/library/pdf/ff0709s.pdf (accessed January 23, 2013).

O'Brien, Eileen. 2001. *Whites Confront Racism: Antiracists and Their Paths to Action*. Lanham, Md.: Rowman and Littlefield.

O'Neill, Geraldine, and Tim McMahon. 2005. "Student-Centred Learning: What Does It Mean for Students and Lecturers?" In *Emerging Issues in the Practice of University Learning and Teaching*, edited by Geraldine O'Neill, Sarah Moore, and Barry McMullin. Dublin: AISHE Readings. Available at: http://www.aishe.org/readings/2005-1/ (accessed January 23, 2013).

Olson, Gary. 2008. "We Empathize, Therefore We Are: Toward a Moral Neuropolitics." *Znet.com*, January 18. Available at: http://www.zcommunications.org/we-empathize-therefore-we-are-toward-a-moral-neuropolitics-by-gary-olson (accessed January 23, 2013).

Orfield, Gary, Susan E. Eaton, and the Harvard Project on School Desegregation. 1996. *Dismantling Desegregation: The Quiet Reversal of Brown v. Board of Education*. New York: New Press.

Orfield, Gary, and Kurlaender, Michal, eds. 2001. *Diversity Challenged: Evidence on the Impact of Affirmative Action*. Cambridge, Mass.: Harvard Educational Publishing Group.

Orfield, Gary, and Chungmei Lee. 2006. *Racial Transformation and the Changing Nature of Segregation*. Cambridge, Mass.: Civil Rights Project at Harvard University. Available at: http://eric.ed.gov/ERICWebPortal/detail?accno=ED500822 (accessed January 21, 2013).

Page, Scott E. 2007. *The Difference: How the Power of Diversity Creates Better Groups, Firms, Schools, and Societies*. Princeton, N.J.: Princeton University Press.

Page, Scott E. 2011. *Diversity and Complexity*. Princeton, N.J.: Princeton University Press.

Page-Gould, Elizabeth, Wendy Berry Mendes, and Brenda Major. 2010. "Intergroup Contact Facilitates Physiological Recovery Following Stressful Intergroup Interactions." *Journal of Experimental Social Psychology* 46(5): 854–58. doi:10.1016/j.jesp.2010.04.006.

Page-Gould, Elizabeth, Rodolfo Mendoza-Denton, and Linda R. Tropp. 2008. "With a Little Help from My Cross-Group Friend: Reducing Anxiety in Intergroup Contexts Through Cross-Group Friendship." *Journal of Personality and Social Psychology* 95(5): 1080–94. doi:10.1037/0022-3514.95.5.1080.

Paluck, Elizabeth Levy, and Donald P. Green. 2009. "Prejudice Reduction: What Works? A Review and Assessment of Research and Practice." *Annual Review of Psychology* 60: 339–67. doi:10.1146/annurev.psych.60.110707.163607.

Parker, Walter C. 2003. *Teaching Democracy: Unity and Diversity in Public Life.* New York: Teacher's College Press.

Parks Daloz, Laurent A. 2000. "Transformative Learning for the Common Good." In *Learning as Transformation: Critical Perspectives on a Theory in Progress,* edited by Jack Mezirow and Associates. San Francisco: Jossey-Bass.

Partnership for 21st Century Skills. 2008. *21st Century Skills, Education & Competitiveness: A Resource and Policy Guide.* Tucson, Az.: Partnership for 21st Century Skills. Available at: http://www.p21.org/storage/documents/21st_century_skills_education_and_competitiveness_guide.pdf (accessed January 23, 2013).

Passel, Jeffrey S., and D'Vera Cohn. 2008, February 11. "U.S. Population Projections: 2005–2050." Washington, D.C.: Pew Hispanic Center. Available at: http://pewhispanic.org/files/reports/85.pdf (accessed January 23, 2013).

Peck, Don. 2011. "Can the Middle Class Be Saved?" *The Atlantic,* September. Available at: http://www.theatlantic.com/magazine/archive/2011/09/can-the-middle-class-be-saved/8600/ (accessed January 23, 2013).

Peet, Melissa, Steven Lonn, Patricia Gurin, K. Page Boyer, Malinda Matney, Tiffany Marra, Simone Himbeault Taylor, and Andrea Daley. 2011. "Fostering Integrative Knowledge Through ePortfolios." *International Journal of ePortfolio* 1(1): 11–31. Available at: http://www.theijep.com/articleview.cfm?id=39 (accessed January 23, 2013).

Pettigrew, Thomas F. 1998. "Intergroup Contact Theory." *Annual Review of Psychology* 49: 65–85. doi:10.1146/annurev.psych.49.1.65.

Pettigrew, Thomas F., and Linda R. Tropp. 2008. "How Does Intergroup Contact Reduce Prejudice? Meta-Analytic Tests of Three Mediators." *European Journal of Social Psychology* 38(6): 922–34. doi:10.1002/ejsp.504.

———. 2011. *When Groups Meet: The Dynamics of Intergroup Contact.* New York: Psychology Press.

Petty, Richard E., Kenneth G. DeMarree, Pablo Briñol, Javier Horcajo, and Alan J.

Strathman. 2008. "Need for Cognition Can Magnify or Attenuate Priming Effects in Social Judgment." *Personality and Social Psychology Bulletin* 34(7): 900–912. doi:10.1177/0146167208316692.

Phelps, Rosemary E., Deborah B. Altschul, Joseph M. Wisenbaker, James F. Day, Diane Cooper, and Carol G. Potter. 1998. "Roommate Satisfaction and Ethnic Identity in Mixed-Race and White University Roommate Dyads." *Journal of College Student Development* 39(2): 194–203.

Pheterson, Gail. 1990. "Alliances Between Women: Overcoming Internalized Oppression and Internalized Domination." In *Bridges of Power: Women's Multicultural Alliances*, edited by Lisa Albrecht and Rose M. Brewer. Philadelphia, Pa.: New Society.

Phillips, Katherine W., and Denise Lewin Loyd. 2006. "When Surface and Deep-Level Diversity Collide: The Effects on Dissenting Group Members." *Organizational Behavior and Human Decision Processes* 99(2): 143–60.

Phillips, Katherine W., Katie A. Liljenquist, and Margaret A. Neale. 2009. "Is the Pain Worth the Gain? The Advantages and Liabilities of Agreeing with Socially Distinct Newcomers." *Personality and Social Psychology Bulletin* 35(3): 336–50. doi:10.1177/0146167208328062.

Phillips, Katherine W., Gregory B. Northcraft, and Margaret A. Neale. 2006. "Surface-Level Diversity and Decision-Making in Groups: When Does Deep-Level Similarity Help?" *Group Processes and Intergroup Relations* 9(4): 467–82. doi:10.1177/1368430206067557.

Pincus, Fred L. 2000. "Discrimination Comes in Many Forms: Individual, Institutional, and Structural." In *Readings for Diversity and Social Justice*, edited by Maurianne Adams, Warren J. Blumenfeld, Rosie Castañeda, Heather W. Hackman, Madeline L. Peters, and Ximena Zúñiga. New York: Routledge.

Pitkin, Hanna Fenichel, and Sara M. Shumer. 1982. "On Participation." *Democracy* 2(4): 43–54.

Powell, Myrtis H. 1998. "Five Recommendations to Build a Multicultural Campus." In *The Multicultural Campus: Strategies for Transforming Higher Education*, edited by Leonard A. Valverde and Louis A. Castenell, Jr., 94. Walnut Creek, Calif.: AltaMira Press.

Pratto, Felicia, Jim Sidanius, Lisa M. Stallworth, and Bertram F. Malle. 1994. "Social Dominance Orientation: A Personality Variable Predicting Social and Political Attitudes." *Journal of Personality and Social Psychology* 67(4): 741–63. doi:10.1037/0022-3514.67.4.741.

Program on Intergroup Relations. 2003. "Intergroup Dialogue Process-Content Outline." Ann Arbor: University of Michigan.

Putnam, Robert D. 2007. "*E Pluribus Unum*: Diversity and Community in the Twenty-First Century: The 2006 Johan Skytte Prize Lecture." *Scandinavian Political Studies* 30(2): 137–74. doi:10.1111/j.1467-9477.2007.00176.x.

Raelin, Joseph A. 2000. *Work-Based Learning*. Upper Saddle River, N.J.: Prentice Hall.

———. 2001. "Public Reflection as the Basis of Learning." *Management Learning* 32(1): 11–30. doi:10.1177/1350507601321002.

Ramachandran, V. S. 2006. "Mirror Neurons and the Brain in the Vat." *Edge: The Third Culture*, January 10. Available at: http://www.edge.org/3rd_culture/ramachandran06/ramachandran06_index.html (accessed July 22, 2010).

Raudenbush, Stephen W., and Anthony S. Bryk. 2002. *Hierarchical Linear Models: Applications and Data Analysis Methods*, 2nd ed. Thousand Oaks, Calif.: Sage.

Raudenbush, Stephen W., and Xiao-Feng Liu. 2001. "Effects of Study Duration, Frequency of Observations, and Sample Size on Power in Studies of Group Differences in Polynomial Change." *Psychological Methods* 6(4): 387–401. doi:10.1037/1082-989x.6.4.387.

Reason, Robert D., Elizabeth A. Roosa Millar, and Tara C. Scales. 2005. "Toward a Model of Racial Justice Ally Development." *Journal of College Student Development* 46(5): 530–46. doi:10.1353/csd.2005.0054.

Reilly, Rosemary C. 2010. "Rendering the Invisible Visible: Lived Values That Support Reflective Practice." *Journal of Applied Research on Learning* 3(Article 11): 1–23. Available at: http://www.ccl-cca.ca/ccl/reports/journal.html.

Richeson, Jennifer A., and Richard J. Nussbaum. 2004. "The Impact of Multiculturalism Versus Color-Blindness on Racial Bias." *Journal of Experimental Social Psychology* 40(3): 417–23. doi:10.1016/j.jesp.2003.09.002.

Richeson, Jennifer A., and J. Nicole Shelton. 2007. "Negotiating Interracial Interactions: Costs, Consequences, and Possibilities." *Current Directions in Psychological Science* 16(6): 316–20. doi:10.1111/j.1467-8721.2007.00528.x.

Richeson, Jennifer A., and Sophie Trawalter. 2005. "Why Do Interracial Interactions Impair Executive Function? A Resource Depletion Account." *Journal of Personality and Social Psychology* 88(6): 934–47. doi:10.1037/0022-3514.88.6.934.

Rifkin, Jeremy. 2009. *The Empathic Civilization: The Race to Global Consciousness in a World in Crisis*. New York: Jeremy P. Tarcher/Penguin.

Rimé, Bernard. 2007. "The Social Sharing of Emotion as an Interface Between Individual and Collective Processes in the Construction of Emotional Climates." *Journal of Social Issues* 63(2): 307–22. doi:10.1111/j.1540-4560.2007.00510.x.

Risman, Barbara J. 2004. "Gender as a Social Structure: Theory Wrestling with Activism." *Gender and Society* 18(4): 429–50. doi:10.1177/0891243204265349.

Rizzolatti, Giacomo, and Corrado Sinigaglia. 2008. *Mirrors in the Brain*, trans. Frances Anderson. Oxford: Oxford University Press.

Rodriguez, Jaclyn, Patricia Gurin, and Nicholas Sorensen. 2010. "Interracial Dialogues: Impact on Identity Engagement." Unpublished manuscript, Occidental College.

———. Under review. "Engaging Racial Identity for Socially Just Intergroup Relations: A Randomized Field Experiment." *Group Processes and Intergroup Relations*.

Rodríguez, Jaclyn, Andréa C. Rodríguez-Scheel, Shaquanda Lindsey, and Ariel Kirkland. 2011. "Facilitator Training in Diverse, Progressive Residential Communities: Occidental College as a Case Study." In *Facilitating Intergroup Dialogues: Bridging Differences, Catalyzing Change*, edited by Kelly E. Maxwell, Biren (Ratnesh) A. Nagda, and Monita C. Thompson. Sterling, Va.: Stylus.

Ross, Lee. 1977. "The Intuitive Psychologist and His Shortcomings: Distortions in the Attribution Process." *Advances in Experimental Social Psychology* 10: 173–220.

Rothman, Stanley, Seymour Martin Lipset, and Neil Nevitte. 2003. "Does Enrollment Diversity Improve University Education?" *International Journal of Public Opinion Research* 15(1): 8–26. doi:10.1093/ijpor/15.1.8.

Rubin, Donald B. 1987. *Multiple Imputation for Nonresponse in Surveys*. New York: John Wiley and Sons.

Rudman, Laurie A., and Peter Glick. 2008. *The Social Psychology of Gender: How Power and Intimacy Shape Gender Relations*. New York: Guilford.

Sabo, Don. 1995. "Pigskin, Patriarchy, and Pain." In *Race, Class, and Gender in the United States: An Integrated Study*, 3rd ed., edited by Paula S. Rothenberg. New York: St. Martin's Press.

Saguy, Tamar, John F. Dovidio, and Felicia Pratto. 2008. "Beyond Contact: Intergroup Contact in the Context of Power Relations." *Personality and Social Psychology Bulletin* 34(3): 432–45. doi:10.1177/0146167207311200.

Saguy, Tamar, Nicole Tausch, John F. Dovidio, and Felicia Pratto. 2009. "The Irony of Harmony: Intergroup Contact Can Produce False Expectations for Equality." *Psychological Science* 20(1): 114–21. doi:10.1111/j.1467-9280.2008.02261.x.

Saguy, Tamar, Linda R. Tropp, and Diala Hawi. 2013. "The Role of Group Power in Intergroup Contact." In *Advances in Intergroup Contact*, edited by Gordon Hodson and Miles Hewstone. New York: Psychology Press.

Sandelowski, Margarete. 2003. "Tables or Tableaux? The Challenges of Writing and Reading Mixed Methods Studies." In *Handbook of Mixed Methods in Social and Behavioral Research*, edited by Abbas Tashakkori and Charles Teddlie. Thousand Oaks, Calif.: Sage Publications.

Saunders, Harold H. 1999. *A Public Peace Process: Sustained Dialogue to Transform Racial and Ethnic Conflicts*. New York: St. Martin's Press.

Saxonhouse, Arlene W. 1992. *Fear of Diversity: The Birth of Political Science in Ancient Greek Thought*. Chicago: University of Chicago Press.

Schaller, Mark, Carrie Boyd, Jonathan Yohannes, and Meredith O'Brien. 1995. "The Prejudiced Personality Revisited: Personal Need for Structure and Formation of Erroneous Group Stereotypes." *Journal of Personality and Social Psychology* 68(3): 544–55. doi:10.1037/0022-3514.68.3.544.

Schlesinger, Arthur M., Jr. 1991. "Writing, and Rewriting, History." *The New Leader* 74(14): 12–14.

Schoem, David, Sylvia Hurtado, Todd Sevig, Mark Chesler, and Stephen H. Sumida. 2001. "Intergroup Dialogue: Democracy at Work in Theory and Practice." In *Intergroup Dialogue: Deliberative Democracy in School, College, Community and Workplace*, edited by David Schoem and Sylvia Hurtado. Ann Arbor: University of Michigan Press.

Schoem, David, and Marshall Stevenson. 1990. "Teaching Ethnic Identity and Intergroup Relations: The Case of Black-Jewish Dialogue." *Teachers College Record* 91(4): 579–94.

Schoem, David, Ximena Zúñiga, and Biren (Ratnesh) A. Nagda. 1993. "Classroom and Workshop Exercises C4. Exploring One's Group Background: The Fishbowl Exercise." In *Multicultural Teaching in the University*, edited by David Schoem, Linda Frankel, Ximena Zúñiga, and Edith A. Lewis, 326–27. Westport, Conn.: Praeger.

Schofield, Janet Ward. 1986. "Causes and Consequences of the Colorblind Perspective." In *Prejudice, Discrimination, and Racism*, edited by John F. Dovidio and Samuel L. Gaertner. Orlando, Fla.: Academic Press.

Scott, Sarah E., and Annemarie S. Palincsar. 2009. "Sociocultural Theory." In *Psychology of Classroom Learning: An Encyclopedia*, edited by Eric M. Anderman and Lynley H. Anderman. Farmington Hills, MI: Gale Group.

Sears, David O. 1988. "Symbolic Racism." In *Eliminating Racism: Profiles in Controversy*, edited by Phyllis A. Katz and Dalmas A. Taylor. New York: Plenum.

Seltzer, Michael. 2004. "The Use of Hierarchical Models in Analyzing Data from Experiments and Quasi-Experiments Conducted in Field Settings." In *The SAGE*

Handbook of Quantitative Methodology for the Social Sciences, edited by David Kaplan, 259–80. Thousand Oaks, CA: Sage.

Shelton, J. Nicole, Jennifer A. Richeson, and Jessica Salvatore. 2005. "Expecting to Be the Target of Prejudice: Implications for Interethnic Interactions." *Personality and Social Psychology Bulletin* 31(9): 1189–202. doi:10.1177/01461672052774894.

Shelton, J. Nicole, Thomas E. Trail, Tessa V. West, and Hilary B. Bergsieker. 2010. "From Strangers to Friends: The Interpersonal Process Model of Intimacy in Developing Interracial Friendships." *Journal of Social and Personal Relationships* 27(1): 71–90. doi:10.1177/0265407509346422.

Shih, Margaret, Elsie Wang, Amy Trahan Bucher, and Rebecca Stotzer. 2009. "Perspective Taking: Reducing Prejudice Towards General Outgroups and Specific Individuals." *Group Processes and Intergroup Relations* 12(5): 565–77. doi:10.1177/1368430209337463.

Shnabel, Nurit, Arie Nadler, Daphna Canetti-Nisim, and Johannes Ullrich. 2008. "The Role of Acceptance and Empowerment in Promoting Reconciliation from the Perspective of the Needs-Based Model." *Social Issues and Policy Review* 2(1): 159–86. doi:10.1111/j.1751-2409.2008.00014.x.

Shnabel, Nurit, Arie Nadler, Johannes Ullrich, John F. Dovidio, and Dganit Carmi. 2009. "Promoting Reconciliation Through the Satisfaction of the Emotional Needs of Victimized and Perpetrating Group Members: The Needs-Based Model of Reconciliation." *Personality and Social Psychology Bulletin* 35(8): 1021–30. doi:10.1177/0146167209336610.

Shook, Natalie J., and Russell H. Fazio. 2008a. "Interracial Roommate Relationships: An Experimental Field Test of the Contact Hypothesis." *Psychological Science* 19(7): 717–23. doi:10.1111/j.1467-9280.2008.02147.x.

———. 2008b. "Roommate Relationships: A Comparison of Interracial and Same-Race Living Situations." *Group Processes and Intergroup Relations* 11(4): 425–37. doi:10.1177/1368430208095398.

Shrout, Patrick E., and Niall Bolger. 2002. "Mediation in Experimental and Nonexperimental Studies: New Procedures and Recommendations." *Psychological Methods* 7(4): 422–45. doi:10.1037/1082-989x.7.4.422.

Sidanius, Jim, Shana Levin, Colette van Laar, and David O. Sears. 2008. *The Diversity Challenge: Social Identity and Intergroup Relations on the College Campus.* New York: Russell Sage Foundation.

Simon, Bernd, Michael Loewy, Stefan Stürmer, Ulrike Weber, Peter Freytag, Corinna Habig, Claudia Kampmeier, and Peter Spahlinger. 1998. "Collective Identification and Social Movement Participation." *Journal of Personality and Social Psychology* 74(3): 646–58. doi:10.1037/0022-3514.74.3.646.

Simpson, Barbara, Bob Large, and Matthew O'Brien. 2004. "Bridging Difference Through Dialogue: A Constructivist Perspective." *Journal of Constructivist Psychology* 17(1): 45–59. doi:10.1080/10720530490250697.

Simpson, Jennifer Lyn. 2008. "The Color-Blind Double Bind: Whiteness and the (Im)Possibility of Dialogue." *Communication Theory* 18(1): 139–59. doi:10.1111/j.1468-2885.2007.00317.x.

Sleeter, Christine E., and Carl A. Grant. 2009. *Making Choices for Multicultural Education: Five Approaches to Race, Class, and Gender*, 6th ed. Hoboken, N.J.: John Wiley and Sons.

Smith, William A., Man Hung, and Jeremy D. Franklin. 2011. "Racial Battle Fatigue and the *Mis*education of Black Men: Racial Microaggressions, Societal Problems, and Environmental Stress." *Journal of Negro Education* 80(1): 63–82.

Snijders, Tom A. B., and Roel J. Bosker. 1999. *Multilevel Analysis: An Introduction to Basic and Advanced Multilevel Modeling*. London: Sage.

Society of American Law Teachers (SALT). 2009. "Letter to Senators Patrick Leahy and Jeff Sessions." June 25, 2009. Las Vegas, Nev.: Society of American Law Teachers. Available at: http://www.saltlaw.org/userfiles/6-25-09_Sotomayor_final.pdf (accessed January 23, 2013).

Sorensen, Nicholas, Richard Gonzalez, Biren (Ratnesh) A. Nagda, Patricia Gurin, and Walter G. Stephan. 2010. "The Road to Empathy: An Empirical Test of a Critical-Dialogic Process Model of Intergroup Communication." Unpublished manuscript, University of Michigan, Ann Arbor.

Sorensen, Nicholas, Biren (Ratnesh) A. Nagda, Patricia Gurin, and Kelly E. Maxwell. 2009. "Taking a 'Hands On' Approach to Diversity in Higher Education: A Critical-Dialogic Model for Effective Intergroup Interaction." *Analyses of Social Issues and Public Policy* 9(1): 3–35. doi:10.1111/j.1530-2415.2009.01193.x.

Sorensen, Nicholas, Biren (Ratnesh) A. Nagda, Patricia Gurin, Walter G. Stephan, and Richard Gonzalez. 2010. "It's Just Not What We Say but How We Communicate that Matters: A Critical-Dialogic Model for Fostering Empathy in Interracial Communication." Unpublished manuscript, University of Michigan, Ann Arbor.

Spanierman, Lisa B., Euna Oh, V. Paul Poteat, Anita R. Hund, Vetisha L. McClair, Amanda M. Beer, and Alexis M. Clarke. 2008. "White University Students' Responses to Societal Racism: A Qualitative Investigation." *The Counseling Psychologist* 36(6): 839–70. doi:10.1177/0011000006295589.

Spanierman, Lisa B., V. Paul Poteat, Amanda M. Beer, and Patrick Ian Armstrong. 2006. "Psychosocial Costs of Racism to Whites: Exploring Patterns through Cluster Analysis." *Journal of Counseling Psychology* 53(4): 434–41. doi:10.1037/0022 -0167.53.4.434.

Steinwachs, Barbara. 1992. "How to Facilitate a Debriefing." *Simulation and Gaming* 23(2): 186–95. doi:10.1177/1046878192232006.

Stephan, Cookie White, Lausanne Renfro, and Walter G. Stephan. 2004. "The Evaluation of Multicultural Education Programs: Techniques and a Meta-Analysis." In *Education Programs for Improving Intergroup Relations: Theory, Research, and Practice*, edited by Walter G. Stephan and W. Paul Vogt. New York: Teachers College Press.

Stephan, Walter G. 2008. "Psychological and Communication Processes Associated with Intergroup Conflict Resolution." *Small Group Research* 39(1): 28–41. doi: 10.1177/1046496407313413.

Stephan, Walter G., and Joe R. Feagin, eds. 1980. *School Desegregation: Past, Present, and Future.* New York: Plenum Press.

Stephan, Walter G., and Krystina Finlay. 1999. "The Role of Empathy in Improving Intergroup Relations." *Journal of Social Issues* 55(4): 729–43. doi:10.1111/0022 -4537.00144.

Stephan, Walter G., and Cookie White Stephan. 1985. "Intergroup Anxiety." *Journal of Social Issues* 41(3): 157–75. doi:10.1111/j.1540-4560.1985.tb01134.x.

———. 1996. *Intergroup Relations.* Boulder, Colo.: Westview Press.

———. 2001. *Improving Intergroup Relations.* Thousand Oaks, Calif.: Sage Publications.

———. 2004. "Intergroup Relations in Multicultural Education Programs." In *Handbook of Research on Multicultural Education*, 2nd ed., edited by James A. Banks and Cherry A. McGee Banks. San Francisco: Jossey-Bass.

Stephan, Walter G., and W. Paul Vogt. 2004. *Education Programs for Improving Intergroup Relations: Theory, Research, and Practice.* New York: Teachers College Press.

Strauss, Anselm L., and Juliet M. Corbin. 1990. *Basics of Qualitative Research: Grounded Theory, Procedures, and Techniques.* Newbury Park, Calif.: Sage Publications.

Stryker, Sheldon. 1980. *Symbolic Interactionism: A Social Structural Version.* Menlo Park, Calif.: Benjamin/Cummings.

Sturgis, Patrick, Ian Brunton-Smith, Sanna Read, and Nick Allum. 2011. "Does Ethnic Diversity Erode Trust? Putnam's 'Hunkering Down' Thesis Reconsidered." *British Journal of Political Science* 41(1): 57–82. doi:10.1017/s0007123410000281.

Stürmer, Stefan, and Bernd Simon. 2004. "Collective Action: Towards a Dual-Pathway Model." *European Review of Social Psychology* 15(1): 59–99. doi:10.1080/10463280340000117.

———. 2009. "Pathways to Collective Protest: Calculation, Identification, or Emotion? A Critical Analysis of the Role of Group-Based Anger in Social Movement Participation." *Journal of Social Issues* 65(4): 681–705. doi:10.1111/j.1540-4560.2009.01620.x.

Stürmer, Stefan, Bernd Simon, Michael Loewy, and Heike Jörger. 2003. "The Dual-Pathway Model of Social Movement Participation: The Case of the Fat Acceptance Movement." *Social Psychology Quarterly* 66(1): 71–82. doi:10.2307/3090142.

Sue, Derald Wing, Christina M. Capodilupo, Gina C. Torino, Jennifer M. Bucceri, Aisha M. B. Holder, Kevin L. Nadal, and Marta Esquilin. 2007. "Racial Microaggressions in Everyday Life: Implications for Clinical Practice." *American Psychologist* 62(4): 271–86. doi:10.1037/0003-066X.62.4.271.

Sue, Derald Wing, Annie I. Lin, Gina C. Torino, Christine M. Capodilupo, and David P. Rivera. 2009. "Racial Microaggressions and Difficult Dialogues on Race in the Classroom." *Cultural Diversity and Ethnic Minority Psychology* 15(2): 183–90. doi:10.1037/a0014191.

Sue, Derald Wing, David P. Rivera, Christina M. Capodilupo, Annie I. Lin, and Gina C. Torino. 2010. "Racial Dialogues and White Trainee Fears: Implications for Education and Training." *Cultural Diversity and Ethnic Minority Psychology* 16(2): 206–14. doi:10.1037/a0016112.

Swart, Hermann, Rhiannon Turner, Miles Hewstone, and Alberto Voci. 2011. "Achieving Forgiveness and Trust in Postconflict Societies: The Importance of Self-Disclosure and Empathy." In *Moving Beyond Prejudice Reduction: Pathways to Positive Intergroup Relations*, edited by Linda R. Tropp and Robyn K. Mallett. Washington, D.C.: American Psychological Association.

Tagg, John. 2003. *The Learning Paradigm College*. Bolton, Mass.: Anker.

Tajfel, Henri. 1974. "Social Identity and Intergroup Behavior." *Social Science Information* 13(2): 65–93. doi:10.1177/053901847401300204.

Tajfel, Henri, and John C. Turner. 1986. "The Social Identity Theory of Intergroup Behavior." In *Psychology of Intergroup Relations*, edited by Stephen Worchel and William G. Austin. Chicago: Nelson-Hall.

Tam, Kim-Pong, Al Au, and Angela Ka-Yee Leung. 2008. "Attributionally More Complex People Show Less Punitiveness and Racism." *Journal of Research in Personality* 42(4): 1074–81. doi:10.1016/j.jrp.2007.11.002.

Tam, Tania, Miles Hewstone, Jared B. Kenworthy, Ed Cairns, Claudia Marinetti, Leo Geddes, and Brian Parkinson. 2008. "Postconflict Reconciliation: Intergroup Forgiveness and Implicit Biases in Northern Ireland." *Journal of Social Issues* 64(2): 303–20. doi:10.1111/j.1540-4560.2008.00563.x.

Tatum, Beverly Daniel. 1997. *"Why Are All the Black Kids Sitting Together in the Cafeteria?" and Other Conversations about Race.* New York: Basic Books.

———. 2007. *Can We Talk about Race? and Other Conversations in an Era of School Resegregation.* Boston, Mass.: Beacon Press.

Taylor, Edward, David Gillborn, and Gloria Ladson-Billings. 2009. *Foundations of Critical Race Theory in Education.* New York: Routledge.

Tjaden, Patricia, and Nancy Thoennes. 2000. *Extent, Nature, and Consequences of Intimate Partner Violence: Findings from the National Violence Against Women Survey.* Washington, D.C.: U.S. Department of Justice. Available at: http://www .ncjrs.gov/pdffiles1/nij/181867.pdf (accessed January 23, 2013).

Toosi, Negin R., Laura G. Babbitt, Nalini Ambady, and Samuel R. Sommers. 2012. "Dyadic Interracial Interactions: A Meta-Analysis." *Psychological Bulletin* 138(1): 1–27. doi:10.1037/a0025767.

Towles-Schwen, Tamara, and Russell H. Fazio. 2006. "Automatically Activated Racial Attitudes as Predictors of the Success of Interracial Roommate Relationships." *Journal of Experimental Social Psychology* 42(5): 698–705. doi:10.1016/j.jesp .2005.11.003.

Trail, Thomas E., J. Nicole Shelton, and Tessa V. West. 2009. "Interracial Roommate Relationships: Negotiating Daily Interactions." *Personality and Social Psychology Bulletin* 35(6): 671–84. doi:10.1177/0146167209332741.

Trawalter, Sophie, and Jennifer A. Richeson. 2008. "Let's Talk about Race, Baby! When Whites' and Blacks' Interracial Contact Experiences Diverge." *Journal of Experimental Social Psychology* 44(4): 1214–17. doi:10.1016/j.jesp.2008.03.013.

Treviño, Jesús, and Kelly Maxwell, eds. 1999. *Voices of Discovery Facilitators' Handbook: Promoting Positive Intergroup Relations at Arizona State University.* Tempe: Intergroup Relations Center, Arizona State University.

Tropp, Linda R., and Robyn K. Mallett. 2011. *Moving Beyond Prejudice Reduction: Pathways to Positive Intergroup Relations.* Washington, D.C.: American Psychological Association.

Tropp, Linda R., and Thomas F. Pettigrew. 2005. "Differential Relationships Between Intergroup Contact and Affective and Cognitive Dimensions of Prejudice." *Personality and Social Psychology Bulletin* 31(8): 1145–58. doi:10.1177/014616 7205274854.

Turner, Rhiannon N., Miles Hewstone, and Alberto Voci. 2007. "Reducing Explicit and Implicit Outgroup Prejudice via Direct and Extended Contact: The Mediating Role of Self-Disclosure and Intergroup Anxiety." *Journal of Personality and Social Psychology* 93(3): 369–88. doi:10.1037/0022-3514.93.3.369.

Tutu, Desmond Mpilo. 1999. *No Future without Forgiveness.* New York: Doubleday.

——— with Douglas Abrams. 2004. *God Has a Dream: A Vision of Hope for Our Time.* New York: Doubleday.

U.S. Department of Commerce and Office of Management and Budget (OMB). 2011. "Women in America: Indicators of Social and Economic Well-being." Washington, D.C.: Government Printing Office. Available at: http://www.white house.gov/sites/default/files/rss_viewer/Women_in_America.pdf (accessed January 23, 2013).

Van Laar, Colette, Shana Levin, Stacey Sinclair, and Jim Sidanius. 2005. "The Effect of University Roommate Contact on Ethnic Attitudes and Behavior." *Journal of Experimental Social Psychology* 41(4): 329–45. doi:10.1016/j.jesp.2004.08.002.

Van Wyk, Clem, Biren (Ratnesh) A. Nagda, and Bianca Robertson. 2005. "A Report on the Desmond Tutu Emerging Leadership Programme." Cape Town: Desmond Tutu Peace Centre.

Van Zomeren, Martijn, and Aarti Iyer. 2009. "Introduction to the Social and Psychological Dynamics of Collective Action." *Journal of Social Issues* 65(4): 645–60. doi:10.1111/j.1540-4560.2009.01618.x.

Van Zomeren, Martijn, Russell Spears, Agneta H. Fischer, and Colin Wayne Leach. 2004. "Put Your Money Where Your Mouth Is! Explaining Collective Action Tendencies Through Group-Based Anger and Group Efficacy." *Journal of Personality and Social Psychology* 87(5): 649–64. doi:10.1037/0022-3514.87.5.649.

Verbeke, Geert, and Geert Molenberghs. 2000. *Linear Mixed Models for Longitudinal Data.* New York: Springer.

Vescio, Theresa K., Gretchen B. Sechrist, and Matthew P. Paolucci. 2003. "Perspective Taking and Prejudice Reduction: The Mediational Role of Empathy Arousal and Situational Attributions." *European Journal of Social Psychology* 33(4): 455–72. doi:10.1002/ejsp.163.

Vorauer, Jacquie D. 2006. "An Information Search Model of Evaluative Concerns in Intergroup Interaction." *Psychological Review* 113(4): 862–86. doi:10.1037/0033-295x.113.4.862.

Walker, Melanie. 2009. "'Making a World That Is Worth Living in': Humanities Teaching and the Formation of Practical Reasoning." *Arts and Humanities in Higher Education* 8(3): 231–46. doi:10.1177/1474022209339960.

Walker, Rebecca, ed. 1995. *To Be Real: Telling the Truth and Changing the Face of Feminism*. New York: Anchor Books.

Walsh, Katherine Cramer. 2007. *Talking about Race: Community Dialogues and the Politics of Difference*. Chicago: University of Chicago Press.

Watkins, Natasha D., Reed W. Larson, and Patrick J. Sullivan. 2007. "Bridging Intergroup Difference in a Community Youth Program." *American Behavioral Scientist* 51(3): 380–402. doi:10.1177/0002764207306066.

Watt, Sherry K. 2007. "Difficult Dialogues, Privilege, and Social Justice: Uses of the Privileged Identity Exploration (PIE) Model in Student Affairs Practice." *College Student Affairs Journal* 26(2): 114–26.

Weiler, Jeanne. 1995. "Finding a Shared Meaning: Reflections on Dialogue. An Interview with Linda Teurfs." *Seeds of Unfolding* 11(1): 4–10.

Werkmeister Rozas, Lisa, Ximena Zúñiga, and Martha Stassen. 2008. "Psychological, Educational, and Dialogue Dimension of Student Engagement: A Literature Review." Paper presented at the Annual Conference of the Northeastern Educational Research Association, Rocky Hill, Conn. (October 21–23, 2008).

Western Interstate Commission for Higher Education. 2008. "Knocking at the College Door: Projections of High School Graduates by State and Race/Ethnicity, 1992–2022." 7th ed. Boulder, Colo.: Western Interstate Commission for Higher Education. Available at: http://www.wiche.edu/pub/11556 (accessed October 15, 2012).

Wilder, David A. 1981. "Perceiving Persons as a Group: Categorization and Intergroup Relations." In *Cognitive Processes in Stereotyping and Intergroup Behavior*, edited by David L. Hamilton. Hillsdale, N.J.: Lawrence Erlbaum.

Wing, Leah, and Janet Rifkin. 2001. "Racial Identity Development and the Mediation of Conflicts." In *New Perspectives on Racial Identity Development: A Theoretical and Practical Anthology*, edited by Charmaine L. Wijeyesinghe and Bailey W. Jackson III. New York: New York University Press.

Wood, Thomas E. 2008. "The Marriage of Affirmative Action and Transformative Education." Princeton, N.J.: National Association of Scholars. Available at: http://www.nas.org/articles/The_Marriage_of_Affirmative_Action_and_Transformative_Education (accessed January 23, 2013).

Wood, Thomas E., and Malcolm J. Sherman. 2001. "Is Campus Racial Diversity Correlated with Educational Benefits?" *Academic Questions* 14(3): 72–88. doi:10.1007/s12129-001-1011-x.

———. 2003. Supplement to *Race and Higher Education*. Princeton, N.J.: National

Association of Scholars. Available at: http://nas.org/rhe2.pdf (accessed June 1, 2003).

Wright, Stephen C. 2009. "The Next Generation of Collective Action Research." *Journal of Social Issues* 65(4): 859–79. doi:10.1111/j.1540-4560.2009.01628.x.

Wright, Stephen C., and Micah E. Lubensky. 2009. "The Struggle for Social Equality: Collective Action Versus Prejudice Reduction." In *Intergroup Misunderstandings: Impact of Divergent Social Realities*, edited by Stéphanie Demoulin, Jacques-Philippe Leyens, and John F. Dovidio. New York: Psychology Press.

Yeakley, Anna M. 2011. "In the Hands of Facilitators: Student Experiences in Dialogue and Implications for Facilitator Training." In *Facilitating Intergroup Dialogues: Bridging Differences, Catalyzing Change*, edited by Kelly E. Maxwell, Biren (Ratnesh) A. Nagda, and Monita C. Thompson. Sterling, Va.: Stylus.

Yellin, Janet L. 2006. "Economic Inequality in the United States." *FRBSF economic letter* no. 2006-33-34. San Francisco: Federal Reserve Bank. Available at: http://www.frbsf.org/publications/economics/letter/2006/el2006-33-34.html (accessed January 23, 2013).

Young, Iris Marion. 1997. *Intersecting Voices: Dilemmas of Gender, Political Philosophy, and Policy.* Princeton, N.J.: Princeton University Press.

Zakaria, Fareed. 2008. *The Post-American World.* New York: W. W. Norton.

———. 2011. *The Post-American World: Release 2.0.* New York: W. W. Norton.

Ziegahn, Linda. 2007. "Critical Dialogue Around the Social Justice and Cultural Dimensions of Globalization." *PAACE Journal of Lifelong Learning* 16: 1–15.

Zúñiga, Ximena, and Adena Cytron-Walker. 2003. *Exploring Differences and Common Ground: A Curriculum Guide for Intergroup Dialogues.* Amherst: Social Justice Education Program, School of Education, University of Massachusetts.

Zúñiga, Ximena, Carey Dimmitt, and Dave Neely. 2011. "The Five College Intergroup Dialogue Initiative: Preliminary Findings." Research Presentation to the Human Resource and Diversity and Equity Directors, University of Massachusetts.

Zúñiga, Ximena, Tanya Kachwaha, Keri DeJong, and Romina Pacheco. 2011. "Preparing Critically Reflective Intergroup Dialogue Facilitators: A Pedagogical Model and Illustrative Example." In *Facilitating Intergroup Dialogues: Bridging Differences, Catalyzing Change*, edited by Kelly E. Maxwell, Biren (Ratnesh) A. Nagda, and Monita C. Thompson. Sterling, Va.: Stylus Publications.

Zúñiga, Ximena, Jane Mildred, Rani Varghese, Keri DeJong, and Molly Keehn. 2012. "Engaged Listening in Race/Ethnicity and Gender Intergroup Dialogue

Courses." *Equity and Excellence in Education* 45(1): 80–99. doi:10.1080/106656 84.2012.644962.

Zúñiga, Ximena, and Biren (Ratnesh) A. Nagda. 1993. "Classroom and Workshop Exercises. C1. Identity Group Exercise." In *Multicultural Teaching in the University*, edited by David Schoem, Linda Frankel, Ximena Zúñiga, and Edith A. Lewis, 323. Westport, Conn.: Praeger.

———. 2001. "Design Considerations in Intergroup Dialogue." In *Intergroup Dialogue: Deliberative Democracy in School, College, Community, and Workplace*, edited by David Schoem and Sylvia Hurtado. Ann Arbor: University of Michigan Press.

Zúñiga, Ximena, Biren (Ratnesh) A. Nagda, Mark Chesler, and Adena Cytron-Walker. 2007. *ASHE Higher Education Report*, vol. 32, issue 4. *Intergroup Dialogue in Higher Education: Meaningful Learning about Social Justice.* San Francisco: Jossey-Bass. doi:10.1002/aehe.3204.

Zúñiga, Ximena, Biren (Ratnesh) A. Nagda, and Todd D. Sevig. 2002. "Intergroup Dialogues: An Educational Model for Cultivating Engagement Across Differences." *Equity and Excellence in Education* 35(1): 7–17. doi:10.1080/713845248.

Zúñiga, Ximena, Biren (Ratnesh) A. Nagda, Todd Sevig, Monita Thompson, and Eric Dey. 1995. "Speaking the Unspeakable: Student Learning Outcomes in Intergroup Dialogues on a College Campus." Paper presented at the Association for the Study of Higher Education Conference, Orlando, Florida, November 1995.

INDEX